KING
WILLIAM IV

Philip Ziegler

CASSELL

Cassell Publishers Ltd
Artillery House, Artillery Row
London SW1P 1RT

Originally published by William Collins Sons & Co Ltd 1971
Published in Cassell Biographies 1989

ISBN 0-304-31793-4

British Library Cataloguing in Publication Data

Ziegler, Philip, *1929* —
    King William IV. — (Cassell biographies)
    1. Great Britain, William IV, King of Great Britain
    I. Title
    941.07′5′0924

Cover portrait by Shee reproduced
by permission of the National
Portrait Gallery

Printed and bound in Great Britain by Biddles Ltd, Guildford and King's Lynn

KING WILLIAM IV

Philip Ziegler was born in 1929 and educated at Eton and New College, Oxford. He entered the Foreign Service in 1952 and served in Vientiane, Paris, Pretoria and Bogotá. In 1967 he became editorial director of the publishers William Collins and Sons, where he worked until 1980 when he resigned to write the biography of Earl Mountbatten of Burma.

His other biographies include *The Duchess of Dino* (1962), *Addington* (1965), *Melbourne* (1976) and *Diana Cooper* (1981).

CASSELL BIOGRAPHIES

To Clare,
Sophie and Colin Christian

Contents

Acknowledgments

By gracious permission of Her Majesty the Queen I have been allowed free access to all the material in the Royal Archives at Windsor and to reproduce certain pictures from the Royal Collection.

I am indebted to the following for allowing me to use manuscript material in their possession or to which they hold the copyright: The Marquess of Anglesey, Earl Mountbatten of Burma, the Earl of Munster, Lady Bedingfeld, Captain Michael Wemyss, Mr Thomas Goff and Miss Cicely Barton.

Several of these have also been prodigal of their time and advice. As well I would like to thank Professor Aspinall, Mr Hugh Cobbe of the Department of Manuscripts at the British Museum, Mr David Duff, Mr Geoffrey Eldridge, Mr Brian Fothergill, Mr Roger Fulford, Mr Gwynne Hargrove, Herr von Jeinsen, Mr Richard Ormonde of the National Portrait Gallery and Mr Derek Tangye.

Mr Robert Mackworth-Young, Librarian at Windsor Castle, and his admirable staff – notably Miss Langton, Miss Gandy and Miss Russell – have never ceased to astonish me by their patience, kindness and efficiency. My debt to the staffs of the British Museum, the National Maritime Museum, the Historical Manuscripts Commission, the Public Records' Office and, of course, the London Library, is so obvious as hardly to need a mention.

I owe my particular thanks to my editor, Mr Richard Ollard, for much help and advice – all the better for being unpalatable; to the Countess of Longford for gallantly working through my typescript and making most valuable suggestions; to Mr Thomas Charrington; and to my wife for unwavering tolerance and support.

CHAPTER I

Childhood

In September 1761, King George III married Princess Charlotte, youngest and plainest daughter of the house of Mecklenburg-Strelitz. Only twenty-three years old and susceptible even for that romantic age, the King was already deeply in love. Those favoured by kings are often more than usually beautiful but even by these standards Lady Sarah Lennox seems to have been exceptional. She was the daughter of the Duke of Richmond, a descendant of King Charles II and the Duchess of Portsmouth. Thus enshrouded in a mist of glamour, her charms were potent enough to survive even an affair with a man called Newbottle and marriage with another called Bunbury. The King wanted to marry her and got close to a formal proposal. His mother and the devious Bute together over-persuaded him and preached the merits of a royal and foreign marriage. Glumly King George consented, making it clear that his heart was broken and that he could hardly be expected to survive for long. If he was not to have his Lady Sarah then any Protestant princess of more or less suitable age would do. The German courts were combed for appropriate candidates and the choice fell on Princess Charlotte.

It did not seem that she had much to help her in competition with Sarah Lennox. At one time it was claimed that she too was beautiful but the legend rested on the activities of an unscrupulous print-seller who put the princess's name beneath the portrait of some imposing but, alas, irrelevant German belle and made a quick killing among the London public. Reality dispelled these illusions. 'Pale and homely', commented Walpole, 'her nose very flat, her mouth very large.'[1] and though a more charitable observer endowed her with 'that inexpressible something that is beyond a set of features'[2] no one pretended that the features themselves had much to commend them. Princess Charlotte was eighteen years old, unsophisticated, slow-witted, with only a smattering of English and totally ignorant of British society, politics and way of life. She took her place in a hostile or indifferent Court;

her only ally, the grotesque and curmudgeonly Madame Schwellenberg, who saw it as her duty to guard her mistress carefully against whatever friendly overtures the English might be inclined to make.

And yet the marriage was an instant and astonishing success. The Queen certainly had qualities – tenacity, good-humour, loyalty – which were of a nature to make themselves increasingly valued as time went on. The King too was monogamous by temperament, he needed a wife in whom he could have confidence and would have been disposed to cast Charlotte for the role whether she were suited for it or not. But the real reason for their happy marriage was that they suited one another admirably. Both were prudent; conservative; dull; disapproving of extravagance, whether financial or emotional; ever conscious of their royal status yet bourgeois in their tastes and habits. Until the King's madness began to put an almost intolerable strain on their relationship, they satisfied each other entirely. Queen Charlotte provided her husband with the stability and continuity which would otherwise have been lacking. She did nothing to moderate his prejudices, indeed she probably did more to strengthen than to break them down, but their mutual dependence was real and moving.

Not that those who arranged the wedding were concerned with whether or not it would lead to happiness. The primary function of a royal marriage was to supply a sufficiency of children, preferably boys, so that the succession to the throne might be secured. To this task the royal couple devoted themselves with the assiduity which was to mark all their activities. George Augustus Frederick, successively Prince of Wales, Prince Regent and King George IV, was born some eleven months after the wedding; Frederick Augustus, later to become Duke of York and Albany, followed a year later; and between three and four in the morning of August 21, 1765, Prince William Henry was born at Buckingham House. He was the third of a family which was eventually to number fifteen: only two of whom did not survive to adulthood.*

*

Any family may be forgiven one profligate but when so many children go badly wrong some degree of parental carelessness must be suspected. Leaving Prince William for the moment to one side, George III's four eldest sons – the Prince of Wales and the Dukes of York, Kent and the

* For a list of the children of George III and Charlotte, see Appendix A.

notorious Cumberland – were to yield a crop of vices fit to fill every
circle of Dante's Inferno. They waged between themselves and with
their parents a warfare savage even by the standards of the House of
Hanover. For this the manner of their upbringing must surely in part
have been responsible. The amateur psychologist of the twentieth
century, versed in the lore of Dr Spock, peers hopefully for signs of
unspared rods or breasts denied, for neurotic compulsions viciously
repressed, bed-wetting held up to public derision, parents coldly remote
or cloyingly possessive, regimented austerity high-lighted by bouts of
gross over-indulgence. Somehow, somewhere, there must have been
something beastly in the royal nursery.

Convenient though so pat an explanation might be, there is unfortunately no evidence to support it. The childhood of the princes
and princesses was tranquil, decorous and, so far as one can judge,
tolerably contented; King George and Queen Charlotte, though somewhat strict and formal by contemporary standards, not far from model
parents. The elder children were brought up almost entirely in the
country, at first at Richmond but increasingly and, after 1772, exclusively at Kew. The Dutch House, now called the Queen's House and
the only surviving residence of the period within the Gardens, had
been acquired by Queen Caroline a half century before. Over the years
it had become the centre of a royal colony, dotted here and there in the
Gardens and clustered around the Green. It was a pleasantly rural
scene but the court at Kew was by no means cut off from the life of the
neighbourhood. Though the majority of the houses around the Green
were lived in by members of the royal family or their appendages no
attempt was made to exclude the public and a few houses and even
shops remained in private hands. The Gardens were generally open to
all those visitors who came up to a minimum level of respectability
and a common entertainment for a Sunday afternoon in London was
to drive out to Kew in the hope of seeing a crocodile of royal infants
taking their walk across the lawns. It was by no means unusual to find
the King himself setting a brisk pace at the head of this procession or,
watering-can in hand, directing operations among the flowerbeds.
'They live as the simplest country gentlefolk,'[3] commented Fanny
Burney, and the comment would have been taken by the King as a
well-merited compliment.

Fresh air and a frugal diet were the hall-marks of Prince William
Henry's earliest years and he throve on them. His sister Augusta, three
years his junior, remarked with some regret that she 'had been brought

up in a cloister rather than a kingdom'[4] but even as a very small child
William seems to have enjoyed quite as much society as was good for
him. His first recorded public appearance came on October 25, 1769
when, aged four, he attended a drawing-room at St James's Palace.
The Prince of Wales was dressed in scarlet and gold, with the Order of
the Garter; Prince Frederick, now styled Bishop of Osnaburgh, wore
blue and gold with the Order of the Bath, while William and his two-
year-old brother Edward were 'elegantly clothed in Roman togas'.[5]
The Princes were said to have received their guests with 'the utmost
grace and affability'[6] but the spectacle of these infants posturing in
fancy dress among the obsequious courtiers led to a few jeers from the
popular press. The Prince of Wales was caricatured flying his kite
among the glories of St James's Palace while William busily spun his
top.

But though Prince William continued occasionally to attend the
Thursday drawing-rooms, such excursions were an inconsiderable part
of his daily life. Miss Albert, some six weeks older than the prince, was
a constant visitor to the royal nursery and found it a little tame; playing
quietly with her young host 'under the eye of dear nurse Chapman'.
Almost the only out-of-the-way event which she recorded came when
the two children were vaccinated at the end of 1768. 'Two punctures
in the arm near to each other were made with the point of a lancet,
through which a thread was drawn several times under the skin, and
this on both arms. The operation was performed by Surgeon Blomfield,
and was one of smarting pain, for we both cried.' Miss Albert had con-
vulsions and was ill for several days; not surprising, perhaps, since it
was many years before Jenner first substituted cowpox for inoculation
with smallpox itself. William, though his arms were covered with
pustules, recovered more quickly.[7] There was an immediate outcry
against the rashness and impiety of the experiment, particularly when
extended to members of the royal family.

Then, in 1772, Prince William's pattern of life was transformed.
Until that time he had shared a nursery with his two elder brothers
under the rule of Lady Charlotte Finch, 'Lady Cha' to all the family, a
woman of brains and culture who knew how to make herself respected
without being feared. Now, however, it was felt that George and
Frederick needed a separate establishment. William's education was
henceforth to be acquired in the company of his brother Edward, future
Duke of Kent. The King, noted Lady Mary Coke, is 'going to put
Prince William and Edward into the hands of Governors, and has

taken the House that Lord Bute lived in on Kew Green for their Habitation'.[8] The house was to be William's home for the next seven years.

'Put into the hands of Governors' is a phrase with an ominous ring, and the young Princes had additional cause for alarm when they learned that their principal tutor was to be a foreign general. But General Budé, despite the title, had seen little fighting. He was a native of the Pays de Vaux who had a passion for anchovies and was a considerable performer on the flute. His personality, however, belied this attractive promise of eccentricity. He seems to have been a dry and disagreeable stick. '. . . his person is tall and showy, and his manners and appearance are fashionable,' wrote Miss Burney coolly. 'But he has a sneer in his smile that looks sarcastic, and a distance in his manner that seems haughty.'[9] He was obsequious to his superiors and coldly offensive to those he deemed below him. One of his flaws as a governor was that he could never make up his mind in which category to place his princely pupils, so that William and Edward found themselves alternately fawned on and sharply reprimanded for trivial faults.

Fortunately the main responsibility for their education rested on Dr Majendie, a classicist of Huguenot stock who was summoned from Exeter to take up this new appointment. Majendie had taught Queen Charlotte English and was already well-known to Prince William, having been involved in the training of all the elder princes before the households were divided. When he felt himself becoming too old for the job he summoned his son Henry from Christ's College, Cambridge, to replace him and the latter, tubby, self-important, but basically well-meaning, did not lose touch with his pupil until he died a fortnight after William's accession to the throne.

*

Budé and Majendie were merely the most conspicuous members of a household which cost the Crown £1,115 a year. For the money the princes enjoyed the services of a housekeeper, two pages of the back-stairs, two rockers (presumably originally engaged to rock the cradle of the still infant Edward), a writing-master, a watchman (at £25 a year) and three hounds (at £20 a year per hound). Gradually, additional experts were added to the staff: a dancing master, a fencing master, two riding masters, and Alexander Cozens, who failed signally to implant even the most elementary principles of draughtmanship in his unenthusiastic pupil.[10]

With the assistance of this little army, Prince William Henry settled down to a tranquil if not altogether relaxed routine.[11] The two Princes rose every morning at six and spent two hours alone, in theory at least in study. At eight precisely they walked over to the Queen's House, knocked at the door of the royal chamber and breakfasted with their parents – a simple though no doubt nourishing meal of milk, sometimes enlivened by a little tea, and dry toast made from Statute bread. Breakfast over, they returned to their house for lessons, a minimum of two hours and usually more, and probably a walk in the gardens. Dinner was taken about three with 'soup if they choose it, when not very strong or heavy, and plain meat without fat, clear gravy and greens'. Fish was always available 'but without butter, using shrimps strained from the sauce or oil and vinegar' followed generally by 'the fruit of a tart without the crust'. On Thursdays and Saturdays, as a treat, they could have whatever flavour of ice took their fancy. Coffee was available only twice a week but there was generally a glass of wine to conclude the meal.

After dinner was over all the children would play games together in the gardens. Cricket, hockey and football were the favourites: Princess Charlotte Augusta, the eldest of William's sisters, recorded proudly that she 'played cricket particularly well'.[12] They also had a model farm in which they were expected to work: in one small field they sowed and reaped wheat and subsequently ground it and made bread from the flour. At five the royal children congregated again at their parents' apartments and read, wrote or made improving conversation. The governesses would arrive at six-thirty to take them off to bed. A light supper was served except on Mondays, an exception presumably related in some way to the fact that every second Monday they were supposed to take a bath.

Their clothes were slightly more lavish than their diet. Each Prince had six suits of full-dress clothes a year and various common suits; new boots 'spring and fall' and a pair of new shoes every other week. Hats were supplied as needed but they always had four silver-looped and gold-looped and two plain.

The Queen took an active interest in every detail of their diet and wardrobe and fussed in particular about their health, two doctors being always in attendance. Indeed, by the standards of the age, both King and Queen were most unfashionably interested in their children. And yet a starchy formality pervaded the meetings of parents and children which were more like courtly audiences than nursery parties. Queen

Charlotte in particular seemed by nature unable to unbend. The children were rarely allowed to sit in her presence and when present at royal games of whist would stand silently behind her chair and some-times fall asleep in that position. It must have been a welcome relief to escape to their Aunt Amelia's house at Gunnersbury. Lady Mary Coke was present at a party there in October 1772:

'After dinner we played two pools at Goose; one of which was won by Prince William, the other by Lady Amelia [D'Arcy]. When that was over She carried them to the passage between the Hall and the Garden, which was fitted up for a Skittle Alley, extremely well con-trived. This diverted them very much for near an hour and a half. We all played, and nobody better than the Prince of Wales . . . We then played at commerce, and about half an hour after eight o'clock they took leave, very much pleased with their reception.'[13]

Outings like this and the occasional appearance at St James's whetted Prince William's appetite for a livelier pattern of life than Kew could provide. 'Prince William and Prince Edward pass the winter in the country,' noted Lady Mary. 'Prince William is not yet reconciled to his new Establishment, and 'tis thought will be ill-satisfied that he is not permitted to go to town . . .'[14] Yet William was not generally a sulky child; on the contrary, he was more likely to exhibit an alarming jollity. On one occasion he and the Prince of Wales were playing some barbarous game with one of the nursery maids. 'Prince William, who was full of humour, contrived to throw her down.' Irritated, the maid retaliated. When she was taken to task another attendant sought to defend her and was called a liar by the Prince of Wales for her pains: '. . . you are both Scotchwomen, and will say anything to favour one another!' His witty riposte, one is told, 'occasioned much diversion'. This odious anecdote was cited by William's biographer to show 'the early affection of the princes for each other'.[15] Such is hardly the moral most likely to be drawn by the modern reader but the story does illustrate well the uncouth and insensitive bonhomie which was to characterize William's behaviour through so much of his life, perhaps, indeed, to the very end.

But though that bonhomie might from time to time manifest itself as insufferable boorishness and rarely made him fit company for the socially squeamish, it was evident even when Prince William was still a child that it was based upon genuine goodwill. Even at his most in-

sufferable his behaviour was usually redeemed by his frank and sincere
liking for other people. He was interested in their activities and concerned about their happiness; he attempted, though without much
subtlety or perception, to understand their point of view. It was this,
above all, which distinguished him from his brothers and was to make
him the only Hanoverian capable of establishing any real relationship
with his people.

When he was twelve the King and Queen took the whole family
over to Farnham to visit Dr Thomas, the Bishop of Winchester, who
was celebrating his eighty-second birthday. 'I was pleased with all the
Princes,' wrote the bishop's niece, 'but particularly with Prince
William, who is little for his age, but so sensible and engaging that he
won the Bishop's heart; to whom he particularly attached himself, and
would stay with him while all the rest ran about the house. His conversation was surprisingly manly and clever for his age, yet with the Bullers
he was quite the boy, and said to John Buller, by way of encouraging
him to talk, "Come, we are both boys, you know".'[16] A rowdy little
boy who makes the effort to be polite to an old gentleman when
he could have far more fun elsewhere deserves some credit. A boy
who understands that his contemporaries may feel at a disadvantage
and does his best to put them at their ease is also not to be despised.
Amiability is not the highest of all virtues but it is a lot to be
thankful for.

Prince William's copy book survives at Windsor. The improving
sentiments which it was thought proper for him to transcribe may
provide some clue at least to the sort of boy his instructors hoped he
would become. The thought for October 19, 1774 was 'that death
which is not far off, when it removes us out of this world, will take
us from all the sufferings of it'. A week later things looked up a little.
The Prince was urged to concentrate on vice rather than the grave.
'Vicious habits are so great a strain to human nature, and so odious in
themselves, that every person, acted [sic] by right reason, would avoid
them, tho' he was sure they would always be concealed both from God
and man . . .'

It could hardly be expected or, for that matter, hoped that a cheerful
schoolboy would pay much heed to such prosy moralizing. His
education, of course, was not confined to a patter of platitudes. Unfortunately, however, whether the deficiency was one of pupil or of
teacher, it left hardly any mark at all. Almost the only exception was a
love of mathematics. Latin and German were drummed into him, but

as quickly tumbled out again, as he was to find to his cost when he
lived in Hanover. His father ruled that English history would be 'a
pleasant as well as a useful occupation';[17] Prince William had no recorded views on the usefulness but a most clear-cut and unfavourable
opinion on the pleasure. Another of the King's tenets was that all
'books of recreation' should be read in French, since in that language
there were more books 'void of evil' than in English. Since the Prince
never read French with total ease recreational reading was excluded
from his life – an omission which would probably have been apparent
in any case. Even his grasp of arithmetic had its limitations: 'though the
Royal Brothers received instruction in Latin and Greek with ease,'
ruefully commented one of their tutors, 'yet they could never be taught
to understand the value of money.'

*

While Prince William grew up, the nurseries at Kew filled with disconcerting speed. The troubles of Zoffany are well known. By the time
he was commissioned to paint a family group nine children had already
been born; the three elder sons and then Charlotte, Edward, Augusta,
Elizabeth, Ernest and, most recently, Augustus. The painter might
reasonably have hoped that so substantial a family would provide a
fairly static subject. He took his time; quickly completing the pre-
liminary sketches but dawdling over the painting itself. The picture was
barely half-way to completion when news came of the birth of a tenth
child, Prince Adolphus. With considerable ingenuity Zoffany squeezed
into the picture the blobbish figure of a new-born baby. The long
drawn-out sequence of sittings was resumed and apparently finished.
The artist was applying what he fondly hoped were the finishing
touches. And then came Princess Mary. Princess Mary, it was clear,
could not be left out. Not more than one child could be dandled on
Queen Charlotte's lap. Reluctantly Zoffany painted out half his figures
and began again. Once again the end was in sight; but Princess Sophia
came in time to confound him. 'Oh! Oh! God bless my soul,' cried
Zoffany. 'This is too much!' Mercifully, however, a burst of speed by
the painter and some dilatoriness on the part of the King meant that
the picture was finished before Prince Octavius was born in 1779.
Octavius lived only four years; Alfred, his younger brother, only
two; Princess Amelia, the last of King George III's children, lingered on
till 1810; but some virtue seemed to have gone out of the stock and
she was always a sickly child.

Prince William knew little of the later arrivals to the family; indeed he can hardly ever have met the ill-fated Octavius and Alfred. Prince Edward was, of course, his closest associate. Sharing a house with him as he did it might have been supposed that the future Duke of Kent would have become and remained particularly dear. In fact William never really understood his sly and moody brother. In childhood Edward was renowned among his relations as being a cheat and a hypocrite. In maturity he blossomed into a ferocious disciplinarian who, to most contemporaries, seemed as much sadistic as misguided. William's attitude towards him varied between grudging tolerance and downright hostility; the latter more and more predominating as time wore on.

It was his sisters, Princess Charlotte and still more Augusta – the most beautiful if also the most colourless of the Princesses – who were William's favourites. 'We had been each others early *friends*,' Augusta once confided. 'I had known every secret of his heart, the same when he was quite a lad, that I could believe and pity all his worries...'[18] It is a curious paradox that this noisy and extrovert youth, whose reputation for foul-mouthed intemperance was to become a by-word in Georgian drawing-rooms, should so consistently have courted the society of women and found the greatest relaxation in their company. His relationship with his sisters was close yet uncomplicated, a model of gallantry and genuine good will which lasted all his life.

Yet though he may have loved his sisters best, it was the Prince of Wales who was most to influence William. Any boy is likely to be something of a hero to his younger brother and when the boy is intelligent, handsome, heir to the throne of England and indecently sophisticated then hero-worship becomes idolatry. From 1773 the Prince of Wales had been assigned a separate household at Carlton House; his life was a full one and he had scant time to waste on a hobbledehoy who must have seemed to him of little interest. In so far as he intervened in William's childish life it was on the side of righteousness: he wrote him patronizing letters in French hoping that he was making good progress with his studies and gave him lavish presents when the mood took him. But King George III was under no illusion that the relationship would long remain so innocent. Already he had more or less written off his eldest son. Even as a child the Prince of Wales had delighted in bellowing 'Wilkes and Liberty' through his father's key-hole; now, aged sixteen, he showed every sign of developing into a debauchee and a profligate. William was ripe to be corrupted and the King had no doubt that the Prince of Wales would revel in the task. It must have been in part, at least, a desire to keep the two boys separated that led the King, in 1778, to come to a somewhat drastic decision about his third son's future. William, he decreed, should go to sea.

CHAPTER II

Midshipman Prince William

THE younger son of a King had a miserable time of it in any monarchy. At first his position might not have been wholly insignificant. It was of the first importance that the succession should be assured, and a supply of twelfth men available in case of need lent stability to any dynasty. But as the years rolled on, as the heir to the throne married and himself produced children, so the younger son dwindled into the background. By the time that he had reached the age at which the normal human being could expect to be most useful he would probably have degenerated into an object of perfect inutility. His upbringing, and his sense of his own importance, conduced inexorably to lavish living – yet it was unlikely that the state would be willing perpetually to maintain him in the style to which he had grown accustomed. He might, if he were lucky, have an army to direct or go out to govern some far-flung colony, yet such functions called for a modicum of training and talent. Sometimes the talent was there, less often the training; all too frequently both were lacking. However absolute the monarchy, it could not long survive if it entrusted its important offices to the incompetent, the ignorant or the idle; and yet rare indeed was the prince who did not feel that a post in the second rank was unworthy of his powers.

Though exceptions were not uncommon, therefore, the luckless Prince was likely to find himself out of a job for most of his life. He was destined to fill the years between puberty and death with gambling, womanizing and seeking in society a solace for his secret doubts about his own importance. Those who entertained him were too often those who sought him as a prince and not a friend, a status symbol to add prestige to any salon. Almost inevitably he slipped into debt, and though the government could hardly allow him to sink into total financial disaster, they equally felt no obligation to ease his mind by providing him with an income sufficient to maintain him at the level he deemed appropriate. His life, in short, was too often ignoble; of a kind designed to exaggerate every defeat and erode every latent virtue, to reduce the good to the barely adequate and the adequate to the disastrous.

Prince William was a third son. The Prince of Wales married late and had only a single child. Frederick, Duke of York, had none. The throne therefore was never impossibly remote. But neither, until the sudden and unexpected death of Princess Charlotte in 1817, could it have seemed a serious probability. For the first forty years of his life William must have believed that he was destined to live and die a prince: and the history of the House of Hanover did not suggest that it was more successful than other dynasties in finding useful employment for its junior members. The prospect can hardly have seemed a cheerful one.

To King George III it was anathema. As a good father, who also deplored every kind of waste, he determined to save his sons from so horrid a fate. They should have a job of work, a real job in which they could serve their country as well as their own best interests. George was to be King of England, and that was surely task enough for any man. Frederick should be a soldier. For William he conceived the idea of a career in the navy. The concept was a daring one – many members of royal houses had been admirals but few indeed midshipmen – yet it had undeniable attractions. It would involve separation not only from the Prince of Wales but from the whole ambience of smart society. King George III was a bourgeois and a puritan – for him the *beau monde* of London reeked of brimstone – but he did not underrate its attractions for a young and susceptible member of the royal family. The world was full of rich and well-connected libertines who would delight in an opportunity to corrupt this innocent youth. If he could spare Prince William the temptation and at the same time instil in him a sounder and more durable scale of values, then surely he would be doing his duty as a King and as a father? And what institution would better be able to teach such values than the Royal Navy?

There is no reason to believe that Prince William's views were considered or even canvassed. In later life he always claimed that nothing had made him happier than the decision to turn him into a sailor, yet it would have been surprising if, at the time, he had not felt some apprehension and a certain chagrin at being removed from the flesh-pots just when it seemed that they were about to be opened to him. If he had expressed such views to his father he would anyhow have got short shrift; King George III was not the man to allow the protests of a thirteen-year-old boy to disturb his plans. William was a noisy, unruly boy – good-hearted, no doubt, but unable to curb his temper or learn the merits of restraint. The navy would put a stop to that, teach him to obey orders, to discipline others and himself most of all. The less William liked the idea, the more it must be desirable.

The Royal Navy at the end of the eighteenth century, like the established church, astonishes more by its similarity to its modern equivalent than by its difference. Then, as now, it was a profession for gentlemen; but then, as now, it was more a case of a naval officer being *ipso facto* a gentleman than of gentlemen alone being eligible for selection as a naval officer. During the Napoleonic wars about forty per cent of naval officers were recruited from the nobility or landed gentry while perhaps half had the professions as their background[1] – in particular the armed services, the church and medicine. This left a mere ten per cent for trade, commerce and the working classes – a small proportion but probably more substantial than was the case in 1779 when Prince William joined the navy. This, however, was not the whole story. Many of those who boasted professional origins in fact came from comparatively humble homes and a few at least of the 'landed gentry' were little more than yeoman farmers. There may have been few first lieutenants like Cochrane's Jack Larmour, 'little calculated to inspire exalted ideas of the gentility of the naval profession . . . dressed in the garb of a seaman, with marlin spike slung round his neck and a lump of grease in his hand . . .',[2] but the type was by no means unheard-of and, on the whole, was accepted without surprise or disapproval.

Even a navy whose officer corps was composed exclusively of the well-established gentry would have provided Prince William with unprecedented opportunities to widen his social horizons. Apart from a few casual visits and occasional brushes with the children of courtiers, his acquaintanceship was limited almost entirely to his own family: brothers, sisters and a few cousins, particularly Sophia and William of Gloucester. To make his new experience still more dramatic, society in the after cockpit was more broadly-based than any other in the ship. Not all first lieutenants would have agreed with Mr Sawbridge[3] that, 'in proportion as midshipmen assumed a cleaner and more gentlemanly appearance, so did they become more useless,' but certainly gentility was not the qualification most prized by naval officers. Midshipmen were as likely to be snobs as anyone else but life at sea would have been intolerable without a fair degree of mutual acceptance and, on the whole, a man's birth was less important on board a ship than in most other spheres.

The conventional picture of the midshipman is of a rowdy teen-ager; probably fresh from his family; half schoolboy, half naval officer. So many of them were; but the typical midshipmen's mess of the eighteenth century would certainly have contained a handful of older men, some of forty years or more, who had been by-passed for promotion or had worked themselves laboriously up from the lower deck.[4] At the other extreme might be a thirteen year old, probably a naval officer's son who had entered the navy at eleven and had already spent two years aboard serving under the gunner's eye. Such a mess would also have been likely to harbour a schoolmaster, the captain's clerk and one or two assistant surgeons. There might be women as well, in theory at least wives of the elder members of the men. These women would go to sea, though it was rare that their presence was endured when the ship was operational and combat a possibility. They were, of course, a very different thing from the whores taken aboard when the ship was in port. These too might be found in the midshipmen's mess and were as hallowed a part of the naval scene as the traditional rum-ration; tolerated by the officers so long as the discipline of the ship was unimpaired.

This curious hotchpotch of humanity, Midshipman Jack Easy dis-covered to his dismay, was boxed up in a hole infinitely inferior to the dog-kennels which received his father's pointers. Conditions may not always have been so insalubrious but the after cockpit would normally have been below the water level and the congestion of hot and dirty bodies must have come as an ugly shock to a boy bred in a palace. Captain Chamier's description of life in the midshipmen's mess was probably typical of most ships in the Royal Navy.

'Cups were used instead of glasses. The soup tureen, a heavy lumber-ing piece of block tin, pounded into shape, was, for want of a ladle, emptied with an everlasting tea cup; the forks were wiped on the table cloth by the persons about to use them, who, to save eating more than was requisite of actual dirt, always plunged them through the table cloth to clean between the prongs ... The rest of the furniture was not much cleaner; now and then an empty bottle served as a candlestick; and I have known both a shoe and a quadrant-case used as a soup plate ... [The midshipman] dressed and undressed in public; the basin was invariably of pewter; and the wet towels, dirty head-brush etc, were, after use, deposited in his chest. A ham-mock served as a bed, and so closely were we all stowed in war, that the side of one hammock always touched that of another; fourteen inches being declared quite sufficient space for one tired midshipman . . .'[5]

Prince William enjoyed certain privileges not offered to the other midshipmen, but in most essentials this was to be his daily life.

*

Having once conceived the idea of sending his son to sea, King George III turned for advice to his naval acquaintances. In the summer of 1778 he visited Portsmouth, discussed the matter with Robert Digby, and subsequently turned for counsel to the Commissioner of the Dockyard, Sir Samuel Hood. It would have been astonishing indeed if either of these gentlemen had done anything to discourage the King's resolve. The decision was taken and in July the King broke the news to the delighted Hood. 'He has begun geometry,' his letter read, 'and I shall have an attention to forward him in whatever you may hint as proper to be done before he enters into that glorious profession.'[6] Hood was asked to provide a list of what the Prince should bring with him and hastened to reply.[7] His suggestions were not extravagant but the quantities involved suggest that they were intended for William's base in the Admiral's house rather than life afloat.

'3 Dozen of Shirts and Stocks
2 Hatts, and 2 round ones (Hatts are liable to be lost overboard)
2 Dozen of Hand Towels
Pocket Handkerchiefs, night caps or Netts,
Basons, Washballs, Brushes, Combs, etc,'

and sufficient other goods to fill a hair-trunk and two chests.

And so, on June 15, 1779, Prince William Henry arrived at Spithead to join the *Prince George*, a line-of-battle ship of ninety-eight guns carrying the flag of Rear Admiral Robert Digby. '. . . I flatter myself you will be pleased with the appearance of the boy,' wrote the King to Hood with unwonted pride, 'who neither wants resolution nor cheerfulness, which seem necessary ingredients for those who enter into that noble profession.'[8] The admiral hastened to assure his monarch that his pride was well-founded. It is a curious reflection on the times, or perhaps on human nature, that the rugged sea-dogs of Britain's navy were second to no one when it came to letting the candied tongue lick absurd pomp and crooking the pregnant hinges of the knee. Nelson was perhaps supreme but few courtiers could have surpassed Hood in his mastery of the obsequious compliment and the fawning phrase. Nor was this confined to mere fulsomeness of expression. Many of his letters to the King reporting the progress of Prince William were deliberately misleading. They leave one in little doubt that Hood was concerned primarily with what he thought the recipient would like to hear and only secondarily with the real facts of the case.

*

When Frederick the Great was petitioned by a nobleman for a commission in the army for his son, he is said to have replied that no men of rank would be admitted because they merely played at soldiers and then retired to less exacting pursuits. 'As our young nobility in general never learn anything, they of course are exceedingly ignorant. In England one of the King's sons, wishing to instruct himself, has not scrupled to set out as a common sailor.'[9]

Frederick slightly overstated his case. Though a 'common sailor' in some respects, the Prince was decidedly uncommon in many others. Few midshipmen, for instance, can have been accompanied aboard their first ship by a private tutor, yet Midshipman the Reverend Henry Majendie figured incongruously on the roll of the *Royal George*. Though William was to become a sailor, his father did not intend him to neglect 'those Branches of Knowledge which are essential to every Gentleman'; Majendie's role on board was to ensure that his charge did not spend his leisure hours in drunkenness or horseplay but applied himself busily to the cultivation of his morals and his mind. The task was not to prove an easy one.

Majendie's instructions were carefully laid down by the King.[10] The first requirement, as was only proper when the tutor was a cleric, even though a reluctant one forced into orders so as to secure a fellowship, was to instruct 'my Dearly Beloved Son . . . in the Christian Religion, to inculcate the habitual reading of the Holy Scriptures, and to accompany these with Moral Reflexions . . .' When Moral Reflexions ran short, Latin followed, and then English composition. The tutor was to correct spelling and style but on no account to tamper with the content of Prince William's letters. History was important; Majendie would do well to stick to the facts and let the political theory wait till later. Translating from Latin and English into French and regular conversations in that tongue would be the best means of 'acquiring a language now

become so universal'. Finally Majendie was urged not to hesitate in
pointing out William's errors. 'I shall be mortified when He returns
from Sea,' wrote the King, 'if not void of the little tricks and rude-
nesses, which ought to be cast off at an earlier age than He is now arrived
at.'

It is doubtful whether the Prince was as grateful for Majendie's
presence as his father would have deemed proper. Probably he appreciated more the essential corollary, a room on board ship sufficiently
light and quiet to make possible this heavy programme of extra studies.
Certainly he must have been gratified by the allowance, lavish by the
standards of midshipmen, which he was given to sustain his way of
life. One record puts it at £1,000 a year.[11] This seems improbably
high; the sum may have included Majendie's wages and living costs.
It can anyhow be assumed that Prince William had more creature
comforts than most of his colleagues. The menu book of the Admiral's
Steward shows that he dined most days at the admiral's table.[12] Nor
was the diet frugal: a typical dinner consisted of: 'Boiled ducks
smuthered with onyons. Purtatoes, French beans, carits and turnips.
Beacken. Albocore [a large tunny-like fish]. Fruit Friters with whipt
cream. Spanish Friters. Boiled Beef and Rst Mutton.' In other ways too
he was certainly granted more consideration than his fellows. But these,
though significant, were still no more than glosses on what remained
the central fact. Prince William was a midshipman like any other. The
King of Prussia had got the essential point.

'The young midshipman will be at the Dockyard between one and
two on Monday,' wrote the King to Hood.[13] 'I desire he may be
received without the smallest marks of parade . . . The young man goes
as a sailor, and as such, I add again, no marks of distinction are to be
shown unto him; they would destroy my whole plan.'

The 'whole plan' was set out in a letter to Admiral Digby.[14] The
gist of it was that the Prince was to be treated exactly like any other
midshipman; made to perform the duties and not given any special
indulgence. Always he was to show, 'due obedience to those above
Him . . . politeness to His equals, and humanity to His inferiors'. He
was not to receive visits and never to go on shore unless in the company
of the Admiral. 'You will direct Him to be treated with civility, but no
visible marks of respect.'

The trouble with the plan was that Prince William was not an
ordinary midshipman and no stroke of his father's pen could make him
so. Even today the prince of the blood royal may find his relationship

with lesser mortals an uneasy one; in the eighteenth century the King was still the repository of immense power and the fount of honour. The divinity that hedges a king had worn a bit thin since the Hanoverians had brought their own style of home-spun and singularly uncharismatic monarchy to England but he was still wrapped around with an awful dignity. With this dignity William was inextricably associated, one day it might be his. Neither he nor his fellows could altogether forget that he was a man apart; that his friendship today might mean promotion in ten or twenty years.

In fact the midshipmen did far more to make the King's plan work than the politick admirals. Life in the mess really does seem to have gone on more or less as normal. James Grant joined the *Royal George* at the same time as Prince William Henry. He remembered that no regular servants were allowed and the two newcomers would take it in turns to do the cooking. They used to get into trouble with the other midshipmen for stealing so much of the scanty ration of flour so as to powder their hair when they dined with the admiral.[15]

But whether the plan succeeded or failed was bound to depend primarily on the prince. Anyone who has endured the torments of a first day at school will feel sympathy with William, faced with the immeasurably greater transition from palace to after cockpit. His new companions were not just unknown; they came from a totally different species. Anyone less extrovert or affable would have found the prospect intolerable. William did not. He must have been apprehensive but he had no doubt that he would like the other midshipmen well enough and never even considered the possibility that they might not like him. He showed from the start a sincere and disarming determination to be what he so eminently was – a boy like them.

Amidst the welter of colourful anecdote which surrounds the Prince's naval days, it is by now impossible to sift the literally true from the embellished, the embellished from the invented. When William was asked his name on his first day aboard did he really reply: 'My father's name is Guelph and you are welcome to call me William Guelph'? When he was behaving with undue self-confidence did one of his fellow midshipmen really say to him: 'Avast there, my hearty, the son of a whore here is as good a fellow as the son of a King'? The latter at least sounds improbably picturesque, and yet something close to it must have been said a dozen times. Prince William joked, shouted, cursed, grumbled like every other boy. He fought Lieutenant Moodie of the Royal Marines, and after peace had been restored, shook him by the hand with the rather patronizing remark: 'You are a brave fellow, though you are a marine.' He drank and gambled whenever the chance was given him – which was not very often – did his work with reasonable conscientiousness, got into trouble from time to time. His life, in fact, was almost entirely normal – in that, of course, lay its abnormality.

*

In 1779 the American War of Independence had already lasted three years. The French and the Spaniards had joined in and Britain was in considerable difficulties. The Admiralty could not afford to leave a ship-of-the-line lying idle and the day after the Prince joined the *Prince George* she sailed to join the grand fleet off Torbay. It would be pointless to describe the arcane manoeuvres by which the British and enemy fleets contrived to avoid each other; William, like any other midshipman, was largely ignorant of the strategy which, in theory at least, guided his movements. Nor did he care – what excited him most about his first cruise was that he learnt to swim. At one moment the *Prince George* was in sight of a considerable French and Spanish fleet but action was avoided and William returned to his more pressing preoccupations. These were not uniquely nautical; by the end of the cruise he had gone three times through the six first books of Euclid, once through the book of logarithms and had made progress with algebra and trigonometry. He had written a short account of the history of England from the Reformation till the Revolution of 1688 and was deep into Sully's *Mémoires*. 'Drawing has not gone on quite so well,' he admitted penitently. 'I am sensible I have been negligent about it; it is at present more attended to.'[16]

Prince William was constantly seeking the approval of his father, and rarely gaining it; on the contrary his naval service was punctuated by blasts of parental disapproval. Letters from the King sometimes contained a modicum of family gossip, but only appended to an intolerable deal of exhortation. The letter which King George III addressed to his son on June 13, 1779 can speak for all the rest, allowing for the strengthening note of acrimony as William seemed to respond inadequately to the admonishments:

'You are now launching into a scene of Life, where You may either prove an Honour or a Disgrace to Your Family. It would be very unbecoming of the love I have for my Children if I did not at this serious moment give You advice how to conduct yourself. Had I taken the common method of doing it in Conversation, it would soon have been forgot: therefore I prefer this mode, as I trust you will frequently peruse this, as it is dictated from no other motive than the anxious feelings of a Parent, that his child may be happy, and deserve the approbation of Men of Worth and Integrity.

'You should never lose sight', urged the King, 'of the certainty that every thought as well as action, is known to the All wise Disposer of the Universe and that no solid comfort ever in this World can exist, without a firm reliance on His Protection . . . these reflections are still more necessary to be foremost in the minds of those at Sea . . . . therefore, I strongly recommend the habitual reading of the Holy Scriptures and Your more and more placing that reliance on the Divine Creator, which is the only real means of obtaining that peace of mind, that alone can fit a Man for arduous undertaking.

'Remember You are now quitting home, where it has been the object of those who were placed about You to correct Your faults, yet keep them out of sight of the World. Now You are entering into a Society of about seven hundred persons, who will watch every step You take, will freely make their remarks, and communicate them to the whole Fleet; thus what would I hope have been cured must now be instantly avoided, or will be forever remembered to Your disadvantage.

'Though when at home a Prince, on board the *Prince George* You are only a Boy learning the Naval Profession; but the Prince so far accompanies You that what other Boys might do, You must not. It must never be out of Your thoughts that more Obedience is necessary from You to Your Superiours in the Navy, more Politeness to Your Equals and more good nature to Your Inferiours, than from those who have not been told that these are essential to a Gentleman.'[17]

The trouble about Polonius was not that he talked nonsense or phrased his sense inelegantly but that he went on so. George III went on too; nor was Queen Charlotte much less persistent. To King George's Royal Hunt and Storm his wife provided piano passages of muted maternal reproach. The penalty of being prosy is to be ignored. The sheer volume of improving and minatory matter which emerged from his parents ensured that William ended by paying no attention. He never lost his terror, or indeed his admiration of his father, but gradually the latter's letters ceased to impress.

Not that this was apparent from Prince William's replies. Nothing could have been more ingratiating than the tone he adopted. In November the cruise was almost over and he could expect soon to see his father again. I hope, he wrote, 'I am in the way of proving an honour to my country and a comfort to my parents; that my moral conduct is not infected by the great deal of vice I have seen, nor my manners more impolite by the roughness peculiar to most seamen'.[18] It is comforting to suppose that after penning these pious reflections under the eye of Midshipman the Reverend Henry Majendie, Prince William plunged back into the midshipmen's mess where he would behave as roughly and as impolitely as any of his fellows.

The Prince quickly followed his letter back to England. The *Prince George* was under orders to take on stores and provisions for a six months' cruise and it seemed at first as if William would have to stay with his ship.[19] This did not please him at all; he appealed to the Queen, who in turn over-persuaded the King. William's mess-mates can not have been best pleased at being left behind to cope with the extra duties but he seems to have spent only a week or so at Windsor and was on board again directly after Christmas.

This time the cruise was to be rather more eventful. On January 8, 1780, the fleet under Rodney captured a Spanish convoy and its escort. The Spanish flag-ship of sixty-four guns was quickly occupied by a British crew and named the *Prince William*, 'in respect to his Royal Highness, in whose presence she had the honour to be taken'.[20] Better still was to follow, for on January 16 Rodney engaged the main Spanish fleet under Don Juan de Langara. 'Won't we give these dons a sound thrashing!' said William gleefully to his neighbour. The battle of Cape St Vincent was duly joined. The fighting was tough and the *Prince George* several times in real danger but the dons were thrashed as soundly as ever Prince William could have wished; seven ships-of-the-line being captured or destroyed and several more severely damaged. The battle began at 4 p.m., wrote the Prince to his father.[21] 'Soon after the *St Domingo* blew up; a most shocking and dreadful sight. Being not certain whether it was an enemy or a friend, I felt a horror all over me . . .'

Don Juan de Langara was captured and visited Admiral Digby on board the *Prince George*. Prince William was presented to him and then retired. When Don Juan was ready to leave, 'his Royal Highness

appeared in the character of a midshipman, and respectfully informed
the admiral that the barge was ready.' Surprised at this apparition the
Spanish admiral exclaimed: 'Well does Great Britain merit the empire
of the sea, when the humblest stations in her navy are filled by princes
of the blood!'[22]

The historian must inevitably feel suspicious of improving anecdotes
which so often prove to have sprung from the pens of official hagio-
graphers. This one appears to be reasonably well attested. But even if
Don Juan had not made the remark, he certainly should have. Prince
William's presence on board and his activities were indeed astonishing
and did credit to the King and to the navy. The Spaniards, or indeed
any other Royal house in Europe, would have done well to note it.

The *Prince George*, with William still aboard, sailed on to Gibraltar.
The Prince happily scrambled all over the rock; in theory inspecting
the defences. With his closest friend among the midshipmen, Lord
Augustus Beauclerk, he did the round of the pubs and became involved in a brawl when he overheard a group of soldiers insulting the
navy. He was arrested and it took the admiral's urgent intervention to
get him out of prison. It was the first of a series, almost a lifetime of
escapades which were to cost him much in the eyes of the sage and the
grave but to win the hearts of many more ordinary mortals.

The return to England also had its share of triumphs. On February
21 a French convoy was intercepted and captured, the French flagship
yielding a highly acceptable booty of £100,000 in ready money. 'Thus
far in the year 80,' wrote Prince William to the King, 'everything has
been successful on our side, as if Providence was resolved to punish our
enemies for having begun the war so unjustly.'[23] Here too was the
first manifestation of a lifetime's habit. William was never to doubt the
fundamental truth – that God, whatever the circumstances, was a
member of the British team.

*

The Prince got back to London to find himself something of a hero.
The ground had been prepared by Admiral Digby who not only sup-
pressed all reference to the contretemps in Gibraltar but told the
gratified if slightly incredulous King that the Prince would make 'a
very great sea officer'. He cannot have had much on which to base his
judgment but William's courage and enthusiasm were undoubted
and the admiral had a better case when he noted approvingly that, 'the
moment he saw that they were preparing for action his spirits rose to

that degree that he was almost in a state of insanity . . . the moment the fleets were separated, his spirits sank very low'. William was allowed to hand over to his father the flags of the French and Spanish admirals and, for perhaps the first and certainly the last time, found himself unequivocally approved of, even admired by both his parents. The London public went further and seem to have assumed that the Prince, perhaps with a little help from Rodney, had personally won the battle of Cape St Vincent. When he went to Drury Lane there was a near riot and a bridge had to be thrown between pit and stage to allow his would-be worshippers to escape without asphyxiation.

The admirable Henry Pye, the Bard of Faringdon, joined in the paean of praise with some of his – mercifully – inimitable verses:

> *'Now last, not "least in love", the Muse*
> *Her WILLIAM's name would fondly chuse*
> *The British youth among*
> *Still may the sailors love thy name*
> *And happy health and blooming fame*
> *Awake the future song . . .*
>
> *E'en now the sea-green sisters bind*
> *A wreath around the growing mind,*
> *And deck their fav'rite son . . .'*

while another poet, alas anonymous, contributed a still more striking testimony to the feats of this marvel-working midshipman:

> *'As the young eagle to the blaze of day,*
> *Undazzled and undaunted, turns her eyes,*
> *So, unappall'd, when glory led the way,*
> *'Midst storms of war, 'midst mingling seas and skies,*
> *The genuine offspring of the Brunswick name*
> *Prov'd his high birth's hereditary claim;*
> *And the applauding nation hail'd with joy*
> *Their future hero in the intrepid boy.'*

If any boy of sixteen is told often enough that he is intrepid, a young eagle and has done something altogether out of the ordinary then he will begin to believe it. All his life William disliked and distrusted flattery, a characteristic which was to stand him in good stead when he was King, but after a month or two of adulation he had become decidedly swollen-headed.

Thomas Byam Martin, who was to figure in William's life for another fifty years, first met him when he was eight and the Prince sixteen. He was, said Martin, 'a fair-looking youth with a florid complexion, light hair and a pleasing countenance, but a squat form.' Martin could not understand the 'respect, ceremony and submission' shown towards Prince William by his father and other officials, '. . . almost doubting if the youth could be of the same flesh and blood as ourselves'. The Prince, he considered, talked too much and too assertively, and it was high time that he again experienced 'the wholesome check of a little man-of-war discipline'. Princely hauteur, however, had not set very deep. A few days later Thomas Martin and his ten-year-old brother Joe picked a quarrel with Prince William in the garden. The lessons of the midshipmen's mess were not forgotten: William cuffed their heads, abused them vigorously and a general set-to was only checked by the arrival of the grown-ups.[24]

And so the Prince's naval career wore on: cruises of two or three months, always uncomfortable, sometimes dangerous, varied by brief periods of leave at Kew and Windsor. He continued his education with tolerable diligence, 'I have begun Opticks . . . and am now able to keep the Ship's reckoning;' 'I have begun Mechanicks'; and hankered as much as ever after a battle: 'If an English Squadron of 28 Sail-of-the-Line . . . cannot beat 32 Spaniards, they ought not to see England again . . .'[25] His parents never stopped exhorting him to greater efforts, Queen Charlotte taking up the cudgels with her plaintive: 'I love You so well, that I cannot bear the idea of Your being only Mediocre. Perfection is the thing you should aim at . . .' Time and again they bemoaned his thoughtlessness, his bad temper, his reluctance to endure any kind of criticism. The favour in which he had basked after his earlier cruises had quickly faded: once the novelty of having a sailor son wore off he reverted to his more accustomed role of hobbledehoy who obstinately refused to mature into a statesman or even a gentleman.

In January 1781 he gave the King and Queen a fresh cause for concern. For the first time in a life pitted with romantic incident, Prince William fell in love. The affairs of princes attract unmerited attention; a friendly word becomes a proposition, a kiss an intimate and long-drawn-out liaison. William, it is only fair to say, gave the gossips much choice material to work on. Little is known about his first love, Miss Julia Fortescue, except that she was an outstandingly pretty girl, 'a more lovely creature never blessed the earth with her presence', and her parents lived in a house looking over Green Park. They met at a ball at St James's, danced all evening together and wooed busily over the following weeks in a series of inadequately secret assignations in the park. The Prince was said to want to marry her – he probably did; he wanted to marry a surprising number of the girls he met – but the affair had not the remotest chance of reaching so happy a conclusion. Miss Fortescue was packed off to Scotland where she married a Drummond and that was the end of her. William went off to help relieve Gibraltar. But this was only a temporary measure. When the next cruise was over it was decided that he should be exiled to still more distant climes.

CHAPTER III

Service Overseas

PRINCE WILLIAM's amatory entanglement was by no means the only, or even the most important of the reasons for his posting to a foreign station. At the end of another vast, didactic letter the King remarked wistfully that, at the beginning of his leave, his son had deplored the improper behaviour of 'one who is dear to all of Us' but that since then things had changed and recently it had appeared, 'You have been more desirous of getting out of the room and perhaps in some degree copying what seemed very properly not to please You when You first came back to Us'.[1] The fact that the King went on to forbid William to write to his brothers without first showing the letter to Majendie proves, if proof were needed, that the 'one' in question was the Prince of Wales.

With Prince Frederick in Germany since the end of 1780 William had become a figure of some consequence in his brother's eyes. The Prince of Wales was now established at Carlton House, had fallen under the influence of his uncle, Henry Frederick, Duke of Cumberland, and was almost totally estranged from his parents. A battle developed, if not for the soul then at least for the society of Prince William. The King, for the moment, carried the bigger guns and William answered his latest outburst with the meek admission that he had undoubtedly been imposed upon by bad advice.[2] 'Very unfortunately,' he wrote priggishly in a later letter, 'the Prince of Wales has taken a terrible course of life, which he might perhaps (had I been home) have induced me to lead, which would have been very much to my own detriment, and very much to Your's, Sir, and the Queen's mortification and grief.'[3] But, whatever he might tell the King, he found the society of the Prince of Wales and his modish cronies infinitely preferable to the starchiness of the court. Whenever he could escape to Carlton House he did. The King, seeing what was happening, was grieved but knew that, in the last resort, he would be powerless to prevent it. A few thousand miles of sea between the brothers might do much good.

When Admiral Digby in the *Prince George* was given command of the American station the King, therefore, decided to let his son go along. With luck some political dividends too might accrue. Things had been going badly in America, morale among the loyalists was low, and the presence on the continent of a prince of the blood royal, however humble his official status, might do something to cheer them up. Prince William himself seems to have accepted the posting with equanimity. Certainly he felt forlorn at his separation from Miss Fortescue, but for a boy of just seventeen the prospect of a brave new world was not to be despised, especially when the journey involved so vast a removal from parental discipline. William wrote to the King of his good fortune in being able to see 'the characters of different nations'[4] and there is no reason to suppose him hypocritical.

New York was also resolved to make the most of it. A huge crowd met him at the quay-side, bellowing 'God Bless King George' with an enthusiasm which might have misled even a less partial visitor into believing that he had come to a continent peopled exclusively by patriots. The Prince noted with pleasure that the dissenters and Quakers seemed particularly well-disposed. One Quaker came up to him and said: 'God Bless Thy Father; it is not for want of respect that I do not take my hat off, but because my Religion requires it.'[5] He was met by the general and admiral, received by a Captain's Guard with Colours, introduced to Benedict Arnold and made the subject of a special sermon by the rector of the Episcopal church. This latter worthy indulged in flattery so sycophantic as to be almost idolatrous. Prince William, he implied, if not actually himself the Son of God, at least stood so high in the company of saints as to engender speculation about the divine origins of the House of Hanover.

Prince William was not particularly struck by New York. 'The town is built in the Dutch way, with trees before the houses,' he told his father. 'The streets are in general narrow and very ill-paved. There is but one Church, all the others being converted into magazines or Barracks.'[6] Society was limited, female society in particular, and, with winter approaching, he saw small comfort in the squalid little port. He hoped he might be allowed a cruise in the West Indies but the idea was quickly crushed and he passed a chilly winter in the admiral's house at New York, continuing his studies and preparing, with the help of Mr Majendie, 'an extract . . . relative to the present state of affairs in this continent'.[7] He found skating too difficult but enjoyed being whisked around a frozen lake on a chair fixed on runners – otherwise his main diversion seems to have been to prowl around the outskirts of the town in search of he knew not what.

It was probably this habit of solitary wandering which first put it into the minds of the American revolutionaries that a prince of the blood royal might be a useful bargaining counter in any future negotiations. A certain Colonel Ogden devised a sea-borne operation involving four whale-boats and a commando of some forty men who were to swoop on New York one rainy night and carry off Admiral Digby as well as the Prince. Washington was delighted by the project:

'The spirit of enterprise so conspicuous in your plan for surprising in their quarters and bringing off the Prince William Henry and Admiral Digby merits applause; and you have my authority to make the attempt in any manner, and at such a time, as your judgment may direct.

'I am fully persuaded, that it is unnecessary to caution you against offering insult or indignity to the persons of the Prince or Admiral . . .'[8]

One theory has it that Washington was playing with the idea of setting up Prince William as king of an independent United States. There is no reason to suppose that any idea so bizarre crossed his mind. Certainly the Prince would never have countenanced it. But the confrontation between the two men would have been striking and a spell as Washington's prisoner might have had interesting effects on William's character. Such speculation is profitless, however; hints of the project somehow came to the ears of the British, guards were doubled, and with the chance of surprise gone Colonel Ogden wisely called off his attempt.

*

Though William played the prince more energetically than before, he was still a sailor. Chief Justice Smyth dined aboard the *Prince George* towards the end of 1781 and found him more agreeable than he had expected. 'Paying our Compliments on departure, the Admiral observed the boat was not yet manned. The Prince instantly started up and took his hat. "I, Gentlemen, will see your boat manned." I told the Admiral that I little expected . . . to have the honour of such assistance from a Prince. "The Prince," said the Admiral, "is a Midshipman on board this ship, and never stops at any part of the duty of his station." [9]

It was as well for him that he had not learned to neglect his duties for in the spring of 1782 he transferred to the *Warwick* under the command of the formidable Captain Elphinstone, later Lord Keith. Keith was no man to pamper princelings and he would not have let William escape an iota of his duties. As it happened, however, the cruise was marred for Prince William by a 'terrible accident' – probably a fall from the rigging – which at one time the King feared might cost him the use of his arm.[10] No doubt the reports were exaggerated; at any rate no permanent harm was done and within three weeks the Prince was convalescent. By the time *Warwick* returned to New York the cure was almost complete and a course of cold baths somewhat surprisingly completed the good work.

During his absence Sir Samuel, now Lord Hood, his father's particular pet among the admirals, had arrived with a separate squadron in the *Barfleur*. Admiral Digby was instructed to hand over his charge – an order which he received with some chagrin but more relief – and the Prince was barely given time to step ashore before the exchange was made. 'We shall now be very curious to hear from Yourself how You like Your present situation,' wrote the Queen. 'Lord Hood besides the great Merits in His Profession bears so excellent a Moral and Religious Character that I feel quite easy to know You in such good Hands.'[11]

In spite of this discouraging thought, Prince William quickly concluded that he was going to like his new situation. He knew that he could manage Hood far more effectively than either Keith or Digby. He decided that his transfer meant that he had now become a man. He was resolved that he should in future be treated as such. The point was underlined by the dismissal of Majendie. Hood had no intention of allowing a potentially meddlesome cleric aboard his ship and packed him back to England at the first opportunity. The Prince rejoiced. Majendie was one of those indeterminate figures that lurk in the wings of history: at best the prompter, at worst a menial shifter of scenes. William quite liked him, even respected him, but he had little influence on his charge and made himself acceptable only by avoiding any direct collision. His chosen tactic, indeed, was to shun not only collisions but any real friendship. 'I have always found my advantage in avoiding entering into Jokes or Satirical Remarks,' he wrote on one occasion. 'When the Banter was innocent I have chosen rather to keep aloof . . .'[12]

What was worse, he tried to keep others aloof as well. 'Close connection or intimacy between His Royal Highness and any person whatever,' he boasted to the King, 'I have always thought it my duty to discourage.' Such chilling austerity can hardly have won the affection of his warm-hearted and impetuous pupil. For the Prince he remained a neuter but on the whole distasteful symbol of parental rôle.

The Prince was not to escape, however, without some supervision. Digby insisted that he should be attended by at least one officer who knew him already. Hood grumbled furiously. He did not want any spy of a rival admiral sticking his nose into what did not concern him. Digby, however, won his point. He selected a certain Captain Napier, 'a Man of Family, a steady Firm Man and a Man of Honor'; as the perfect companion for the Prince: 'I flatter myself, when Captain Napier is a little better known to him [Hood] He will be of my opinion. Though I rather think he will not rest till he gets him removed.'[13] The first part of this prophecy was over-sanguine, the second disastrously correct.

Poor Captain Napier never had a chance. Prince William quarrelled with him almost from the first day. The two men had fundamentally different concepts of their relationship. Napier considered that he was William's supervisor; a senior officer deputed to direct his studies and correct his conduct, with courtesy and consideration certainly but also firmly and with authority. To the Prince, Napier was no more than an attendant, something between a jumped-up valet and a private secretary. Add to this that Napier was brash and tactless, William quick to resent the best-deserved reproof, and it was evident that trouble must lie ahead. Before the end of their first cruise together, in January, 1783, William was complaining to Hood about Napier's 'disgusting conduct . . . so very different from what he had been accustomed to' while Napier counter-charged that the Prince was impossible to control or even to advise.

Hood not surprisingly took Prince William's side. He roundly told the unfortunate captain that '. . . there was a manner and Language to be made of to [sic] His Royal Highness very different from what a dogmatical country Pedant would use to one of his scholars', and that he had 'neither seen nor heard anything of the Prince, but what was truly amiable and proper . . .' William was not to be treated as a child; being so 'volatile, it was necessary He should be *reasoned* into what was right, and not be treated with an austerity and harshness of Language'.[14] When Napier asked to leave the ship he sped him on his way and wrote to the King in glowing terms of the Prince's nobility and patience under the almost intolerable affronts of his companion.

The King was not prepared to swallow so one-sided a story. 'I cannot admire the warmth He has shewn in the disputes that have arisen between Him and Captain Napier,' the King wrote to Hood.[15] 'William has ever been violent when controlled. I had hoped that by this time He would have been conscious of his own levity.' Napier might have been too hasty yet that could not excuse the violence of his son's reaction.

One may admire the objectivity which could make a father so swiftly accept the more critical of two reports upon his son. There is little doubt that the King's view of the affair was more nearly correct than Hood's. Nevertheless impartiality can be at times a chilling virtue and understanding more important in a relationship. If George III had been less ready to see the bad side of his sons it is possible that they in their turn might have been less determined always to turn their bad side towards their father.

For William this trivial contretemps had an important consequence. George III made up his mind that the navy alone could never turn his son into a worthy prince. A period on land was needed to give him the polish and self-restraint which marks a gentleman and to complete his military education. He must go to a country where the soldiers' arts were properly appreciated; a country where a British prince would be treated with proper deference and where he could remain to some extent under his father's eye; a country, above all, where the Prince of Wales was not. As soon as he returned to Europe, the King resolved, Prince William should go to Hanover.[16]

*

The cruise with Hood, however, still had some time to run. It started with a disappointment when the preliminaries of peace were signed in Paris in November 1782. Hostilities gradually spluttered out as the news filtered through to the various fields of battle. 'Prince William is in the dumps about peace,' wrote Hood to Budé, 'as His heart was sett upon seeing service in this country . . .'[17] But a trip to the West Indies more than made up for this deprivation. The fleet was based on Port Royal in Jamaica; most of the time was spent at sea but there was quite enough on shore to allow William some reasonably innocent dissipation. At Havana he is supposed to have lost his heart to Doña Maria Soleno, the lustrous daughter of his host, the Spanish admiral.

The Prince was extricated before he became seriously compromised. The story was probably exaggerated by the gossip-mongers, its interest lies in the fact that the naval officer who looked after him was the twenty-five-year-old commander of the *Albemarle* frigate, Horatio Nelson.

Prince William had first met Nelson a few months before when the *Barfleur* was lying off Staten Island. 'He appeared to be the merest boy of a Captain I ever beheld,' William told Dr Clarke many years later.[18] His first reaction was one of suspicion tinged with faint hostility, but the suspicion wore off after only a few moments' conversation: 'There was something irresistibly pleasing in his address and conversation; and an enthusiasm, when speaking on professional subjects, that showed he was no common being.' It was not surprising that William should have been dazzled and impressed, more interesting that Nelson appeared genuinely attached to the young Prince and had a high opinion of his abilities. He did not merely fawn on him in public but wrote of him with equal enthusiasm in letters to his closest friends.

'He will be, I am certain, an ornament to our service. He is a seaman, which you could hardly suppose, with every other qualification you may expect from him; but he will be a disciplinarian, and a strong one ... with the best temper and great good sense, he cannot fail of being pleasing to everyone.'[19]

Hood urged the Prince to turn to Nelson for help or advice whenever he felt the need and William had the sense to do so. It is intriguing to speculate what would have happened if he had had a Nelson rather than a Napier as his official mentor. Even as it was Nelson's influence was considerable and always beneficial but the two men did not see enough of each other to make the impression profound or lasting.

And so back to England, to the uncertainties of a continental visit, above all to reunion with his parents. Prince William was as obsessed as ever by his relationship with the King and Queen. Towards the beginning of his last cruise he seemed at last to have won their approval. Hood, he knew, had reported on him enthusiastically and the King had been delighted. '. . . this is the first time,' he wrote wistfully to his father in April 1783, 'I have had the pleasure of receiving a letter from Your Majesty as from a tender parent to his son grown up.' It was also close to being the last, for even before he acknowledged the letter the Napier affair had once again aroused his father's darkest thoughts. He was returning, if not in disgrace, at least in disfavour. For someone who believed that his conduct deserved more praise than blame it was a hard homecoming.

It predisposed him, of course, to make common cause with the Prince of Wales, who by now provided a rallying point for the Opposition. There is no reason to believe that the Prince had given any serious thought to political affairs. Nevertheless it does seem that at this point in his life, before his political arteries had begun to harden, or the generous impulses of youth die down, he was more disposed than ever again to welcome radical ideas. A curious letter survives from a Captain Maxwell, written shortly before the Prince left for England and intended to enlist his aid in pressing various reforms on the King and thence the Board of Admiralty. 'The time is not far distant,' wrote the captain, 'when the voice of the people will be para-mount in the country, and the improvements in the administration of their affairs will depend on other persons than that of the sovereign or a junta of men, who preside over the most important branch of the public service . . .'[20] There is no reason to believe that William shared such heretical beliefs, equally Maxwell would hardly have risked putting them forward if he had not expected the Prince to receive them with some sympathy. It would be absurd to make too much of this. Naval messes are traditionally conservative and William can never have heard much revolution preached. Still, his mind was not yet wholly made up and he was at least ready to question some of those first principles which to King and ministers seemed so immutable.

But though Prince William might have been politically well-disposed towards his brother's camp, it was more doubtful whether he would prove socially acceptable. He was still not quite eighteen when he returned to England and except for brief periods of leave had been at sea or abroad for the last four years. He lacked totally the polish and *savoir-faire* that was prized above all in the circle of the Prince of Wales; raucous practical joking was more his line than witty repartee, school-boy riots in the midshipmen's mess than drawing-room debauches. When he first saw his brother Frederick wearing a coat of bright gamboge yellow with large steel buttons, light blue trousers and puce waistcoat he took it that this was fancy dress. Assured with some hauteur that, on the contrary, it was the latest fashion, he bellowed with laughter and cracked a laborious naval joke about 'Yellow Admirals', which must have been entirely lost upon Prince Frederick.

His brothers, however, did not intend to miss a chance to score off the King. Prince William arrived at St James's to be told that his parents would receive him at a designated hour in the not-too-immediate future; Prince Frederick and the Prince of Wales rushed to welcome him. They found that, though he lacked finish, he was by no means unacceptable as a companion. The standards applied to the charms of eighteenth-century princes were traditionally pitched pretty low but there seems no reason to doubt that he was a personable young man, at pains to please all who encountered him. Horace Walpole, who met him in July at Princess Amelia's, prided himself on being 'not apt to be intoxicated with royalty'. Nevertheless he found Prince William charming; 'Lively, cheerful, talkative, manly, well-bred, sensible, and exceedingly proper in his replies . . .' '. . . he was in great spirits all day,' commented Walpole, 'though with us old women – perhaps he thought it preferable to Windsor!'[21] He took to London society with what his father could only consider alarming alacrity and by so doing fortified the King's resolve to get him out of England as soon as possible.

*

The two years or so which Prince William spent in Hanover were perhaps the least satisfactory of his life. Every weakness in his character seemed to have been exaggerated, every virtue nullified. And yet he left London with the best possible intentions and a most promising blue-print for his improvement. 'My great object,' the King told Budé, 'is that my dearly beloved son may learn the German language, the law of nations, the grounds of civil law, engineering, artillery and military tactics . . .'[22] But that was, in fact, only part of the grand design. Hanover was to achieve the miracle which the navy had failed to perform; William was to be transformed into a sage, suave and accomplished statesman. He was to go there a sailor; to emerge an officer, a gentleman and a prince.

The debacle which followed can be blamed in part at least on the choice of his companions. Prince William was to be closely attended by Captain William Merrick, a cheerful extrovert with limited force of character whose titular function seems to have been little more than to help the Prince inspect the Neapolitan fleet if he should ever happen to get that far. Merrick, however, counted for little: for anything except the most trivial details, the Prince's conduct and train of life was the responsibility of the bleak and unimaginative Budé. The appointment was calamitous, if only because William associated Budé with his childhood and resented fiercely the latter's reappearance now that he felt himself a man. Budé had not the least idea how to manage this sensitive and short-tempered youth, who would indeed have been a challenging proposition for a man far more talented. He would try to impose his will by threats and bullying; then relapse into baffled and defeatist acquiescence. In the first mood Prince William resented and opposed, in the second ignored him. His presence was indeed counter-productive since some part of William's wilful misbehaviour can be traced to his determination to annoy the General.

But to keep William in the paths of righteousness, the King depended quite as much on Prince Frederick. The lay Bishop of Osnaburgh had now spent the best part of three years in Germany, was thoroughly at home there and in theory should have been the obvious person to show his younger brother the ropes. Why the King had such confidence in and love for his second son will always be a mystery; that the confidence was misplaced was demonstrated brutally over the next few years. Greville described him as the only gentleman among the princes: a reflection possibly unjust to his brothers and certainly over-flattering to him, for whatever connotation the word 'gentleman' may carry it cannot properly include the boorishness and dishonesty which marked Frederick's conduct. He regarded William with a faintly contemptuous affection, patronizing him as only a worldly-wise roué of twenty can patronize a hobbledehoy of eighteen. He told the Prince of Wales that he found his brother boringly fond of practical jokes and excessively rough and rude;[23] Prince William, who almost simultaneously was begging his eldest brother for cocked-hats, shoe buckles and an elegant watch chain, would barely have recognized the description.

Perhaps Frederick's least attractive feature was his tendency to gamble. It was not just that he lost money – which he did in profusion for his play was both reckless and incompetent – but that he hated to pay his debts when he had done so. Prince William was no more successful and laboured under what his brother would have considered a laughably bourgeois preoccupation with settling his losses. Since his allowance was a mere £100 a year he soon got into trouble. Within a year his debts amounted to some fifteen hundred crowns, incurred as much on clothes and houses as at the tables, and Budé asked the King for permission to pay them off. The King agreed, accompanying his consent with a solemn blast of reproach to his erring son:

'. . . I cannot too strongly set before your eyes that if you permit yourself to indulge every foolish idea you must be wretched all your life, for with thirteen children I can but with the greatest care make both ends meet and am not in a situation to be paying their debts if they contract any, and to anyone that has either the sentiments of common honesty or delicacy, without the nicer feelings which every gentleman ought to possess, the situation of not paying what is due is a very unpleasant situation. In you I fear that vanity, which has been too predominant in your character has occasioned this, but I hope for the future you will be wiser.'[24]

Prince William had another unpleasant experience when he became involved with Baron Hardenberg, an adventurer who specialized in fleecing tyros at the gambling tables. William won a considerable sum, presumably laid out as bait by the Baron, and then disconcerted his opponent by retiring from the game. Hardenberg solaced his feelings by insulting the Prince and Captain Merrick challenged him to a duel. William tried to take the quarrel on himself and in turn challenged the Baron. Budé then hurriedly intervened, threatened to have Hardenberg denounced for some long-forgotten scandal in Berlin and induced him to apologize to William and quit Hanover. The affair was over, but it left an unpleasant memory. Perhaps in part because of it, the Prince never became a serious gambler; even when money had ceased to be a problem, Pope Joan for one shilling stakes remained his favourite game. He assured his father that he would be out of debt by the end of the year. 'Promises, I will no more make, as Your Majesty hints that my parents are not to be deceived by such things. Believe me, Sir, my intention was not to blind the eyes of my best friends, as I hope I may call my parents ... I have too much honour to leave my debts unpaid.'[25] This time at least he seems to have kept his word.

*

Prince William quickly settled down to a routine as effortless as it was uninspiring. On a typical day, he would get up at about eight, spin out the process of rising for as long as possible, then breakfast with his brother preparatory to an interminable visit to the royal stud. This would usually be followed by an inspection of the troops on the market place. Dinner would be taken with some high official: no women, no conviviality and a minimum of conversation. What there was related almost exclusively to horses. A visit to the theatre would often follow. Since, for the first few months at least, he found great difficulty in following the German, his evenings can hardly have been merry. Only the fall of the final curtain released him for the gambling houses or other, still less reputable, pleasures.

The trouble was that he did not enjoy the same things as his hosts. He did not like horses, about which the lives of so many Hanoverians revolved. He did not like boar-shooting; the recoil of the rifle hurt his shoulder and he always seemed to miss. He did not care for military matters, and life in Hanover was largely tailored to meet the soldier's needs. Above all he did not like the Hanoverians. Hanoverian society was arid, formal and governed by inexorable good taste; Aldershot aping Versailles. Prince William, who at that time cared mainly for whores and naval officers, was horribly out of place in these stagnant salons. He quarrelled with most and was deplored by all the leading lights of the Hanoverian establishment.

The result was that Prince William became more of a social pariah than would have seemed possible for a son of the King of England. He was lonely and disgruntled. Nor was he making any striking progress with his studies. He picked up German and acquired a smattering of military knowledge but there it stopped. He was still open to new impressions, ready to be engaged in new occupations, yet Budé made no effort to interest him in the constitutional or social condition of the country. When he visited Berlin, Baron Walstein took him to visit a slum quarter. He was genuinely shocked and distressed by what he saw; he had never suspected that the poor lived like that. There were slums enough in Hanover and the Prince could certainly have found them for himself if he had taken the trouble. But he needed encouragement and advice; it is typical of Budé that he never considered for a moment that they might constitute a field of study proper for a prince.

Gradually William settled down; he found a circle of more or less congenial friends, manufactured a few occupations, and decided life was not so bad after all:

'To say I preferred Germany to England would be false,' he wrote to the Prince of Wales in January 1784, 'yet at the same time I must allow I pass my time very agreeably . . . I at first, like so many of my countrymen, abored everything that was German for no other reason in the world than because it was not English. I now begin to see things in general with different eyes from what I did at first. An honest man, whether an Englishman or a German, is still an honest

man and there are a great many such here, it is my own fault if I
keep company with bad ones. You will very likely say that [this]
is an hipocritical letter,' he concluded disingenuously. 'By no means,
I assure you. I have two reasons for writing in this manner; the one
is to show you that when I chuse I can write as sensible letters as
anybody, the other is to give you a just idea of his Majesty's subjects
at Hanover.'[26]

His tribute to the Hanoverians was becoming but perhaps a more convincing explanation of his new-found content came in another letter,
written a month or two later. 'I have introduced myself,' he said
ominously, 'into the private parties of the women.'[27] In spring, summer,
autumn and winter alike, the Prince's fancy lightly turned to thoughts
of love. It is hard to understand entirely his attitude towards women.
The two long and, on the whole, satisfactory liaisons which marked
his life show him as a model of constancy, selfish and inconsiderate at
times but convincedly monogamous. Yet at other periods of his life,
by no means only in his youth, he leapt from pinnacle to pinnacle of
female charm with the addresse of an agile if overweight gazelle.
More Don Quixote than Don Juan his advances rarely ended in success.
He lacked the cool professionalism of the accredited seducer. Each
time he genuinely believed himself in love – perhaps, therefore, *was* in
love – yet he would rebound with ebullience and disconcerting speed
so that the old love was still recovering her breath when she observed
him in energetic pursuit of the new.

Prince William had barely arrived in Hanover before he fell in love
with the fourteen-year-old Princess Charlotte of Mecklenburg-Strelitz,
his mother's niece. Budé wrote to the Queen in high alarm; he was
doing what he could to check the affair but was doubtful how far he
had succeeded.[28] The Queen was not gravely concerned. 'Your attachment to my niece,' she wrote, '. . . does not for the moment surprise
me, as you are of an age when young men are apt to fancy themselves
in love with every sprightly young woman they see.'[29] Budé was urged
to watch Prince William carefully and the Queen's instructions showed
how little confidence she had in her son's capacity to keep his word.
She stressed her fear lest 'Notre jeune Homme, sous l'apparence de la
Sommission aux Arrangements que Vous avez prise avec mon Frère ne Nous
joue un mauvais Tour et en parle à la Princesse . . . Il en est bien capable car
sa vivacité et ses passions l'emporte toujours sur son jugement.'[30]

Prince William recovered from this set-back with alacrity. By the
K.W.

end of 1783 he was vigorously courting Maria Schindbach, the pretty daughter of a rich merchant. He took her for drives in a sledge drawn by one of the celebrated cream-coloured horses from the royal stud at Hanover. Such delights, however, failed to blunt her bourgeois caution; she resisted his advances, opted for the second best and emerged as the fiancée of Captain Merrick. The Prince felt some relief as he had been becoming dangerously entangled. 'I am happy to find Your Royal Highness got so well over the Affair of *La Petite Fille*,' wrote a friend from London. 'They are Dangerous things to deal with, and when worth looking after, require a great deal of Secrecy and trouble in the Pursuit.'[31]

Then there was the mysterious, perhaps even mythical, affair with Caroline von Linsingen. Caroline was the daughter of General Wilhelm von Linsingen of the 12th Hanoverian Infantry. She was a sickly romantic of the Werther school who left a detailed account of her frustrated passion.[32] She and Prince William, she recorded, loved each other deeply and were married in a mountain chapel near Pyrmont. 'But, William, say now if we should one day be parted, what then?' 'Then grief and misery and woe will be our lot through life . . .' After the ceremony her young husband knelt before her: 'Whether or no Fate's chill shadow fall upon us, our bond of union is eternal – you are mine and I, I am Caroline's blissful husband.' He was – for about three weeks and long enough to sire a son, Heinrich – then departed. Caroline wasted away, was laid out as dead, plucked back from the verge of the grave by a young surgeon and married him in lieu of a fee. Her action relit all William's passion. 'I rave, I tremble, am again the William I was before I knew you . . . He has kindled your heart? Warmth of affection! Fire! Loudly, loudly do I scoff at them . . . Wife surpassed by none, wife that alone filled and will for ever fill my heart, wife with a soul of fire, *you* love for eternity; and only William, only your earliest love, can suffice for you.'

Apart from the implausibility of the prosaic Prince wooing in such terms, the main flaw in this romantic tale is that none of the dates fit. William was not in Hanover during the period in which he was supposed to have been courting Caroline; when he was said to have met her he was in fact at Plymouth, the day of their 'marriage' he was watching a boat race in Richmond. Nor does his continued friendship with the Von Linsingens suggest that he had previously married and then abandoned a member of the family. The story must be dismissed as the ramblings of an over-active imagination.* And yet an obstinate crumb of doubt remains to nag the biographer. The story is so circumstantial, so filled with inconsistencies that could easily have been avoided if Caroline had taken even a little trouble, that one can hardly doubt that she was at least sincere. And if she were sincere, is not the most likely reason for her delusion that Prince William had done something to justify it? It would come as no surprise if it were shown that the ever-impressionable William had been bowled over by this languishing beauty and had laid heart, debts and princedom at her feet.

'Women as poxed as whores were the reason I am in disgrace,' wrote William sorrowfully to the Prince of Wales in April, 1785. Cut off from the aristocratic salons, denied the relief he craved by the middle-class beauties whom he courted, he turned hungrily to the brothels of Hanover or, less satisfactorily still, pursued his amours 'with a lady of the town against a wall or in the middle of the parade.'[33] Though hardly a paradigm of sensibility, it did not take him long to sicken of such delights. The squalor and tedium of his life at Hanover appalled him, yet he could not escape it.

Through the schoolboy bawdy that permeated his letters to his brother there runs a bitter undercurrent of resentment that he was being cut off from the finer pleasures of life. He wrote that he hated being 'in this damnable country, smoaking, playing at twopenny whist and wearing great thick boots. Oh, for England and the pretty girls of Westminster; at least to such as would not clap or pox me every time I fucked'.[34] His imagination did not run to a Nirvana more enticing than a pox-free Hanover with prettier girls and thinner boots, but at least he had no doubt that his present train of life did not meet either his needs or his inclinations.

*

Though three-quarters of Prince William's stay on the continent was passed in Hanover he managed to fit in a certain amount of travel. He went twice to Berlin, was taken on manoeuvres by Frederick the Great and sharply rebuked for not having read *Candide*. Moving back to Göttingen he attended a lecture by the great Michaelis. The historian, inspired by his audience, delivered an impromptu harangue on the sovereignty of the people. The Prince, with some naïvety, reported on

* I am indebted to Herr Henning v. Jeinsen of the Von Linsingen family for the assurance that, contrary to what has sometimes been stated, no information proving the existence of this marriage exists in the family archives.

this with approval to his father and suggested that it be translated into English. King George III reacted briskly; Michaelis was dismissed and another nail hammered into the coffin of William's reputation. In the autumn of 1784 he went on tour with Frederick. The two brothers, thinly disguised as Lord Fielding and Count Hoya, ended up in Prague for the Imperial Review. They were genially received by the Emperor Joseph but William claimed to have found the city sadly dissolute. After one masquerade he is said to have ended up with forty-seven cards slipped into his hand by different ladies seeking assignations. The bishop, he noted with some chagrin, had accumulated fifty-three.

During the last twelve months his parents' letters had grown increasingly acrimonious. The Queen found it hard to take her son altogether seriously when he spoke plaintively of his 'disposition towards Melancholy'. 'It is a thing so little known in your family,' she observed, 'that I cannot think it so serious, particularly as you say it arises from the dislike you have to the place you are at, and that you are sensible of not being liked.' The reason for his unpopularity, she pointed out, could only be his own behaviour and he made himself absurd by talking of hidden enemies who worked secretly to destroy his good name.[35] On an earlier occasion she reproached him with saying one thing and doing another: 'You have been a little like a *Cameleon*, I want you to be like an *Owl* that is wise . . .'[36]

If the King had been disposed to cull his own analogy from animal life he would probably have compared the Prince to an unkempt dog, inadequately house-trained and of uncertain temper. As the reports flowed in of his son's misbehaviour, his whore-mongering, his idleness, his incivility, George III's indignation mounted. 'I was most extremely hurt by the last letter Your Majesty thought proper to write to me,' the Prince wrote in April 1785. 'It gave me very great uneasiness to find my conduct had been so highly displeasing to my father.'[37] His father's chilling reply can have done nothing to mend his injured feelings.

Constantly he reverted to the same plea; let him leave Hanover, let him go to sea again, all would then be well. He tried to recruit Hood on his side but the admiral refused to be involved; the Prince should remain demurely where he was until the King thought fit to move him. The Duke of York did rather better; in part at least, one suspects, because he was heartily sick of his brother's presence in Hanover. He wrote to his father to pass on William's regrets for some unspecified folly. 'But pardon me, Sir, if I add, that there can never be any real alteration for the better in him till he has been kept for some time under severe discipline, which alone can be done on board of ship, for his natural inclination for all kinds of dissipation will make him, either here or indeed in any place by land, run into any society where he can form to himself only an idea of pleasure.'[38] Reluctantly the King gave way. It was unthinkable that the Prince should now be let loose in London; nothing remained but to send him once more to sea.

Prince William was delighted and wrote in ecstasies to his father.[39] His pleasure must, however, have been damped by the ostentation of his disgrace. When he got to England the King made him stay at the Queen's House at Kew where he could be strictly supervised and spared the temptation of St James's.[40] His first night at home the Prince of Wales was having a resplendent fête at Carlton House. Not unnaturally he hoped his brother would attend. 'Eh! what!' said the King, 'Eh! what! Take William away! Take William away! He shan't go – he shan't go! Just arrived from Hanover – Want to know how things are going on there. Fine stud! Fine stud!' The Prince of Wales persisted. 'Shan't go! Shan't go! Better with his mother tonight.' A furious family row ensued and Prince William stayed at Kew.[41] But he could not perpetually be so confined. Not a day must be lost before he was packed off again out of reach of his eldest brother.

CHAPTER IV

Shipwreck of a Career

❦

ON June 17, 1785, a full board of Admiralty approved Prince William's promotion to the rank of lieutenant. 'Had I been the son of an admiral instead of a King, I should have been a lieutenant long ago,'[1] he remarked wryly; and certainly he had received no special favour for, even though he had spent two years on shore, his six years as a midshipman would have been considered excessive by most of the well-connected. Lord Howe, who presided over the board, assured the King that his son 'was every inch a sailor' and had passed with flying colours. It would have been a striking gesture of independence if they had failed him but also unjust, for even Prince William's most embittered critics admitted that he was a perfectly competent junior officer. The Prince of Wales had just time to crowd in a celebratory breakfast at Carlton House before William was rushed away to join his ship at Portsmouth.

The *Hebe*, of forty-four guns, had originally been captured from the French. To the Prince she was the finest frigate in the Royal Navy. His only wish was that she were better manned; there were only a handful of trained seamen in the crew and he noted with disapproval that few were as tall or as stout as he was.[2] Almost before he had had time to settle *Hebe* was away on a mammoth tour of the British Isles. William knew little of his homeland beyond the immediate environs of London and a few seaports. The trip was a revelation to him, and by no means always a pleasant one. '. . . we have made a very extraordinary passage,' he wrote to his father. 'We have sailed around Scotland and touched in the Orkneys and the Hebrides and are now in Ireland.' He had been dismayed by the Orkneys where, 'everything is miserable beyond description: the common people go without shoes or stockings . . .' and not much better pleased by the Highlands: 'I think the inhabitants here are in a more miserable state than the negroes in the West Indies . . . this curious people. They do not talk English, it is not even understood here: they all talk Erse and wear the highland dress . . .'[3]

It was while *Hebe* was at Kirkwall that Prince William encountered John Moodie, an old shipmate who had done him some service while he was aboard *Prince George*. Finding that he was out of a job and likely to stay so the Prince offered him a pension of £40 a year, payable until it was no longer needed.[4] To be generous with money, usually other people's, is not a particularly endearing trait. There was, however, a good-heartedness about William's philanthropy which made it attractive. He did not casually scatter largesse and then forget about it but saw his good deed through. In Newfoundland a few months later he took over a penniless child who came to his notice, clothed him, trained him as a midshipman and, on return to England, sent him to school and back into the Navy.[5] He did the same thing with an orphan in Plymouth and in the end had the pleasure of signing his commission as Rear Admiral.[6] Not all his bounty was as well disposed. At Greenwich, when the governor tried to show him the Painted Hall, he instead insisted on visiting another old shipmate, John Adams, who had been placed in the hospital by his intercession. Adams addressed him with effusive gratitude as 'My Royal William' and the Prince pressed two guineas into his hand. The money was spent on gin, and Adams was hideously drunk the whole of the next day. But even if the Prince heard of this it is unlikely that he would have regretted his gesture: Adams had presumably had some fun with his money and his benefactor would not have felt it ill spent.[7]

Not that he had much money to spare. His letters to the Prince of Wales were full of appeals for help – £500 at one time, £1,000 at another. Sometimes he got it, more often he did not. It is hard to see why he needed such large sums. Once at least it was to lend it to a fellow officer.[8] Otherwise his life should not have been particularly expensive. Most of his time was spent at sea, when on shore at Portsmouth he usually stayed with the commissioner, Sir Henry Martin; he entertained little and gambled less. Expeditions to London were rarities. There is a story of a masked ball in the autumn of 1785 at which two of the guests came to blows. They were marched off by the guard and unmasked. 'Aye, William, is it you?' 'Aye, George, is it you?' and the embarrassed guards hurriedly released their princely prisoners. If the incident ever happened, it must have been exceptional, for William can hardly have visited the capital more than two or three times during his twelve months on a home station.

Not content with his recent advancement Prince William soon felt hat it was time to take another step up the naval ladder. In November,

1785, he wrote to his father to ask for the command of the *Phaeton*: 'I wish to be promoted, I do most anxiously; every officer does the same. It is for the good of the publick; ambition makes us vie with one another and ambition promotes the glorious spirit we have in our corps.'[9] The King refused the request with some brusqueness: William, he made it plain, had to prove himself a lieutenant before he could aspire to anything grander. 'My father, I am sorry to say, has not acted kindly towards me . . .' complained William, but it is hard to see that he had the smallest reason to feel himself ill-used. There'll be no promotion this side of the ocean was a lesson princes had to learn as well as commoners.

Inevitably the Prince solaced his desolation by falling in love. This time it was with Sarah Martin, the daughter of his host, Sir Henry Martin, 'young, handsome, exceedingly attractive and interesting in her manners, with an excellent understanding and a well-cultivated mind.'[10] To the Prince of Wales William spoke archly of his amusements on shore and dismissed with dismay any idea that he could possibly be considered 'a sedate Presbyterian'.[11] The accusation, if ever made, must indeed have seemed fanciful, but the Prince does appear to have conducted his wooing with exemplary propriety. Though he was as highly sexed as he was susceptible, he was a model among princes when it came to the seduction of the innocent. '. . . do not imagine that I debauched the girl,' he wrote indignantly a few months later. 'Such a thought did not once enter my head. The highest crime under Heaven next to murder is that of debauching innocent women; and is a crime I can with a safe conscience declare I never committed.'[12] So far as one knows he could have made the same boast on the day he died.

He was indeed deeply in love, showed it decorously but emphatically, and in due course suggested marriage. Sarah, who seems to have been a thoroughly nice and sensible child, was gratified but sceptical; her father frankly horrified. Martin knew that there was no possibility of a permanent relationship between his daughter and the Prince which would have given the former any chance of a full and happy life, and he very properly packed her off to London before she had time to draw breath. William rushed to Windsor to tell his father of his idyll, found the King hunting and poured out the story to a cool but not totally unsympathetic mother. '. . . very unpleasant and unexpected', commented the King,[13] and swiftly removed his son from the Martins' house and, a few days later, from Portsmouth to Plymouth.

Given the circumstances, everyone seems to have behaved with decency and dignity. The King and Queen let their son off with a relatively tolerant reproach.[14] Commissioner Martin wrote to William praising the nobility of the Prince's behaviour.[15] William himself deplored repeatedly the disturbance he had caused. 'My heart bleeds for my poor unfortunate Sarah, whom God bless and give strength of mind to support this misfortune . . .'[16] He was genuinely if somewhat superficially in love, remained faithful to her for at least six weeks, and even a year later was writing that, though subsequent affairs might have yielded 'higher gratification', Sarah's place in his heart remained secure.[17] From Prince William, aged just twenty-one, this was constancy indeed.

Though his parents did not take his latest escapade too tragically, the King had no intention of seeing it repeated or compounded. The Prince must go off again to America. Unfortunately, Lord Howe still did not feel he should be more than a lieutenant. His love blighted, exile imminent, and now even denied command of a ship: it was all too much. 'What shall I do?' he asked his brother. 'Quit the service is a hard thing after having laboured seven long years.' And if he did give up the navy, how was he to live? 'Give me your advice. I will try the Army line. I have a letter prepared to Lord Howe with my resignation.'[18] To his parents he pleaded that a posting to America could only do him harm. 'You suspect the American manners to be very vicious,' the Queen commented, with what one feels may have been mild irony. 'Alas, where is not vice to be found? I am so little acquainted with it in general that I cannot much enter upon that subject . . .'[19]

Eventually a compromise was reached. The posting to America should stand but Prince William was to have his precious promotion. On April 10, 1786, he received his commission as post-captain of the twenty-eight gun frigate *Pegasus*. Some three months later he sailed for the Americas. He was to spend fifteen months there before he returned to England.

On the whole they passed pleasantly enough. He found little appealing at St John's: 'The face of the country is truly deplorable . . . a small brushwood for the first five hundred yards inshore and then a most dreadful, inhospitable and barren country . . .'[20] and Placentia, where he had to quell a riot of drunken Irish fishermen, was hardly more attractive. He was particularly offended by the weather: for ten days running at the end of August thick ice formed over the puddles which covered the main street. Halifax, however, was warmer in every sense, 'a very gay and lively place, full of women and those of the most obliging kind'.[21] Whatever his experiences might have been in Hanover, he quickly learned that in the New World a prince of the blood was a considerable catch. When, in addition, the prince was young, friendly, cheerful and tolerably good looking, then every door was permanently open.

He reached the West Indies in September to find that *Pegasus* formed part of the command of Horatio Nelson. Prince William often said that it was Nelson who taught him how to be a sailor and would accept from him advice and direction with a docility, even enthusiasm, which Napier or Budé would have viewed with incredulity. It was not that these were bad men – on the contrary they were decent and honourable – but only remarkable qualities of character could have overcome the prickliness and intractable pigheadedness which were William's heirloom from his Hanoverian ancestors.

'. . . as an individual I love him,' rhapsodized Nelson, 'as a Prince I honour and revere him.'[22] Still, from time to time he must have wondered whether he had not taken on rather more than he had bargained for. 'This Prince hunting is but a bad sort of business,' he wrote forlornly to his fiancée, Fanny Nisbet. 'I had much rather be quiet . . .'[23] Quiet was not a condition often experienced in the Prince's company. Wherever he went there were balls, and wherever there were balls William would stay till all hours. If he dragged himself away before dawn it was as often as not to pursue less reputable pleasures. To his father he argued that all this roistering had been unfairly forced upon him because of his position and that his income, now £3,000 a year, was quite inadequate for his expenses. 'So long as it does not hurt my health, it is well and good, but I am afraid I shall fall a sacrifice to this feasting.'[24]

His health in fact was far from perfect. He suffered from a series of fevers; prickly heat caused him intense irritation and stopped him sleeping; large blotches formed on his skin, giving place to inflamed boils when he moved to a cooler climate; rheumatic pains racked his right side and thigh until he was no longer able to stand: in short, reported his surgeon Fidge at the end of his tour, 'I cannot recommend it for His Royal Highness to return where he has suffered so materially.'[25] Much of his suffering was self-inflicted. Though far from a habitual drunkard he often drank too much and, in May, 1787, he was on a mercury cure for 'a sore I had contracted in a most extraordinary manner in my pursuit of the *Dames de Couleurs*',[26] and Fidge reported at least two. onsets of venereal disease within a few months of the Prince's leaving England.[27]

Drunkenness and lechery are not the most savoury of characteristics but Prince William was young and the temptations great. It is difficult to be so forgiving when one hears of him jeering at a colleague for being the son of a schoolmaster from Hackney and asking why his fellow captain had not followed the same career. 'Why, sir,' retorted the admirable Captain Newcombe, 'I was such a stupid, good-for-nothing fellow, that my father could make nothing of me, so he sent me to sea.'[28] Nor is it possible to sympathize with the sort of man who could have an unpunctual German painter thrashed with a cat-o'-nine-tails.[29] Such anecdotes, it is fair to say, are as likely to be exaggerated as the recitals of his ceaseless benevolence, but there is no doubt that Prince William in 1787 was bad-tempered and even sometimes brutish. It did not make him an easy master for those unlucky enough to serve under him.

Yet he was by no means an incompetent naval officer. 'In his professional line,' wrote Nelson, 'he is superior to two-thirds, I am sure, of the list; and in attention to orders, and respect to his superior officer, I hardly know his equal.'[30] 'The *Pegasus*,' he told the same friend some time later, 'is one of the finest-ordered frigates I have seen.'[31] Nelson may have been prejudiced in William's favour, but there is no reason to suspect the same of Joseph Yorke, a future admiral and no particular friend of the Prince, who said that the ship was in excellent order and that 'the officers gave the Prince a very high character'.[32] With the vices of his family Prince William also inherited their ebullient energy. He could dance or make love till three in the morning, return on board and be on deck at seven, spick and span, complaining furiously about the turnout of his officers. In the West Indies, where dissipation was at its height, he is said never to have spent a night ashore .[33] He felt for his men the personal responsibility that must be the mark of every good officer. When a member of his crew was unjustly accused of obstructing a Customs House Officer he pulled endless strings to protect him and engaged Thomas Erskine for his defence, 'for I would sooner give every farthing I am worth than that this honest man should suffer.'[34] Another time he complained stormily that the food the crew were offered was 'Mouldy, Rotten, Rancid, Stinking and' – striking conclusion – 'unfit for men to eat'. He refused to accept the scions of noble families as midshipmen when old shipmates or naval officers had sons to offer, and once such a boy was taken on he spared no pains to ensure that he became an efficient officer. 'I never met with a captain,' wrote Byam Martin, who heartily disliked the Prince, 'more anxiously devoted to the improvement of his youngsters in all professional matters . . . It will be well for the service if all who served under his Royal Highness followed his example . . .'[35]

This dedication had its disagreeable side. Prince William's rigorous strictness, Martin went on, amounted 'almost to torture, so that as growing boys we had scarcely strength for the work he took out of us.' In command of his own ship he had matured into a disciplinarian, making no concession to the frailties of individuals. It was not only the seamen or the midshipmen who suffered. In ship's orders of August, 1788, he denounced the 'scandalous and disgraceful laziness' of his officers and ruled that hammocks should be lashed up and taken down by six bells in the morning. In the West Indies all officers, before going ashore, had to sign a book giving their reasons for the visit. Midshipmen were spared this humiliation since they were not allowed ashore at all.

Prince William found it impossible to combine the aloofness inevitably imposed upon the captain of a ship, King's son or not, with any sort of reasonable relationship with those beneath him. The only way he knew to maintain his superiority was to treat his officers as an inferior breed. 'I see with pleasure,' he wrote to Lord Hood, 'that by my having been very severe at first, and by my constant attention to my own conduct on board, I am respected and feared . . .'[36] To be respected is fair enough, but the naval officer who flatters himself on being feared by his men is unlikely to run a happy or even a particularly efficient ship.

The Prince's disciplinary zeal may have contributed to the curious conduct of the ship's schoolmaster, Mears. One afternoon William awoke from a tropical siesta to find Mears crouched over him with a drawn penknife pointed at his throat. 'Good God, Mears, what are you about?' asked the Prince. 'I was merely going to tell your Royal Highness that you would be likely to lose your life by sleeping here with the windows open.' Mears then retreated muttering from the cabin. Though not entirely satisfied by this explanation, William, with considerable sang-froid retired once more to bed. Mears soon after announced that he must go to warn the Prince that the ship was about to run aground. Since the ship was then a hundred and fifty leagues from the nearest land it was suggested that this advice was hardly called for.

Undeterred, Mears seized a carving knife and was on the point of breaking into the Prince's cabin when disarmed by a marine sentry.[37]

*

Mears's antics can plausibly be ascribed to an overdose of tropical conditions. No such plea can be made in the case of Isaac Schomberg. A squabble between the captain of a frigate and his first lieutenant may lack significance in the eye of eternity but for Prince William it was a turning point. It came near to souring the pleasure he found in his career; it shook the faith of those senior officers who believed that one day he could be a great asset to the service; and it displayed that disastrous inability to work with other people which was to destroy him forty years later as Lord High Admiral and could have destroyed the country if he had not learned his lesson by the time he became King.

Schomberg was a protégé of Lord Hood's. He was twelve years older than William and vastly more experienced. The relationship of fledgling commander and mature subaltern is never an easy one; in this case it was made more difficult by the fact that Schomberg had been told privately to keep an eye on his youthful captain and steer him away from mischief. Schomberg might still have made a success of it if he had possessed even a modicum of tact. Unfortunately however he proved to be a worthy, capable but totally insensitive prig, acutely aware of his superior seamanship and resolved that Prince William, for the sake of his soul and the Royal Navy, should be equally conscious of it. In the Prince's phrase, 'he wished to carry on the duty of the ship entirely,' and though William's account of the affair was heavily, indeed naïvely loaded in his own favour, on this point there is no reason to doubt him.[38] It characterized Schomberg that, within two years of his battle with William, once again theoretically right, once again acting with blundering indiscretion, he barely escaped court-martial by Cornwallis in Madras.

The actual heads of conflict were trivial. Prince William accused Schomberg of disrespect by giving his opinion unasked 'on the propriety of punishing William Hinstone, seaman, and William Madden, marine, for hanging up their clothes to dry between decks'; by omitting to send for some sheets when told to do so; by protesting when William over-ruled his instructions forbidding midshipmen to hang up their wet clothing in the mizzen rigging. The real trouble was that the two men could not stand each other and ill health and the unspeakable climate stepped up their mutual resentment to explosion point.

As early as December, 1786, Nelson had spotted that there was something badly wrong. The Prince had grumbled about all the officers, in particular, 'your friend Schomberg as he calls himself, but I don't believe you know much of him'. Nelson protested that he had a high opinion of Schomberg. The latter then came up and William immediately complained that the ship's company were not wearing uniform jackets as he had ordered. Schomberg said that the day was too hot but that if William wanted he would have them put on. 'The manner in which this was spoke made a much greater impression upon me than all that happened afterwards for I plainly saw all was not right.'[39]

All got rapidly worse. In mid-January Prince William threatened Schomberg with court-martial. The unfortunate first-lieutenant was forced to apologize for his crimes in front of his brother officers, but promptly offended again by sending a boat ashore without permission. More public reproaches followed and this time Schomberg was stung into demanding a court-martial. Reluctantly Nelson ordered his arrest but, as soon as Schomberg had apologized once more and asked for the court-martial to be rescinded, he urged the Prince to forget all about it.[40] With bad grace William disgorged his prey, charges were dropped and Schomberg returned to England.

It is impossible to establish any exact balance of right and wrong in this discreditable affair. Both men behaved foolishly and intemperately but the Prince, in the position of strength, could best have afforded to be generous. Provocation certainly existed, yet his behaviour was still of altogether unreasonable harshness. Certainly Hood must have thought so, for on Schomberg's return he appointed him first-lieutenant on his flagship, the *Barfleur*. When William protested Hood replied, somewhat disingenuously, that he could not imagine anyone of the Prince's 'humanity and condescending goodness' would wish to be the ruin of another officer, however much the latter might accidentally have offended.[41]

Nelson, too, was not as unequivocal a supporter as the Prince would have liked. In September, 1787, William was reproaching him with giving Schomberg a favourable recommendation. Surely it was Nelson himself who had first told him that one should never forgive an officer for disrespect?[42] And when Lord Howe, in his turn, criticized Prince William's unduly harsh treatment of another officer on *Pegasus*, the third-lieutenant William Hope, it all became too much. 'Much as I love and honour the Navy,' he wrote to Hood, 'I shall beyond doubt resign if I have not a satisfactory explanation from both your noble

lordships.'[43] For a very junior captain to demand 'satisfactory explana-
tions' from the First Lord of the Admiralty and the Commander-in-
Chief, Portsmouth, was a circumstance in itself sufficiently unusual to
suggest that his naval career was unlikely to run smoothly.

*

By the autumn of 1787 Prince William was at Quebec again, grumbling
to his brother about the King's neglect. His debts were more crippling
than ever and Colonel Hotham, William's pet hate among his father's
court officials, seemed to delight in denying him what was necessary.
'He has no more business to regulate my expences than the Pope in
Rome,' wrote the Prince indignantly to his brother,[44] but the King
paid not the slightest attention to his protests. For some weeks he was
also extremely ill; some tropical fever aggravated by the sudden change
in climate kept him to his bed and cost him several nights of delirious
raving.[45] Having failed to soften his father with an account of his
sufferings he sought to engage his interest with picturesque if not
particularly authoritative accounts of the 'magnitude, beauty and
fertility' of the province of Canada. 'The ground is rich and if the
industrious Englishman tilled it instead of the lazy Canadian, it would
be inestimable.'

Then, abruptly, Pegasus set sail for England. This is an obscure
passage in Prince William's life. Biographers have always accepted
that he suddenly sickened of his bleak near-Arctic exile and fled without
permission for the fleshpots of home.[46] This was certainly the popular
gossip of the day. Yet the Prince himself stated categorically to the
Prince of Wales that he had received orders to return to Plymouth and
refit, and that this had been confirmed by a letter from Lord Howe.
It is hard to see why he should have told a lie to his brother, especially
a lie which could so easily have been detected. 'There can be no great
pleasure in going,' he commented gloomily, 'with a certainty that my
Christmas box or New Year's gift will be a family lecture for im-
morality, vice, dissipation and expence, and that I shall meet with the
appellation of the prodigal son.'[47]

The most probable explanation is that he was called back in disgrace,
for reasons which he preferred to keep to himself. His debts may have
been partly responsible, but an even more common cause for recrimina-
tion seems to have existed. '. . . between ourselves,' he confided in his
brother, 'a certain affair is likely to take place that will spoil the whole.
These damned women cause me more uneasiness than enough . . .'[48]

The 'damned woman' in this case was probably Mrs Wentworth, wife of the surveyor-general, an American who had lived a great deal in England and had the reputation of 'preferring men to women'.[49] Not surprisingly, she also preferred princes to commoners and a twenty-four-year-old prince to her staid and pompous husband of fifty. William stayed frequently in her house and the pair were generally held to be passionately in love. It is unlikely that there was much passion on either side, certainly little on Prince William's, but the pleasures of a handsome and sophisticated mistress may well have drawn him into indiscretion. Colonial officials, however complaisant, are only men and John Wentworth's patience was tried very high. A protest to the King about his libertine son's behaviour would have fallen on receptive ears and it would not be surprising if the Prince's immediate recall had been ordered to avert a worse scandal. At the beginning of December *Pegasus* arrived in Ireland; on December 27, 1787, she docked at Plymouth.

CHAPTER V

The Duke of Clarence

PRINCE WILLIAM's reception was in keeping with his crimes. From Windsor came a chilly silence, from the Admiralty brusque instructions to remain at Plymouth until ordered to the contrary. The Prince promptly offered his services to Lord Howe for an expedition that was fitting out for the East Indies.[1] So remote a posting did not fit in with the King's idea of what was proper; for the moment he was to be left in Plymouth to expiate his sins in solitude.

Unfortunately for the King's intentions his elder sons delighted in taking their brother's side. By this time the long-simmering quarrel between King George III and his heir had exploded into ferocious warfare. The Duke of York, as Frederick had now become, had finally sided with the Prince of Wales. The two brothers now decided to visit William and thus flaunt their indifference to their father's will. They arrived in Plymouth on January 8, 1788, and devoted two days to dinners, balls and miscellaneous inspections. Prince William had seen little enough of his brothers in the previous ten years and was dazzled by the gorgeous apparition. Their visit whetted his appetite for the life of the metropolis and at the same time taught him to feel something near indifference to the displeasure of the King. '... the old boy is exceeding out of humour,' he wrote to the Prince of Wales a few weeks later.[2] '... Fatherly admonitions at our time of life are very unpleasant and of no use; it is a pity he should expend his breath or his time in such fruitless labour.' He would not have written so blithely even six months before.

The Prince may have felt a touch of wistfulness as he saw his brothers depart for London but he had his own fish to fry in Plymouth. He was in love again. This time it was to Sally Winne (occasionally Wynne, Wynn, or Winn) the pretty daughter of a prosperous merchant. Her father encouraged the affair, not so much in the hope that it would lead Sally to happiness or the altar, as to further his ambition of becoming Agent Victualler to the Navy. This was the first of William's affairs

K.W.

to win any sort of national notoriety. Peter Pindar was quick to hymn Plymouth as:

> '*A town where, exiled by the higher pow'rs*
> *The Royal Tar with indignation lours;*
> *Kept by his sire from London and from sin,*
> *To say his catechism to Mistress Wynn*'

The Prince wooed her with his customary energy and sent the Prince of Wales a lock of his hair with instructions to have it set in diamonds and returned forthwith.

But he could not devote himself exclusively to dalliance for on March 13, 1788, the crew of *Pegasus* was transferred to *Andromeda*, of thirty-two guns and seven hundred and fifty tons; 'a nice sort of frigate in those days', though William had hankered after something grander.[3] For the first time he was enabled to indulge that obsession with military and other uniforms which was so marked among members of the House of Hanover. His midshipmen were required to wear 'white breeches so tight as to appear to be sewn upon the limb – yellow-topped hunting boots pulled close up and strapped with a buckle round the knee . . . a pigtail of huge dimensions dangling beneath an immense square gold-laced cocked hat . . .' with frizzed hair stuffed with powder and pomatum and a sword two-thirds the size of the boy who wore it. The main flaw about this slightly unseamanly rig was that the breeches were apt to burst whenever the midshipmen had cause to climb the rigging.[4]

What with his white breeches and Sally Winne, he was reasonably content. Certainly he felt no wish to go abroad again.[5] Meanwhile, however, word of his latest entanglement had got back to Windsor. To the harassed King it must have seemed that he was destined to keep his son, like an out-sized yo-yo, whipping up and down in flight from his various mistresses. Prince William had crossed the Atlantic to forget Miss Martin, returned to escape Mrs Wentworth and now was made to cross it once again so as to extricate him from the arms of Miss Winne and the would-be Agent Victualler. 'Aye, what – what – what,' said the King, 'William playing the fool again; send him off to America and forbid the return of the ship to Plymouth.'*[6]

The result was that the unfortunate Prince was shanghaied as he

---

* Or so Byam Martin recorded. It is hard to believe that he knew George III's actual words but the remark is sufficiently in character to be worth quoting.

came in sight of the Lizard after a three-week cruise and brusquely ordered to set sail for the New World. With chagrin, he obeyed; complaining to his father, 'the men are in a peculiar hard situation . . . the most part of them are married, and have left their wives and families unprovided for.' He already knew all about the West Indies, he protested, and was fully competent to command any class of ship. What he needed now was to participate in the command of fleets, and where was that better done than the British Isles? 'London, believe me, Sir, is the last place in your Majesty's dominions I wish to visit. I do not deny my partiality for Devonshire; my connections there are such as I am by no means ashamed of and after having been so long in that part of England I confess I am attached to it.'[7]

*

And so, sulkily, Prince William set forth on what was to be his final posting as an active sailor. He headed for Halifax and, no doubt with some relish, spent his first night ashore at the house of Mrs Wentworth. The liaison – if, indeed, there had ever been one – was not resumed however and he reported wryly that his former mistress was amusing herself with another officer and seemed to have thrown all decorum to the winds.[8] His squadron was under the command of Captain Charles Sandys, a vulgar, drunken dolt whom the Prince found unconscious in bed when he paid his first official call.[9] The presence of the Captain turned the celebration of the King's birthday on *Andromeda* into a Saturnalia; a salute of a hundred and sixty guns was fired and a ship ablaze five miles away, firing distress signals in every direction, was suffered to founder without the rescue of a single man.

Even without Captain Sandys, however, William showed a considerable appetite for the more raucous entertainments. An unusually clear picture of his daily life in Halifax in 1787 and 1788 is available through the diary of his friend and drinking companion Lieutenant William Dyott.[10] It provides a daunting portrait of a hunt after pleasure; a little group of bored and boring men seeking distraction in wine, women, more wine, more women and the occasional, usually bawdy song.

The Prince himself, Dyott states repeatedly, did not much enjoy drinking and rarely ventured beyond a bottle of Madeira. What he liked was for other people to become drunk. Dyott recalls one banquet at which the Prince gave twenty-three bumpers without a halt; bellowing, whenever he saw a glass not entirely full, 'I see some of God

Almighty's daylight in that glass, Sir; banish it!' By the end of the
evening, governor, general and commodore were all too drunk to
stand and had to be hoisted on to their chairs to drink the toasts.
Twenty guests drank sixty-three bottles of wine. 'His Royal Highness
saw we were all pretty well done up and he walked off . . . I never saw
a man laugh so in my life.'

An unattractive picture; yet in William's defence – if defence it is –
it should be said that he was often enough 'outrageously drunk',
'wondrous drunk', 'completely drunk', to show that he participated in
the delights of society as well as smugly observing its follies. The
Prince clearly contributed to the gaiety around him; singing, telling
stories, joking. He would give exquisite balls and suppers on board
Andromeda, followed by cold breakfast with a vast selection of cold
meats and game; in particular his special fancy, cold turkey. He was
an excellent host – 'it was wonderful to see the attention his Royal
Highness paid to everyone present, not neglecting a single midshipman'. He adored dancing and would dance 'Country Bumpkins'
for hours at a time; switching partners among all the pretty women.
And yet this cheery portrait was marred by that characteristic, hateful
in those in high places, of inviting intimacy and then snubbing it once
it was offered. 'His character is, where he takes a liking he will be free,'
noted Dyott, himself a victim; 'but if ever any man takes the smallest
liberty, he cuts instantly.'

Bouts of drinking were interspersed with fornication: casual, loveless liaisons without even a Mrs Wentworth to lend them individuality.
'He would go into any house where he saw a pretty girl, and was
perfectly acquainted with every house of a certain description in the
town.' According to another, more picturesque though even less
reliable account, Prince William would 'whet his carnal appetites by
watching the women engage in lesbian exhibitions'.[11] And yet this
rich vein of dissipation did not stop him being as conscientious a
captain as ever, his ship as well-found and his men as well trained, nor
did it check his habit of taking vast walks in the heat of the sun which
left his companions reeling with exhaustion.

'He is,' wrote Dyott, when Prince William was on the point of
sailing for Jamaica in November, 1788, '. . . as honourable a man as ever
held a commission in the British service. He has a generous and noble
spirit and will, I am convinced, when an opportunity may offer,
render an essential service to his king and country. I had the honour, I
may say, of living with him for three months, and in that time one

may be able to judge of a man's character. I believe I never shall spend three months in that way again, for such a time of dissipation, etc, etc, I cannot suppose possible to happen . . .'

The Prince found time while in Jamaica to attend debates in the House of Assembly and to take an interest in the problems of slavery. He accepted without demur that this institution was essential for the economy of the island, applauded the somewhat desultory steps that were being taken to better the condition of the slaves and generally so much endeared himself to the Jamaicans that they seriously mooted the idea that he should be their Governor. The views which he imbibed were to remain with him all his life. But he did not allow such activities to cut deeply into the hours he set aside for balls, dinners, drunkenness and lechery. It seemed that he had become bound fast in a train of life which would never loose him; from which, indeed, he did not seek release. And yet it was a joyless feasting, a satisfaction of the senses that seemed less and less to satisfy. Just before he left Halifax he wrote: 'I am sorry to say that I have been living a terrible debauched life, of which I am heartily ashamed and tired. I must in the West Indies turn over a new leaf, or else I shall be irrevocably ruined . . . I have made a determined resolution to abstain from excess of all kinds . . .'[12] The resolution was not kept but for once the *cri de coeur* rings true.

It was while still in the West Indies that he heard the news of his father's illness. There is today much ingenious speculation as to the exact nature of King George III's affliction. It is held, on medical evidence which, to the layman, appears impressive, that the King was not 'mad' in any proper sense of the word but instead suffered from porphyria.[13] To readers of this book the significance of the point is mainly that there is no proof, or even evidence, that William could have inherited the disease from his father. For most of us it will suffice that George III babbled to the trees, chatted confidentially with those far absent, often indeed long dead, and suffered from manifold delusions which, in the eyes of his contemporaries, proved him mad.

The Prince's absence spared him participation in the discreditable squabble that took place around the King's sick-bed. If he had been in London it is probable that he would have taken the side of the Prince of Wales in his battle to secure full powers as Regent. By doing so he would have embittered still further his relationship with his father. As it was he was able to write to his brother in no doubt perfectly genuine dismay: 'Sincerely do I love the good and worthy man and long may he yet with his usual firmness reign over us,'[14] while at the

same time congratulating the Prince of Wales on the impressive unity
with which he and his brothers were confronting Queen and Ministers.
'. . . I only hope to be admitted of the party,' he concluded.

The Prince of Wales at once ordered William's recall and the Prince
obeyed with relish, according to John Walter of *The Times*, in the hope
of being appointed to the Admiralty in his brother's first government.
On April 29, 1789, *Andromeda* arrived at Spithead. Three days later
Prince William was at Windsor. It was said that the Prince of Wales
had earlier tried to secure a peerage for his brother but that Pitt had
blocked it.[15] If so it could only have been because the Prime Minister
wished to leave the decision till after the King had recovered. With
William's return the matter was quickly settled. On May 16 he was
gazetted Duke of Clarence and of St Andrews and Earl of Munster in
the peerage of Ireland. The honour virtually marked the end of his
career as an active naval officer.

*

In 1789 there were three things which William needed urgently if he
were to lead a prosperous and satisfying life: a regular job, a sufficient
income and a wife. He was to be denied all three.

His naval career had reached a point at which he either had to be
groomed for stardom or discarded. As a royal duke he could no longer
be fobbed off with a frigate. He might have been satisfied with a
larger vessel for a few years yet but this could only have been on the
understanding that in the reasonably near future he would command a
fleet. To this the Lords of the Admiralty were resolutely opposed.
King George III acquiesced in their verdict; probably indeed he would
have rejected any other. No one, looking at the facts of Prince William's
career, could argue that the Admiralty were unjustified.

And yet he was not quite twenty-four years old. He had been
subjected to every kind of temptation and deprived, even though
largely through his own fault, of the guidance and authority which
could have redeemed him. Now he was ready to dedicate his limited
but not negligible talents, his tremendous energy and his influence as a
prince of the blood to the service of the navy which he loved so much.
Whether he would have served it wisely is uncertain, that he would
have served it faithfully is beyond question. From the point of view
of the navy the risk might have been unwarrantable but for the sake of
the Duke of Clarence one must regret that he was never given another
chance to prove his worth.

Not that, viewed purely on grounds of professional merit, his worth would have been great. Byam Martin, who observed him closely with a knowledgeable if unkindly eye, was categoric: 'He was deficient in almost all the qualities necessary for a person in high command. An unguarded way of speaking upon all subjects and to all persons, made him very unsafe to be trusted with any confidential duty. A flightiness and want of sound judgment left him without any settled opinion upon any point, and he was turned and twisted just according to the advice of the person who happened to be last with him; it was therefore better he should be on shore than at sea.'[16] Yet against this damning judgment one must quote Nelson, who had worked several years with the Prince and stated repeatedly that William was an excellent seaman and a highly competent officer. His opinion cannot be ignored.

Probably both were right. William impresses as a capable junior officer who might have matured into a more than competent captain, but also as one who lacked the qualities required from those who command great fleets. He could not have advanced much further without some risk to the navy, at any rate in time of war. If he had been an ordinary mortal he could still have rendered the navy good and distinguished service; as a royal duke he probably best served it by his retirement.

The tragedy was that he had nothing else to do. His brother, the Duke of York, had pre-empted the military role in the family, and, anyway, the Duke of Clarence would have been no more welcome as a general than as an admiral. He might have governed some province – Hanover, or his beloved Jamaica – but the rapid deterioration of his relationship with the King made it seem more and more unlikely that any such office would be offered him. On the threshold of maturity, his energies at their greatest, his will to apply himself for the first time stronger than his taste for frivolity and dissipation, he found himself permanently unemployed.

His second need, a sufficient income, should have been met when he became Duke of Clarence. He was granted £12,000 a year, together with an apartment at St James's and many valuable extras in the form of food, light and heating. For a man who did not gamble; who was, on the whole, more entertained than entertaining; and who was required to live in dignity, certainly, but not in lavish state; this should have been a reasonably generous provision. It proved insufficient. He never ran up debts to be compared with the monstrous accumulations of the Prince of Wales and the Duke of York but it was to be many years before he found it possible to live within his income.

Some at least of the blame must rest with his elder brothers. Even before he returned to England he had become enmeshed in the web of debts which was spun by and about the Prince of Wales. In particular he was involved in the loan of 3.6 million guilders (about £1m sterling at contemporary values) which the Prince was seeking to raise in Holland. He seems to have derived little if any benefit from the loan, acting only as a collateral security. Mercifully, therefore, it is unnecessary to elucidate this complex and discreditable affair.[17] But it and similar manoeuvres ensured that William began life as a duke with considerable liabilities already pressing on him. He was never to shake them off until Adelaide took his finances firmly in hand some thirty years later.

Finally, and most serious, was his need for a wife. William, like most men of his family, had a seemingly insatiable sexual appetite. He was also a romantic, eager to idolize and to prove himself loyal to whomsoever he might be in love with. The fact that the objects of his love had in the past changed with bewildering speed could be ascribed more to the circumstances of his wooing than to any inherent fickleness. Marriage seemed the obvious answer.

Unfortunately the third son of the King of England had a very limited range of possible spouses open to him. The English aristocracy was excluded from the start: even if the King had been prepared to contemplate a commoner as a daughter-in-law, her selection from some leading family, inevitably with political associations, would have proved endlessly embarrassing. English princesses were few and far between, Princess Sophia of Gloucester was the obvious candidate but William viewed her with small enthusiasm and hoped that she might fall prey to the Duke of York. All that was left was foreign royalty; and here the richest, grandest and most beautiful princesses tended to be reserved for the more important dynastic alliances. The French Revolution and ensuing war could only make the hunt more difficult.

If the Duke had felt a burning urge to marry some unknown and possibly unattractive bride he could probably have secured one. If the King had believed it essential for the nation that his third son should marry, he could certainly have brought it about. But a loveless match attracted William little and his father did not consider the question of the first importance. The matter was allowed to drift and soon was lost sight of altogether.

The role of unattached and unemployed bachelor is a difficult one to play with distinction. Some measure of cultural attainment, for instance, is desirable if time and money are to be spent with good results. William had no such accomplishments. Musically he never progressed beyond the Irish jig: 'O'Carrol, O'Rafferty, O'Carey, all his *delights*'.[18] He was reported as having visited the Academy and studied the pictures with attention[19] but he dismissed his brother's admirable acquisitions as expensive nicknacks[20] and himself added little to the royal collection except portraits and a bevy of naval scenes. Poetry he eschewed, though he found some of the battles in *The Iliad* stirring stuff. He enjoyed acting, and played Prince Hal to Lieutenant Storey's Falstaff and Mistress Page to Lord Augustus Beauclerk's Mistress Ford in the midshipmen's mess of the *Prince George*; but even in this pursuit it was the incidental fun and games which most appealed to him. As stage-manager for *The Merry Wives of Windsor* he poured pitch over the heap of rags and oakum which represented the Thames so that the unfortunate Falstaff emerged literally tarred and feathered.

He read a certain amount of history, naval history in particular, and was ready to take an interest in any practical work, as for instance a manual for the more scientific construction of lighthouses, but literature as such he regarded with suspicion. 'I know no person so perfectly disagreeable and even dangerous as an author,' he protested,[21] and his biographer can hardly doubt the disfavour with which his own activities would have been regarded. Beyond this he played a competent game of chess and had mastered some of the simpler card games – talents which completed the gamut of his intellectual diversions.

Travel rarely broadens the mind: usually the most it achieves is to substitute one set of prejudices for another. In William's case it did not do even this. He had travelled farther and seen more than any other member of the royal family, yet had imported not one new idea into the English scene. A conviction, misplaced, that he understood certain colonial problems, was the solitary fruit of his wanderings.

Otherwise a foul mouth and a strong head were his two most notable legacies from the navy. His vast repertoire of dirty stories made him the terror of every genteel drawing-room and, though generally abstemious, he could drink startling quantities with little effect. Creevey records a gargantuan drinking bout with the Dukes of Clarence and Norfolk and the Prince of Wales (who cheated by drinking less than the rest). After dinner Norfolk and Creevey slumped into a stupor – the latter waking some hours later to find William, still drinking, 'in a very animated discussion as to the particular shape and make of the wig worn by George II'.[22] Drunk or not, he was interminably loquacious. At dinner at Houghton he drank two bottles of wine single-handed and proposed six toasts, each prefaced by a speech. Before proposing Lord Spencer's health he indulged in a harangue which included biographical sketches of all the principal naval officers who had served during Spencer's lengthy tenure of office.[23]

He was, in short, something of a boor; and yet in almost all the anecdotes which illustrate his boorishness there is a twist which makes him somehow endearing. When, for instance, he saw a Quaker girl looking wistfully through a shop window, he nudged her familiarly and said, 'So, I see thou art not above the vanities of the world!' Uncouth behaviour enough, but when he saw he had upset her, he hurried into the shop, bought an expensive work-basket and persuaded the girl's mother to accept it on her behalf. He was present one day when James Northcote was painting his protégé 'The Young Roscius'. Being bored he idly twitched Northcote's dirty collar and dandruff-ridden hair. 'You do not devote much time to the toilette,' he remarked, with offensive accuracy. 'Sir,' replied the outraged painter, 'I never allow anyone to take personal liberties with me; you are the first that ever presumed to do so, and I beg your Royal Highness to recollect that I am in my own house!' The Duke left in pique but returned next day to say: 'Yesterday I took a very unbecoming liberty with you, and you properly resented it. I really am angry with myself, and hope you will forgive me and think no more of it.'[24]

William thus emerges as a brash and cheerful extrovert, by no means stupid but insensitive to the feelings of others. He was loyal to his friends and absent-minded about his enemies – often, indeed, it never occurred to him that they were enemies at all. He enjoyed the society of other people and expected other people to do the same by him; any more complicated relationship usually proved outside his emotional range. He was honest and straightforward to a degree so startling that some people assumed his guilelessness must be a cloak for deep cunning. Others held that he was soft in the head. Both were wrong. To say bluntly what he thought and to stick to his word came naturally to him; anything else would have smacked of indecency. And William was, for all his vices, a thoroughly decent man.

*

The Duke's most urgent need, now that he had become a civilian, was to find a home. As a first step he took Henry Hobart's house, Ivy Lodge, on Richmond Hill; '. . . in the middle of a village with nothing but a green short apron to the river; a situation only fit for an old gentlewoman who has put out her kneepans and loves cards.'[25] Accounts of his way of life in Richmond are curiously varied. To Horace Walpole he was so popular that 'if Richmond were a borough and he had not attained his title, but still retained his idea of standing candidate, he would certainly be elected there. He pays his bills regularly himself, locks up his doors at night that his servants may not stay out late, and never drinks but a few glasses of wine.'[26] Such decorum sounds a little too good to be true. George Selwyn was probably nearer the mark when he noted darkly '*Il tient des propos trop indécentes* – thinks that sort of discourse will give him the reputation of wit. It may, on the forecastle deck, but our Richmond ladies do not relish it.'[27]

What the Richmond ladies relished even less was his choice of a companion. In September 1789 he installed in Ivy Lodge a certain Polly Finch, a courtesan of some repute whom he had won away from a rival in Berkeley Square. His acquisition gave rise to a feast of arch puns from newspapers and society wits. Polly, said *The World*, 'from the price may properly be denominated á *gold finch*'; to Selwyn she was a Green Finch, reluctant to be '*un oiseau de cage*, although fed and caressed by a Prince'.[28] She seems to have been a nasty little gold-digger whose craving for society did not at all suit the cosy domestic nature of the Duke. She left him in the end because she could not stand another evening of his reading aloud from *The Lives of the Admirals*. With some complaint she put up with Volume One, but when she found there were more to come she set off on the return journey to Berkeley Square.[29]

In November, 1789, the Duke left Ivy Lodge, lived for a few months in St James's Palace, and then bought for 12,000 guineas Lord Camelford's house at Roehampton.[30] He changed its name from Petersham Lodge to Clarence Lodge and spent more money than he had on its embellishment. It is uncertain at what point he shed Polly Finch but probably she did not survive the retreat from Richmond. He never had recourse to her kind again. The meaner beauties of the night were bundled unceremoniously from his memory as the moon rose imperiously above him. Some time in the spring or summer of 1790 William fell in love with Mrs Jordan.

CHAPTER VI

Mrs Jordan

THE phrase 'star quality', usually qualified by some such adjective as 'elusive' or 'indefinable', is one of the more irritatingly imprecise of theatrical clichés. It is doubly so since in fact the quality does defy definition. It is the curious inner force which makes an actress of mediocre talent and unspectacular beauty indubitably a star; can turn dross to gold and suffuse trivial acting with the glow of greatness. Mrs Jordan enjoyed it. Without it, indeed, she could never have risen from her unpromising origins to the top of her profession.

Dorothy Bland was born in London in 1761.[1] Both her Irish father and Welsh mother – who were never legally married – had been involved with the stage, and it was not surprising that her destitute mother should urge her in that direction. Before she was twenty she was working in Richard Daly's Dublin company, within another year she had been seduced and 'ruined' by her employer. Daly comes down to us as so much the conventional cad and villain that even the most partisan supporter of his victim may doubt the accuracy of the portrait. Whatever their relationship, however, it is certain that Dorothy Bland soon fled, pregnant, to England. It was at this point, when she found herself playing roles in a condition which made her billing as Miss Bland a little indiscreet, that she took the name of Mrs Jordan. Her manager had suggested the name, apparently, because she had 'crossed the water'.

Dorothy did not appear in London until October, 1785, when she played Peggy in *The Country Girl*. Her début was triumphant and she quickly established herself as a successful comedy actress. Her fame brought her a new and more reputable lover. Richard Ford was the son of a court physician who curiously doubled his profession with co-ownership of the theatre at Drury Lane. Dorothy Jordan believed that he planned to marry her and she may well have been right for Ford was a decent if fundamentally flabby young man. His father's disapproval, however, made him play for time. In the meantime Dorothy and he lived in a fair imitation of the matrimonial state and she bore him three children, two of whom lived.

By 1789 Dorothy had risen to the peak of her profession. It is hard to be sure how good an actress she was. Her range was limited. She played Ophelia and earned a curiously phrased tribute from Leigh Hunt to the 'complacent tones and busy good-nature' in her performance of the mad scene,[2] but in general she wisely eschewed the tragic roles. Her *forte* lay more as a principal boy in parts calling for high spirits and the display of her admirable legs in tight-fitting breeches. And yet such a description suggests a coarseness about her performance which did not exist. To Charles Lamb she seemed 'one whom care could not come near; a privileged being sent to teach mankind what he wants – joyousness',[3] and it was above all her capacity to communicate happiness, to lift an audience above itself, which her critics most admired. Her weapons were her appearance, 'the exquisite witchery of her tone', above all, perhaps, her laugh. Hazlitt was among her most ardent admirers. In his *Dramatic Essays* he described her:[4]

'Her face, her tones, her manner, were irresistible. Her smile had the effect of sunshine, and her laugh did one good to hear it. Her voice was eloquence itself – she seemed as if her heart was always at her mouth. She was all gaiety, openness and good nature. She rioted in her fine animal spirits, and gave more pleasure than any other actress, because she had the greatest spirit of enjoyment in herself . . .'

Small wonder that the Duke of Clarence, romantic, susceptible, and seeking wistfully some permanent liaison, should have seen in her the answer to his needs.

*

There is little to show when the Duke became aware that Dorothy Jordan was out of the ordinary run of his amours. In October 1791 he wrote to the Prince of Wales of 'a course of eleven months endless difficulty' during which she had behaved like an angel.[5] It seems most likely that the romance ripened gradually throughout 1790 and culminated in a definite understanding by the end of that year. The main difficulty was how to dispose of Mr Ford. Eventually a settlement was arrived at by which virtually all her earnings were set aside for the maintenance of her and Ford's two daughters.

Curiously enough, the Press does not seem to have concerned itself greatly with the new liaison until it had almost matured into an established institution. It was not till July, 1791, that *The Morning Post* announced with relief: 'We hear from Richmond that an illustrious Youth has at length passed the Ford, yet is not likely to be pickled by a legal process' ('Little Pickle', the girl who loved a merry tar, was one of Mrs Jordan's most celebrated roles). Even in October the same paper noted: 'A celebrated Actress, who has withdrawn from her late nominal Spouse, has not yet formed her Princely connection . . . Her terms are £1,200 a year annuity, an equipage, and her children by all parties provided for.' It was not till almost the end of the year that the relationship was accepted as an established fact.

The Duke's wooing had not been allowed to proceed uninterrupted. Early in 1790 the Spanish attacked a fishing settlement at Nootka Sound on the coast of Vancouver Island. £1m was voted by parliament as a military credit and the fleet was mobilised. Once more William found himself in command of his own ship, this time the *Valiant* of seventy-four guns. For four months the fleet hung around Torbay and Plymouth. In August Lord Howe insisted that the fleet should put to sea, even though there was no prospect of action, many ships were badly under-manned, discipline was poor and gales were on the way. '. . . a chapter of absurdities and inconsistencies,' wrote the Duke crossly to the Prince of Wales. 'It is ridiculous to see how far vanity can lead a stupid old fool eat up with the gout and various other bad humours.'[6]

It was a gloomy period for William. His fellow officers seemed to distrust, even to shun him. Royalist to a man, they knew that he had sided with his brothers against the King and did not hesitate to show their disapproval. He was bored, lonely and depressed. He missed his comforts, he missed society, he missed Mrs Jordan. 'Am I to have any chance of being again amongst Christians, or am I to linger the rest of my life with the Philistines?'[7] It was a far cry from the fervour with which he had joined the navy, far too from the romantic glow with which his memories of the service were later to be suffused.

Ashore he solaced himself in the ways to which he had grown accustomed. 'Last night I followed those passions my godfather and godmother would not renounce [*sic*] and retired into the arms of a chaste Irish whore whose breath was impregnated with gin and tobacco . . .'[8] But the charm had faded, that first fine careless rapture was not to be recaptured. 'It is what the French very properly call *La Misère*.' The threat of war passed, the fleet was disbanded, William was once more at liberty. He had had his last fling and had not enjoyed it. With relief he closed this messy postscript to his naval life.

*

From the beginning of 1791 the Duke of Clarence and Mrs Jordan were to all intents and purposes man and wife. They lived together, entertained together, went everywhere together except, of course, to court, above all made love together. They were indeed a thoroughly loving couple. Mrs Jordan's letters to the Duke betray a touching and incoherent affection which could not be hypocritical. '. . . my heart and best affections are and ever must be *yours* and yours alone,' she wrote some time towards the end of 1791. 'You are all goodness, all generosity, all feeling.' 'God bless *you do love* me, I know you *now do* but continue to do so, for mine can never never feel less ardour for you than that which now so entirely possesses my heart and soul. What love you have to me, it is more than love, love is too faint an expression for the sensations I feel to you.'[9] William was somewhat less ardent. There was a note of complacency in his description of her as '. . . a very good creature, very domestic and careful of the children. To be sure she is absurd sometimes . . . But there are such things more or less in all families.'[10] But even such moderate criticism was rarely voiced. In general he extolled her as 'one of the most perfect women in this world'.[11]

In one respect, however, their alliance differed radically from the more conventional marriage of the age; still more, perhaps, from the traditional relationship between prince and courtesan. Mrs Jordan continued to go out to work. Partly this must have been because she enjoyed it – nobody who has tasted glory can renounce it without a qualm – but the more important reason was that she and the duke needed every penny that she could earn.

Not that William profited from their liaison. The bulk of her earnings was reserved for her children by previous connections, in addition to which, every quarter for twenty years, she received from the Duke a regular payment of two hundred guineas.[12] Certainly nothing on this scale came back to her lover and though she often sent him the fruits of her provincial labours, more often than not the payments were designed to settle her own personal debts. Nevertheless, there were occasions when Mrs Jordan's contribution made the difference between solvency and disaster. The Duke made no attempt to hide the fact. He reported a loan of £420 to his banker, Thomas Coutts. 'Mrs Jordan is getting both fame and money;' he commented, 'to her I owe very much.'[13]

To contemporaries the idea that a son of the King owed even part of his prosperity to the labours of his mistress was repellent.

> *'As Jordan's high and mighty squire*
> *Her playhouse profits deigns to skim*
> *Some folks audaciously enquire:*
> *If he keeps her, or she keeps him?'*

Today the idea of a wife contributing to the household expenses is not so strange; even in 1790, it is worth remarking, nobody would have felt anything but admiration for William's acumen if he had contrived to marry money.

His mistress's mite could do no more than mitigate the Duke's problems. He was already heavily in debt; paying out between £3,000 and £5,000 a year in interest. Both of them were generous to a fault, lavish in entertaining, and reluctant ever to discharge even the most superannuated servant. After five years of cohabitation he was reduced to borrowing £12,000 from the Landgrave of Hesse Cassel and, only five years later, was seeking a further £20,000.[14] By 1793 his debts were estimated at £52,000 and, though he set aside half his income to satisfy his creditors, the total in September 1797 had only dropped to £46,543. Given this background it was not astonishing that the King felt he was being too generous rather than too miserly with his mistress.

'Hey, hey: – what's this – what's this,' he is recorded as saying. 'You keep an actress, they say.' 'Yes, sir.' 'Ah, well, well; how much do you give her, eh?' 'One thousand a year, sir.' 'A thousand, a thousand; too much; too much! Five hundred quite enough! quite enough!'[15]

If the anecdote were true it would be of interest as showing that King George III accepted his son's liaison with resignation if not enthusiasm. Certainly this was so with most of his family. To the Prince of Wales and the Duke of York, Mrs Jordan was to be treated as much like their brother's wife as the Royal Marriages Act would allow. When the Prince of Orange dined with the Duke of Clarence, she did the honours and missed a performance as Ophelia as a result.[16] The Prince of Wales and the Dukes of York, Kent, Sussex and Cambridge all attended a birthday party for William, not to mention the Lord Chancellor and a host of other dignitaries. 'At seven o'clock the second bell announced the dinner, when the Prince took Mrs Jordan by the hand, led her into the dining-room, and seated her at the top of the table. The Prince took his seat at her right hand, and the Duke of York at her left . . .'[17] Lady Elizabeth Feilding derived malign satisfaction from the Prince giving precedence to his brother's courtesan when the Duchess of Bolton and the Countess of Athlone were present. 'I say,' she commented loftily, 'that the Duchess and the Countess were very well served for putting themselves in such company.'[18]

King George III seems at first to have objected to Mrs Jordan playing the hostess in what was to all intents and purposes a royal house, but even this scruple was eventually dispelled. By 1797 Lord Liverpool reported that everything was now changed, '. . . the Duke of Clarence has managed so well that the King jokes with him about Mrs Jordan.'[19] The King and Queen together even attended a performance at Drury Lane in which Dorothy was playing one of her most popular roles while the Duke of Clarence lurked solicitously in the wings.

It would have been amazing if such glory had not gone somewhat to her head. The livery of her footmen, her crested coach (an anchor in honour of her lover – 'If it is at all wrong, do not hesitate to tell me; indeed, I *love* everything that has the least reference to *you*.')[20] made her a little ridiculous. From time to time she could not resist playing the *grande dame*. She dined with Mrs Lefanu in Dublin: '. . . hospitality was the order of the day, but the stile of living so very *different* from what I have been accustomed to, that I really was obliged to have recourse to my *very* best acting to conceal my surprise.'[21] But such aberrations were the exception; her quite extraordinary niceness and her sense of humour ensured that she rarely gave offence and that the Duke of Clarence had good grounds for the almost child-like pride he took in her possession.

The couple were never to be invulnerable to those periodic fits of moral indigestion which in the past have, still do and presumably always will afflict the British people. Cobbett, the self-appointed conscience of the nation, from time to time trumpeted forth his denunciations; devoting himself with particularly heavy-handed sarcasm to the royal birthday party at which Mrs Jordan had played hostess to the Prince of Wales.[22] But the authentic vein of rectitude coupled with frenetic fantasy was struck most richly by *The Times* which some years later described the unfortunate Dorothy as: '. . . a woman who . . . had been admitted into the secrets of harems and palaces, seen their full exhibition of nude beauty and costly dissolute-

K.W.

ness; the whole interior pomp of royal pleasure, the tribes of mutes and idiots, sultans and eunuchs, slavish passion and lordly debility . . .'[23] When this was the current mood, no absurdity was too great. Mrs Jordan was said to have brutally abandoned her children in her hunt for the royal crock of gold while the Duke was accused of seducing one of the self-same children and getting her with child.[24]

On the whole, however, even the most malicious critics of the royal family were gradually won into acquiescence. The harmony and obvious respectability of the union was indeed used as a stick with which to beat the other princes. Even the radical journalist Charles Pigott, in what the Prince of Wales stigmatized as '. . . the most infamous and shocking libellous production yt ever disgraced the pen of man',[25] admitted that the Duke of Clarence was 'not so deeply immersed in vicious destructive folly' as his brothers. On the contrary, his relationship with Mrs Jordan deserved praise as 'a proof of his taste and feeling and as preserving him from really criminal and disgraceful pursuits'.[26]

The truth of the matter was that it was extraordinarily difficult to denigrate any relationship so happy, domestic and virtuous. They were two likeable people, anxious to do no harm to anybody and devoted to each other. It would have been surprising if the public had not learnt to look on them, at first with tolerance, in the end with affectionate approval.

*

For the first few years the Duke and Mrs Jordan divided their time between Clarence Lodge and the Duke's apartments in St James's Palace, which Dorothy 'made a riot of colour with blue sarsnet hangings relieved by crimson panels'.[27] Then, in January 1797, the Duke was appointed Ranger of Bushy Park, a sinecure which carried with it the use of Bushy House. Bushy was a pleasant and substantial country house, set in the middle of the park a mile or so from Hampton Court. Handsome without being grand, comfortable but not luxurious, it was admirably suited to its new occupants. William loved it as no other house and it remained his home until he succeeded to the throne. For thirty years it bulked large in his thoughts and he spent endless hours planning its improvement.

In 1797, however, it proved something of an embarrassment. Though the Government put up some money for the installation, a lot of work still had to be done at the Duke's expense and the home farm in particular was gravely dilapidated. Thomas Coutts, his friend and banker, fortunately obliged with a loan.

The Duke took to farming with fervour. The record suggests that his financial advisers did not consider it an extravagance. 'I am glad to find you are turned farmer,' he wrote to an old friend. 'I believe officers of the navy make the best, as they are always active.'[28] He had no time for the landlord who let his agents get on with it while he himself lived in London or frittered away his life in country sports. 'As a farmer I am well aware of the necessity of the presence of the master; but at this time of year, when the harvest is going on, he ought not to be absent a minute . . . I never am out of the field the whole day.' Whenever he travelled, his letters home were filled with anxious enquiries about crops and cows and, on his return, it was never certain whether children or cattle would first receive a visit.

'We shall have a full and merry house at Christmas,' wrote Mrs Jordan to an old friend; "tis what the Duke delights in.'[29] Anyone who doubted that William felt most at home in a domestic setting had only to see him with his children. One he already had before he even met Mrs Jordan, a son named William who was drowned off the coast of Madagascar early in 1807.[30] Who the mother was remains a mystery, probably the child was the result of a furtive affair in Hanover for which the bill was rendered a few years later. Another was credited to him by the *Gentleman's Magazine* but was his only if he had slept with a woman when no more than thirteen – an achievement remarkable even for a precocious Hanoverian princeling.[31] But whatever the truth about these casual by-blows, his real family was the one he shared with Mrs Jordan.

Dorothy Jordan had a miscarriage in August, 1792; noteworthy chiefly because it kept her for several weeks off the stage – an unprecedented and financially deplorable lapse. Then on January 29, 1794, at her house in Somerset Street, she presented William with a son. He was christened George and was herald of a procession of siblings.* Sophia followed in 1795, Henry in 1797 and by 1807 the family consisted of ten, five boys and five girls, who to make matters tidier still had been born alternately according to sex from George at the head to Amelia in the rear. Their births at first were punctuated by mildly ribald comment from the journals: 'Mrs Jordan is shortly expecting to produce *something*, whether a young Admiral or a Pickle Duchess it is impossible yet to tell.'[32] But as the happy event was rapidly repeated,

* For a list of the children of William and Mrs Jordan, see Appendix B.

so public interest waned, until hardly an eye was turned to the ever more crowded nursery at Bushy.

The Duke was a kind father; over-indulgent perhaps, but if so it was an understandable reaction to his own dour upbringing. George he certainly spoiled. A visitor to Bushy was attacked violently by this 'infant Hercules' and was told proudly by Mrs Jordan that 'his fine-tempered father' always allowed such conduct.[33] Lord Glenbervie, who had a sharp eye for hypocrisy, was impressed when William brought his eldest son, then aged eleven, to a dance and the following night appeared with four children at Mrs Riddell's. 'His care of these children and marked affection for them is certainly very amiable,' he noted with approval. '*Si sic omnia*.'[34] His eldest son was his favourite. He refused a pressing invitation from the Prince of Wales to visit him in Brighton on the grounds that, 'tho' not absolutely ill,' George was expecting a visit from the doctor and William wished to hear the result.[35] By today's standards this may not seem remarkable; in an aristocratic family at the end of the eighteenth century, paternity could hardly have been more extravagantly doting.

Ten children in thirteen years would be taxing for any mother; somehow Mrs Jordan managed simultaneously to sustain a violently energetic theatrical career with the endless travel that that entailed. Up to within a week or two of every birth she would continue to squeeze herself into the breeches which were so much her stock-in-trade – rarely more than a month later she was on the boards again. Lady Bessborough recorded seeing her in September, 1807, a few months after the birth of her tenth child. 'Mrs Jordan was received with boundless applause; she is terribly Large, but her voice and acting still delightful.'[36] Somehow the charm and vitality remained, some-how too she contrived to remain a good wife and a devoted mother. Her life called for loyalty, determination and boundless stamina. She had them all, and a capacity for love which made her one of the marvels of the age.

They had their troubles. William was made to feel jealous by the Duke of Richmond and Dorothy by the widowed sister-in-law of the Bishop of Rochester. And then there was the illegitimate child brought over with its mother from Hanover by a group of well-wishers. *The Times* took the case up, referring to 'a certain royal Duke' who was the reputed father, and stating that the mother had come '. . . to seek that redress from her unprincipled seducer, to which she is so justly entitled'. William at first denied paternity but was said later to have agreed to pay the return fare of mother and child to Hanover and £100 until the child was twenty-one.[37] Mrs Jordan could console herself with the thought that the affair, if indeed it had ever existed, had been ancient history long before she had met the Duke. It may have disquieted her, though, to reflect how many similar skeletons might be lurking in William's cupboard.

But these were minor blemishes on a relationship which was by and large without flaws. For twenty years Mrs Jordan and the Duke of Clarence made their lives together in the utmost contentment. It was not the happiest period of William's life: as we shall see, he felt himself neglected, slighted, sometimes even persecuted. That he endured it without intolerable strain was due above all to the security, the stability and the affectionate warmth of his family circle. His debt to Mrs Jordan was indeed great; greater perhaps than he ever knew.

CHAPTER VII

The Wasted Years

FROM the moment that he left the Navy, the Duke of Clarence vanished almost completely from public view. His disappearance could hardly be total – the third son of the King of England must always merit a certain amount of attention, if only in the gossip columns. But his roles were unobtrusive; a bemused but willing Rosencrantz hovering in the wings or just an attendant lord – 'Enter the Prince of Wales with group of courtiers.' This was not in the least what William wanted. He considered himself more than competent to play a major part in the national life and would have felt no office beyond his powers. He was denied the chance to prove himself; in part because of the limitations imposed by his royal birth, his indiscretion and his lack of talent, but most immediately by the fact that the King was determined to keep him from any position of importance.

The Duke had some cause to feel chagrin at his father's attitude. His innocence of any complicity in the Prince of Wales's efforts to secure power during his father's illness should have won him at least a temperate welcome at Windsor. Indeed, at first things went well. On his return to England he had dutifully rushed to Windsor and won Fanny Burney's heart by knowing about and congratulating her on her brother, 'As long as she has a brother in the service, ma'am, I look upon her as one of us. Oh faith I do! I do indeed! She is one of the corps.'[1]

For the next few months he was assiduous in his attentions. He accompanied the King on the royal tour of 1789 and was present for part at least of George III's sojourn at the 'clean, agreeable and opulent' town of Weymouth.

> 'Weymouth! Behold the hour arrive
> Ordain'd to crown thy fame!
> Contending towns shall vainly strive
> To emulate thy name!'[2]

One cannot be certain whether he bathed alongside the King when the latter took to the sea at seven o'clock every morning – 'at the same time a machine accompanied him with music, playing "God Save The King"' – but at least when Plymouth was illuminated in honour of the visit it was noted that the Duke of Clarence's hatter boasted the most elegant transparency. His device was 'Neptune with his Trident, drawn in his Car upon the Ocean by Tritons, over which was a Medallion of his Royal Highness.'[3]

But though the Duke made a real effort, and no doubt his parents did too, they found each others' company at the best exhausting, at the worst actively painful. The factor that above all poisoned their relationship was William's inability to behave with what his father considered to be minimal dignity and decorum. The King and Queen were prudish and strait-laced, the Duke noisy and vulgar; when they met the parents felt embarrassment and even outrage, the son constraint. It was not a happy base on which to build.

An instance is recorded by Fanny Burney. Her account[4] is worth quoting at length because it gives so vivid a portrait of the Duke at the period – explaining not only why the King and Queen found him hard to tolerate but also, in part at least, what there was for Mrs Jordan to love. Fanny was dining at St James's with Mrs Schwellenberg, the Queen's odious Keeper of the Robes, Monsieur de Luc and Mr Stanhope, a pair of equerries, and a couple of Ladies in Waiting. The Duke had been with the King and burst into the room in search of diversion. He looked, wrote Fanny, 'remarkably well, gay, and full of sport and mischief, yet clever withal as well as comical.'

'Pray, have you all drunk His Majesty's health?'

'No, your Royal Highness: your Royal Highness might make dem do dat,' said Mrs Schwellenberg.

'O, by —— will I! Here you (to the footmen); bring Champagne! I'll drink the King's health again, if I die for it! Yet, I have done pretty well already: so has the King, I promise you! I believe His Majesty was never taken such good care of before. We have kept his spirits up, I promise you . . .'

When the champagne came Fanny tried to pass it. William noticed, clapped his hand on the table and called out 'O, by ——, you shall drink it!' She did not argue the point.

'Come, let's have the King's health again. De Luc, drink it! Here, Champagne to Le Duc.'

De Luc wore a mixed simper – half pleased, half alarmed. He drank, and the Duke took a bumper for himself.

'Poor Stanhope,' he cried. 'Stanhope shall have a glass too! Here, Champagne! What are you all about? Why don't you give Champagne to poor Stanhope?' Stanhope drank, and at once: 'Hark'ee! Bring another glass of Champagne to Mr le Duc.'

Le Duc knew how unwise it would be to protest. He shrugged his shoulders and drank.

'And now poor Stanhope! Give another glass to poor Stanhope, d'ye hear?'

'Is not your Royal Highness afraid,' ventured Stanhope, displaying the full circle of his borrowed teeth, 'I shall be apt to be rather up in the world, as the folks say, if I tope on at this rate?'

'Not at all! You can't get drunk in a better cause. I'd get drunk myself if it were not for the ball. Here, another glass of champagne for the Queen's philosopher!'

'Oh, your Royal Highness,' cried De Luc, whose courage grew as he drank. 'You will make me quite droll of it if you make me go on – quite droll!'

'So much the better! So much the better! It will do you a monstrous deal of good. Here, another glass of Champagne for the Queen's philosopher!' He then decided it was time to drink the Queen's health again. 'Here are three of us,' he cried, 'all belonging to the Queen. The Queen's philosopher, the Queen's gentleman-usher, and the Queen's son; but, thank Heaven, I'm nearest!'

'Sir,' cried Stanhope, a little affronted, 'I am not now the Queen's gentleman-usher; I am the Queen's equerry, sir!'

'A glass of Champagne here! What are you all so slow for? Come, a glass of Champagne for the Queen's gentleman-usher,' laughing heartily. Mrs Schwellenberg now decided to restore order.

'Your Royal Highness, I am afraid for the Ball!'

'Hold your potato-jaw, my dear!' cried the Duke, patting her. Then he recollected himself. He took Mrs Schwellenberg's hand, kissed it abruptly, flung it hastily away, laughed and called out: 'There! that will make amends for everything, so now I may say what I will. So here! A glass of Champagne for the Queen's philosopher and the Queen's gentleman-usher. Hang me if it will not do them a monstrous deal of good!'

His carriage arrived and William got up to go.

'Oh, your Royal Highness,' cried De Luc. 'Now you have made us droll, you go!'

Off, however, he went. 'Is it not a curious scene?' commented Miss Burney temperately.

Most curious and slightly unpleasant. Those who try to make other people drunk are nuisances. In defence of the Duke it can be said that Stanhope and De Luc were a pair of sycophantic prigs and that William was half-drunk already, intended to get a lot drunker, and saw nothing degrading or even inconvenient about being in such a state. He wanted to make fun of the equerries, perhaps, but, more important, also to have fun *with* them. He reckoned to leave the diners more cheerful than when he arrived and, with the possible exception of Mrs Schwellenberg, he certainly succeeded.

The King and Queen, however, would hardly have seen the incident in so charitable a light. How could a man who would so demean himself be trusted with any position of responsibility? The question was a reasonable one. It would have taken a wiser and more tolerant man than the King to reverse it and wonder whether responsibility might not bring sobriety; whether it was not idleness and a sense of futility which encouraged his son in his wilder flights of folly.

*

Shortly before William was created Duke of Clarence he threatened to stand for the House of Commons and took steps to secure a seat at Totnes in Devon. It is doubtful whether his election would, in fact, have been valid, but the possibility seems to have alarmed the King, As he signed the patent, George III is said to have remarked gloomily. 'I well know that it is another vote added to the Opposition'.[5]

It is difficult to list with any confidence the principles which inspired the opposition in 1789 and 1790; impossible to establish any relationship between them and what little is known of the opinions of the Duke of Clarence. If to be a Whig was to believe in parliamentary reform, then he could certainly not be numbered among their more enthusiastic members. If to be a follower of Charles James Fox it was necessary to applaud the French Revolution, then the Duke was his inveterate foe. As with so many illiberal Whigs of his generation, who had sponsored reform mainly because it was anathema to the Tories and the King, the excesses in France quickly proved too much for his squeamish stomach. '. . . this pernicious and fallacious system of equality and universal liberty must be checked,' he wrote to Nelson, 'or we shall here have the most dreadful consequences.'[6] His attitude opened a deep breach between him and the more radical Whigs, led by Fox and Grey, who viewed with professed if sometimes uneasy enthusiasm all that was happening on the continent.

Nevertheless, the Duke believed himself a Whig, and since membership of that party involved more an affirmation of faith than a declaration of policy, it is reasonable to accept that he was correct in his diagnosis. '... He said the *Whigs* had brought His family to the throne of this Country,' noted Farington, 'and He would always give His support to them.'[7] No argument could have seemed more forceful to William, who placed loyalty and a sense of tradition close to the summit in the hierarchy of the virtues. Furthermore, to have paraded himself under any other political label would have been to defy the Prince of Wales, and the Duke still regarded his brother with love and admiration. 'The Prince of Wales is taking all possible pains to form a strong party against the Government...' wrote Lord Sydney in January 1790. 'H.R.H. governs His two Brothers.'[8]

Perhaps the most important single factor in shaping his attitude was his animosity towards William Pitt. For no good reason, he was convinced that Pitt had wilfully delayed his acquisition of a dukedom. On better grounds, he believed that Pitt had adopted a distinctly pawky attitude towards the settlement of his outstanding debts and was responsible for his income being limited to a mere £12,000 a year. In 1790 he joined with his brother in a campaign to defeat Pitt's candidate, Lord Euston, in the University election at Cambridge; and though this, and other similar forays, caused little trouble to the all-powerful minister, he succeeded in turning Pitt into the enemy which he imagined him already to be.

But though he took his seat among the Whig peers, he was never consistent in his politics. In 1789 there was, of course, no organized 'opposition' comparable to that which exists today. Even allowing for this, however, the Duke of Clarence was more than usually erratic. On any given issue it would have been rash to predict his attitude by arguments based on party or any other set of principles. The progress of the French Revolution quickly convinced him that the radical wing of the Whig party was to be eschewed. As early as 1791, in a confidential chat at Brooks's, he was telling Bentinck that he 'blamed the Prince of Wales for falling into the principles of the democrats of the day'.[9] When the Whigs split and the Foxite rump was left dolefully to contemplate its allies deserting to the ministry, he applauded the schism and rejoiced at the discomfiture of those misguided men who could not or would not see the dangers spreading from across the channel.

*

The political activities of the Duke of Clarence, therefore, though sometimes distasteful to the King, can hardly have seemed treasonable. Money provided a more potent source of conflict; the King deplored his mounting debts and gave him little credit for the fact that they were small in comparison with those of his elder brothers. The relationship was rarely better than chilly. The proprieties were observed, but the Duke kept his appearances at court to a barely respectable minimum. Away from court, even respectability was sometimes forgotten. Lady Bessborough, herself no pattern of propriety, professed herself shocked when she heard William abusing the King 'in the most indecent manner'. 'Is it not too bad?' William appealed to her. 'It must be bad indeed when even your Royal Highness cannot deny it', she countered coolly.[10] From time to time things would look a little brighter, usually when parent or son was ill or in pain. In 1793 the Duke broke his arm; the King expressed his infinite sorrow and made soothing noises about his son's future in the British Navy.[11] It seems doubtful however whether either sorrow or good intentions survived the discovery that William's accident had been incurred when tumbling drunk down the steps of Mrs Jordan's house in Somerset Street.

It is hard to be sure how far the coldness between father and son was the work of the Queen. Queen Charlotte is indeed a mysterious figure. She was ferociously hated by her enemies – '. . . the basest and most abandoned of women . . . every crime and enormity was sanctioned in her reign.'[12] Even a sober observer like Sir Gilbert Elliot believed that the Queen dominated the King, forced him into hostility with his children and poisoned his natural affection for the 'frank, sincere, spirited, honourable' Duke of Clarence.[13] And yet her birthday letter to her son on August 19, 1792, does not read like the deceit of a practised plotter: 'When the Heart speaks, few Words will be sufficient to express one's Mind. May You see many returns of this Day and may every Earthly Bliss and happiness fall to Your Share. This is the Sincere and ardent Wish of, my dear William, Your very affectionate Mother and Sincere Friend.'[14] What is certain is that she viewed far more severely than the King, William's way of life and, above all, his cohabitation with Mrs Jordan. It would have been surprising if the constant burden of her disapproval had not worn away the King's inclination to make it up with his erring son.

Almost whether he liked it or not, therefore, the Duke found himself forced into close association with his brothers. If one judged only by the diarists it would seem that, in the closing years of the eighteenth century, the Prince of Wales and the Dukes of York and Clarence were never separated. Three overweight *enfants terribles*, they prowled the ball-rooms and the salons of London, abusing their parents, huffing and puffing about the iniquities of Mr Pitt, terror of the conservatives, the sobersides and the prudes. Yet William was always slightly out of place. Often he was getting into trouble for blurting out what would have been better left unsaid. 'William has been saying some very foolish things to the King respecting us . . .' the Prince complained to the Duke of York. 'He is as good natur'd a fellow as exists; means no harm, but has not the smallest regard to the truth . . .'[15] Certainly few were better qualified than the Prince of Wales to judge.

From the outbreak of the war with France in 1793 the Duke of York became deeply involved with his military duties. William succeeded to the doubtful privilege of acting as his brother's confidant and closest ally. He comforted the Prince as the latter's marriage to Caroline of Brunswick tottered towards total collapse and advised him while Moira and Loughborough busied themselves with patching up a reconciliation. For a time – to the Prince's mingled relief and alarm – it seemed as if they might succeed; '. . . the whole matter,' wrote Moira with striking sang-froid, 'should be treated as a light disagreement, exaggerated by incorrect representations.'[16] Then Caroline changed her mind. The terms for a separation were hammered out at a conference at Bushy where the Prince had been staying with his brother for the previous two weeks. '. . . nothing can be more perfect than William's own conduct is towards me', wrote the Prince to the Queen enthusiastically.[17] It is doubtful whether perfection in such a cause did much to raise the Duke of Clarence's stock at Windsor.

*

But however low the opinion held of him by King and ministers, the Duke confidently supposed that, in time of crisis, the country would make use of his services. The Prince of Wales, as heir to the throne, was left to fret at home but the other royal brothers were quickly playing their part. The Duke of York went off to command the British contingent in Flanders; Prince Edward, now a major-general, fought

with Sir Charles Grey in the West Indies; Prince Ernest went into
battle with the Hanoverians. The Duke of Clarence alone, able-bodied,
intrepid, and with far more active service behind him than any of his
brothers, was left without a job.

It does not seem that this was what the King had at first intended.
As late as June, 1793, the Duke believed that he was to serve under
Howe in the Home Fleet, probably in command of the *London*, a
first rate of ninety-eight guns.[18] But for one reason or another his
appointment was delayed: his injury held up matters by a few months,
other vessels were given priority, there was bickering about his allowances. He lost patience and showed his independence of ministers by
preaching against the war. 'The Duke's idle and indiscreet abuse of the
war,' wrote Glenbervie, some time later, 'and of the characters and
conduct of his Majesty's Ministers, particularly Mr Pitt, in every
promiscuous company, at balls, to women, young officers and boys, is
a matter of scandal and discomfort . . .'[19] When the 'promiscuous
company' was extended to include the House of Lords, some official
notice had to be taken. On June 17, 1793, the Duke argued in the
House that, since Holland was now safe, ministers should make peace
at once.[20]

His speech caused consternation, even among those who joined
with him in his dislike of ministers. 'As to William, I never was so
hurt at his declaration . . .' wrote the Prince of Wales; his sense of
outrage caused as much as anything by his brother having dared to
take an initiative without his prior authority. 'He is much ashamed of
it . . .', the Prince went on.[21] If he was, he concealed it well. Several
months later he was writing to Thomas Coutts that every day convinced him more and more of the propriety of his objections. His wish,
if the chance were ever given him, would be to rule as a peaceful
monarch. And yet he believed the revolutionary movement in France
to be a total evil and was satisfied that the safety of the British state
depended on its being swiftly scotched. Essentially, he never wavered
in this view. His objections to the war were generally confined to
individual continental forays which he believed cost more in men and
money than could be justified by their potential value. His pacifist
phase lasted less than a year and even during that period was not consistently maintained. When pique led him into outright denunciation
of British policies he generally regretted it and did his best to prove
that he had meant something else.

His speech proved disastrous for his immediate prospects. Pitt took

umbrage and told the King he could not support the employment of a
'political Admiral'. The King does not seem to have pleaded his son's
cause with any enthusiasm. The Duke's appointment was shelved indefinitely. 'I am sorry he is not employed,' wrote Nelson to Fanny.
'What does it matter to him whether the war is right or wrong? As an
officer who I would wish to see rise in the esteem of his country, I wish
he was at sea where I am sure he would acquire honour . . .'[22]

By the following year he had changed his tack. In the debate on the
Address he vigorously defended the ministry and the war. England
would deserve the contempt of all the nations of the world if she did
not show the regicides that they could not cut off the heads of Kings
and Queens, 'like so many poppies in a garden' without having their
own heads cut off in return. The speech was neither pithy nor lucid,
yet at least it showed ministers that his heart, however belatedly, was
in the right place.

After so handsome a gesture, the Duke confidently awaited an offer
of employment. No such offer came. Impatiently he wrote to the
Lords of the Admiralty. 'Conscious that during my naval career, I
never committed an act which could tarnish the honour of the flag
under which it was my pride and glory to fight, I solicit in this hour of
peril to my country that employment in her service which every
subject is bound to seek . . .'[23] Their Lordships did not even reply and
William turned to his father, begging that they should be forced to
employ him or state publicly why. Any job, however lowly, would
satisfy him, provided it enabled him to serve his country.

Though the Admiralty's discourtesy cannot be condoned, the Duke's
request must have put them to great embarrassment. Whatever he
might say William would not have been fobbed off with some minor
job. His real views on the matter were those expressed to Moira:
'H.R.H. said he was ready to serve, could it be put upon terms any
way decent, which he explained by saying, that the being sent out
sixth or seventh in command of the Channel Fleet, or on any mission
obviously contrived for the sole purpose of keeping him out of the
way, would not be a situation becoming a son of his Majesty's who
had seen a considerable share of active service.'[24] The trouble was that
the Admiralty had a war to win. Though the Duke had proved himself
competent to command a frigate, they saw no more reason now than
previously to believe him fit to be in charge of a fleet.

The Duke now turned to the possibility of a post in the ministry.
In mid-1796 it seemed that Lord Spencer would soon be forced by ill

health to resign. The Duke suggested to the King that he should succeed him at the head of the Admiralty, either as First Lord or under any other title that was preferred.[25] Evidently the King delayed replying; at any rate William's hopes were still alive in the autumn, when he wrote to Nelson: '. . . the time must come when I shall be where both my rank and my experience with the Navy ought to place me, I mean when I am entrusted with the executive management of the Admiralty.' Then indeed, he promised Nelson, the latter would get the promotion he deserved.[26]

Spencer remained in office, but three years later the Duke's hopes soared again. Lord Bridport was to resign and William had been told that he would then be appointed to command the Home Fleet.[27] Once more his optimism was proved folly. Spencer was again the stumbling block: this time because he appointed St Vincent to the post.[28] Irrepressible, the Duke declared that he would accept to serve as second-in-command. Spencer and St Vincent would soon fall out and he would then take over. The vision was rosy but the offer was never made. Eventually he humbled himself and applied directly for the job, only to receive a reply 'of the most Jesuitical Kind' whose opaque phrasing still could not conceal St Vincent's determination to keep him at bay.[29]

Thwarted again, he was left with no role more satisfactory than to provide the nucleus of a disestablished ginger group. 'I am ready either for the Cabinet or the Fleet, but I have no reason to expect either situation, and must do all the good I can in Parliament.'[30] More active employment was provided by a force of yeomanry which he raised around his home at Bushy. He dressed them in fancy uniforms – sumptuous red, gold and blue – drilled them and harangued them grandiloquently: 'My friends and neighbours! Wherever our duty calls us, I will go with you, fight in your ranks, and never return home without you.' But he did not delude himself that this botched-up body of largely unarmed farmers and grocers was likely to be of much use in case of invasion. To General Hawker he described them as useless: '. . . the sooner Government can or will get rid of the Volunteer Force, the better. If we are to carry on war against France we must have a regular army . . .'[31]

In 1798 he became an Admiral; a titular promotion which did nothing to increase his chances of active employment. Nevertheless, when Pitt resigned in 1801 to make way for Addington, *The Times* reported that the Duke of Clarence was vying with the Marquis of

Buckingham for Spencer's vacant office at the Admiralty. '. . . we are well assured that neither will obtain it,' said *The Times* with some satisfaction, and neither did.[32] Perennially optimistic, however, he remained convinced that not only employment but an honourable peace lay just around the corner. The fear of invasion was absurd, he told Nelson, and condemned to inactivity the French army would rust away. This attitude predisposed him to support the uneasy truce which was patched up in 1801 by the Treaty of Amiens. He defended its terms in the House of Lords, arguing that since neither England nor France could strike effectively at each other, an adjustment of their differences was the only sensible course. The treaty would provide 'a safe and honourable peace' which he hoped and believed would prove permanent.[33] It did not, of course, and the war was resumed in the summer of 1803. This too he defended as the lesser of two evils,[34] and he stuck loyally by Addington's administration, which Pitt had now turned on and was seeking to destroy.

It would, indeed, be true to say that he stuck by Addington's administration *because* Pitt was seeking to destroy it. He bluntly stated that he would support ministers, if for no other reason, then so as to keep their predecessors out of office.[35] Addington was grateful for any help but the Duke of Clarence did not carry guns big enough to hold the government's enemies at bay. The administration foundered, and Pitt was minister again. The Duke reserved his hottest anger for the Admiralty whose leader, Henry Dundas, now become Lord Melville, was one of Pitt's closest associates and in part responsible for the Duke's earlier humiliations. In 1805 Melville was accused of malversation of funds during his long tenure of office as Treasurer of the Navy. William was genuinely concerned about the finances of the navy but so legitimate a preoccupation could neither explain nor excuse the gleeful venom with which he now pursued his prey. It was political vendetta, of the nastiest sort. 'Lord Melville talks of passing the summer in the Highlands of Scotland,' he proclaimed, 'but I hope he will pass it in the Tower.'[36] Such words came ill from a member of the House of Lords who would shortly be required to pass judgment on the object of his denunciation. When the trial ended William, with the Dukes of Kent and Sussex, voted Melville guilty on nine out of ten counts. William can hardly have imagined that Pitt would employ him in Melville's place, but his chagrin was redoubled when Sir Charles Middleton was appointed to the Admiralty – 'a man turned eighty,' he wrote indignantly 'and solely employed about religion and farming.'

The death of Pitt early in 1806 did something to improve the Duke's relations with ministers, but neither the Whig Ministry of All the Talents nor the predominantly Tory administration which succeeded it seemed in any hurry to offer him employment. At one point, when Collingwood's health broke down, he confidently offered himself for the command in the Mediterranean. '... my Flag flying will give satisfaction to many Officers, Seamen and Royal Marines,' he assured the Prince of Wales, '... if employed I shall have the agreeable task of commanding by love and not through fear.'³⁷ Alarmed by this threat, the Ministers persuaded Collingwood to remain in command. Gloomily he assured them that he was ready to die at his post and, a few months later, suited his actions to his words. Again the Duke's hopes rose, again he was disappointed. His ambitions spluttered out ignominiously. Uncourted, unwanted, almost forgotten, he embarked upon his middle age with fifteen years of inactivity behind him and a limitless vista of the same to come.

*

His inactivity did not preclude occasional forays into public life. His parents considered that it was the duty of the princes to support the servants of the king. Where else should ministers look for staunch supporters?³⁸ This the Duke could not accept; yet equally his profound distrust of everything which smacked of radicalism would not allow him to commit himself wholly to opposition. His compromise was a surly isolationism, from which he would periodically emerge to intervene on issues close to his heart. Of these the most conspicuous was the future of slavery.

Today it is so much a truism that slavery must be evil that it is hard to recapture the atmosphere of an era when humane, decent and by no means stupid men could argue in its defence. This however was the case, not only with the Duke of Clarence, but with many people who on other issues were ranged, if not with the liberals, at least with the more moderate of the conservatives. Among this group the Duke, because of his long service in the West Indies, was listened to with a respect which his opinion on other issues did not usually command.

During his stay in Jamaica he had become convinced that a plentiful supply of slaves was essential to the island's economy; to cut off the trade, still more emancipate those who were already there, would

K.W.

imperil an investment of £80 million and destroy the livelihood of the very people it was intended to help. Though there were injustices to be rectified, the slaves were 'comparatively in a state of humble happiness' and most of the planters were fully alive to their responsibilities.[39] To supplement this reassuring information the Duke could adduce his experience as a naval officer. A strong navy in war depended on a strong merchant fleet in peace, and the slave trade was one of the greatest, if not the greatest single factor in keeping our merchant navy prosperous.

To these arguments were added, of course, the welter of subsidiary points with which proponents of the trade bolstered up their case: the right of property; the imbalance of sexes among the slaves which made further imports essential; the fear of insurrection; the advantage other, less scrupulous nations would reap if we abandoned our share of the lucrative market. The line which William pursued with the greatest relish was that 'the gross barbarism of the Africans on the slave coast' so endangered the less warlike members of the community that these had to be enslaved to save their lives – a *recherché* variant on the conservationist defence of blood sports which commands such support today. But always he reverted to what was for him the salient point: 'Without this trade, the West Indies must be lost to Britain, and without the West Indies, not only the dignity and prosperity of the nation was gone, but its very existence as an independent empire would cease.'[40]

The Duke was active in the debates of 1792 and 1793. His speeches, particularly that of 1793, were judged a striking success by all who happened to agree with them. 'William made a most *incomparable speech*,' rhapsodized the Prince of Wales. '. . . Lord Thurlow assured me it was as good as possible.'[41]

He did not slacken in the cause. In 1799, when danger again threatened, he was 'earnestly engaged in Parliament upon the Slave Trade for several weeks.'[42] Liverpool used him as a go-between to explain his position to the King[43] and he was generally considered to be one of the most formidable enemies of abolition. 'It is shocking,' wrote Zachary Macaulay, 'that so young a man, under no bias of interest, should be so earnest for the continuance of the Slave Trade . . .'[44] It is curious that he found the Duke's attitude more shocking because disinterested, but one can sympathize with his dismay. 'It seems to be a main object of the Royal Duke to prove us visionaries, Dissenters and Democrats . . .'[45] It was a dangerous line of attack and one which Macaulay had difficulty in repelling – especially at a moment when even mild reform seemed tainted with the blood of revolutionary France.

The Duke continued the battle to the bitter end, and for him it was bitter indeed. 'Lord Grenville, at one blow, destroys by the abolition of the Slave Trade, the Maritime Strength of the Country', he wrote disconsolately in 1807.[46] From then onwards he regarded with uneasy suspicion any evidence which suggested that the Royal Navy was still afloat and doing well.

His attitude on slavery can perhaps be condoned, but not even the most pious hagiographer could hold it to his credit. On most other issues he was ranked with the more liberal members of his family. He supported, for example, Lord Stanhope's bill to repeal the penal statutes against those who failed to attend divine service. 'All compulsion sits uneasily upon the necks of individuals ...' he remarked; an impeccable sentiment which might with advantage have occurred to him during the debate on slavery. To punish a man for not going to church was 'grossly and unjustifiably interfering in the solemn compact which a man might have entered into with his Maker, who claimed to himself the natural privilege of worshipping that Maker in the way most agreeable to himself.' The Archbishop of Canterbury hurried to expostulate with the King. 'Very bad, very bad indeed!' agreed the indignant father. 'I'll speak to Pitt about it.'[47]

His broad-mindedness was evident in a still more unexpected context during the debate on adultery in April, 1800. Lord Auckland moved a bill to prevent anyone divorced for adultery from marrying the other guilty party. The Duke denounced the adulterer as 'an insidious and designing villain ...' but pointed out that it would merely make bad worse to stop the sinners subsequently marrying. Such a ban would leave the woman with no resort but suicide or prostitution. In a second speech he dilated at length on the Mosaic Law, took the House briskly through Greek and Roman precedents, moved on to Montesquieu, and concluded with an almost complete sermon borrowed from the Bishop of Rochester. Bathurst concluded that his stand was the first step in a campaign to establish 'a sort of princely influence in the House which ... will in time become troublesome.'[48] He credited the Duke with too much guile. This was an issue about which he felt strongly and when William felt strongly it was not in his nature to remain silent.

If he had been more calculating he might have held his tongue. It was widely felt that none of the sons of King George III were well placed to condemn adulterers and William was on thinnish ice when it came to striking moral attitudes in the House of Lords. It is a tribute to his innocence, or perhaps a reflection of his naïvety, that no such thought entered his head. He would not have altered his speech an iota if it had. William often did the wrong thing but can rarely be accused of failing to do what he believed was right. His principles were sometimes quaint, always idiosyncratic, but by them he abided.

CHAPTER VIII

The Breach with Mrs Jordan

SUNDAY, December 16, 1810: 'I could perceive by your letter,' wrote Mrs Jordan to her lover, 'that you were more than usually irritated against the *Ministers*, and indeed, who can wonder at it?'[1] Most of his fellow citizens seemed to share the Duke's irritation. The disastrous Walcheren campaign had destroyed what was left of the government's credit and its titular leader, the Duke of Portland, had finally declined from decrepitude to death. His successor, Perceval, hopefully courted the Whigs but was rejected with less than minimal civility. Few people yet foresaw that Wellington in the Peninsula was to turn the tide of war, though the Duke of Clarence was surprisingly prescient. 'Lord Wellington,' he wrote, 'is *willing* and *capable* of doing his duty. I understand our army is the finest in all ways that ever was seen . . . In a very short time the season will prevent the French from acting, and I cannot think that any minister in this country can be weak enough not to have our forces in Portugal . . . in that state of defence before next spring that it would be madness in the French to attack in that quarter.'[2]

But long before Wellington's victories were to bolster the morale of ministers, a new crisis arose. In November 1810 the death of George III's youngest daughter, Princess Amelia, helped once more to shake the old King's tottering wits. Within a few weeks it became clear that he was incapable of governing and that this time there was little chance of his recovery.

The Duke was genuinely distressed. 'It is impossible to know the King and not to love him . . .' he had written to his son in mid-October. 'His conversation with me today was perfection itself, and I wish the whole world could have heard it.'[3] It would be a heartless son who could watch undismayed while his father sank into irreparable insanity, but the tragedy also carried with it interesting possibilities for the future. The Prince of Wales would take over the reins of power, he would bring in the Whigs, new blood would surge through the sclerotic veins of government: surely at last there would be a place for

him? The gossips told of his exuberance, of his gloating boast at Sir
Thomas Sutton's dinner table that Perceval had 'turned the key upon
the King. He'll come back no more!'[4] It is an unpleasant story, no
doubt made more unpleasant by the malice of the narrator, but it is not
wholly unconvincing. If William could have cured his father he would
have done so, but he could not chase from his mind the glittering
prospects which the King's illness might open to him. And anything
that was in his mind was almost certain to come tumbling out of it
within a very short space of time.

Before there could be any question of a new government, however,
the powers of the Prince of Wales had first to be defined. Predictably
the Tories, following the precedent of 1788, introduced a regency bill
which gave the Prince only limited powers for the first twelve months.
No less predictably, the Whigs argued that the Prince must be accepted
as Regent with unrestricted powers. In conclave the royal dukes protested against the proposal to fetter their brother's freedom of action.
The Duke of Clarence signed with the rest; but that almost concluded
his contribution. During the debates he spoke only once and then with
uncharacteristic brevity. 'Great and momentous as the present crisis
was,' he told the startled peers, 'he would now abstain from fully
uttering his sentiments upon it.'[5] It was left to the Duke of Sussex to
make the running for the royal family.

It is at least possible that his attitude betrayed loss of faith in his
brother's intentions. He was committed to the need for a change of
ministers. 'He still remains *a firm Whig* and *hates* the Ministers ...'
recorded Princess Charlotte.[6] Yet rapidly it became apparent that the
Prince Regent, as the Prince of Wales had become in February, 1811,
had doubts about making a clean sweep. He procrastinated, he offered
compromises which he knew would be unacceptable to the Whigs, he
kept his former friends in a state of dubious hope until the end of his
probationary year. By then it was clear that the King was most unlikely ever to recover. Fortified by this the Regent finally declared his
position. The most that the Whigs could have would be a share in
government, and a pretty small share at that. The offer was rejected;
the Whigs resigned themselves to another sojourn in their wilderness.
Their hopes died, and with them died the hopes of the Duke of
Clarence.

It is from this period that the special relationship between William
and his eldest brother began to wither. The two men never quarrelled
but their intimate association was over. The Duke was less often at

Carlton House. More and more he passed his time at Bushy while the Regent found other companions. Almost the only serious exception was the occasional tour which he would undertake with the Prince. On one occasion at least he contrived to cause some embarrassment to his brother. 'My royal Brother and Myself,' he is said to have told his hosts in some Yorkshire town, 'have been not a little grateful at finding so much civilization in this out-of-the-way country. We expected barbarism, but really you seem a civilized people, after all!' But the occasion for such follies came ever more rarely; it seemed that there was no longer a role for the Duke of Clarence to play on the national scene.

*

It was not his relationship with his brother, however, which most occupied the Duke's mind in 1810 and 1811, but his liaison with Mrs Jordan. Her letters show that she was as loving as ever. 'You have more sense and genious than any one of your family, but less self entrest,' she wrote with enthusiasm, if erratic spelling. The arrival of his 'dear letters' was anxiously awaited whenever she was away from home.[7] Few of William's letters survive but from those that do and from Mrs Jordan's replies, there is no reason to think that he, on his side, was any less affectionate.

But there were troubles ahead. The Duke was already deeply in debt. He had cut back his establishment, to the extent where he could not even afford to have a party on his birthday. Mrs Jordan was still earning a good income but she was portly and well on into middle-age. She could not indefinitely sustain the *jeune ingenue* roles which had been her speciality. There were signs that she was no longer the box-office attraction she had used to be.

Nor were the debts likely to do anything but swell. The mischief lay with his growing family, five boys, five girls, each one more expensive every year. George FitzClarence, the eldest son, had been since 1808 on active service in the Peninsula. He had done well. 'I am sure he has every quality to make a good officer,' wrote General Stewart to the Duke, 'great Quickness, Intelligence and Activity'.[8] But most of his fellow-officers were far richer than he. In February 1811 he arrived unexpectedly in England and alarmed his father by his fast friends and his taste for drink and gambling. 'I love you most sincerely,' William wrote to him, 'but must not forget you have four brothers and five sisters who have an equal claim on me. I must provide for all, I have made great sacrifices and am ready to make more for the good of you all, but you must not distress me . . .'⁹ His second son, Henry, he put into the Navy. It was not a success. His Captain was said to be a martinet and a flogger of midshipmen, and Henry did not take kindly to the idea. By May, 1811, he had left the navy and shortly afterwards received a commission in the Fusiliers. It all meant more expense for his father.

But though the boys might run up debts they could be expected, in the end, to contribute something to their expenses. Daughters were another and in some ways still more intractable problem. By now Sophia was fifteen. It was already evident that she was a pretty and clever girl, but she would need more than looks and wit to compensate for a bar sinister and a non-existent dowry. If she was to marry well, the Duke would have to scrape together at least something of a fortune. But then there were Mary, Elizabeth, Augusta and Amelia to come. The problems of a father never ended; yet somehow William was determined to provide for his children. 'Money is, as you know, my object,' he told Lord Mayo, 'and I am now come to that time of life that I must make those sacrifices I would not formerly have done; but then I am the father of ten children and it is my duty to provide for them.'¹⁰ The money was to come from a rich wife; the sacrifice to be Mrs Jordan.

If one had to date exactly the beginning of the end of what, for the last twenty years, had been in all but law a marriage, it would be June 19, 1811; the day on which, at a fête at Carlton House, the Duke met Miss Catherine Tylney-Long. Everyone agreed that Miss Tylney-Long was worth at least £40,000 a year, some put it as high as £60,000 with £300,000 accumulated in funds. Added to this she was cheerful and attractive, if scatter-brained, and owned a palace at Wanstead built in the height of fashion by Colen Campbell. These qualities made her the target of every fortune-hunter in Town, including 'Romeo' Coates who wooed her with some of the worst among his invariably execrable odes.¹¹

Undeterred by this opposition the Duke of Clarence at once opened negotiations with Lady de Crespigny, Catherine's aunt. He was left in no doubt that his suit could never prosper so long as he was linked with Mrs Jordan. By now he had convinced himself that he loved Miss Long as well as desired her fortune. He assured her, through an intermediary, that he would part with Mrs Jordan and surrender the latter's place in his affections to his new passion; '. . . the poor little girl thought that she was intended to officiate *in the same capacity* with her predecessor: so she fell a crying, and called the unlucky ambassadress all the bad names that she could think of.'[12] The misunderstanding was quickly straightened out; indeed the Duke assured his heiress that the Prince Regent had promised to withdraw all restrictions on royal marriages as soon as he had the power. 'What will become of poor Mrs Jordan and all her children, I wonder?'[13] asked Lady Bessborough; and all London society wondered with her.

Mrs Jordan, on tour in the provinces, was one of the last to be told what was going on. In August, 1811, she complained of never receiving letters from the family. 'I believe when I am out of the gate at Bushy Park I am very soon *forgot*. Well, I cannot help it – it is only a continuation of my strange fate.'[14] It would be wrong to read too much into such remarks yet she cannot have been taken entirely by surprise when, early in October, she was summoned from Cheltenham to Maidenhead to discuss the terms of a separation. Forewarned or not, however, the shock was painful. In the play in which she was appearing that night she was supposed to laugh uncontrollably, on which another character would comment: 'Why, Nell, the conjurer has not only made you drunk, but he has made you laughing drunk.' When the scene was reached, however, all Mrs Jordan could do was cry. With aplomb the actor adapted his lines: '. . . the conjurer has not only made thee drunk, he has made thee *crying* drunk.'[15] And crying drunk the poor woman remained for several weeks.

The Duke called on Princess Charlotte on October 11, 1811. He was on his way to spend four weeks at Ramsgate with his daughter, Sophia. Charlotte noticed that he was in high spirits.[16] The reason was quickly plain for he was on his way to woo 'the bewitching Catherine'. He poured out his hopes to Lady de Crespigny: '. . . I really flatter myself the lovely little nice angel does not positively hate me. I walk with her and of course never leave her, and she does not dislike my devoting my public attendance on her . . . her dear little eyes sparkled with pleasure at many things I said.'[17] He courted her energetically and was probably speaking something near to the truth when he protested that, 'it is not the fortune, but the *little dear angel* I love and esteem.'[18]

Though no one can doubt Mrs Jordan's distress, her role was curiously equivocal. She seems not only to have made no attempt to dissuade the Duke from his new endeavour but almost to have encouraged him. At the most, she counselled prudence: 'I again repeat, *be cautious* for fear of a *disappointment*. All *women* are not to be taken by an open attack, and a *premeditated* one stands a *worse chance* than any other.'[19] To the Duke of Cumberland she referred to it as a lamentable business but still seems to have been hoping that her lover would bring it off.[20] William contrived to convince himself that Mrs Jordan was almost as much in favour of the match as he was himself. She 'has behaved like an angel . . .' he told Lady de Crespigny. 'Miss Long therefore cannot be afraid of any *éclat* from that quarter.'[21]

Even before he offered this reassurance, however, he was becoming uneasily aware that the path of true love was likely to prove as bumpy as ever. It was flattering to be courted by a prince of the blood but when the prince was forty-six and looked every year of it; portly, balding and uncouth with no small talk, a mountain of debts and ten illegitimate children; a romantic girl might be forgiven for finding that blood alone had only limited charm. Besides, a far less suitable and hence more glamorous suitor was in the field. William Wellesley-Pole, nephew to the Duke of Wellington, was twenty-four, handsome, witty, a spendthrift and a cad. The combination was irresistible. The Duke should have been warned when, one evening, he refused to let Miss Long dance with his rival whereupon, 'She hurt one of her beautiful little feet and gave up dancing . . .' However, he would not accept that such meretricious attractions could prevail until the news of her engagement with Pole was actually broken to him by the heiress herself.[22]

The newspapers were surprisingly slow in exploiting this latest royal embarrassment. *The Times* waited until November 2, when the affair was almost over, before it recorded that the Duke 'had paid his suit . . . with the magnificence and ardour of an English tar.' In general the Press was less sympathetic and a welter of bad verse condemned his enterprise:

> '*What! Leave a woman to her tears?*
> *Your faithful friend for twenty years.*
> *One who gave up her youthful charms,*
> *The fond companion of your arms!*'

Miss Tylney-Long was portrayed as upbraiding him for his faithlessness and sending him about his business:

> '*Return to Mistress J——'s arms*
> *Soothe her, and quiet her alarms;*

> *Your present differences o'er,*
> *Be wise and play the fool no more!'*

Far from ceasing to play the fool, however, William now began to play it with a vengeance. 'I trust that all the historiettes about the Duke of Clarence are lies and waggeries,' wrote Lord Auckland, 'but when we are told that he first offered himself to Miss Long, and immediately afterwards to Miss Mercer, and then to Lady Berkeley . . . It is difficult not to apprehend that there may be more business for Messrs. R. and T. Willis.'*[23] Other stories credit him with also proposing to the Dowager Lady Downshire and Lady Charlotte Lindsay. Certainly there was malicious exaggeration in the rumours but it does seem that William, whose pride would not allow him to be on with the old love again and yet who had been irrevocably cheated of the new, now cast about desperately for any match which would save his face. There is no doubt at least that he made an offer for the hand of Meg Mercer Elphinstone, the wealthy daughter of his old captain, Lord Keith. The offer was rejected briskly and all he earned was the disapproval of his niece Charlotte, Miss Mercer's confidante.[24]

All such tentatives ended in failure. Indeed it does not seem that, with the exception of Miss Tylney-Long, he can have pushed them very seriously. Between him and the throne stood the Prince Regent, the Prince's only child, Princess Charlotte, now sixteen years old and unbetrothed; and the Duke of York, twenty years' married and without the prospect of an heir. Though the Duke of Clarence therefore only had an outside chance of coming to the throne himself, even this was worth the consideration of an ambitious woman. What was more, he was well placed to inherit Hanover, from which Princess Charlotte was debarred by the Salic Law. He was, in short, a highly eligible *parti*. 'I have no doubt he will marry someone if he does not her,' commented Lady Bessborough when his wooing of Miss Long was beginning to go awry.[25] In general terms she was right, but the Duke found it difficult to conjure up much enthusiasm for these lesser beauties and must have compared them wistfully with the mistress whom he had enjoyed for more than twenty years.

*

There was however no question of taking up again his life with Mrs

* Doctors who specialized in the treatment of lunacy and had treated King George III.

Jordan. Throughout the autumn of 1811 discussions went on about their separation. The Duke was anxious to be generous within his means, but the means were limited; Mrs Jordan showed a disturbing tendency to pitch her value high. 'Here I *stick*,' she wrote to her eldest son, George FitzClarence, from Bushy, 'and I will be well paid for leaving it. *Generosity* and *liberality* will not always do in this world – but I have justice on my side and shall be able to fight my own *battles*.'[26] At one point, it seems, she threatened to publish the letters which the Duke had written to her over the years.[27] However hard pressed, it is unlikely that she would in fact ever have done so. Dorothy Jordan was no Mary Anne Clarke, to gloat as the British public laughed over her royal lover's naïvely doting scribbles. But the thought of it must have given the Duke sleepless nights.

At last a compromise was worked out. In strictly financial terms Mrs Jordan had reason to be satisfied. For her own use she was to receive £1500 a year with a further £800 for her children by the earlier liaisons. Another £1500 was allowed for the maintenance of the four younger FitzClarence daughters, with £600 for their house and carriage. William added the not unreasonable stipulation that, if Mrs Jordan went back to the stage and the daughters were thus left without a parent, they should return to his care and the allowance designed for them should stop. '. . . the arrangements for the future provision of myself and ten children are entirely settled,' wrote Mrs Jordan, probably to the Prince Regent, 'and . . . I am. happy to add, in a manner that does high honor to the Duke of Clarence'.

But though Mrs Jordan felt she had been treated with generosity, all the riches of Miss Tylney-Long could not have reconciled her to her lot. It cannot be pleasant for a woman of fifty to be abruptly ousted from her home, separated from her sons and deprived of the status which she had enjoyed for so long. Her children did little to solace her. Sophie, the eldest daughter, decided that her mother was an embarrassment and must consequently be ignored. 'To say that Sophy's conduct towards me is *reprehensible* is too gentle a word for it,' moaned poor Mrs Jordan. 'It is *shocking* to reflect how a young *creature* can without the smallest remorse *break* through the *first* and most sacred tye of human nature.'[28] But the sons were not much more dutiful and she had good reason to feel herself abandoned.

Her allowance should have been sufficient to keep her in comfort but she already had debts. Thomas Alsop, the husband of her daughter by Richard Daly, through his folly and extravagance, embroiled her still deeper. She returned to the stage in the hope of increasing her income, and, by so doing, lost control even of her four younger daughters. Then her art failed her, she found every appearance more taxing, the audiences seemed strangely unappreciative. Worst of all, her health was deteriorating; more and more performances had to be cancelled or tours curtailed. By the summer of 1815, her position made far worse by the embezzlement of what fortune she had left by another of her sons-in-law, she had come to the end of the road. Advised by John Barton, the Duke's most trusted man of business, she fled the country to escape her creditors.

Forlornly she dragged herself across France and by the beginning of 1816 was installed in rooms at St Cloud. Over the next few months her hopes of a return to England dwindled, gradually her health ebbed away. Occasional messages came from her children but far more often she passed her days waiting for letters that never came. Abandoned, almost destitute, she had nothing left to live for. Early in the morning of July 5, she died.

'Barton has written me the particulars attending your mother's misfortunes and death,' the Duke told his son George. 'The infamy and rascality of March and Mrs Alsop . . . will prevent my further intercourse with them.'[29] One can only speculate how far he was ignorant of Mrs Jordan's fortunes after their separation. Sir Jonah Barrington, a close friend and admirer of Mrs Jordan, denied indignantly that the Duke had deserted her; '. . . though separated, for causes in no way discreditable to either, he never lost sight of her interests or her comforts. It was not the nature of his Royal Highness, he was incapable of *unkindness towards Mrs Jordan*.'[30]

So comprehensive a piece of white-washing is unacceptable yet it does at least seem likely that Barton, wishing to avoid a dangerous run on the ducal coffers, deliberately kept his master in the dark. The Duke of Clarence could fairly be accused of many vices but he was rarely mean: it is almost inconceivable that if he had realized how desperately she was in need of money he would not have found her some. That it was his business to find out is a fair comment, but it is only of thoughtlessness that he was guilty.

No letters indicate what grief he felt at her death but all his life he spoke of her with great affection. Whenever a portrait of Mrs Jordan came on the market he would acquire it and add it to his collection. When he became King he sent for the sculptor, Chantrey, and told him he had a commission to which he attached particular importance. He wanted a bust of Mrs Jordan, now dead for more than fifteen years. He 'then went into a thousand particulars of their private life, always ending that she had been an excellent mother to her children'.[31] When the work was done the King asked Chantrey where he felt it should be placed. The embarrassed sculptor made no suggestion, whereupon William announced that it was destined for St Paul's. To his chagrin the chapter politely refused the proffered honour and the bust remained under the tolerant eye of Queen Adelaide.[32] Around it clustered other relics of a past which the King never forgot or looked back on with anything but pleasure.

*

'Money, money . . . or the want of it, has, I am convinced, made *him* at this moment the most *wretched* of men . . . His distresses should have been relieved before.'[33] Mrs Jordan at least had no doubt that it was financial reasons alone which had led to the separation. No other explanation can be advanced with confidence. And yet a nagging suspicion remains that something more was involved. If the Duke's need for a rich marriage was really so desperate it is surprising that he largely lost interest in the quest by the end of 1811 and did not achieve his end for another seven years.

Inevitably one is drawn to the conclusion that – even though the Duke himself would not have admitted the fact, perhaps was hardly conscious of it – his relationship with Mrs Jordan had ceased to satisfy. Sex had always been an important element and though his hearty Hanoverian appetites had perhaps abated, they had certainly not yet withered away. Mrs Jordan, stout, matronly, short of breath, could offer little stimulus to his flagging powers. She had few other talents with which to beguile him. The four years by which she was his senior suddenly began to seem important. Ennui, even distaste, ate into his life. If they had been married it would never have occurred to William that they might separate, as they were not the operation was disastrously simple.

To abandon after twenty years somebody who has been to all intents and purposes one's wife and has borne one ten children is inexcusable by any standards. If it had been essential that the Duke of Clarence should produce an heir to the throne then he might have pleaded this as a justification; but such was not the case. A legitimate heir was of course to be desired but, until Princess Charlotte died a few years later, the future of the dynasty seemed relatively secure. He acted from expediency, because a rich wife was desirable for himself and for the future of his children.

But though inexcusable, his conduct was not inexplicable. At first one is amazed by the casualness with which the Duke sloughed off his entanglement and the ready acquiescence of Mrs Jordan. It was as if arguments might be possible over timing or terms, but the principle was taken for granted by both parties. And so indeed it was. Their behaviour only makes sense if it is realized that the role of royal mistress in the eighteenth century was almost by definition a temporary engagement. Neither the Duke nor his mistress had ever believed that they were united till death them did part. On the contrary, William, if accused of inconstancy, would have felt genuine surprise and resentment. In his eyes his relationship with Mrs Jordan was remarkable because it had lasted so long, not because it ended when it did. He had been faithful to her for twenty years, had ended the affair on the most generous terms that he could afford, and had shown some, if not much consideration for her dignity and comfort. In so doing he had behaved not well but rather better than might have been expected.

CHAPTER IX

The Search for a Wife

THOUGH the placid domesticity of the Duke's life had thus been shattered, his activities did not become noticeably less humdrum. The loss of Mrs Jordan's company did not lead to any corresponding increase in his appearances at court, and though from time to time he accompanied the Regent in his progresses around the stately mansions of Britain's aristocracy, he rarely found such outings to his taste. The Duke of Clarence would come from time to time to Stowe, commented Buckingham, with a loftiness characteristic of his odious family, but would never have been endured except as an 'appendage' of his brother.[1] The more elegant and witty the society believed itself, the more he was felt to be out of place. 'It was a heavy matter to have the Duke of Clarence *sur les bras* all the day . . .' groaned Lady Bessborough, though she conceded him an endless fund of stories, some of them amusing, and a neat touch at taking off the Queen.[2]

The picture emerges of a bluff, affable and loquacious boor – a man whom the sensitive would shrink from and the dandies disdain but the life and soul of any party composed of his intellectual peers. He was foul-mouthed, but meant no harm by it. When he was staying with Lady George Murray at Weymouth she plucked up her courage and asked him not to swear in front of the children. On leaving he proudly said: 'Lady George, have I not been very careful. I am sure your boy has not learnt any naughty words from me!' 'I do feel very grateful,' his hostess rather sanctimoniously replied, 'but if your Royal Highness could refrain for a week, why not give up a bad habit altogether?'[3] His sense of humour was limited and crude – jokes running the small gamut from banana-skin to lavatory. Lady Granville recorded seeing the royal brothers at a performance by the great clown, Grimaldi. The King was in such fits of laughter that his stays hurt him, 'York roared again, Clarence was dull and did not twig them'.[4]

Such were not the qualities to win favour in 'that Mahomet's Paradise, Carlton House'[5] or to make him a member of that rarefied group, the Cottage Coterie, so called after the *cottage orné* in which the Regent increasingly entertained. Englishmen, indeed, were in a minority in that inner circle. More often to be found were Count Münster from Hanover, the Austrian ambassador, Prince Esterhazy and Prince Lieven,* the Russian ambassador, with his assertive and scheming wife.

The Duke had a brush with Princess Lieven in the winter of 1814 when both were dining at the Pavilion at Brighton. The Princess was an incorrigible liar but her account has the ring of at least partial truth.[6] The Duke 'as usual after dinner, a little lively and unsteady on his legs,' conducted the Princess to her carriage. Suddenly he pushed the footman to one side, leapt in and ordered the coachman to drive on:

'Are you cold, *Madame*?' he began the unexpected *tête-à-tête*.

'No, *Monseigneur*.'

'Are you warm, *Madame*?'

'No, *Monseigneur*.'

'Permit me to take your hand.'

'It is needless, *Monseigneur*.'

The Duke nevertheless grasped the Princess's hand. 'Fear seized me,' she recorded improbably, 'for he was evidently drunk . . . I racked my brains for something to distract his attention. I have said he was very stupid, very ignorant of everything. He took no interest in anything, great affairs preoccupied him not at all. He had only one fixed idea in politics – Hanover.' The Princess therefore had the happy idea of telling her companion that the Congress of Vienna, which was then in session, had decided to give Hanover to Prussia and compensate England with a slice of Westphalia. William was aghast:

'God Damn! Does my brother know this?'

'I don't think so yet, and I beg you, *Monseigneur*, not to tell him. It is a secret which I tell you now.' Overwhelmed by the enormity of the threat, the Duke forgot the Princess entirely: 'amid a torrent of great words'. Next day the Princess told the Regent what she had done. He 'laughed like a madman', kept up the joke by telling his brother that he had agreed to swop Hanover for Westphalia, and in future always escorted Princess Lieven to the carriage himself.

*

His relationship with ministers improved. Lord Liverpool, prime

* So called for simplicity though in fact he did not become a prince till October 1826.

K.W.

minister since 1812, had no more intention than his predecessors of giving the Duke any substantial employment but at least took the trouble to wrap up his refusal in decent courtesy. When William, at the end of 1813, pressed to be allowed to visit the British army then fighting in the Low Countries, Liverpool raised no objection. The spectacle of the royal admiral taking to sea again after so long an interval invited attention that was not always entirely respectful:

> *'I own it, since my promotion*
> *I've not ventured much on the ocean;*
> *For great men in our creed*
> *To themselves should take heed,*
> *Nor rashly run into commotion.'*

But now, went on the poet, all was changed:

> *'I'll frighten the sharks and the seals*
> *At the sight of my multiplied keels;*
> *The dolphins and soles,*
> *Shall fly us in shoals,*
> *And the grampuses take to their heels.'*

The Duke himself took the expedition very seriously. He paid Princess Charlotte an endless visit and 'was quite ridiculously *consequential* and close about his journey ... The real truth is he goes for his own amusement, but does not allow of that and thinks proper to make everyone believe that Ministers have sent him on a secret mission of importance ...'[7] In fact his mission, undertaken, as he assured his son, 'with the desire of the Prince Regent and with the concurrence of the Cabinet',[8] was to woo the widowed Grand Duchess Catherine of Oldenburg, twenty-five-year-old sister of the Emperor of Russia.

Unfortunately the Grand Duchess had different ideas. Charlotte claimed that the project had been absurd from the outset, since both the Emperor and his sister would have considered the Duke unsuitable.[9] This seems on the whole unlikely. William's confidence must have had some basis and up to the moment of his return to England, escorting the Grand Duchess across the channel, he remained convinced that she was to be his. He exploded with rage when the Admiralty tried to fob off 'this elegant and fascinating lady' with anything less than a ship-of-the-line: 'George the First sent an Admiral and a whole British Fleet to fetch Peter the Great, her ancestor, and *now* a *cutter* is sent for the Grand Duchess.'[10] But his gallantry did him no good. When the Grand Duchess got to London she complained of his vulgar familiarity. The Prince Regent she dismissed as '*un voluptueux*'. Indeed the only member of the royal family she cared for was the Duke of Sussex; presumably because he had, at that moment, the merit of being hardly on speaking terms with any of his brothers.[11]

Unaware of this disappointment to come, the Duke meanwhile thoroughly enjoyed his continental jaunt. The British army under Sir Thomas Graham was pushing the French out of the Netherlands. William, so long condemned to watch the war from the side-lines, was at last able to feel himself embattled. On the way to headquarters his horse fell and he had to walk five miles through the dark and icy cold. He clambered up a steeple to watch the bombardment of Antwerp and was almost blown up when the church was struck by several shells. In the final attack he had a bullet through his coat.[12] It was all most gratifying. The Dutch greeted him with enthusiasm – 'If I had been their own prince they could not have treated me with more distinction.'[13] He was the hero, the representative of Britain's might. For one who had been so long in obscurity, neglected if not despised, it was a heady experience.

By February he was in Brussels, to receive the plaudits of two thousand people. 'I think I have not any reason to be dissatisfied with my expedition . . .' he wrote complacently.[14] With Bülow and the Duke of Brunswick he attended a Te Deum in the Cathedral. All glory, laud and honour . . . not *his* glory, he knew, but still some little wisp of it seemed to hang about him. William the Liberator would ride at the head of his army to Paris, would enter it side by side with the Russian and Prussian commanders. 'The game is up with Bonaparte and I shall be in at the kill.'[15] Then the bubble was pricked, abruptly the Regent recalled him to England. The excuse given was the forthcoming session of Parliament: ready though he always was to believe himself needed, even the Duke can hardly have supposed that his presence at Westminster would be of much significance.[16]

A consolation was quickly offered him. King Louis XVIII was to return in bedraggled triumph to his country. On April 23 he set sail from Dover in the *Royal Sovereign*, escorted by *Jason* which flew the flag of the Duke of Clarence. A hymn, set to the tune of 'God Save the King', was composed for use in case the Duke accompanied the King ashore:

'Thanks to Royal Clarence
Who guides our King to France
Thanks to Clarence.
He maintains the glory
Of the British navy,
Oh, god, make him happy,
God save Clarence!

Stirring stuff, but sadly there is little chance that it was ever delivered.[17]

Better still was to follow. '... to my great joy and satisfaction,' wrote the Duke after he had transferred his flag to *Impregnable*, 'the Emperor of Russia and the King of Prussia embark with me in this Ship: their suites are large but with activity and regularity I shall arrange everything,'[18] All did not go smoothly. The Admiralty, in a fit of misguided economy, countermanded his order for fifty extra beds and he had to send a cutter posting back to Deal so as to save the dignitaries a sleepless night in a hammock.[19] Then he was ordered to haul down his flag after the sovereigns left his ship at Portsmouth. 'I cannot express how very deeply and keenly I do feel this cruel treatment which I really do not deserve.'[20] Melville's answer seemed to leave him no loophole but the Duke firmly misunderstood and kept his flag flying till the royal party returned to Portsmouth.[21]

But, such contretemps apart, it was a happy time for William. In a flurry of largely futile activity he refound the sense of being wanted which had deserted him for so long. 'I get up at six and till dinner time the pen is hardly ever out of my hand,' he wrote to his son from on board *Impregnable*. 'In short, an Admiral is a slave, but the King's service *must* be carried on and I am the last man not to do my duty.'[22] The note of exultation in his lament could hardly have been more clear. As he was greeting the Emperor, the King of Prussia and the Prince Regent for the return journey, he spotted something which displeased him about the set of the top-gallant yards. A torrent of oaths was directed at the sailors responsible. The Emperor winced, the Regent found the happy phrase. 'What an excellent officer William is!' he remarked benignly.[23]

Frustrated in his quest for a Russian bride, the Duke now looked nearer home. His cousin, Princess Sophia, was again put forward. He liked her but she was already forty-two and old for child-bearing. 'Under these circumstances,' he told the Regent, 'I cannot see any advantage in marrying Princess Sophia.'[24] His attitude was hardly gallant, but he never pretended that he was looking for more than an heir and a grant from Parliament. Almost simultaneously he seems to have made some advance – proper or improper – to his former quarry, Miss Mercer Elphinstone. Princess Charlotte wrote sympathetically: 'The Duke of Clarence's conduct to *you* is just what it *ever* is, ungentle-manlike and blackguard. It is not worth thinking or caring for a second. He deserves being treated with due contempt.'[25]

In the House of Lords he continued active, liable to erupt discon-certingly in any debate which took his fancy. Catholic Emancipation was a new theme. On the whole his heart was in what most people today would consider the right place. 'I hope not many years will elapse before I see all religious distinctions done away with in the Empire,' he wrote to Lord Mayo.[26] An admirable sentiment, and one for which at first he seemed disposed to do battle; but when the Prince Regent switched camps and opposed reform, William began to trim. His main contribution to the problem impressed at least by its simplicity. 'The great obstacle and danger after all is the Pope,' he concluded. The Prince Regent, the King of Prussia, the Emperor of Russia and the Prince of Sweden all had great influence in European affairs. 'I think these four might *at least* try to persuade the Catholics to do away with the Pope . . .'[27]

*

'I hope,' wrote the Duke to George FitzClarence in May 1813, 'you will carry on as successful and efficacious a war in the Peninsula as Warner is waging in the kitchen and offices against the black beetles.'[28] But George, and his younger brother Henry, were soon in trouble. They were among a group of officers of the Tenth Hussars who accused their commanding officer, Colonel Quentin, of cowardice and neglect of duty. At a court-martial Quentin was acquitted and the rage of the establishment turned against his accusers. The Prince Regent, for some reason, took the participation of the two FitzClarences as a personal affront. Not only did he pack them off to India but instructed Lord Moira, the Governor General, to treat George strictly and not bring him into the family circle until he had expiated his sins in outer darkness. Moira paid little attention to the Regent's instructions; he took a fancy to George FitzClarence, treated him kindly, and told McMahon, no doubt to the Regent's disappointment, that the Captain's behaviour had been admirable.[29]

Henry FitzClarence was not so lucky. Towards the end of 1817 the

Duke was told that his son had been ill but was now recovered. Moira, however, did not think he would ever really be well in India and had decided to send him home. William was delighted and began to make plans to welcome the prodigal. Then Lord Bathurst received a package from Moira enclosing a letter '. . . for the Duke of Clarence which I wish should not come upon his Royal Highness abruptly. The death of Lieutenant Henry FitzClarence is announced in it. The young man was proceeding with me on my personal staff; and he has been carried off by fever after four days illness.'[30] Henry was the first to die of William's children by Mrs Jordan. He was not his father's favourite but the Duke was a loving and conscientious parent and was distressed by the tragedy. It was fortunate that in February 1818, when the news reached him, he was fully occupied with other matters. A few months before, something had happened which had totally transformed his prospects.

*

In May, 1816, Princess Charlotte, heir presumptive to the throne, had married Prince Leopold of Saxe Coburg. The Duke of Clarence led the bride to the altar and must have reflected as he did so that the marriage was likely finally to eliminate his chances of succeeding to the throne. In due course, she became pregnant. The Duke was with the old Queen at Bath when news was received that the baby had been born prematurely and had died but that the Princess was not in danger. After some hesitation they decided nevertheless to attend a great banquet that was being given that night in their honour. In the middle of it a messenger hurried in and gave a letter to the duke. '. . . he rose from table and struck his forehead as he read it, and then hurried out of the assembly with inexpressible trepidation and dismay.'[31] Princess Charlotte was dead.

William was genuinely fond of his niece; he would have been astonished and hurt if he had known of the malice she habitually vented on him in her correspondence. But he would have been more than human if he had not felt some exultation at the future which this tragedy opened up to him. The Regent and the Duke of York were all that stood between him and the throne, he was by far the most healthy of the three and it was highly unlikely that either could produce an heir. From an obscure royal duke he had become suddenly a figure of the first consequence. The most immediate result was that his marriage, hitherto considered by all except himself as a matter of minor moment, became suddenly of urgent importance. One by one the would-be brides of Europe were taken off the shelf and dusted down, not for him only, but for his brothers the Dukes of Kent and Cambridge.

The Regent reviewed the field in a letter to his mother about what he patronizingly referred to as 'William and his little concerns'. The best bet seemed to be the elder Princess of Hesse but there was another Princess, of about the right age, who was the only daughter of the King of Denmark.[32] With some hesitation – after all, as he pointed out to Martin, he *had* seconded the vote of thanks to Nelson for his conduct during the attack on Copenhagen – the Duke agreed to the latter. But he was determined to extract a good price for his acquiescence. He set out his terms in a letter to his mother:

'. . . If the Cabinet consider the measure of my marrying one of consequence they *ought* to state to *me* what they *can* and *will* propose for my establishment: for *without previously* being acquainted with *their* intentions as to *money* matters I *cannot* and *will* not make any positive offer to any Princess. I have *ten** children *totally* and *entirely* dependent on *myself*: I owe *forty thousand* pounds of *funded* debt for which of course I pay interest, and I have a *floating* debt of *sixteen thousand pounds*: . . . *thus* situated and turned *fifty* it would be madness in me to marry without previously knowing what the settlement *would be*. If *that* settlement is made which I can consider *adequate* I shall only have to explain my real situation as the *fond* and *attached* father of *ten* children to the Princess whom I am to marry: for without a *complete* understanding of my full determination to see *when* and where I please *my daughters* I cannot and will not marry.'[33]

Busy negotiations now went on: the Duke of Cambridge with the Danish court on the one hand, the Regent with Lord Liverpool on the other. The latter went surprisingly well. Even the Duke of Clarence could not find much wrong with Liverpool's proposal to raise his parliamentary grant from £18,000 to £40,000 a year, to provide £22,000 for outfit upon marriage and to write off £17,000 of funded debt.[34] So far so good, but now plans went awry, for the Danish Princess announced that she did not feel ready to leave her parents: '. . . for which I certainly admire her,' wrote the Duke with regret but also considerable relief.[35]

The relief was easily explicable. While the royal match-makers were

* In fact Henry was already dead though this was not yet known in England.

at work William had been quietly striking off on a line of his own. Now he felt free publicly to avow it. '. . . *honour, love and virtue* are my guides,' he wrote to Barton, 'and the lovely dear heiress of Oxfordshire may be my reward.'[36] The lovely dear heiress of Oxfordshire was Miss Wyckham (sometimes Wykeham, or Wickham) of Thame Park who had inherited from her uncle, Lord Wenman, an estate estimated at some £16,000 a year. Not all observers found her so lovely or so dear. Henry Fox called her vulgar and dull,[37] while Greville, still less gallantly, deemed her disreputable and half-mad.[38] She seems in fact to have been a noisy eccentric; good-hearted, assertive and by no means stupid. She was attracted by the distant glamour of the throne, the Duke by the more immediate pleasures of her fortune – but the couple, almost incidentally, seem to have been genuinely fond of each other. William's distress when he lost her was not uniquely that of the thwarted treasure-hunter. '. . . I think and exist only for Miss Wyckham,' he told his son, and the words strike true.[39]

'On its being told to the Regent,' reported Lady Jerningham, 'H.R.H. *groaned* – which is it seems his way of disapproving.'[40] Undismayed, the Duke told the Duchess of Gloucester that 'the Prince's consent will be *wrung from him at last* so he [had] better give it at once.'[41] He was convinced that the Royal Marriages Act allowed him, after the age of twenty-five, to marry as he liked. In fact, if the King did not consent, twelve months' notice had to be given to the privy council and the two Houses of Parliament given a chance to disapprove. The Regent referred the question to the Cabinet who at once concluded that the marriage was unthinkable. They urged the Regent to dissuade his brother; if he failed, they threatened, then they would have to advise Parliament of the proposed match and of their own disapproval of it.[42]

'The unfortunate business concerning the lovely and all-accomplished Miss Wyckham is over,' mourned the Duke. 'She thought it impossible to go on after the Cabinet had taken up the matter and we parted the best friends but in the most distressing manner to both.'[43] As a consolation he tried to secure a peerage for his would-be-bride. Blandly Lord Liverpool replied that so unusual a step would attract attention to what had surely better remain secret.[44] It was not till 1834, after almost four years on the throne, that William finally coerced his ministers into creating her Baroness Wenman.

The marital merry-go-round did not slacken its pace. The once rejected Princess of Hesse was next to be sounded out but negotiations were quickly blocked by the Princess's father.[45] The Duke of Cambridge, who was conducting the business, was undiscomfited; the fact that his own wedding plans were hanging fire until his elder brothers were safely married ensured that no effort would be spared in the quest. Immediately he switched his attention to Saxe-Meiningen; a small, dim duchy to the north of Bavaria. There was not much money but the ducal family was of excellent blood and there was a twenty-five-year-old daughter, Princess Amelia Adelaide, who was said to be presentable. To his relief the suggestion was accepted with alacrity. At the age of fifty-two the Duke had found a wife.

It was not yet all plain sailing however. As Canning said with brutal clarity in the House of Commons: 'the Duke of Clarence would not have thought of contracting this marriage ... if it had not been pressed upon him as an act of public duty.'[46] The time had now come for Parliament to provide the *quid pro quo*. But, faced with the request to provide additional money for four royal dukes, the House of Commons proved distressingly truculent. First Lord Liverpool, under pressure from his supporters, reduced the proposed increase to £10,000 a year; then there was a back-bench revolt and the increase was cut still further to a mere £6,000. All hope of the marriage was now over, Castlereagh informed the House, while the Duke took the line that so pitiful a grant was irrelevant to his needs and that he would therefore refuse it altogether.

If he contemplated calling off the match, however, he quickly changed his mind. There were some cogent arguments in its favour. Princess Adelaide was said to be personable and home-loving and after eight years as a bachelor the Duke was more than ready for the pleasures of domesticity. Her family were supposed to be good breeding stock, and William dearly longed to father the heir to the throne. Finally, it was pledged that she would tolerate, indeed positively welcome, his brood of bastard children. This was the clinching factor, for few princesses would be so generous. 'I may by proper *settlements* and *arrangements* not only *not* injure my family but *eventually* put myself into that situation which will enable me to prove to the world my *real affection* for you all,' he reassured his son George. 'Had I one hundred children I could love them equally and you must know my heart *too well* to think I *could* forget those I have, I do, I shall and I must love.'[47]

And so the marriage was arranged. Yet the Duke did not go gentle into that good night; on the contrary he approached the altar with fixed and apprehensive gloom. He did not know whether to be more sorry for himself or for his bride. 'She is doomed, *poor dear innocent young* creature, to be my wife,' he wrote disconsolately. 'I *cannot*, I *will not*, I *must* not ill use her . . .'[48] The sentiment was impeccable as far as it went but it did not offer much hope for a conspicuously joyful married life.

CHAPTER X

Princess Adelaide

THAT Princess Adelaide turned out to be the ideal wife for the Duke of Clarence, owed nothing to the perspicacity or taste of the Duke of Cambridge, who would happily have betrothed his brother to Messalina if she had been available. He would have been perspicacious indeed if he had seen through to her qualities for Adelaide, though not ugly, was far from immediately impressive.[1] Her unassuming presence evoked everything that was most odiously patronizing on the part of the English: 'A small, well-bred, excellent little woman,' commented Lady Granville, in one of the more favourable judgments;[2] 'your amiable little Duchess', said the Prince Regent;[3] 'a poor little bad-ish concern', was Lady Anne Barnard's[4] unkinder opinion. Always the emphasis was on her smallness – a matter of impression rather than measurement since she was in fact well up to average height.

Beneath this mouse-like exterior she had courage, clarity of purpose and, above all, tenacity. She rarely disputed but never gave way. Calmly, modestly and with daunting inflexibility she reiterated her prejudices until at last opposition was worn down and her point of view accepted. Her prejudices were those which she had absorbed in youth, unleavened by humour, unshaken by the merest flicker of intellectual curiosity. She was intelligent enough to defend them but not to question them: a blindness which was to prove disastrous to many of the political causes which she had most at heart.

Her sense of duty was one of the wonders of the age. Brought up in a narrow and provincial court, she had a clear vision of how life ought to be run and no idea of modifying her view to suit an alien land. On her husband her influence was to be almost wholly beneficial. She set his finances in order, cut down his drinking, cleaned up his language and generally tidied him up and made him presentable.

Princess Adelaide accepted the burden of the Duke's bastards with genuine enthusiasm, since she was devoted to children. When the elder

FitzClarences slighted her she retorted with forbearance and resolved to be even more magnanimous towards their younger siblings. There was genuine kindness in this, indeed in much that she did, and yet a curious joylessness permeated all her life. An artist, noticing during a sitting how red her eyes were, asked whether the light was troubling her. 'It is not that,' replied Adelaide. 'It is that I have veept much.' Somehow she never seemed to be far from tears. She had many admirable qualities; and yet the total effect was dispiriting. She was the sort of woman whom every man maintains would make an excellent wife for somebody else.

*

In spite of his doubts the Duke managed to put on a reasonably good face for the outside world. Lady Williams Wynn spotted him passing Adelaide's picture around at one of the royal concerts, 'and bowing to each person when they passed it on, giving them credit for their Approbation of his choice.'[5] He wrote to his son that he had heard the most flattering reports of his fiancée,[6] and did what he could to convince himself that the reports were true. But he seemed in no hurry to put them to the test. When the Prince Regent's secretary, Knighton, wrote to him at Aldenham Abbey to tell him that Princess Adelaide and her mother were to arrive on the evening of July 4, he replied coolly that, 'sooner than eight o'clock it will be impossible for me to leave this lovely hospitable mansion though I am certainly most anxious to meet this Princess.'[7] The visitors found themselves deposited at Grillon's hotel and it was only late that night that the Prince Regent and, finally, the Duke himself arrived to pay their respects.

The marriage took place at Kew just over a week later, on July 13, 1818. It was a double affair, with the Duke of Kent and Princess Victoria Maria Louisa of Saxe-Coburg making up the party. The weather was perfect, the royal family on their best behaviour, and Queen Charlotte lasted through the ceremony before retiring to be sick in the next room. William and Adelaide then retreated to the former's rooms at St James's Palace and settled down to the perilous business of getting to know each other. Both parties were determined to make a success of it, good-natured and anxious to please, but it still caused surprise when the marriage proved an instant, total and lasting success. The Prince Regent, who called on them two days after the wedding, found them 'sitting by the fire exactly like Darby and

Joan'.[8] The Duke discovered to his delight that his new wife was quite as domestic and as socially unadventurous as he was himself. She loved the country, was delighted by Bushy, and was anxious to make the acquaintance of all the children.[9] He wrote to his banker, Coutts: 'I really believe,' he concluded, '. . . I have every fair prospect of success.'[10] It is not difficult to detect the relief in this cautious summary of a fortnight's marriage.

The reluctance of the House of Commons to satisfy his financial needs meant that the Duke believed himself unable to live in England in anything like appropriate state. Clearly they had to move to the continent, for a year or two at least. Hanover was their destination. This was hardly ideal, if only because the Duke of Cambridge was Governor General and firmly settled in the official palace. It was galling for William to yield precedence to his younger brother, even if only on official occasions. But nowhere else could they be so cheaply and yet respectably looked after. After some debate he was offered the Fürstenhof, a handsome house belonging to the Crown, £2000 a year and various extras like fuel, game and garden produce.[11] Certainly he could not complain that he was being ungenerously treated.

The Duke of Cambridge, too, did his best to make things agreeable. A cavalry escort met the travellers at the frontier, the roads were put in order, a battery of guns saluted them, a guard of honour paraded for the Duke's inspection. But he was not to be so easily consoled. 'England, fortunately for us, is the *first* and best part of the world,' he told his son.[12] Other countries, he conceded grudgingly, might have their good points, but those of 'detestable and unhealthy' Hanover were hard to find. The fact was that he was in exile and felt himself miserably misused; 'necessity and not inclination keeps me *here* till I can live without incurring fresh debt.'[13]

His heart remained at Bushy. He had great confidence in Daniell, his steward, but could not bear to let control slip from his hands. 'I will not have *any* alteration in the *Park*, *Farm* or *Garden without* my *previous* Consent', he wrote truculently.[14] No detail was below his notice: some pigs were to be sold; certain servants were to be cut off candles and soap; a bulletin was called for on the parrot's health; 'I am glad Betsy Budd is *made* an *honest* woman notwithstanding the anger of Mr Weaver,' – a tantalizing fragment of a no doubt improving tale. He bought and dispatched by the official messenger a hundred pounds' worth of 'very superior and cheap linen'. 'Do not mention this . . .' he added coyly, 'as it is in fact against *law*.' The bargain was not so striking as the Duke had hoped; Mrs Oak, the housekeeper, found the linen shoddy stuff.

*

In November, 1818, the Duke wrote exultantly to his steward that he was looking forward to the event that would crown the success of his marriage.[15] 'The Duchess of Clarence,' the Duke of Kent remarked more bluntly, 'certainly is, I believe, in the family way.'[16] His jubilation was as much financial as dynastic; surely Parliament could not deny a living income to the father of the future monarch? For seven months his exultation was unabated; then the Duchess caught a cold, the cold led to pleurisy, pleurisy involved bleeding; the worry and disturbance provoked a premature birth. Charlotte Augusta lived only a few hours and was buried '*in aller Stille*' beside the body of King George I in the crypt of the palace.[17] For several days the life of Adelaide too was in danger.

This was only the first of a long and melancholy procession. Barely four months later the Duke was writing anxiously to Liverpool that he had 'every reason to believe the Dutchess once more with child'.[18] This time she miscarried at Calais on the homeward journey. The Duke reproached himself with having treated her with too little consideration. Next time he would ask less of her. At last patience was rewarded. 'The Duchess of Clarence is delivered of a Princess,' recorded Lady Jerningham in December, 1820. '. . . it is to be a future Queen Elizabeth – but, I trust, not so sanguinary.'[19] The name was the Regent's choice, William and Adelaide would have preferred Georgina.[20] Lord Eldon was present at the birth and found the baby disturbingly small.[21] It was indeed six weeks premature. The doctor, Sir Henry Halford, contemptuously remarked that the mother was a 'poor *wishy-washy* thing' but that the baby would live provided it survived the first dangerous month or so.[22]

Princess Elizabeth lived for four months and seemed to thrive. Then the Duke wrote in anxiety to his steward at Bushy cancelling a visit because of the baby's illness. The worst, he thought, was over but there was still danger.[23] Two days later, at 1 a.m. on March 4, the baby died of 'inflammation in the Bowels'. On the same day William found time to write to Mrs Clayton, the woman responsible for looking after the Princess, to assure her that the tragedy was no fault of hers.[24]

Even this was not the end. Early in 1822 the Duchess was again pregnant.[25] On April 8 she once more miscarried, this time of twins.

'I want words to express my feelings at these repeated misfortunes to this beloved and superior woman,' wrote the Duke to George IV, as the Regent had by now become. '. . . I feel what I cannot express for her . . . I am quite brokenhearted.'[26] Rumours that the Duchess was with child were still being spread long after she had become Queen but for her husband the question was all but closed. He had married Adelaide for financial security and for an heir. He had secured neither. It is to his credit that his first thought was for her distress.

The Duke found some solace in being a grandfather. He was particularly fond of Adelaide, the eldest daughter of George FitzClarence who had married Lord Egremont's illegitimate daughter, Mary Wyndham. 'As your birthday is next Saturday', he wrote to her, 'I wish you to come here to breakfast at half past nine and remain till dinner. I will order the nicest roast fowl and potatoes and the best rice pudding . . .'[27] Princess Victoria too was a great favourite with both the Clarences. 'My children are dead,' Adelaide wrote to the Duchess of Kent, 'but your child lives, and she is mine too.'[28] Nothing could compensate Adelaide for her loss but the little princess was a comfort in her desolation.

*

The death of their first child had convinced the Duke that Hanover was no place for him. After an extended visit to Adelaide's family in Saxe-Meiningen they set course for London. Unfortunately their journey coincided with the Duchess's second pregnancy. William was determined that the child should be born in England; the consequence was a miscarriage at Calais and six weeks' convalescence in Walmer Castle at Dover.

It was not the most promising preamble to Adelaide's first sojourn in her husband's land. The poor woman found London society alarming and often inexplicable. She dined with Lord Dudley, whose habit of speaking his thoughts aloud, alternately in a deep bass and a high falsetto, had disconcerted many people with socially far more *savoir-faire* than her. 'What bores these Royalties are!' he mused aloud. 'Ought I to drink wine with her as I would with any other woman?' Deciding he should, he gracefully asked the honour of taking a glass of wine with her. Towards the end of dinner he asked her again. 'With great pleasure, Lord Dudley, but I have had one glass with you already.' 'The brute! And so she has,' commented his Lordship loudly.[29] Lord Dudley was agreed to be odd, even by the English; more typical were Lady Jersey,

Princess Lieven and the Ladies of Almacks who snubbed her with ferocious chilliness.[30] She did her best, dutifully refusing to speak anything but English, busying herself over innumerable charitable concerns, but only in the seclusion of Bushy did she feel at home.

In January 1820 the Duke of Kent died at Sidmouth. Within two weeks George III had followed his son. For ten years he had been secluded in his gilded mad-house at Windsor and his final disappearance merely put the formal seal on a transformation which had taken place long before. Such distress as William felt can hardly have been profound. For him, and indeed for the new King and his ministers, the most important consequence was that it precipitated the crisis which had long been brewing between George IV and his estranged wife, Caroline. If the Queen had chosen to remain abroad she could have enjoyed her pension and her pleasures for the rest of her life, but the lure of the throne was too strong and in June, 1820, she returned to England to demand her rights.

The bedraggled farce which was played out in the House of Lords has been described *ad nauseam*. The Duke associated himself wholeheartedly with the King and trumpeted loudly in his defence. It was alleged, indeed, that he had written to the captain of the ship in which Caroline had left England in 1814 suggesting that both princess and Regent would be delighted if he were to seduce his royal passenger. Lords Brougham and Denman, the Queen's champions, offered to prove the existence of this letter but the Secret Committee ruled that it was no affair of theirs.[31] Thwarted, Lord Denman had to satisfy himself with a bitter attack on the Duke in the House of Lords. Certain people in the highest circles, he said, had been industriously circulating 'the most odious and atrocious calumnies' against the Queen. Then, with a dramatic gesture towards the Duke: 'Come forth, thou slanderer,' he declaimed,' and let me see thy face!'[32]

Brougham and Denman must have had something to support their case but it is hard to believe that William had either the guile or the malice to act in such a way. Indeed, until Caroline actually returned to London he spoke of her, if at all, with guarded friendliness. But he had undoubtedly been warm in his championship of his brother and would not have been backward in adding his mite to the gossip which enshrouded the wretched Queen. When the time came for him to vote on the Divorce Bill, 'he shouted, "Content" with a yell that would quite have become a savage,'[33]

Caroline's cause was a popular one and the Duke found himself in

disfavour with the crowd. Ben Backstay, in *Black Dwarf*, spoke for
many of his readers:

> '*Admiral Tarry Breeks, a Royal Duke,*
> *The moral brother of a moral King,*
> *Is anxious 'mongst the Lords to look*
> *A sapient, nautical and moral thing.*
> *But ere he points at Britain's Queen a shaft,*
> *Or steps (the ship that chases her) aboard on;*
> *He should remember memory looks aloft,*
> *And read his morals in the hapless Jordan.*'[34]

Apart from this one foray into public life, he conducted himself
unobtrusively after his return to England. Most of the time was spent
at Bushy, poring over naval histories, confusing the farm manager
and playing Pope Joan for one shilling stakes. When he went to
Brighton he was equally decorous. Lady Granville portrayed him
among the rarefied splendours of the Pavilion, languid from the heat
and the over-eating, complaining about his gout, while Rossini – 'a fat
sallow squab of a man' – sang to them after dinner.[35]

The Duchess had had the most beneficial effect upon his behaviour.
He was still bluff, still outspoken, still apt to speak first and wonder at
some later time exactly what he had meant, but his vocabulary had
been considerably cleaned up and he was far more sensitive to the
susceptibilities of other people. W. H. Lyttelton met him at dinner at
Portsmouth and was amazed by the transformation. The Duke 'behaved perfectly well, was civil to everybody, even gentlemanlike in
his manner, did not say a single indecent or improper thing'.[36] Lyttelton was not alone in observing the dramatic results of matrimony. 'You
would be surprised at the Duke of Clarence if you were to see him';
confirmed Lord Colchester, 'for his wife, it is said, has entirely reformed him; and instead of that *polisson* manner for which he used to
be celebrated, he is now quiet and well-behaved . . .'[37]

One consequence of his return was that he was forced to swallow his
pride and accept the annual £6,000 which he had so disdainfully
refused three years before. The increase was backdated to 1818 so the
Duke found himself with a pleasant bonus of £18,000 with which to
settle some of his outstanding debts. Better still was to follow for, two
years later: 'It is cried out against the Ministers,' wrote Lady Holland,
'for giving something in the Marines to the amount of £4,000 pr. an.

to the D. of Clarence.'[38] The 'something' was the post of General of
the Marines; the place was more or less a sinecure and there must have
been some heart-burning among the senior Admirals at seeing it so
bestowed.

*

Almost the only distinguishing feature of the next few years was the
continental travel which the Duke and his wife three times indulged in.
The journeys were made in 1822, 1825 and 1826 but all followed more
or less the same pattern so that the details blend together and even the
most assiduous biographer may be forgiven for forgetting during which
trip they saw Blanchard's balloon crossing from Dover to Calais and
in which the carriage was nearly upset on the road between Stuttgart
and Liebenstein. William endured it all with a good grace but he found
little to please him in the resorts which his wife liked so well. 'Pleasure
and a total forgetfulness of everything that is business are the order of
the day at a German Bath,' he wrote disapprovingly to his steward at
Bushy; then, in an addition which showed where his interests were
really centred, 'I dread the fate of the Turnips'.[39]

On their travels they took with them an obsequious young doctor
named Beattie whose journal of the expeditions, though a sickening
exercise in sycophancy, still presents a life-like portrait of their train of
life.[40] Frugality, simplicity and a rigid adherence to bourgeois standards
were its hall-mark. When travelling the Duke breakfasted at seven upon
tea and a slice of dry toast. Luncheon was a picnic, consisting of cold
fowl, Westphalia ham, veal or *gibier*. He rarely dined, contenting
himself on arrival with a pot of green tea. Nor was his usual diet much
more lavish when he arrived in Saxe-Meiningen. Here, as in England,
he dined habitually off roast or boiled mutton. 'Sherry is his favourite,
and I may say only wine. I never saw him taste port; and seldom French
or Rhenish wines. He rarely eats roots or vegetables, not even a
potato.' The only drink he consumed in quantity was barley water
flavoured with lemon.

As befitted a man deeply in debt he was economical, even parsi-
monious in his personal affairs. 'He looks over all the accounts himself,
sums up, calculates, adjusts and compares, nicely balancing every item.'
Often he would send back a bill for amendment – though on one
occasion at least it was because he was being undercharged.

His daily routine was no more extravagant than his diet. He was up
and dressed by seven and, after his breakfast, walked till eight. He

would then devote two or three hours to his correspondence, always answering letters in his own hand. When Beattie tried to persuade him to do less he replied meaningfully: 'I must keep up the practice of letter-writing . . . one day or other I may have still more occasion for it.' He would then walk till dinner time; if it were raining never venturing out without his galoshes. Nor were these walks mere genteel strolls. The King of Prussia's *aide de camp* came to pay his respects and William suggested that they might take a turn together – promising that the walk would be a short one. It lasted more than two hours and when the Prussian returned he told Beattie 'that, perfectly unaccustomed to such pedestrian feats, he was ready to drop with fatigue; and must, he feared, in the event of another visit, be obliged to perform his duty by proxy'. With no such guest to consider, the Duke would think nothing of a four hour walk, generally in the hottest part of the day. If the weather were really bad then he would pace up and down the drawing-room with the windows wide open.

Given this régime it was not surprising that he enjoyed excellent health. His solitary ailment, with the exception of periodic pains in the legs which were ascribed to gout, was an annual attack of asthma. Every year, at some date between May 26 and July 1, William was afflicted with this miserable malady. Sometimes he was let off lightly, at others he suffered severely and his life was felt to be in danger. He was, said Dr Beattie, an excellent and docile patient. Once Beattie had been unwisely optimistic about the duration of an attack. 'Well, Doctor,' said the Duke philosophically, 'you thought this fit would abate by nine o'clock; now, you observe, it is near ten. Well, well, it can't be helped.'

*

In the summer of 1826 the Duke of York, gouty, dropsical and barely capable of coherent thought, slipped into what the doctors said was likely to be his last illness. 'The King is deeply distressed,' wrote Princess Lieven. 'The Duke of Clarence will be a fine King! The King said to me at table the other day: "Look at that idiot! They will remember me, if ever he is in my place." '[41] The King's disapproval of his brother can hardly have been violent since, at the moment of which the Princess was writing, he was busily organizing a substantial gift for him from the privy purse.[42] Nevertheless, he felt the Duke of York, temperamentally and politically, would make more suitable a King.

It was not till January 5, 1827, that the Duke of York finally succumbed. In obituary vein William told his son George that he had long been looking forward to seeing 'poor dear Frederick ... filling the Throne to the advantage of all us his future subjects ... But alas that fond hope is now over and I have therefore if possible stronger reasons to pray to the all-mighty to prolong the *life* and *health* of His present Majesty.'[43] It would be unfair to tax him with insincerity; but the immensity of the consequences can never have been far from his mind. At the funeral Peel noticed with some disapproval that: 'The Duke of Clarence did not act the part of Chief Mourner very decorously. He spoke to everyone very much as usual. I heard him enquire from Lord Hertford how many head of game he had killed at Sudburn.'[44] Creevey maliciously noted that several peers paid more attention to the Duke than had been their habit in the past and claimed that, whenever there was a gap in the proceedings, he turned to the Duke of Sussex with the observation: 'We shall be treated now, Brother Augustus, very differently from what we have been.'[45]

The first notable difference was financial. By the death of the Duke the nation was saved some £26,000 a year. Lord Liverpool wanted the Duke of Clarence's income to be raised immediately by £8,000 a year, and the Duchess's by £4,000.[46] Once again he came under pressure from his colleagues to reduce the payments and the final result was a jointure of £6,000 for Adelaide but only an additional £3,000 for her husband. Still, William was well content. Under the tutelage of his wife he had been reducing his debts for several years and the latest gift from the King had enabled him to cut them down to a few thousand pounds.[47] With his augmented income he could look his creditors in the face with confidence and even consider what steps he could take permanently to benefit his children. Cheerfully, William settled down to wait out the years before he should become King at last.

CHAPTER XI

The Lord High Admiral

IN February, 1827, the Prime Minister, Lord Liverpool, had an apoplectic fit and was found unconscious in his library. It was soon known that he would never recover sufficiently to carry on the government. A new government without Canning would have been impossible and, since he would serve under nobody, the only solution was to make him prime minister. This, however, created almost as many problems as it solved, for Canning had numerous enemies. Among those who declined to serve was Lord Melville, from the Admiralty. To replace him Canning conceived the idea of reviving the ancient office of Lord High Admiral, last held by the Earl of Pembroke in the early eighteenth century, and offering it to the Duke of Clarence.

'Of this his friends boasted as a *coup de maître*,' noted Henry Hobhouse in his diary, 'inasmuch as it at once shut the door against Lord Melville's return, and so punished him, and conciliated the Duke (who has lately expressed himself very contemptuously of Canning) both as heir presumptive and as future Sovereign.'[1] Not everyone agreed that it was such a master stroke. Knighton, the King's private secretary, was said to have called the appointment 'sad and foolish',[2] while Bathurst considered it hazardous and felt that the King would be jealous of his brother's new distinction.[3] Not surprisingly no such doubts occurred to William himself.

The Duke's tenure of office at the head of the Navy was not of the first importance, either for the nation or for the service which he commanded. For him, however, it was of critical significance. After nearly forty years of retirement he suddenly found himself in a position of high responsibility. The value of the experience as a dress-rehearsal for the monarchy can hardly be exaggerated. He made mistakes which he was not to repeat and learned lessons which he was not to forget; all at a relatively trivial cost to the country. If he had played out his probationary role during his first crucially important years on the throne, the results for England could have been disastrous.

In fact his task was made difficult from the start by a fundamental difference of outlook between him and the rest of the ministry. Canning saw his appointment as a neat trick to confound the opposition and lend his government the apparent weight of royal support. The question of whether or not it would be good for the navy hardly entered his head. The Duke's role was to be that of a figure-head, not even a member of the cabinet, docilely rubber-stamping the decisions of his council. William, on the other hand, took his duties most seriously. As a professional sailor, with strong views on the needs of the service, he had every intention of making his own decisions and imposing them upon the council. Indeed, he was not sure that the council served any useful purpose, at the most its function should be to advise him or to work out in detail the policy which he had previously laid down. The patent setting out his powers, it was true, stated that in London he could act only with the knowledge and approval of his council, while at sea he must always be accompanied by a member of the council or else transmit his orders to them for endorsement. To this the Lord High Admiral resolved to pay little heed.

The tactic might have worked if the Duke had had a properly subservient group of councillors. Unfortunately this was far from being the case. Its senior member was Sir George Cockburn: obstinate, conservative, a subtle expert in naval law, who was quick to resent any encroachment on his own position or the powers of the council. The Duke had disliked and distrusted him for years, considering him incompetent and an upstart.[4] 'I can only say that he never was fit to be at the Admiralty' he told Martin, 'any more than my old Grandmother.'[5] It was hardly the most healthy basis on which to build a partnership.

Croker, the secretary to the council, was supposed originally to have conceived the idea of offering William the job.[6] If so, he must soon have regretted it for he wrote malevolently of the Lord High Admiral's inadequacy. The contempt was reciprocal; the Duke described Croker as lacking judgment, discretion and good taste.[7] But he was a dangerous enemy. Once at the Pavilion William was provoked into exclaiming that '. . . were I King, I'd be my own First Lord, and you should *not* be my secretary.' Croker pointed out that the last person to fill the two roles had been James II and that the precedent was hardly a healthy one. There was a general laugh and King George IV asked what the joke was. 'Nothing,' said Croker blandly, 'but your royal brother is saying what he will do when your Majesty is no longer King.' George IV moved off without saying a word.

Curiously enough the Duke's closest ally on the Council proved to be an old enemy from the Schomberg affair, the 'very troublesome, disrespectful and violent' William Hope.[8] When he took office William wrote to Hope:

'I ask it as a favour of you to stay here. You may remember that when you were a lieutenant in the ship I commanded, we had a violent quarrel, and that you quitted the ship; and that our quarrel was not made up for ten years; but the world at large, who know of the quarrel, may not have known of our reconciliation; and I wish that, by your staying now, they may become fully acquainted with it. Moreover you cannot know that, after you left my ship, I thought you in the right and *myself in the wrong*, and that is another reason, so you must stay and be of my council.'[9]

It was an appeal few men could have resisted and Hope gratefully succumbed.

After the first meeting of the council Cockburn must have thought that all was well. The Duke modestly stressed 'how little professional knowledge could be expected from *him*; and how much he had to look to from them.'[10] He asked whether previous First Lords had used to entertain and was gratified to hear they had: 'That's quite right. I delight in hospitality and mean to practise it here.' Nothing could be more satisfactory; a Lord High Admiral who would busy himself with giving parties while the professionals got on with running the Navy.

The council was quickly disillusioned. Not that the Duke failed to live up to his word. On the contrary, he spent enormously; according to his comptroller running up £23,000 of debts in less than eighteen months. He revelled in the formal side of his office; the parades and the fancy uniforms, the balls, banquets and regattas, but brought his individual touch to the starchiest occasions. No one could criticize him for lack of pomp when all the ships of Spithead fired a salute to mark the two hundred yard walk from his launch to church and then boomed out again an hour later when he walked back again;[11] and yet when the new Prussian minister attended a party at the Admiralty he searched everywhere for his host to find him in the end 'in a little room where they were washing up the china'.[12] Not the least of the pleasures of office was the frequent chances it gave him to speak in public. At one typical 'splendid, sumptuous and costly' banquet given by the Mayor and Corporation of Portsmouth, the Duke answered the toast to his health with a 'very neat and sensible speech'. He spoke again when his name was coupled with that of the Royal Marines, proposed Lord Spencer's health 'in a felicitous speech', did the same by Mr Baring and only reluctantly left Mr John Bonham Carter to the Mayor. From this last disappointment he recovered quickly, rising to propose the health of the Mayor.[13]

But this was only the beginning of his activities. At Plymouth, for instance, he not only gave a lavish ball but was in the dock-yard early the next morning, inspecting the offices, examining the books, visiting every part of the storehouses and keeping an elaborate record of all his criticisms.[14] He astounded Lady Brownlow by spending every day at the Port Admiral's office, returning only for dinner.[15] He interfered in questions of promotion, asked awkward questions about the level of stocks, was endlessly active in schemes to improve the standard of naval gunnery. Nervously the members of the council began to wonder whether their chief was going to prove quite as amenable as they had hoped.

*

In August 1828, less than four months after he had taken office, Canning died. Goderich came, winced and departed, leaving government in the powerful hands of the Duke of Wellington. The Duke of Clarence's position was unchanged but Wellington, nurtured on the pure milk of military discipline and good order, would be far more sympathetic to the orthodoxy of the career sailors than to the maverick skirmishing of the Lord High Admiral. William, for his part, foresaw no difficulties. 'I augur *well* of the *new* Government,' he wrote to Knighton and, a few days later, 'I know the *greatness of mind of the Duke*'.[16]

Yet already the event had occurred which was to strain relations between the Lord High Admiral and the other ministers. Sir Edward Codrington was in charge of the British fleet in the eastern Mediterranean. His orders, in un-nautical terms, were to hang about, liaise with the French and Russians, keep an eye on the Turkish fleet and try to stop any massacre of the Greeks. 'Discretion, prudence and perfect deliberation will be your guide, and we must hope for the best . . .' wrote William, instructions which one may doubt whether the admiral found satisfactorily explicit.[17] Princess Lieven, among others, reported that the Duke of Clarence added to this dispatch a private codicil reading 'Go it, Ned!' or, according to another version, 'Go it, my boy!',[18] but Codrington himself denied this and nothing among his papers[19] belies his word.

On October 20, 1827, Codrington, interpreting his instructions with some liberality, destroyed the Turkish fleet in the Bay of Navarino. 'I believe the Turk never before felt the British eloquence of our Guns,' wrote the Lord High Admiral enthusiastically.[20] For him there was no question: a brilliant triumph had been gained, British honour upheld, the infidel smitten. To Codrington he was categoric: 'I am to congratulate you on the splendid victory . . . I admire your perfect conduct on the day of battle.'[21] He made his view manifest by promoting a bevy of Codrington's senior officers and recommending to the King that the admiral himself should be rewarded with the Grand Cross of the Bath. He wrote so eloquently of the victory to his brother that the latter's 'old English heart bounded again and again with delight'.[22]

But the Duke spoke only for himself. Sir John Gore called on the Admiralty and found them cold and close.[23] When he went on to see William, the latter stressed that he was not a member of the cabinet. Even to secure the promotions he had had to do battle with his council. 'Ministers would gladly shelter themselves . . . by throwing the blame on Codrington', he told Gore, 'but he has done nobly.'[24] In the Speech from the Throne of January 29, 1828, Navarino was ominously described as an 'untoward event'. William could not save Codrington from recall and dismissal. Wellington for his part made it plain that the Lord High Admiral's precipitate welcome of the victory had been embarrassing to his colleagues.

On issues like this, though the council members might profess neutrality, they still felt privately that the Duke's heart was in the right place. In July 1828 came the first direct clash between council and Lord High Admiral. William was appalled by the low standard of naval gunnery. He set up a standing commission of naval officers to enquire into the problem. The council took umbrage and ruled that the terms of reference were too wide. Promptly the Duke hoisted his flag in the *Royal Sovereign* and summoned the commission to Portsmouth. Battle was joined. Your order, complained Cockburn, is 'neither in accordance with the spirit of the Act of Parliament . . . nor consistent with the real nature of the . . . office . . .'[25] He referred the question to ministers and, without hesitation, they decided to back the council. The Duke's aim was to assert his independence. 'We resist the Lord High Admiral's attempt . . .' wrote Lord Ellenborough.[26]

The Duke now embroiled the matter further. To Cockburn he wrote a sharp letter, pointing out that the function of the council was to advise, not to dictate to him.[27] When this had no effect he demanded Cockburn's instant dismissal and the appointment of Sir Charles Paget in his place.[28] Wellington was genuinely anxious to avoid a clash with William, but his sympathies lay with Cockburn and he knew anyway that other members of the council would themselves resign if the Lord High Admiral had his way. He invoked his ultimate weapon and asked the King to reason with his brother. George IV had no doubt where his duty lay. To Knighton he wrote sadly that his poor brother had 'bamboozled himself and bothered himself into a sad dilemma'.[29]

On July 15, after a few days for meditation, King George IV struck. His letter must have caused his brother acute dismay:

'It is with feelings of the deepest Regret that I observe the embarrassing situation in which You have placed Yourself. You are in Error from the beginning to the end. This is not a matter of Opinion, but a positive fact.

'You must not forget, My dear William, that Sir George Cockburn is the King's Privy Councillor, and so made by the King, to advise the Lord High Admiral.

'What becomes of Sir George Cockburn's Oath ... if he fails to offer such Advice ... ? Am I, then, to be called to dismiss the most useful, and perhaps the most important Naval Officer in my service for conscientiously acting up to the Letter and Spirit of his Oath and his Duty? The thing is impossible. I love You most truly, as You know, and no one would do more or go farther to protect and meet Your feelings, but on the present occasion I have no alternative. You must give way ...'[30]

This letter reached the Duke at Portsmouth and he had hardly read it before he was on the way to town. In the letter which preceded him he told the King that, if he could not convince him that Cockburn had erred, he must resign himself. His message was dignified, even moving but he could not resist one dig at his enemy: 'Sir George Cockburn *cannot* be the *most useful* and the *most important* officer in Your Majesty's service, who *never* had the ships *he* commanded in *proper* fighting order.'[31] Arrived in London, a series of stormy interviews took place. He saw Cockburn and failed to get the retraction which he wanted, saw Wellington and was offered no sympathy.

On July 18 William visited Wellington and Cockburn together. An uneasy truce seemed to have been declared. It is noteworthy that none of the participants addressed himself to what might reasonably have been thought the principal question. The future of naval gunnery and the urgent need for reform were forgotten, overlaid by a futile debate about whether the Lord High Admiral had or had not exceeded the terms of his patent. The fact is that, on the main issue, the Duke was embarrassingly right and, that though his methods might have been irregular, he was still trying to do something which badly needed doing.

The truce did not last long. Essentially, the Duke was not prepared to work with Cockburn and considered it intolerable that this should be asked of him. It was inevitable that he should soon renew hostilities. On the last day of July he made a further break for freedom. 'I think our Lord High Admiral is getting into another scrape,' wrote Aberdeen. 'He has gone to sea, without any of his Council, and has sent some extraordinary orders to the Admiralty . . .'[32] Sir Henry Blackwood had been collecting a squadron of manoeuvre at Plymouth and the Lord High Admiral, profiting by his late arrival, had hoisted his flag and sailed on his way rejoicing. He stayed at sea with two three-deckers and some smaller vessels for ten days, and no one had an idea where he had gone. His behaviour was totally irresponsible.

Indignantly the Duke of Wellington reported to the King. 'If the Lord High Admiral cannot make up his mind to fill his station according to the laws of his country,' replied George IV, 'it will be quite impossible for the King to retain him in his present situation.'[33] Wellington interpreted this as meaning that the Duke was to be forced into resignation. When the Lord High Admiral returned from his jaunt he found a letter awaiting him, pointing out in the brusquest terms that he was again violating the terms of his patent.[34] The Duke pleaded that his Council was competent to advise him only on financial matters; '. . . unless it is clearly understood between your Grace and myself that I am to be *in future* the judge, *except in matters of expense*, on what matters I shall consult my Council, *I must resign*.'[35] Since the prime minister had already made it clear that his understanding was exactly the contrary, it seemed that the end of the road had at last been reached.

In elegiac tones the King mourned his brother's obstinacy:

'Can the Lord High Admiral suppose that the laws are to be infringed ... without notice or remonstrance by the responsible advisers of the Crown? Can the Lord High Admiral suppose that his best friend and his Sovereign is to have no feeling under such circumstances? I am quite aware that I am drawing fast to the close of my life; it may be the will of the Almighty that a month, a week, a day, may call the Lord High Admiral to be my successor.

'I love my brother William, I always have done so to my heart's core; and I will leave him the example of what the inherent duty of a King of this country really is. The Lord High Admiral shall strictly obey the laws enacted by Parliament ... or I desire immediately to receive his resignation.'[36]

On August 14 the Duke attended his final council and announced that he was about to resign. He spoke, said Croker, 'with an eager look and an impassioned voice; and it was doubtful whether anger or a feeling of regret was predominant in his mind.'[37] If it was anger he concealed it well, for he invited Cockburn and his other enemies to his forthcoming birthday party at Bushy. It seems that, after his brother resigned, George IV had a belated change of heart. Studying the terms of the patent with care for the first time he concluded that they really were excessively restrictive. He sounded out Wellington about the possibility of amending them. Wellington had no intention of reopening an affair which he was convinced was better closed. Firmly he replied that he could recommend no change.[38] Undoubtedly he was right, for the Duke could never again have worked harmoniously with his council. William, however, might still have felt him harsh and unforgiving. In fact, as he left the room after formally handing in his resignation, William turned to Wellington and said: 'Though the Lord High Admiral and the Prime Minister may differ in matters of policy; the Duke of Clarence and the Duke of Wellington must ever be friends. God bless you!'[39] Nor was he less forbearing in the case of Cockburn. When William became King the North American station fell vacant and Cockburn was appointed. Sir James Graham told the new incumbent that, in view of past history, he would never have dared himself propose such an appointment; it was made solely thanks to the earnest wish and interference of the King.[40]

*

'Of all the mighty tricks, magic, spells, and witch-craft that have been used to unship the Duke, you will hear much,' wrote Sir John Gore darkly to Admiral Codrington.[41] There is no need to look to the occult for an explanation. William's catastrophe was the inevitable result of an intemperate and impatient man colliding with a doctrinaire conservative who was master of the rule book and played strictly according to its directions. There is no doubt that the Duke had run amok and become a liability to the navy. Frustrated by the impossibility of forcing through much needed reforms and goaded by his dislike of the triumphant Cockburn, he was near to breakdown. 'His family are afraid the fatigue will kill him. He is now and then mad – or very nearly so,' wrote Ellenborough.[42] His own son, George FitzClarence, told his doctor that he was getting greatly over-excited and must resign in the interests of his health.[43] From everyone's point of view it was best that he should go.

But this tragi-comic finale should not obscure the fact that he had been a great deal more successful than he is generally given credit for. In spite of the indifference or active opposition of his Council he pushed through several measures of considerable importance.[44] He overhauled and streamlined the promotion system. He sent out to sea, for exercise and gunnery training, guard ships which had been static for so long that some of the officers resigned rather than face the perils of life on the ocean wave. He insisted on half-yearly reports on the battle-worthiness of every ship in the Navy as well as quarterly reports on gunnery exercises and the expenditure of ammunition. He forbade the use of the cat-o'-nine-tails except in extreme cases such as mutiny at sea. He put into commission the *Lightning*, the first steam vessel on the naval list. The concept of steam-powered warships was, of course, not his own, but he sponsored it eagerly and urged the construction of many more. It is notable that his successor, the experienced professional Lord Melville, at once reversed this policy, pleading that the introduction of steam 'was calculated to strike a fatal blow to the naval supremacy of the Empire.'

Even more important, perhaps, the Duke with his enthusiasm, his open-handed generosity and his readiness to discard outmoded fetishes, did much to raise the morale of a service which had lost heart since the end of the Napoleonic wars. His integrity was an example to every officer. 'I hate presents,' he told his son, 'and shall send back the truffles to Captain Rich as I have the Cask of Cape Wine to Captain Christian.'[45]

It would be absurd to maintain that the Duke was a great administrator or that his innovations were of critical importance for the Royal Navy. Equally it is unfair to dismiss him as a mischievous buffoon with no understanding of his duties. Within the limitations imposed upon him he did a good job, without such limitations he might have done an excellent one. He could legitimately look back upon his period of office with a certain pride.

*

From the time of his resignation the Duke was marking time, waiting – though he would never have admitted it even to himself – for the corrupt and dropsical body of the King finally to subside into the grave. By the beginning of 1829 his reconciliation with Wellington was complete: the only difference between them, he told Dr Philpotts, was in the construction of a patent, in which each had a right to his own opinion.[46] But another issue was soon to come up which was to test his loyalty to ministers.

His views on Catholic Emancipation had grown more decisive since he had meekly followed the Prince Regent's lead nearly twenty years before. As early as June 1826 he had stated decidedly to Dr Beattie that the Catholics of Ireland must be emancipated. Then, in 1827, he seemed to hedge. At a dinner of the Society for the Promotion of Christian Knowledge he declared sonorously: '. . . to the sound and strict principles of the Church of England, I am unalterably attached – and it will be at all times and under all circumstances my first desire and duty to maintain those principles.' The statement seemed unequivocal yet, a few days later at a naval dinner, he triumphantly recounted: '. . . I dined with sixteen Bishops the other day . . . and humbugged them gloriously, to their very heart's content. It was delightful to see how they swallowed it. But I am for the Catholics . . . heart and soul to the very backbone – yes, I humbugged the Bishops well!'[47]

The only doubt was whether he would take the same line in the House of Lords. He told Croker that previously he had hung back out of respect for the King and the Duke of York, but that if the King's ministers could be persuaded to support the measure he would be with them whole-heartedly.[48] But Creevey, hob-nobbing with the Duke of Norfolk, still doubted whether he could be relied on even in such circumstances. '. . . our Billy is a wag,' he commented sourly.[49]

In 1829 the Duke of Wellington was finally convinced that emancipation must come and introduced a bill to that effect. The night before the critical debate the Duke of Clarence dined with Ellenborough. 'He got into a long story about Lord St Vincent, and I know not how many other admirals, with little episodes attached to each, and supposed them all to put up their heads, and express delight at seeing the Irish sailors who had fought the lower deck guns emancipated.'[50] Fortified by this claque of nautical ghosts, the Duke spoke stoutly in the House of Lords. 'He had never given a vote with so much pleasure and satisfaction as he should feel in supporting the contemplated measure.' He turned ferociously on the opponents of the Bill, in particular the Duke of Cumberland. When the time came for the latter to reply he said that he objected strongly to having his conduct described as 'factious and . . . and he had forgotten the other epithet'. 'Infamous', put in his brother helpfully.

On this issue King George IV would normally have aligned himself whole-heartedly with Cumberland. The Duke had, indeed, been nervous about the King's reaction to his speech and had defiantly told his sister, Princess Mary, the morning of the debate, that he did not need royal consent before he voted according to his conscience.[51] In fact, however, George IV was by now almost too old and ill to care what anybody did. By the early spring of 1830 it was clearly only a matter of months before he died.

It was fashionable to portray the Duke as waiting impatiently for the end. The King, for his part, was said furiously to resent his brother's attitude. Neumann, the Austrian chargé d'affaires, claimed that when William called at Windsor George IV, though in extreme pain, 'had himself dressed and put on his wig in order to appear in a better state of health and to destroy any hope his brother may have of succeeding him soon.'[52] In fact, though there is no reason to take at their face value the somewhat stereotyped cries of dismay with which the Duke punctuated his letter to Sir William Knighton,[53] there is the ring of truth about Lord Erroll's statement that 'Billy has a real affection for Prinney, and . . . never returns home after seeing him without being greatly affected and crying like a child.'[54] Certainly one cannot doubt the sincerity of the gloom which the Duchess showed as the throne grew closer. 'Our position keeps getting more trying,' she wrote on June 11, 'and we are passing through a very dark time.'[55] For one who was totally devoid of royal ambitions, the light at the end of the tunnel must have been hard to see.

But though William's grief at his brother's illness was sincere he could not avoid a feeling of rising excitement. His correspondence with Wellington became more confidential and he spoke increasingly in the tones of one who was already half-way up the steps of the throne. People who had snubbed William for thirty years now hurried to pay court. Lady Jersey arrived at Bushy, exclaiming with delighted surprise at the beauty of the house and park. Lord Anglesey descended like a latter-day Polonius and lectured William on the need to keep a brilliant court, to live down his reputation for wildness, to eschew frivolities of dress.[56] Every day the taste of kingship seemed to grow stronger.

At 6 a.m. on the morning of June 26 the Duke was woken at Bushy and told that Sir Henry Halford and Sir William Waller wished to speak to him. As he walked down the stairs to meet them he can hardly have doubted the reason for their call. After sixty-five years he had become King of England. It is tempting to believe that he shook his startled guests by the hand and then announced that he must go back to bed 'as he had long wished to sleep with a Queen',[57] but the story is too picturesque to be anything but apocryphal. What at least seems sure is that within a few hours he was on his way to Windsor 'with a bit of crape on a white hat, grinning and nodding to everybody as he whirled along.'[58] It was sad about poor George but the best job in the world had fallen to his lot and he found it impossible to hide the fact that he was an exceedingly happy man.

CHAPTER XII

The Blissful Dawn

In the forty-odd years between the French Revolution and the accession of King William IV the political institutions of Great Britain had remained frozen in a posture which every year became more anachronistic. It was the revolution itself which was largely responsible for this misfortune. In the 1780s the cause of parliamentary reform had been, if not universally accepted, at least respectable. It was espoused not only by such men as Fox but by William Pitt, with all the enthusiasm of which his prudent soul was capable. It seemed likely that, before the end of the eighteenth century, at least the worst of the current abuses would be cured.

Then came the storming of the Bastille. Almost overnight the cause of moderate reform was discredited. As the Terror mounted, so the fervour of the anti-Jacobins rose with it, until even to imply that the British constitution was other than perfect seemed tantamount to treason. A few stalwarts refused to be panicked but even their enthusiasm dwindled when Wordsworth's blissful dawn gave way to the sullen twilight of an authoritarian Empire. If this could happen at the fountain-head of liberty, what hope was there for the remote rivulets across the channel?

With the end of the Napoleonic wars, reform might again have come into fashion, but the civil disorders of 1815 and 1816 proved disastrous. Once again the establishment recoiled from a first step which might launch Britain down the bloody path towards the tumbrels and the guillotine. It was still admitted by most sane men that a measure of reform was in principle desirable. Yet somehow the moment for introducing reforms never seemed expedient. By 1830 nothing had happened. The consequences of this inertia in parliament itself will be considered later; for the country at large it entailed the almost complete failure of the legislature to grapple with the problems posed by the economic and social development of the early nineteenth century. The structure of British society was profoundly modified, above it the superstructure of the establishment remained blandly inviolate.

Between 1789 and 1830 the population rose from some ten to sixteen and a half million. This was striking enough, but in the lives of the people the shift from countryside to town was still more significant. Agricultural depression and the needs of the rapacious new industries combined to make what social historians sometimes call the 'Early Railway Age' into a period, above all, of urban expansion. Villages grew into towns, towns bloated cities, and all without the benefit of forethought about the needs of the new citizens. Without the reform of the antiquated municipal corporations any serious effort to change the situation was certain to fail, and without prior parliamentary reform the stubborn inertia of the legislature doomed the municipalities to continue in their primeval gloom.

To live in squalor may be more readily supportable if one is well paid to do so, yet the new industries often did not offer even this consolation to the lower classes. The vast increase in the number and size of factories – particularly in the worlds of wool and cotton – of course brought wealth to the proprietors and, in the long run, was to better the economic lot of all who worked in or around them. In the early stages, however, mechanization and the application of new technologies, led often to a smaller need for unskilled labour. The labourer was told – if anyone bothered to tell him anything – that boom times lay ahead, but this was scant consolation for those who were out of work and near starvation.

Nor was life much more satisfactory for those who remained in the country. The agricultural boom of war-time was followed by recession. Enclosures led to the elimination of many small-holdings. New agricultural techniques reduced the size of the labour-force while mechanical threshing cut into the farm labourer's traditional winter occupation. Everything combined to produce chronic under- and often un-employment. A bad harvest in 1828 and a still worse one in 1829 exacerbated an already painful situation and 1830 produced a wave of agrarian disturbances which – as Hobsbawm and Rudé have shown in their recent most penetrating study[1] – often seemed on the point of ripening into national revolution. Confronted with burning ricks and smashed machines, a sullen hostile peasantry, the landed gentry had recourse to violent repression. What Romilly described as the 'savage spirit' infused in the British upper classes by the French

Revolution was revived with a new fervour and the peasant paid with compound interest for his unwise indignation.

And yet, of course, the majority of the aristocrats, gentry and *nouveaux riches* were not wicked or vicious, and though their short-sightedness sometimes seems almost wilful it was based on a genuine failure to understand that the state of the world had changed and a new set of social needs and responsibilities had evolved. Byron's vision of an aristocracy which roared and dined and drank while the 'blood, sweat and tear-wrung millions' toiled to maintain their masters in luxury was not wholly a caricature, yet few of those aristocrats realized the scope of the disaster which had overtaken their country and fewer still contemplated for an instant that it was their duty to see that things were put right. To this myopia the new King was as much a victim as any of his subjects. In his letters to his prime ministers and home secretaries there were plentiful references to crimes, riots and other forms of disorder but few indeed to unemployment, inadequate hygiene, the shameful lack of schools and hospitals, the widespread malnutrition which underlay the surface froth of violence. Confronted with the evidence of national misery the King felt much distress. Personally he was capable of great charity. Nevertheless, the concept that he and his ministers should seek out the misery and tackle its causes was altogether beyond his grasp. In this he was no better, but equally no worse than almost all those who habitually surrounded him.

*

Though William might have no understanding of social or economic problems he was far from ignoring his duties as a king. To suggest that he had thought deeply about the nature of his royal duties would be to claim for him a capacity for philosophical study to which he did not aspire. Still, as his brother crumbled slowly into decrepitude and death, he had become increasingly preoccupied with the issues that would confront him. He had laid down in his mind certain principles to which he felt he should adhere, had evolved a pattern of conduct to fit, as he hoped, every eventuality. Allowing for certain lapses of varying gravity he followed this pattern with fair consistency. In doing so he earned the right to be considered the first truly constitutional monarch of Great Britain.

The first broad principle on which he based his conduct was that it was the King's duty to support his ministers, whether or not he liked their policies. This duty only lapsed if it seemed evident that the ministers were out of touch with the feeling of the nation.

To those bred in the twentieth century this modest doctrine will hardly appear sensational, yet to either King George III or George IV it would have seemed almost revolutionary in its implications. The battle for monarchical control over government had, of course, been fought and lost long before. Whatever he would have liked, George IV had been far from an autocrat. But if his ministers displeased him, if they pursued policies contrary to those which he advocated, he felt no loyalty of any kind. His preoccupation was to destroy them, to replace them by others more amenable to his will. That the facts of political life in the early nineteenth century often frustrated this intention did not mean that it was any the less sincerely held. King William would have considered even the thought improper. His actions were not always as pure as his principles, at times his rancour against ministers was so great that he virtually denied them his support. But such phases were exceptional and usually stopped short at the point where overt dislike was translated into active counter-measures. By and large he held true to the course he had mapped out for himself.

As a corollary to this doctrine he believed that a monarch should take advice only from his own ministers and that contacts with the opposition should generally be limited to the social.[2] 'King William,' wrote Croker, 'with all his faults, had a very constitutional scruple against receiving advice except from a constitutional adviser.'[3] So long as the prime minister retained the confidence of the House of Commons then he was *his* prime minister, to be treated as his principal adviser. To those who remembered the dislike and scorn with which George IV had treated Lord Liverpool, this was indeed a striking departure from precedent – though whether it would have survived the appointment of a prime minister less congenial than Grey or Melbourne is at least open to question.

King William too, consciously and cheerfully, set aside rights which had been jealously guarded by his predecessors. '. . . the King cannot be accused of advocating *the Rights of the Sovereign*,' he wrote to Melbourne, 'as it is well known that He reserves to Himself no Patronage, seldom interferes in the disposal of any, and that it is vested in the Minister for the time being, and is applied, as far as may be reconciled to justice and reason, to the support of the Government.'[4] He perhaps pitched his self-abnegation a little high, but there is ample evidence to show that he did not consider the use of patronage a proper way of securing influence for the crown. Though he drew the line at certain individuals who were particularly obnoxious to him he was in general scrupulous in allowing ministers to fill all available offices as they thought best, even when this related to appointments in the royal household. The direct influence of the crown in the House of Commons had of course been shrinking for many years[5] but under William IV the King's men, in the sense of a body of placemen totally committed to the royal cause, virtually ceased to exist.

It does not follow from this, of course, that the King did not enjoy powers immeasurably greater than those of the modern monarch. Not till after the Reform Bill was the balance between King and Cabinet radically altered to the benefit of the latter. Even then, and for a generation thereafter, the monarch's right to select his ministers remained theoretically distinct from the elections which returned a majority to the House of Commons. When William dismissed Lord Melbourne in 1834 it was felt by some that he had been unprincipled and by many that he had been unwise, but few indeed suggested that his action had been in any way unconstitutional. After 1834 he never tried again.

On the whole, therefore, the King did not seek to use his still massive powers. Nevertheless, he conceived it his duty to influence his ministers. He saw his role in public life as that of the great conciliator; above faction, above party, preoccupied solely with the interests of the nation. Those interests could best be served, he was convinced, by a reconciliation between government and opposition, so that a policy would be evolved acceptable to men of goodwill on both sides. Whenever a controversial piece of legislation was introduced he devoted his energies to inducing those who sponsored it to remove all clauses wholly unacceptable to the opposition and urging the latter to accept what was left. But this he saw as no more than a palliative; his ultimate vision was that of a Britain in which all matters of serious controversy would be banished from political life. Every time that a change of administration seemed a possibility, he urged the merits of coalition – ignoring with sublime short-sightedness the issues of principle, as well as the personal rancours, which made his plan no more than a futile dream. The vision never faded. Even at the end of 1836, when he was fast losing his zest for politics, he was still alert to promote it if he saw a chance. It seemed that Melbourne might be going to resign. At once he dictated and signed a memorandum in which he spoke of his

determination to eschew all prejudice and partiality and think only of
the prosperity of the country:

'In order to attain this desirable end, The King deems it very essential that endeavours should be made to prevail upon the most respectable Members of the Two Great and Influential Parties in the Country
to lay aside the feelings which have so long produced a Spirit of
Political Hostility between Them . . . and to unite in the Service of the
State those of both Parties whose general character, abilities, experience
and Patriotism would offer to the Country the happy prospect of a
Government founded upon a secure and permanent Basis.'[6]

The crisis passed, and Taylor enquired whether the memorandum
should now be destroyed. Keep it, the King ruled; it was, after all,
'applicable to any contingency'. Applicable or not, it was certainly
invoked by him at every contingency. If he had left a political testa-
ment it would have been this.

*

But in June, 1830, his thoughts were far from testaments. He was
preoccupied with the altogether delightful business of ascending a
throne and devoted little time to the political problems which lay
ahead. He threw himself into his new life with a zest and energy that
could hardly fail to be endearing. 'The King,' wrote Princess Lieven,
'for whom the proverb "Happy as a King" seems certainly to have
been invented by anticipation, imparts to all about him this extraordinary animation. He shows by his manner, his good-nature and
cordiality, a sense of gratified pleasure which is quite contagious.'[7]
The whole nation, she wrote, was suddenly infected by this new gaiety
and movement.

King William IV had inherited the throne from a man who had
been almost uniquely unpopular among British monarchs. George IV,
ten years before, had been Swellfoot the Tyrant, the high priest of
reaction, a figure to be feared and hated by all with even mildly
liberal opinions. The ensuing decade had seen fear dwindle to indifference, hatred to contempt. This bloated, sorrowful figure, skulking
under heavy guard around the Great Park at Windsor, was monstrous
now only in extravagance and in looks. To his ministers he could still
be a painful trial, but to his other subjects he was no more than an
obscene shadow, out of sight if not yet totally out of mind. His disappearance was a matter for indifference tinged with relief. 'No

monarch,' commented *The Times* with devastating candour, 'will be
less generally mourned.'

William therefore took on an institution in sad disrepute. Driving
to and fro between Bushy and Windsor it was very evident that the
crowds felt small concern at his passage. But the contrast which he
presented to his brother ensured that the reaction would be swift and
violent. 'Tho' our adored Sovereign is either rather mad or very
foolish,' commented Emily Eden uncharitably, 'he is an immense improvement on the last unforgiving animal, who died growling sulkily
in his den at Windsor. This man at least *wishes* to make everybody
happy, and everything he has done has been benevolent . . .'[8] William
had only to be natural to win the hearts of his people; and since it
would never have occurred to him to be anything else, the way ahead
seemed clear.

Informality, economy, patriotism: these were to be the hall-marks of
his reign; the style, or perhaps more correctly the deliberate lack of
style which he imposed upon the act of kingship. Informality, indeed,
was hardly a matter of choice for the grand manner was never within
his repertoire. 'A little old, red-nosed, weather-beaten, jolly-looking
person, with an ungraceful air and carriage,' remarked one objective
but by no means unkind observer.[9] Another spoke of his 'Wapping
air'[10] while Washington Irving watched him at a ball given by the
Duke of Wellington and noted: 'His Majesty has an easy and natural
way of wiping his nose with the back of his forefinger, which, I fancy,
is a relic of his middy habits.'[11]

He was not grotesque or even conspicuously eccentric but extraordinary in his very ordinariness. Physically, his only freakish feature
was his head. Traditionally this was said to be shaped like a pineapple
but in fact his nick-name of 'Coconut', derived from his pointed and
red-thatched skull, seems to have been more apt. Even a servant as
dutiful as Sir Herbert Taylor referred to 'the peculiar shape of His
Head:' congratulated himself on it indeed, since the King's hats had to
be heavily padded and this saved him from injury when a man threw a
stone at him during an Ascot race meeting.[12] Few monarchs can have
looked less like a King and none put themselves to smaller pains to
play the part according to the rules.

William, indeed, made a merit of his ordinariness. Shortly after his
accession Hobhouse met him bowling along the roads near Brighton
in a plain and strikingly unmajestic carriage while the Queen hacked
about on the downs. At the levee the King gave his hand with a brisk

'How d'ye do?' Hobhouse just restrained himself from replying 'Very well, thank ye'. 'In short, the worthy couple are like wealthy bourgeois . . .' he mused. 'All this is worth recording only in contrast with our late Asiatic monarch.'[13] He eschewed formality with a zeal that was at times almost frantic. 'Our Citizen King,' as Lady Elizabeth Feilding called him with mild dismay,[14] made a mockery out of court etiquette. He kissed women on one cheek, both cheeks or no cheek according to some private scale of values based more on their appearance than their grandeur. When his subjects arrived to sign the book at the palace he dismissed the practice as ridiculous and said they ought to call on him like any other civilized person. He chatted affably with fellow promenaders on Brighton Pier, spat out of the window of his carriage (though probably not, as was commonly alleged, when in formal procession on the way to prorogue parliament); told one of his guests who looked bored to go to bed and, when the guest expostulated that the King must leave first, replied cheerfully, 'Oh, damn it, I'll smuggle you out!'

His most celebrated exploit occurred the day that he swore in the privy counsellors and Lords Lieutenant. Wearied by the ceremonial, he decided to take a turn in the streets and pottered off alone into Pall Mall and St James's. A friendly but boisterous crowd collected and when he was kissed by an Irish whore outside the window of White's Club a group of members came to his rescue. He was convoyed back to the palace, but was not in the least discomfited by his reception. 'Oh, never mind all this: when I have walked about a few times they will get used to it, and will take no notice.'[15] The Duke of Wellington lectured him on his folly but could make little impression. Then Queen Adelaide was invoked to exert the influence which she alone possessed over him.[16] Grudgingly the King was brought to agree that, though such liberties might be permitted at Brighton or Windsor, the heart of London was no place for a monarch to wander alone. The King 'is very original in his behaviour,' remarked the Prussian Ambassadress in a tactfully selected phrase. 'He is already exceedingly popular.'[17]

But the King's bid for his people's affection was not confined to empty gestures. He threw open the East Terrace at Windsor to the public, though even he objected when they scribbled their names on the statues. He opened a passage for the public where the Duke of York's Steps today stand between Waterloo Place and the Park. He authorized the destruction of the royal mews to clear a large part of what is now Trafalgar Square. On his birthday, August 21, 1830, he gave a banquet at Windsor for the poorer inhabitants. Tables were laid for three thousand and boiled and roast beef, roast veal, hams and plum puddings were served. The King sat at the centre table amidst his subjects.

Nor was his hospitality confined to the lower classes. 'He entertained on an average two thousand persons a week,' recorded the Duke of Buckingham. 'These social reunions were remarkable in other respects; a nautical freedom prevailed which often gave a peculiar heartiness to the conversation, though strict etiquette was not unfrequently entirely lost sight of.'[18] He kept up this lavish entertaining throughout his reign. A year later the Duke of Wellington was said to be 'shocked and alarmed' by the hectic spending, twice at least what could be afforded by the civil list. In 1834, thirty-six thousand bottles of wine were drunk at St James's alone.[19] Yet in fact the King kept well within his parliamentary income – proof not so much of his own austerity as of the grotesque prodigality of his elder brother.

Hospitality was in fact the only field in which he was guilty of extravagance. Patriotism and economy were nicely blended in the onslaught which he made on the various royal establishments. He saved £14,000 a year by dismissing George IV's German band and replacing it by a homespun if less skilful substitute. He sacked the squadron of French cooks who had previously followed the King from residence to residence – a piece of frugality deplored by some of those who ate habitually at the royal table. 'Detestable,' wrote Philipp van Neumann of the royal cuisine; while Lord Dudley uttered one of his celebrated *sotto voce* grumbles: 'What a change to be sure – cold patés and hot champagne.'[20]

Everywhere pomp was discouraged, the luxurious structure of the late King's way of life dismantled. The royal yachts were cut down from five to two; George IV's sumptuous cottage at Windsor in large part demolished. The stud was reduced to half its former size; the King remarking that personally he would have liked to dispense with it altogether but he supposed he was in duty bound to encourage the breeding of good blood stock.[21] A hundred and fifty exotic birds and beasts which had belonged to George IV were presented to the Zoological Society.

It was not so much what he did as the way he did it which won the people's hearts. He seemed to exude humanity and good cheer so that every anecdote which was told about him – whether it came from friend or enemy – contributed to the legend. During a dinner party at Windsor a 'little, fat, red-faced footman named Sykes', conducted his private celebration behind the serving screen, tossing back a tumblerful of claret at each of the royal toasts. Unfortunately the arrangement of the mirrors was such that, to the startled guests, it seemed as if a whole regiment of Sykeses was performing these enormities. George IV's vengeance would have been terrible; the following day King William mildly said to Lord Albemarle: 'As I am afraid you and I were not the only witnesses of Sykes's indiscretion, I wish you would manage to keep him out of sight till the whole affair is forgotten.'[22] Even when he blundered or was unnecessarily rude, his contrition was so evident that the effect was still endearing. A Mr Smith, a clergyman, was by mistake invited to dine at the Pavilion. 'And who the devil are *you*, Sir?' the King accosted him. 'I never asked you!' Appalled, Mr Smith produced his letter of invitation. Little less dismayed, the King went out of his way to be nice to his guest and later at dinner proposed, 'The health of my new friend, the Rev. Mr Smith, and to our long friendship.'[23]

'Two miracles at once,' wrote Lamb when the news came that the Bourbons had been chased from France:

> '*Two miracles at once! Compell'd by fate,*
> *His tarnished throne the Bourbon doth vacate;*
> *While English William – a diviner thing –*
> *Of his free pleasure doth put off the King;*
> *The forms of distant old respect lets pass,*
> *And melts his crown into the common mass.*
> *Health to fair France and fine regeneration!*
> *But England's is the nobler abdication.*'

It was a striking compliment coming from a man who only a few months before had quoted with approval Coleridge's aphorism that England in the past had had wicked kings, foolish kings, wise kings, even good kings, 'but never till now . . . a blackguard king.'[24]

Everyone, Whig or Tory, radical or reactionary, agreed that in the first few months of the new reign the monarchy had become immeasurably better loved. There were some who questioned the permanence of the popularity, others who doubted its value, but on the achievement itself all concurred. 'This is not a new reign, it is a new dynasty,' said Wellington, in one of the few complimentary remarks about King William which he is ever known to have uttered.[25] It would have been more accurate to say that it was not a new king, it was a new concept of monarchy. Few would have denied that change was overdue.

CHAPTER XIII

The Wellington Administration

ALMOST the first of William's public appearances as King was at the funeral of George IV. It provided a foretaste of what was soon to become accepted as the royal style. 'He behaved with great indecency,' commented Greville sharply. All the company were as merry as grigs and the new King the merriest. 'He darted up to Strathavon . . . shook him heartily by the hand, and then went on nodding to the right and left.'[1]

But though this exuberance was not to slacken, the court of King William and Queen Adelaide was a dull and dowdy place. In this it largely reflected the personality of the Queen. Adelaide was a Victorian before her time; indeed in many ways the court which Victoria inherited in 1837 was more 'Victorian' than was to be the case for another twenty years. It was exclusive, but not in any worldly sense. She declined to receive the fashionable and immensely rich Duchess of St Albans, widow of Coutts the banker, since previously she had been a Miss Mellon, an actress of doubtful reputation (a piece of discrimination which must have caused some discomfort to her husband).[2] When Lady Ferrers, who had notoriously lived with her husband before her marriage, dared to present herself before the Queen, Adelaide turned away, though contriving – for she was a kindly woman – not to make the insult too obvious to those around.[3]

As befitted the woman who introduced the Christmas Tree,* the Queen was *gemütlich* to the point almost of suffocation. 'You know well enough what life is like at Court,' wrote Princess Lieven. 'Dinners of forty people, who are not all of them remarkably interesting; and no possibility of having any reasonable conversation. In the evening we all sit at the round table. The King snoozes, the Queen does needle-work, talks a good deal and with much amiability, but never a word of politics.'[4] The endless hours trickled by; the ladies-in-waiting tittering

* A claim disputed, *inter alia*, by Princess Lieven and the Duchess of Kent.

discreetly over their needle-work; the King waking with a sudden start, peering around, uttering 'Exactly so, ma'am', and falling asleep again; the scrape of a chair leg as an attendant lord shifted his position and looked around with guilt. No wonder Lord Camden found the evenings so severe a trial that he vowed he would do all he could to avoid a second invitation.[5]

Life at Brighton only varied in that the sea air made the King even drowsier. William first went to Brighton as King in August, 1830, and next morning was observed in the grounds of the Pavilion with John Nash sketching out plans in the gravel with the point of his cane. Gloomily the more cost-conscious citizens predicted a plethora of building but the King in fact confined himself to a North and South Lodge. The former survives as the North Gate, and is by no means unhandsome; the latter, now demolished, was said to be more like a gate house prison than an appendage of the most exotic palace in England.[6]

Thomas Drummond visited Brighton a few months later to present a copy of his paper on lighthouses to the King. He told his mother rather wistfully that he had prepared a little speech for the occasion, 'but somehow or other I could not get it in'. He dined at the Pavilion. The King took wine with all his thirty guests in turn; 'Indeed he asked me twice – the second time probably because he had forgotten the first.' After dinner was over the men joined the ladies in the drawing-room. The ladies were mostly at work and conversation, such as it was, was conducted *sotto voce*, no voice being heard except the King's. Since the King was most of the time asleep an evening of really formidable torpor must have ensued.[7]

The Queen's prudishness contrasted oddly with the constant presence at court of a group of young FitzClarences. For the daughters the situation was by no means disagreeable; one by one they were married off into the nobility and produced a string of grandchildren for their royal father to delight in. The sons were far worse off. Acutely conscious of their royal blood yet without any formal status; brought up in an atmosphere of affluence yet with an income that must have looked ridiculous to most of their friends; princes by their pride yet bastards by their blood: the strains they bore must almost have been intolerable. Their lot was made no easier by the vicious sniping of the Press. 'The by-blows of a King ought not to be his bodyguard,' railed the *Morning Post*. 'Can anything be more indecent than the entry of a sovereign into his capital, with one bastard riding before him, and another by the side of his carriage? The impudence and rapacity of the FitzJordans is unexampled even in the annals of Versailles and Madrid.'[8]

In the months after the accession relations between the King and his male children grew inexorably more bitter. George FitzClarence, it was said, hoped to be made a duke, the younger sons pined for honours and pensions. 'They want to renew the days of Charles II,' commented Greville, 'instead of waiting patiently and letting the King do what he can for them and as he can.'[9] In fact the King could not do much for them. He had no intention of creating them peers without somehow finding the money which would let them live in the appropriate state. It was not unreasonable of his sons to seek to keep him up to the mark, but their pressure soon became counter-productive. In November, 1830, George, Frederick, Adolphus and Augustus launched a grand remonstrance. 'We are well aware of the cruel position in which we are placed as natural children,' they opened plaintively, 'and feel too acutely that in the eyes of the Law we are at present nameless and devoid of many rights and advantages of our Fellow Subjects.' Now, they insisted, they should be enabled 'to take that reasonable rank in society which we may expect.'[10] When the King still failed to give satisfaction, the brothers carried out what the Queen described as 'their mad threat of leaving him. Frederick and Lady Augusta* left our house in the morning without my knowing anything about it.'[11]

The gesture was a futile one, since they could expect help from nowhere else and would eventually have to accept whatever the King chose to give them. For their father, however, the situation was peculiarly painful since he genuinely loved his sons and felt a sharp sense of guilt on their behalf. George threatened suicide; Frederick – a menace still more alarming – announced that he would seek a seat in the House of Commons. The quarrel lasted six months before a compromise was reached. George FitzClarence was created Earl of Munster and his brothers and sisters given the rank of children of a Marquis. Even then George was not satisfied. Constantly he demanded more money and, in July 1831, wrote to plead: 'Let me carry your crown at the Coronation ... Who is more fit than your own *flesh and blood*?' He suggested that the Garter would be an acceptable reward for such a service.[12] Taylor told the Duke of Wellington that he had never seen the King more annoyed than by this letter.[13] When William made his eldest son Constable of the Round Tower at the end of 1832, George graciously consented to speak to him again but even then their relationship was

---

* Formerly Lady Augusta Boyle.

punctuated by a series of savage and, for the King at least, painful quarrels.

In spite of being thus plagued, however, the existence of the Fitz-Clarences – in particular his daughters and their husbands – was on the whole a source of happiness to the King. 'It sounds immoral,' wrote Lady Louisa Percy, 'but the quantity of natural children the King has certainly makes *la cour* pleasanter. They are all, you know, pretty and lively, and make society in a way that real princesses could not.'[14] For William, however, the chief pleasure lay in the presence of his grandchildren. At Windsor, in particular, there were rarely less than five or six of these in evidence, careering around the corridors and being mothered by Queen Adelaide. The King would kiss them every morning before breakfast and would often attend the parades in the Octagon Room when they were drilled every morning by Sergeant Winterbottom. His inner sanctum, where only he and his valet were allowed to enter, was lined with portraits of his children and grandchildren jostling with mementoes of his own naval life.

*

The King's relationship with his brother, the Duke of Cumberland, was even less happy than that with his eldest son. Cumberland was variously accused of rape, murder, sodomy, incest, adultery and blackmail. So grotesque a Bluebeard must, one feels, be more a figure of fiction than of history. The only charge which seems to have been effectively substantiated was that he frightened two girls by riding his horse too close to them in Richmond Park. What is certain, however, is that he was an assiduous and by no means unskilful politician, a leader of the extreme right wing of the Tory party. His influence in the last years of George IV's reign had been considerable and he was installed firmly at Windsor as Gold Stick in command of the Household Cavalry. 'The effect of the King's death will . . . be to put an end to the Duke of Cumberland's political character and power in this country entirely,' wrote Wellington with satisfaction,[15] but Cumberland did not concur. So long as he kept his base at Windsor he was confident that he could impose himself on the new King as he had upon his predecessor.

King William realised that the presence of Cumberland at Windsor presented a threat to his concept of kingship. Almost his first decision was to reorganize the Household Cavalry so that its commander was responsible to the Commander in Chief and no longer directly to the

King. Cumberland interpreted the decision as a direct attempt to humiliate him. Indignantly he resigned and wrote his brother a hectoring letter, setting out a few salient points about the functions of a King. The King's reply was a curt acknowledgment.[16]

A second clash swiftly followed. The Queen wished to stable her horses in the regulation place, only to find the Duke of Cumberland in occupation. King William, through the Duke of Leeds, ordered his brother to remove the horses. Cumberland replied that he would be damned if they should go.[17] He was then told that, if they were there the following morning, they would be removed by the royal grooms. Grudgingly he gave way. A few days later the King at dinner gave the celebrated toast: 'The land we live in, and let those who don't like it, leave it!' No one present doubted that the barb was intended to speed Cumberland on his way to Hanover.

Cumberland remained a menace but he could make relatively little mischief. It is possible that the danger was any way exaggerated. If he had stood his ground and retained a place in the inner circle around the King it is doubtful whether history would have taken another course. But during the crucial negotiations over the Reform Bill confidence between King and ministers was all important. To achieve it was difficult enough; with the baleful figure of the Duke brooding over Windsor it might have proved impossible.

*

The King would have been no Hanoverian if he had not taken an almost obsessive interest in the details of uniforms. Within a few days of his accession it was decreed that the collars and cuffs of the uniform coats of naval officers should be changed from white to scarlet.[18] This was only a start. The cavalry was his next objective; the Hussars were robbed of some of the more sumptuous items in their wardrobe and the other regiments put into red. Some time later he was designing a new uniform for the Master and Brethren of Trinity House. But he was less pleased when his subjects indulged the same passion. When Lord Mulgrave went as Lord Lieutenant to Ireland he consulted Frederick FitzClarence about a suitable uniform and was given the – possibly frivolous – advice that green should prove a suitable colour for Dublin. The King's indignation was enormous. 'Although it is·satisfactory to His Majesty,' he wrote to Mulgrave, 'to know that the Lord Lieutenant has not worn His Fancy Coat, His Majesty regrets that His Excellency, when he followed the absurd advice given by Lord

Frederick FitzClarence, did not recollect that Green is the *Rebel* Colour of Ireland.'[19]

Uniforms were not the only feature of his soldiers' appearance which engaged his interest. In August 1830 an order from the Horse Guards decreed the abolition of moustachios for all the cavalry except the Life Guards, Horse Guards, and Hussars. The hair of non-commissioned officers and men was in future 'to be cut close at the sides and back of the head, instead of being worn in that bushy and unbecoming fashion adopted by some regiments.' Cornet Jack Spalding, the greatest dandy of the day, left his pet regiment rather than accept the rape of all that he held most precious.

Ministers were well satisfied that he should thus concern himself with trivialities and leave the serious business of government to them. They were less enthusiastic when he indulged in his other pet pursuit, that of making speeches. The King was not a bad orator, in so far as oratory is a means of filling an indefinitely expandable period of time with more or less meaningful rhetoric. He was indeed intolerably long-winded and repetitious but he had a gift for turning phrases and was capable of whipping up a fair enthusiasm among his listeners. The trouble was that he whipped up still greater enthusiasm in himself, and, once enthusiastic, all control over his tongue was lost. 'Really, my master is too stupid,' Wellington was alleged to have said to Princess Lieven, 'so that when at table he wishes to make a speech I always turn to him my deaf ear, so as not to be tempted to get up and contradict him.'[20]

His indiscretions could be dangerous. His ministers winced when he referred to the King of the French as 'an infamous scoundrel'. 'Very unfortunate, and still more improper', commented Grey,[21] while the Duke of Wellington gave the King a stiff rebuke that kept him quiet for several weeks. But he was irrepressible; it was at another delicate moment in Anglo-French affairs that he startled a military banquet at Windsor by hoping that, if his guests had to draw their swords, 'it would be against the French, the natural enemies of England'.[22] The King hardly redeemed his indiscretion when he said afterwards to Sir George Scott, 'You damned rascal, it was all your fault; if you had not made me drink so much grog, I should not have made such a fool of myself.'[23]

His most celebrated gaffe came at a dinner at St James's given for the diplomatic corps. After the ladies had gone the King elected to make his second speech of the evening in French, a long rambling discourse covering whatever came into his head. He concluded with the rousing toast: '*Les yeux qui tuent, les fesses qui remuent, et le cul qui danse, honi soit qui mal y pense.*' As the nervous titters died down Lord Sefton turned to the French ambassador, Prince Talleyrand, and enquired, '*Eh bien, que pensez vous de cela?*' Impassively the old man replied '*C'est bien remarquable*'.[24]

*

For Wellington the King's most significant oratorical flight came at a dinner at Apsley House on July 25, 1830, which the Duke gave in honour of the King of Württemberg. William devoted the greater part of a vast harangue to the exploits of his host and concluded by stating that he had found the duke in office when he had come to the throne, that he had kept him there because he thought the administration highly beneficial to the country, that he gave him his fullest and most cordial confidence and that 'he announced to all whom he saw around him, to all the Ambassadors and Ministers of foreign Powers, and to all the Noblemen and Gentlemen present, that as long as he should sit upon the throne he should continue to give him the same confidence.'[25]

Many people were surprised by the King's attitude. They remembered how Wellington had chased the Duke of Clarence from his post as Lord High Admiral and had assumed that the latter would now be quick to exact a tit-for-tat. They totally misunderstood the King. William had never thought the worse of Wellington for doing what he believed to be his duty and would anyway have thought it wholly improper to dismiss a prime minister on no more than personal grounds.

Where the King erred was in his estimate of Tory strength. He accepted as a fortress of great strength a castle which was not only built on sand but whose superstructure was largely made of cardboard. The Whigs, knowing this, took his speech far from tragically. Lord Holland wrote to Lord Anglesey that the King's language and conduct had strengthened 'the Great Captain more than you or I could wish – but yet I do not think Ministers are comfortable or content.'[26] They were not; and discomfort and discontent were growing daily.

Wellington's position, indeed, was weak. He had lost the liberal, or Canningite wing of the Tory party in the spring of 1828 shortly after he first took office. A year later, when he surrendered over Catholic Emancipation, it was the turn of the Ultra Tories. This mafia of malcontents, under the unappealing leadership of Cumberland and Eldon, pledged themselves to destroy the Duke. To achieve this they would happily have allied themselves with the Whigs, almost with the Radicals themselves. Wellington was left to look for support from a rump of apprehensive country squires and place men. In the House of Commons Peel stood virtually alone as the Tory champion. The ministry survived as much through the inadequacy of the opposition as its own powers. By the beginning of 1830, however, the Whigs were again emerging as an effective force, pledged to some measure of parliamentary reform. It became more and more clear that the government had lost its hold on the country. The antiquated system of parliamentary representation ensured that this unpopularity would not be fully reflected in the general election which necessarily followed William's accession, but Wellington still did not look to the polls with any confidence. Everyone except the King appeared to realize that the government's days were numbered.

In the memorandum which he drew up some years later, setting out the political principles which had guided him throughout his reign, the King stated bluntly that he had 'without any hesitation, determined to maintain in the administration ... those who had been the confidential servants of his late brother, those whose political principles and measures had continued to be ... such as had been approved by his late father.'[27] This impressive filial and brotherly loyalty was in fact little more than a picturesque figure of speech. Wellington's government had already defied George IV over Catholic Emancipation and King William knew well that his brother had disapproved of many of its policies. To those close to him he spoke freely of 'the late King's error in not frankly supporting his Government, and of his own determination to do so.'[28] So unfamiliar was this concept of kingship that many of his subjects assumed the King was the captive of his ministers, totally committed to their support and to the exclusion of the Whigs. Curiously enough, it took a Russian to perceive the limitations of his loyalty. 'He acts on the principle,' wrote Princess Lieven, 'that the King's duty is to support the Minister until Parliament by its vote determines that the Minister no longer possesses the confidence of the nation. For this reason he will do nothing to upset him, but he will be at no pains to pick him up when he falls.'[29]

*

Certainly Wellington found it a pleasure to deal with William after the sloth and obsessive evasiveness of the late King. More than forty-eight thousand documents had accumulated which required a royal signature; night after night, his arthritic hand creaking painfully, William laboured through them until all was in order. He was an excellent man of business, commented Brougham with enthusiasm. King George III had been so intent on expressing his own point of view that he never paid attention to any other, King George IV was so ashamed of admitting ignorance that he would never put questions to his counsellors; King William listened patiently, asked for what extra information he needed, then gave his own view with perfect candour and fairness. Above all, wrote Brougham wonderingly, he was not only ready to tolerate contradiction but seemed positively to relish it, 'in order that he might come to a full understanding with his Ministers.'[30]

It was perhaps this readiness to listen to another point of view which marked him out most clearly from his predecessors. A few weeks after his accession, King William recommended Sir Andrew Halliday to Peel as a Commissioner in Lunacy. With some nervousness Peel argued against the suggestion and the King did not press the point. Peel wrote to Sir Herbert Taylor, hoping that the King was not offended:

'His Majesty,' replied Taylor, 'is not only open to Representation and Objection upon any Matter which suggests itself to Him or upon which He may have stated a Wish or an Opinion but will be pleased with those who offer their Opinion or the Objection which may occur to them frankly and without hesitation. He takes up Matters *readily* and is disposed to act *eagerly* upon such fresh idea or impression, but He listens kindly and patiently to whatever may be submitted in Opposition to what He may have proposed and more than once I have heard Him say, "He is right and I am wrong".'[31]

To be amenable to argument is not in itself a proof of statesmanship. King William's denigrators have represented him as a weak, indeed fatuous figure: bluff and jolly enough but with no opinions on any subject except the colour of a uniform and the appropriate sinecure to bestow upon his bastards. Even a glance at his enormous correspondence, first with Wellington, Peel and Aberdeen and later with Grey, Melbourne and Palmerston makes it obvious that this portrait is unreal. There was no field of government into which the King did not enquire and on which he failed to express his views. It by no means follows that his views were necessarily right or that he always expressed them with lucidity, still less brevity. On the contrary, his correspondence was horrifyingly verbose. But the letters were those of a conscientious and thoughtful monarch who worked at his job and was by no means to be despised for his understanding of the issues.

It was claimed by some that all these letters were the work of Sir Herbert Taylor and that the King's role was to throw out some vague and ill-considered generalization at the beginning and add a scrawled initial at the end. This too is patently untrue. Taylor himself was an old-fashioned Tory but when he wrote to Peel, 'Whatever may be my private feelings and Opinions, I conceive that they must be placed out of the question',[32] he spoke no more than the truth. If William can be called the first constitutional King, Taylor certainly set the pattern for the devoted band of royal servants who have followed him. Quiet, cautious, discreet, industrious to a degree which seems alternately admirable and appalling, his influence was vast but was used, as Grey attested, 'for the purpose of allaying the feelings of irritation created at times in His Majesty's mind, and of smoothing any difficulties that arose between him and his Ministers.'[33] The form and prolixity of the King's correspondence owed much to his efforts but he affected the content remarkably little. This is proved eloquently by the host of complementary letters which he found it necessary to write, elucidating what the King had said, explaining the background to the decision and occasionally confessing in despair that, though he had tried to deflect the King, he had had no success. The recipient rarely indeed had reason to doubt that though the hands were the hands of Taylor, the voice was William's voice.

*

The new King's first formal meeting with his ministers took place at the privy council on June 27. His discourse was appropriately noble in tone, if unadventurous in content, and the dignity with which he took the declaration was generally admired. But he could never sustain the grand manner for long. 'This is a damned bad pen you've given me,' he commented affably, and looked around for a better instrument. He was particularly friendly with Croker and Cockburn, two old enemies from his Admiralty days who might well have feared a chillier reception. The clerk of the council, James Bullen, 'the best but stupidest of men', began to swear in the councillors in the name of King George IV. 'William, if you please,' said the new King firmly, but appeared to feel the mistake a natural one.[34]

In spite of the support which he was resolved to give his ministers he hankered after some form of coalition. He seems to have sounded out Lord Holland for the Whigs and Wellington for the government to see if the latter might not be reinforced by a few of his more eminent adversaries.[35] But Grey and his followers had no wish to help keep afloat a palpably sinking ship. The project was forgotten before it had been properly launched and both parties took up their positions for the forthcoming election. The Tories would have done badly anyway but the cause of the Whigs and Radicals was immeasurably aided by the July Revolution in Paris which occurred as the election entered its opening phase. No one in England had much to say in defence of Charles X or the Polignac ministry and the moderation shown by the victorious Orleanists stilled any fears that 1789 might be here again. 'The battle of English liberty has really been fought and won at Paris,' rejoiced the *Edinburgh Review*. In the upshot the Duke's majority diminished by some fifty seats, but more significant were the sweeping victories won by the opposition in the open constituencies, above all the triumph of Brougham in Yorkshire.

When parliament reconvened in the autumn of 1830 it was at the end of three months of mounting disturbances in industrial and agricultural Britain alike. Watching nervously from Windsor, the King offered to send off his dragoons at a moment's notice.[36] But dragoons, he was beginning to realize, could never provide a lasting answer. Something more was needed – and it was at least open to question whether Wellington could provide it. The Whigs suspected that he might be going to try, by sponsoring a modest measure of reform which would rob them of their respectable supporters without in the least satisfying the Radicals. Then, on November 2, he stilled their fears. In one of the most ill-timed utterances that can ever have been made by a political leader in this country he announced that he was not only well satisfied with the state of the legislature but that, if required to invent a new body to do the same work, he would humbly seek to reconstruct the present model. He denied categorically the intention of introducing any measure of reform and concluded, 'I will at once declare that . . . as long as I hold any station in the Government of the country, I shall always feel it my duty to resist such measures when proposed by others.' By those few sentences he doomed his government.

A few days later there was to be a great dinner at the Guildhall for King William and his ministers. Then came the Duke's declaration. It was followed by a frenzy of insurrection and, though much of it was probably mere surface froth, ministers were alarmed at a possible massacre if they tried to force their way through an angry mob to eat their dinner. On the other hand, to admit that their unpopularity was so great that they did not dare venture under strong escort into the City of London would be so humiliating as almost to destroy their standing in the country. After anguished debate the cabinet decided to call off the dinner. Wellington and Peel went off to tell the King while the other members awaited their return. To their relief Wellington assured them that the King had expected the advice and had, indeed, been relieved to accept it.[37]

Wellington deluded himself. Even though, ten days later, the King was still assuring Ellenborough that he was perfectly satisfied with his ministers and felt it his duty to support them, in his mind he had accepted that they must soon go.[38] To Peel he made it clear that he felt concessions over reform were essential.[39] His affability remained unimpaired but Lady Granville was probably not far off the mark when she reported on November 9 that she had dined, 'at Billy's last night. He was all fondness and civility to the Beau [Wellington] and drank his health four or five times . . . [Wellington] looks upon Billy's civility as conclusive, says he never heard of it being otherwise from a King to a Premier at the last gasp.' She quoted Lord Haddington as saying that 'all the Royalties were at Billy's last night, talking the most open, unguarded defiance and dislike of the Duke.'[40]

The last gasp was not long extended. As petitions for reform poured into Westminster, the Commons met to debate the Civil List. Sir Henry Parnell moved an amendment and, to the general surprise, all elements of the opposition combined to pass it by 233 votes to 204. Conceivably the government might have survived but worse would certainly have followed and Wellington had no intention of letting himself be harried any further. The news of his defeat was taken to St James's. The King had a note which he opened, and left the room, but soon returned, recorded Miss Clitherow. 'Colonel Fred FitzClarence came in, and told the Queen of it in German . . . nothing transpired, not a comment. It's the great secret at Court, to smile and be cheerful and attentive to the circle round you when the heart is sad . . .'[41] By the end of the evening the decision had been taken and the following day, November 16, 1830, Wellington and Peel announced in their respective Houses that the administration was at an end.

CHAPTER XIV

The Advent of the Whigs

WHEN Mary Clitherow spoke of sadness at heart at Windsor she had in mind above all the Queen. Adelaide was a high Tory who believed that even the timidest step towards reform heralded the march of revolution. Worse still, she was a hero-worshipper who had convinced herself that Wellington was the solitary bulwark against disaster. For her his fall was a tragedy, both personal and political. After a senti-mental farewell she confided to her diary: 'I assured him . . . how grieved we were at what had happened, and that I was sure the King would always have in him a faithful Friend! I saw tears in the hero's eyes, a rare sight which rejoiced me . . .'[1]

The King was less lachrymose and very reasonably disinclined to see the replacement of one set of aristocrats by another as the presage of inevitable bloody turmoil. Once his irritation over the Guildhall fiasco had worn off he genuinely deplored the loss of Wellington. On November 18 he spoke to Martin of the Duke's 'upright and manly conduct, and much regretted his going out, which he attributed to that *cunning old Rascal Eldon* (to use His Majesty's gracious words) . . . and to that abominable fellow the Duke of Cumberland who he said ought to be ashamed of himself . . .' Yet he also talked in warm terms of Lord Grey and viewed with equanimity his allegedly radical ambitions.

But it was still inevitable that the King should look somewhat apprehensively towards the approaching Whigs. At first he was not even certain whether Grey should be the leader; Lansdowne, Spencer, or even the pitiful Goderich might be safer men. But both Lyndhurst and Spencer assured him that nobody else would be acceptable to the party and the country and he took the advice without much hesitation. George IV, it was true, had considered Grey little short of anti-Christ incarnate, but William had small respect for his brother's judgment. He is said to have asked Wellington what sort of a man Lord Grey was. 'The Duke said he really did not know. He had the reputation of being an ill-tempered violent man; but he knew very little of him.'[2] It does not sound a likely conversation. Apart from anything else, the King had no need to ask Wellington about Grey, for he had himself known the Whig leader for nearly fifty years.

If King William had had serious doubts about the revolutionary proclivities of his new government, they would surely have been stilled by the presence at their head of this prudent veteran. In his youth Grey had been something of a Jacobin but over the years he had graduated into a grand and austere dignity, marked chiefly by a sense of social obligation, a fine disdain for the mob, a longing for the countryside, and distaste for the hurly-burly of political life. The political scene is habitually beset by would-be nature-lovers, earnestly professing that they despise success and yearn only for a tranquil life of contemplation. Almost all of them are liars. In Grey and Althorp the Whig party could boast two men who genuinely disliked office and courted defeat as a long-sought-for mistress. It was notorious that towards the beginning of every session, when his beloved Howick seemed intolerably remote, Grey would be seized by a resigning fit and would seek to cajole his fellow ministers into admitting that the government must be broken up. Always he was talked out of it and as the session wore on and the vacation grew nearer he was found almost to be enjoying himself in office.[3]

There was little in this reticent, unambitious man to alarm even the wariest of Kings, and his closest political associates were not much more fearsome. Melbourne, Althorp, Palmerston, were all men with whom King William was confident he could get on; reliable aristocrats and land owners who would be properly prudent when the real interests of the country were at stake. Lord Holland, whose son Charles had married Mary FitzClarence, was probably the King's closest friend in the political arena. Durham and John Russell were said to be more turbulent, but the King had no particular reason to view them with suspicion. The only prominent Whig who caused alarm was Henry Brougham. Brougham was a maverick of genius, a man who stood head and shoulders above his colleagues in intellect and oratorical powers but was marred by instability and vanity so overweening that it was close to madness. 'Dirty, cynical and coarse,' the Duchess of Dino called him,[4] but he had a force which drove him irresistibly to the fore, he was adored by the people, he was the spirit of reform. No Whig government could be formed without him.

In the afternoon of November 16, William IV sent for Grey. 'The

King seems to have behaved perfectly throughout the whole business,'
wrote Greville, enraptured, 'no intriguing or underhand communica-
tions with anybody, with great kindness to his Ministers ... The fact is
he turns out to be an incomparable King, and deserves all the enco-
miums that are lavished on him. All the mountebankery which
signalised his conduct when he came to the throne has passed away
with the excitement which caused it, and he is as dignified as the
homeliness and simplicity of his character will allow him to be ...'[5]
The interview itself went as well as its preambles. Grey undertook to
try to form a Ministry, making as his only condition that he should
pledge himself from the start to introduce some measure of reform.
The King seems to have accepted the condition with alacrity. Both
men left the meeting well pleased with each other. Grey wrote enthusiastically that nothing could have been more gracious than the
King's manner or more satisfactory than what he said,[6] while Frederick
FitzClarence told Durham that 'the King was delighted with Lord
Grey and with all that has passed in their interviews.'[7]

Grey had every reason to be satisfied since William had given him
carte blanche to form a new administration, including all the officers of
the royal household.[8] It did not take him long to fill the main places
with Palmerston at the Foreign Office, Melbourne at the Home Office,
and Althorp, perplexed but willing, at the Exchequer. The Duke of
Richmond was brought in as the uneasy emissary of the Ultra Tories
who had helped so signally in Wellington's destruction. The only
serious problem was Brougham. He wanted to be Master of the Rolls,
a position which would have given him an income for life and left
him free to exert his colossal influence in the House of Commons. The
King would have none of this, being convinced that so long as Brougham
remained in the Commons he would be in effective control of the
administration.[9] Grey was glad of the excuse to refuse Brougham this
office and instead tried to fob him off with the Attorney Generalship.
The offer was brusquely rejected. The fearful prospect opened of
Brougham outside the Government conducting his private crusade for
reform. Nervously Grey suggested to the King that Brougham might
be Lord Chancellor. The King agreed at once. Brougham was almost
equally prompt to accept. He was received at court with honeyed
courtesy and preened himself on this mark of royal favour. He might
have been less gratified if he had heard the King say to Lord Holland:
'You are all under great obligations to me. I have settled Brougham;
he will not be dangerous any more.'[10]

On November 23 the new ministers came to St James's to receive their seals. Their predecessors had handed theirs back only a few moments before and there was an uneasy pause while the two parties waited in adjoining rooms. 'The effect was very droll, such a complete *changement de décoration*', noted Greville, darting amusedly from one to the other. The King brushed aside the formal rigmarole and made a – for him – brief speech of welcome. The new Government, he promised them, would receive his most cordial, unceasing and devoted support.[11] It was a propitious start to the relationship.

*

The customary few months of honeymoon followed. The Whigs were running themselves in and wondering what they ought to do about reform while the Tories licked their wounds. Not that the wounds were very deep. They felt that they had been destroyed by their own internal divisions and that it would not take too long for these to heal. Then the power that was rightfully theirs could be regained. In the meantime they did not take too seriously the threat that the Whigs might introduce a substantial measure of reform. Grey was a gentleman who could be relied on to play the game by the gentlemanly rules. For them the urgent issue was the civil disorder which was engulfing so much of Britain. Once tranquillity had been restored it might be time to consider a modest degree of reform. That the surest way to restore tranquillity might be to grant reform was a concept which hardly entered their heads.

On the whole, the King shared their view. Shortly after Grey took office he sent the King a cabinet minute setting out what action was being taken against unlawful assemblies and acts of outrage. The reply was a clarion call for sterner measures: 'the present State of the Country imperiously calls for every possible Demonstration of firmness in the Resolutions of His Government, for the utmost Vigour and Energy in its Measures, and for Promptness and Decision in the Execution of those Measures.' But he did not lose his common sense and was dismayed by a proposal to form bodies of discharged soldiers into vigilante squads to protect the public peace. Such bodies, he pointed out drily, might all too easily prove better calculated to promote violence than to check it.[12] In Melbourne he found a home secretary after his own heart; not prone to panic yet quite as harshly repressive as he felt the circumstances required.

Exquisite harmony, indeed, reigned between King and ministers and Grey rhapsodized about the kindness of the King and Queen. 'I am quite fallen in love with the latter,' he wrote fondly – a statement which he may have remembered with some wryness in the future.[13] The King responded with equal friendliness. Cheerfully he agreed to receive Grey at three 'or at any other hour that may suit him. His Majesty indeed wishes it to be clearly understood ... that he will never suffer any engagement or his convenience to interfere with the attention which His Majesty considers to be due to public business.'[14] But from time to time, through all this affability and mutual admiration, a warning note could be heard. The day after the King had so lavishly placed himself at the disposal of his ministers a proposal was put forward to reorganize the Ordnance. William agreed that the change was desirable, 'much as His Majesty dislikes even the appearance of yielding to clamours for reform, which have often been, and may still be, urged by individuals who ... do not take the trouble of making any distinction between that which is useful and necessary, and that which is wasteful and superfluous.'[15] Reform for the sake of reform, he made it clear, was not going to be tolerated.

The King was not to escape without any trial. One of the electoral cries of the Whigs had been the traditional slogan of every opposition: retrenchment and economy in public life. Now that they were in office, the rank and file displayed a dismaying desire to see these pledges redeemed. The Court, of course, provided a tempting target. First came the problem of the Queen's outfit. Taylor had pointed out that unless certain expenses were met from public funds, the Queen would start the new reign heavily in debt.[16] Grey felt the demand to be reasonable but was doubtful about the feelings of the House of Commons. Before it ever reached that body, however, Charles Grant at the Board of Control bluntly threatened to resign if the Queen's outfit was paid for by the nation.[17] Grey confessed to the King that, in the light of this, he did not dare raise the matter in Parliament. Lord Althorp, when the Civil List was debated, would do full justice to the King's nobility in meeting the cost himself. William's reply was generous. He urged that no reference should be made to the matter by Althorp for: 'He does not wish to be considered as claiming the least merit for abandoning a claim to which an objection could possibly be urged.'[18] But though the King was sincere when he told Grey that he did not blame him for the debacle, yet still his respect for the prime minister was diminished. A leader who could not keep his troops in order must be an uncertain quality when the battle grew really hot.

Ministers did rather better when it came to the civil list. Althorp proposed that certain expenses, now paid from the list, should be put under parliamentary control. To this the King happily agreed. In the debate, however, opportunity was taken to attack expenditure in the royal household and to propose reduction of the salaries paid to various court officials. The King was indignant and, since only some £12,000 a year was in question, Grey was anxious to avoid an unnecessary clash. Althorp was entrusted with the question in the House of Commons. His tactics were characteristic. He cheerfully admitted that he too, when he had first considered the cost of living in the royal palace, had been surprised to find that, though the price of almost every commodity had gone down, total expenditure had risen steeply. Nevertheless, he went on, 'no reduction can be made in this class of expense without compelling his Majesty to alter his style of living or to incur debt. I am convinced the House has no wish to compel his Majesty to do either'.[19] Astonishingly the House accepted this striking conclusion, and the matter of the cuts was pressed no further.

The King was gratified and all went on smoothly; but he was never entirely easy to deal with. There was an unpredictable quality about his responses which kept ministers nervously on the alert. He could never be relied on not to do things in his own way. Lord Durham asked leave to drive his carriage through the royal parks. Ministers should have been consulted but Taylor told Peel that he feared the King had already agreed. 'My great object . . .' he wrote wistfully, 'is to keep business in the regular Channels, and I may perhaps effect it in time but it is uphill Work . . .'[20] Impetuosity was allied to an obstinate determination to have his way. The Queen of Württemberg was to visit England and he told Byam Martin that a large chair would be needed to hoist her in and out of the yacht. Martin complacently said that he had just the thing:

'No such thing. You have no notion of her size!'

'Sir, the chair is of dimensions to receive any two women in the kingdom.'

'I tell you, it won't do; she is larger than any three women, aye, than any four women.'

'Sir, what I speak of is more like a sofa than a chair.'

'I tell you again, it won't do, and I desire you will get a larger!'[21]

When crossed in such whims his fury was sometimes appalling. Martin was lucky not to be berated like the unfortunate President of the Royal Academy who pointed out to William a portrait of Admiral

Napier at a time when the latter was in deep disfavour. 'Captain Napier may be damn'd, Sir!' roared the indignant King. 'And you may be damn'd, Sir! And if the Queen was not here, Sir, I'd kick you downstairs.'[22] Outbursts of this kind served to endear him to the general public, but they can hardly have made life more tranquil for those who had to work with him.

*

Shortly after the Whigs came to power a committee was formed consisting of Lord Durham and Sir James Graham from the Cabinet and Lord Duncannon and Lord John Russell from outside it to work out a measure of parliamentary reform which would be large enough to satisfy public opinion, yet would maintain 'the essential character of the constitution'.[23] Most people thereupon dismissed the matter from their minds but the King could never escape a sense of nagging alarm at this timebomb ticking away quietly in Lord Durham's drawing-room. This Grey seemed more anxious to foster than to allay. 'The perilous question is that of Parliamentary Reform,' he wrote to Taylor in January, 1831, 'and, as I approach it, the more I feel all its difficulty. With the universal feeling that prevails on this subject,' he continued, 'it is impossible to avoid doing something.'[24]

Such unenthusiastic phrases hardly befitted the man who should have been Reform's most ardent champion. The King however was not discomfited. Grey, he was certain, would oppose 'the wild and mischievous projects of the Radicals', while he for his part would refrain from 'frivolous or captious objections'.[25] Two days later Taylor assured Grey that the King was 'convinced that your Lordship would have postponed the question if you could have done so',[26] – a statement of the position which was probably correct but would have read oddly to Grey's more ardent colleagues. The King made only two conditions: that the duration of parliaments should not be abridged nor the number of members increased. Grey replied that the intention had been to reduce the period between elections from seven to five years but that this was not important; as to the members, their strength was actually to be cut to six hundred.[27]

But the King still doubted whether the bill was really needed. With satisfaction he surveyed the scene of tranquil apathy presented by the House of Commons; two parties with hardly an issue of principle between them and divided only by the desire for office. Surely this was as it should be? Surely it was foolhardy, criminal almost, to disturb the peace at Westminster when peace everywhere else in the country was so severely threatened? 'He looks forward with more anxiety to the proceedings in Parliament than to any other circumstance,' Taylor told Grey.[28]

Grey paid no attention to these qualms. But letters of this kind confirmed his almost paranoic fears that the King, though himself well-intentioned, was surrounded by a clique of Ultra Tory conspirators busily engaged in filling his ears with poison and leaking to the Press whatever court gossip was helpful to their case. To Grey's fearful mind, Wellington, Camden, Londonderry, Buckingham, were perpetually around the palace, lurking in the closet, hissing dark prophecies about the lunatic rashness of the Whig proposals. Taylor did his best to still their suspicions with his usual calm common sense. When Grey protested that information was being passed from the Court to *John Bull* he replied that it was the King's duty to see a large number of people of varying points of view and to listen to what they had to say. But the fact that the King listened to visitors did not mean that he offered his opinions to them in return, still less that he expounded or criticized the views of his ministers. Politics were never touched on at social gatherings.[29] This was certainly true. The diaries and letters of Tory leaders make it clear that, though the King would always listen, he rarely discussed, while the complaints of regular guests, like Princess Lieven, who lived for political gossip, show that the table-talk at Windsor or Brighton held little to interest them.

But this, for Grey, was not enough. 'There were persons having access to the King,' he wrote darkly, 'who were eager to avail themselves of every opportunity of endeavouring to injure his Ministers . . .' Here he was on stronger ground. The King's intimate circle – his family, his courtiers, his closest friends – had a decidedly Tory tinge. Queen Adelaide, in particular, was a high Tory of the most reactionary cast; in Lord Wellesley's words, 'educated in the very worst principles of passive obedience and Divine Right.'[30] She never ventured to speak her opinions in public. On one occasion, it is said, she tried to put in a word and was slapped down by the King with a firm: 'Women should not mix in politics.'[31] But who can be sure that she was equally reticent when in bed with her husband rather than at dinner with the King? The persistent drip of her prejudices was to erode William's frail loyalty to the cause of liberalism.

The same is true of the other intimates at Court who sought to turn the King against Reform. The Duke of Gloucester, William's first cousin, Silly Billy,* told him that the Whig proposals must infallibly cost him his crown. 'Very well, very well!' snapped the King pettishly. 'But, Sir,' continued the alarmist Duke, 'your Majesty's head may be in it!'[32] The FitzClarences, too, were at this point hot against reform, though the quarrel with their father meant that their voices were now mercifully little heard at Court. Grey therefore had a point, but at the beginning of his administration it was still a remote one. It was to take time before this constant reiteration began to tell. On January 21, 1831 – only ten days before the Durham Committee's recommendations on parliamentary reform were laid before the King – Taylor reassured the prime minister that: 'The general impression here is, and with strict reason, that His Majesty is very partial to his Government, very much pleased with all their Proceedings, determined to support them, and anxious that these sentiments should be known.'[33]

Certainly the saner sections of the opposition did not share Grey's doubts. On the contrary, the Duke of Wellington told Croker that the King, 'from pique or fright or folly', would consent to anything that the Whigs chose to suggest. 'When the Crown joins the mob all balance is lost,' he commented gloomily.[34]

On one point alone it seemed that the Tory propagandists had alarmed the King. Someone had pointed out to him that reform could never pass the House of Commons with its present membership. Grey's next step must be to demand a dissolution. The King had a rooted fear of general elections, above all, as Taylor told Brougham, at a moment 'when so much excitement prevails; when the disposition to violence and outrage, to the almost indiscriminate and unprovoked destruction of property, has with difficulty been checked.'[35]

> '*I consider Dissolution*
> *Tantamount to Revolution.*'

– a piece of doggerel allegedly scrawled by the King on a scrap of paper – is memorable as marking the only occasion on which passion provoked him into a flight of poesy.[36]

To Grey, who knew quite well that he would indeed be seeking an

---

* Many people seem to think that Silly Billy was a nickname of William IV. During his reign at least it was used exclusively for the man Creevey referred to as 'that damned slice Gloucester'. His lack of any noticeable chin probably inspired the nickname.

election within the next few months, the King's attitude was an ominous presage for the future.

*

On January 29, 1831, Grey wrote to Lord Anglesey: 'I am going tomorrow to Brighton to propose our plea of Reform. It is a strong and effectual measure. If the King agrees to it, I think we shall be supported by publick opinion. If he does not – what is to come next?'[37] It was indeed a strong measure, almost too strong for Grey to swallow, too strong by far, he feared, for the delicate stomach of the King. His spirits cannot have been raised by the special prayer offered in the royal chapel on the day he arrived, to God '. . . who in Thy heavy displeasure didst suffer the life of our late gracious Sovereign King Charles the First to be this day taken away by the hands of cruel and bloody men . . .'[38] Nervously Grey sketched out the main heads of Lord Durham's project. The King 'entered into every part of the plan, asked questions wherever he found any difficulty and ended by understanding it thoroughly.'[39] Only then did he tell his apprehensive Minister that he would support the project in all its details.

A paean of joy broke out all over Britain as the great Whig lords congratulated each other. 'Never was there such a King,' rhapsodized Holland to Anglesey. 'He not only acquiesces in but espouses the measures deemed necessary by His Ministers, however disagreeable they must in their nature be to Royal Palates. Our Reform (and I promise you it is not mawkish milk-and-water stuff) is taken without a wry face . . .'[40] It was indeed a striking achievement by Lord Grey – quite how striking Lord Anglesey was only to realize when the details of the Reform Bill were published a few weeks later. But the King's conversion to reform was not so unequivocal as Grey had hoped.

For a few days after Grey's visit King William cogitated in silence. Then, on February 4, he sent his prime minister a long memorandum which set out his views, not on the details of the proposed Reform Bill, but on the principles which underlay it.[41] He stated bluntly that the dangers which he foresaw in introducing such a measure far outweighed any possible advantages. Nevertheless, he accepted that his ministers were pledged to reform. If their proposals had included such fantastical measures as voting by secret ballot 'a practise which would . . . abolish the influence of fear and shame, and would be inconsistent with the manly spirit and the free avowal of opinion which distinguish the people of England' – or, worse still, universal suffrage – 'one of the wild projects which have sprung from revolutionary speculation' – he would have felt bound to oppose them. As it was, and because he recognized that the present system was far from perfect, he would, with some reluctance, support the Bill. What he dreaded most, he made it clear, was that a substantial measure of reform would be passed by the Commons only to be rejected by the Lords. The quarrel that would ensue between the two branches of the legislature would be a great national calamity. 'The King conceives', he added in a passage which gave deeper insight into his fears than all that had gone before:

'. . . that the most strenuous advocates for reform, those whose object it may be to introduce a preponderance of *popular* influence, will not be disposed to deny that the influence of the House of Commons has increased more than that of the Crown or of the House of Peers; and the question is, Whether greater danger be not to be apprehended from its encroachments than from any other evil which may be the subject of speculation, and whether it is not from this source that the mixed form of government of this country has to dread annihilation.'

Though Grey can have gained little pleasure from this missive, it did not qualify the King's readiness to accept reform. The government could go ahead. The King was not as reliable an ally as Grey had hoped but at least there was no cause to fear that he might prove an enemy.

If there was any reason to believe that secrets confided to the King were automatically passed to the opposition, it was now dispelled. Grey expounded his plan to him on January 30, Lord John Russell did not introduce the Bill into the Commons until March 1, yet between these dates no word of its contents was known outside the tiny circle of the initiated. Tories and Radicals, the first with complacency, the second with dismay and disgust, alike anticipated an anodyne measure designed to satisfy the moderates that something was being done without affecting the essentials of the existing system. But for the daring of Durham and Lord John Russell and the striking open-mindedness of the King they would certainly have been correct. As it was their disillusion was to be dramatic, swift and total.

CHAPTER XV

Reform: The Battle Joined

VIEWED from the lofty pinnacles of twentieth-century democracy, it is hard to realize how dramatic, even revolutionary, the provisions of the first Reform Bill must have seemed to our forefathers. When one considers them against the background of the constitutional position in 1831, the situation is very different. In the previous fifty years the economic and social structure of British society had been dramatically modified, yet the political institutions of the country were virtually unchanged; had been unchanged, indeed, if Ireland is left to one side, since the Act of Union in 1707. A few minor modifications had been made, but on the whole the position had grown steadily more remote from reality as the sicklier boroughs had putrified into full rottenness. The members of the House of Commons in 1831 were elected on a basis which seemed designed to ensure that none of those forces responsible for the dynamic growth of the country should find any kind of representation within their ranks.

The enormities of the system are too well known to call for much description.[1] No statistics can have any finality, but Croker was unlikely to have exaggerated when he estimated that, in 1827, 276 members were returned by patrons of which the Tories appointed 203.[2] This imbalance meant that the Whigs could only hope for a majority when the country was overwhelmingly in their favour, and that even then their tenure of office would often be dependent on the whim of a handful of voters. It was hard to say which was more absurd: the numbers of the voters or the geographical distribution of the seats. Cornwall, for instance, returned forty-four members while industrial centres, such as Leeds, Birmingham and Manchester, already large and growing with alarming speed, did not enjoy a single member between them. Even where a large town might be lucky enough to have a representative, only a handful of its citizens would be entitled to a vote. The franchise however could hardly have been more narrow than at Old Sarum, where the two members were returned by seven votes. Since the seven votes were attached to empty fields, the seats were in fact in the gift of the landowner.

The phrase 'in the gift of' was frequently inappropriate since seats were freely bought and sold on the open market. In 1830 £6000 was a reasonable price to pay for a seat during the life of a parliament; while between £1500 and £1800 was the usual annual fee. Where members did not pay, it was generally expected that their voting would be to the taste of their patron. As a result, the poor man who yearned to be in politics either risked being given orders by a rich patron or had to seek one of the few constituencies with something like a popular franchise. Even if he were lucky enough to find the latter it was rarely indeed that he would escape without major electoral expense.

It hardly seems necessary to say that the system was indefensible, yet it would be dangerous to forget that it was in fact defended, and defended ably, by men of intelligence who were by no means preoccupied only with their selfish interest. The conservative case against reform rested on several arguments. Perhaps the most vigorously advocated was the right of property. These boroughs *belonged* to someone, no doubt to the heirs of some heroic figure who had deserved well of his country, and could no more be taken from them than their house or land. Then there was the fear of revolution; the obsession that interpreted everything in the pattern of 1789 with Burdett for Mirabeau; Place, Robespierre; Cobbett, Danton; and the Whigs as Philippes Égalité setting themselves up for a trip to the guillotine. There was the belief that no government could enjoy stability unless it were backed by a plethora of docile placemen, and the somewhat incompatible conviction that the independence of the individual member would be lost if he were constantly looking over his shoulder to observe the reactions of his electors. If the system were overhauled there would be no room left for the boldly free-minded statesman of genius whose presence in the House was so desirable, instead there would be rank upon rank of subservient mediocrities, drawn predominantly from the cities and swamping that landed interest which, as every Tory knew, was the true repository of Britain's greatness.

But the most unanswerable of the conservative arguments was that, illogical though it might be, the system worked. It was unanswerable because it conceded the whole of the reformist case and rested only on affection for existing institutions, a thin but potent compound of patriotism, respect for tradition and sentimentality. The argument was doubly insidious because in fact the system *had* worked pretty well.

England was regarded by European liberals – with generous if ill-informed enthusiasm – as the home of liberty and the touchstone for progressive thought. The political structure of the British Isles was invested with sacramental significance, far greater than the sum of its various parts. 'The rights and liberties of a nation,' said Disraeli, 'can only be preserved by institutions. It is not the spread of knowledge or march of intellect that will be found sufficient sureties for the public welfare in the crisis of a country's freedom.'[3]

It was this above all which struck a chord in the heart of the King. He saw the force of the reformist case but was not shaken in his obstinate conviction that the British constitution was the best in the world and should be treated with due love and reverence. 'He is aware . . .' he wrote wistfully to Palmerston in another context, 'that the Spirit of the Times may be pleaded against Him, that He is constantly against Doctrines generally diffused and daily gaining ground in favour of what is called the *liberal* System . . . as opposed to the existing order of things.'[4] But to be aware is not to be convinced. He was persuaded by the Whigs that public opinion made reform essential; he agreed that he must support their measures, but never could he escape the fear that in so yielding he did not serve the long-term interests of his country. '. . . as the Objects of Change or Reform necessarily are the Subversion or at least the limitation of Institutions, Rights and Prerogatives, those who are attached to, or who, from Principle or Interest, are desirous of maintaining the established Order of things, naturally dread the designs of those who cannot introduce what they consider Improvements in the order of Society . . . without disturbing the Tranquillity of States and the Peace and Prosperity of the country . . .'[5] Palmerston would have been naïve indeed if he had failed to realize that the King numbered himself among those who were 'desirous of maintaining the established Order of things'.

*

Given this prejudice, it is all the more remarkable that he should have been brought to support measures as drastic as those now introduced by Lord John Russell into the House of Commons. Brougham had suggested the disfranchisement of five boroughs and he was believed by the Tories to be the most extreme proponent of reform among the Whig ministers. Not even the most radical of politicians had dared dream that more than a dozen seats would be affected. Now Russell calmly read out a list of sixty boroughs which were to be totally abolished. As the angry laughter died away and the Tories eyed each other with stupefied alarm; 'More yet,' put in Russell, and moved on to a second schedule of forty-seven boroughs which were to lose one member each. Not all the bill was so radical – indeed, certain changes to the property qualification meant that in some constituencies future elections would be less and not more democratic – but such minor blemishes could hardly mar the revolutionary splendour of the new proposals.

Many Tories – and, indeed, Whigs too – believed that if Peel had refused even to debate so preposterous a measure and had at once divided the House, then the Whigs would have fallen and the Tories been left free to introduce whatever moderate measure of reform might take their fancy. He missed his chance. Battle was formally joined on the floor of the House. Grey had little hope of success with the present membership; his majority was flimsy at the best of times and would soon melt away in the heat of debate. In the end he knew he would need a dissolution and a fresh election. But he knew too that the King would strongly oppose any such proposal, believing that elections, in the present febrile state of the country, would be an invitation to violence. Cautiously he sounded out the King, bemoaning the ferocious opposition he was already meeting. The reply was affable but non-committal. He was quite prepared, he said, to do what he could to help the government over its difficulties, but no hint did he give that dissolution might be one of the weapons which he would put at his prime minister's disposal.

On March 18 the Tories, flexing their muscles, defeated the Government by forty-seven votes on a trivial question relating to the Timber Duties. The vote was taken as a declaration of intent to destroy the Reform Bill. Princess Lieven asked Wellington if this would not lead to serious trouble in the country. 'Bah! Bah!' retorted the Duke loftily. 'It does not appear to me a very powerful argument.'[6] The King would not have agreed. He was as anxious that the Tories should allow the Whigs to govern as that the Whigs should not provoke the Tories too far. But the chances of averting a direct clash were fast dwindling. Grey now wrote to Taylor, asking what the King's views would be if he were asked to dissolve parliament. Taylor, tactlessly as Grey believed, passed on the letter to the King, whose reply was as chilling as it was categoric. In the present disturbed state of the country, particularly Ireland, he told Grey, he would feel it his sacred duty to refuse his sanction for an election;[7] if he yielded, 'this country would be thrown into convulsion from the Land's End to John of Groats.'[8] Rather grudgingly Grey agreed not to press the matter for the moment but reserved his right to do so if the situation grew worse. To this William could hardly object but Taylor warned the prime minister that the King's objections were final and conclusive.[9]

What disturbed Grey was not just the King's refusal to contemplate a dissolution but the fact that his attitude quickly became public knowledge. This confirmed Grey's suspicion that the King, though himself well enough disposed, was surrounded by a mafia of Tory plotters. He was not wholly wrong. Cumberland was particularly active at this time; plotting with Buckingham to reunite the Tories and to organize the brain-washing of the unfortunate King by those patriarchal reactionaries, Lord Eldon and Lord Sidmouth.[10] The Queen, the Princess of Hesse Homburg and the Duke and Duchess of Gloucester, according to *The Times*, were also busily at work. 'We have been well aware from the beginning,' reported that omniscient journal, 'of the degree to which an Illustrious Person has been tormented by the intrigues of certain old courtiers.'[11] But in fact this pressure did not yet amount to very much. Lord Holland, who knew the King far better than any other minister, put the matter in its true proportions when he wrote to Lord Anglesey: 'It is possible that the Old Courtiers and even the Princesses (whom some irreverently call the Begums) may be frightened at the measure, but I doubt very much their . . . having any influence on the King who is fairness and straitness personified.'[12]

That the crisis was postponed was due above all to the Whigs' masterly handling of the Reform Bill in the House of Commons. Partly this was thanks to the energy and dedication of Lord John Russell; but far more the Whig success was the work of Althorp. Althorp, slow, bungling, uncouth, a lamentable speaker and a worse economist, was arguably the most decent man ever to achieve high place in a British government. He hated Westminster and loathed the trials of office. In moments of crisis his face was a barometer of the government's standing; dejected at success, suffused by joy at the prospect of defeat. He served with absolute loyalty out of a sense of duty to his party and his country. He enjoyed in the House of Commons the personal authority and influence which falls only to the man of total integrity whom every member trusts as well as loves. Once, in the course of the debate on the Reform Bill, Croker argued ingeniously in favour of a damaging amendment. Lord Althorp assured the House 'that he had made some calculations which he considered entirely conclusive in refutation of the Hon. Member's arguments, but unfortunately he had mislaid them . . .' His word was accepted without demur.

So well did the debate go for the Whigs that, when the second reading of the Bill was moved on March 22, the Tory triumph which had seemed so sure a few weeks before was in the balance. Still, most observers believed the reformers would be narrowly defeated. Macaulay's description of the scene when it was learned that the Whigs had won by a single vote is well known but is too good not to be quoted once more:

> 'You might have heard a pin drop,' he wrote to Ellis, 'as Duncannon read the numbers. Then again the shouts broke out, and many of us shed tears. I could scarcely refrain. And the jaw of Peel fell; and the face of Twiss was as the face of a damned soul; and Herries looked like Judas taking his necktie off for the last operation. We shook hands, and clapped each other on the back, and went out laughing, crying, and huzzaing into the lobby. And no sooner were the outer doors opened than another shout answered that within the House. All the passages and the stairs into the waiting rooms were thronged by people who had waited till four in the morning to know the issue. We passed through a narrow lane between two thick masses of them; and all the way down they were shouting and waving their hats, till we got into the open air. I called a cabriolet, and the first thing the driver asked was, Is the Bill carried? Yes, by one. Thank God for it, Sir. And away I rode . . .'[13]

Though the King was not as enraptured by his ministers' victory as the ardent Macaulay, he was still profoundly relieved. He believed that, if the Tories had won, they would have shelved their differences and united to form a government. In such a case he would either have had to accept them as his ministers or agree to Grey's wish to dissolve parliament. Both thoughts appalled him. Durham believed that the King was blind to the 'feelings of disappointment, of almost reckless despair . . . hatred and vengeance against those who have refused their claims', which would possess the people if the Whigs were supplanted by the forces of reaction.[14] In this he was wrong. William had no illusions about the risks involved. But he was equally preoccupied by the risks of an immediate election. It was a choice between two daunting evils and, as always when in such a situation, he refused to admit that a choice needed to be made. Now the House of Commons had proved him right. He at once told Grey that he was sorry the majority had not been larger but was sincerely happy about the result. It meant that time had been gained for further consideration.[15] His prime minister can hardly have failed to divine that, in the King's view, this time should be spent on deciding what concessions might be made which would render the bill less odious to the Tories.

Grey knew well that no compromise he might honourably propose would be remotely acceptable to Peel or Wellington, let alone Eldon or Cumberland. He knew too that the bill would never survive the committee stage without being mauled by the opposition. 'The alternatives then will be Dissolution or Resignation;'[16] and with the first a remote prospect he prepared himself bleakly for the second. But the King seemed determined to show that, short of dissolution, he would do anything he could to help his ministry. Horace Seymour and Captain Meynell were dismissed from the royal household for voting against the government in the recent debate.[17] The Queen, presumably on a hint from her husband, treated Grey with honeyed courtesy (which Grey believed to be sincerely felt, though Princess Lieven commented that Adelaide obviously hated every minute of it).[18] It seemed that Reform Billy, as the Radical journals were hopefully calling him, was genuinely anxious to see his ministers successful.

For several weeks everything hung fire as the parties prepared for the next phase of the battle. The King was formidably discreet, yet the opposition noticed with glee that, as the opening of the committee stage drew near, the Whig leaders grew more despondent. Ministers expected to be beaten and to be obliged to go out, Wellington stated confidently.[19] On April 18 debate began. Almost at once General Gascoyne moved that the number of members for England and Wales should not be diminished. The point was significant but not one on which the whole future of the bill need have depended; the cabinet however decided that there was nothing to be gained by delay and made it clear that Gascoyne's amendment would be unacceptable. To the King, Grey wrote that he expected to have a majority but that, if he did not, 'immediate and anxious consideration' would be called for.[20] Perceiving only too well what was meant by this characteristically shrouded phrase William replied briskly that his views on a dissolution were unchanged.[21]

Gascoyne's motion was adopted by eight votes and the following day the cabinet drew up a formal minute advising the King to dissolve. His failure to follow the advice would mean that he was to look for a new set of ministers.

The Tories were confident that the King would let his ministers go with barely a pang of conscience and send for the Duke of Wellington. The Whigs had small cause to disagree. 'Our reasons for apprehending that the King will not agree to the Dissolution,' Lord Holland wrote to Lord Anglesey directly after the Cabinet meeting, 'is that he has uniformly told us so, though at the same time professed (and acted up to his professions) to support the bill manfully and to confine to us any expression of aversion to dissolution ... The consequence of his adherence to his opinion is obvious, that we must resign, which I have little doubt will happen in the course of a day or two ... We shall ... separate from the court itself without any sore feeling either of the King towards us or of us towards the King – for though I think he is sadly mistaken in his view of the subject ... I must in my conscience declare that I think he has acted throughout most fairly and honourably by us ...'[22] With government and opposition thus agreed about his likely course of action, it only remained for the King to fall into line.

It would, indeed, have been a perfectly rational and proper thing to do. Parliament had only been sitting for some six months and there was no reason to believe that the popular frenzy which had been whipped up since the introduction of the bill would be reflected in the polls. Certainly any substitute government would have had to pledge itself to some measure of reform, but this was not a major problem. Wellington and Peel might still mutter that any such course would be unthinkable but few politicians doubted that if the terms of the bill were modified and compensation given to the owners of the disappearing boroughs, then all except the die-hards would concur. Plenty of Tory trimmers had already shown themselves eager to sponsor such a project.

It is probable that the King had never intended to allow his ministers to resign. What he wanted them to do was so to amend their bill as to make it acceptable to the more moderate Tories. There was no chance of their doing this if they knew that their intransigence would be rewarded by a dissolution. Only when all hope of compromise had passed could he afford to reveal his true intentions. The feeling of the people 'avowedly and manifestly' was in favour of his present government, and therefore he was resolved to support them so long as he could reconcile it with his conscience.[23] He told Grey frankly that, 'as an individual, consulting merely his own feelings and prejudices, he would probably have taken and maintained a different position. As a Sovereign it was his duty to set those feelings and prejudices aside.'[24] In the end it was all a question of his duty as a King towards his subjects and as a gentleman towards his ministers. As he had said to Sir Henry Halford: 'I shall give these men fair play. It they can succeed, well and good ...'[25] So far they had not had a reasonable chance; until they had had it and failed he considered that he should stick by them.

On April 21, 1831, the King wrote to his prime minister gloomily accepting dissolution as the 'lesser of two evils'. But he made it clear that he was not abandoning his role as conciliator. It was understood, he said, that the Government would resist any attempt to broaden the principle of the present bill. Rather, their object after the election should be: 'to introduce such modifications as without producing any essential departure from the principle of the measure, shall be calculated to conciliate the opponents of the Bill.'[26] Somewhere, he would never cease to believe, there must be enough common ground between the parties for a monarch and a few other men of good will to stand on.

An ecstatic clamour of approval rose from the Whigs. '. . . the King has behaved like an Angel,' wrote Grey to Anglesey. '. . . there is no extent of gratitude that we do not owe him for the confidence and kindness with which we have been treated.'[27] Their joy was the more unbounded because they had been completely deceived about his intentions. With equal abruptness the Tories were plunged into the blackest gloom. 'I don't believe,' fulminated Wellington, 'that the King of England has taken a step so fatal to his monarchy since the day that Charles I passed the Act to deprive himself of the power of proroguing or dissolving the Long Parliament ... ';[28] while the Duke of Gloucester more concisely jeered at his cousin: 'Who is Silly Billy now?'[29] Only the most passionate enemies of reform really believed that the King had taken the first step down the steep slope to revolution and the scaffold but many more had doubts about the wisdom of his conduct. At the Duchess of Kent's that night, Prince George of Cambridge turned to the Queen. 'What has the King been about, has he not done something odd?' 'The King can do odd things,' replied Queen Adelaide with careful ambiguity.[30] But to her diary she confided her private fears. 'May God will,' she concluded, 'that this step be not dangerous for the welfare of the country.'[31]

Events now began to move with violent speed. Lord Wharncliffe announced his intention of sponsoring in the House of Lords a motion against dissolving parliament. If passed, this would at once accentuate the breach between the two Houses which was so much dreaded by the King. In such circumstances Brougham even feared that the King might go back on his promise to dissolve. A few hours before Wharn-cliffe's motion was to be introduced, Grey and Brougham hastened to St James's to try to persuade the King at once to prorogue Parliament in person and thus stop all discussion. When Brougham explained how the Lords were seeking to impede dissolution, the King flared up at what seemed to him dangerous interference with his exercise of the prerogative.[32] He was, indeed, so eager to act that he did no more than express mild surprise when Brougham admitted that he had already ordered an escort of the Horse Guards to be in attendance. Getting ready the state coach proved more complicated. Lord Durham was sent off to warn Lord Albemarle, the Master of the Horse, whom he found still at table.

'You must have the King's carriage ready instantly.'

'Very well, I will just finish my breakfast.'

'No, no, you must not lose a moment. The King ought to be in the House.'

'Lord bless me! Is there a revolution?'

'Not at this moment, but there will be if you stay to finish your breakfast!'[33]

The harassed Master of the Horse rushed to the palace. It was un-thinkable that the state coach should set out at such short notice, he pleaded. The manes of the greys could not be properly plaited. 'Then I will go in a hackney cab,' retorted the King furiously.* From behind the arras the sepulchral voice of Townshend, the Bow Street Officer on duty, was heard applauding:

'Well said, sir. I think your Majesty is damned right.'

'Is that you, Townshend?' asked the King.

'Yes, sir. I am here to see that your Majesty has fair play.'[34]

When the royal procession arrived at the Houses of Parliament the

---

* This anecdote illustrates well how impossible it is to sift the apocryphal from the true in the life of King William, or indeed any other public personality. Lord Albe-marle's son does not refer to it in his memoirs and Brougham does no more than note, 'I cannot say whether this is true or not'. Greville makes the King say 'Then I will go with anybody else's horses', but he was in Newmarket on that day. On the other hand Grey told his son, Lord Howick, that he believed the story to be true and Robert Grosvenor, the Comptroller of the Household, told Lord Broughton he had heard the words. All one can say with certainty is that the remark sounds characteristic, that, if the King did not make it, he should have, and that, in the event, no cab was needed.

opéra bouffe moved into riotous finale. The Lords were in uproar: the Duke of Richmond trying to delay debate by a series of bogus points of order; Lord Londonderry brandishing a horse-whip and restrained from violence only by four or five colleagues clinging to his coat-tails; Lord Mansfield bellowing insults at the government. The noise was such that the King heard it as he entered the robing room and asked what was going on. 'If it please your Majesty,' replied Brougham with commendable sang-froid, 'it is the Lords debating.'[35] It was doubtful whether the King should properly have worn the crown before his Coronation but he had nevertheless sent for it. Lord Hastings made as if to place it on the King's head but William checked him. 'Nobody shall put the crown on my head but myself,' he decreed. He put it on and turned to Lord Grey: 'Now, my Lord, the Coronation is over.'[36] In a vivid phrase George Villiers described the scene as William settled himself upon the throne with the tall grim figure of Lord Grey beside him, sword of state in hand. 'It was as if the King had got his Executioner by his side, and the whole picture looked strikingly typical of his and our future destinies.'[37]

*

With the dissolution the King found himself a popular hero, the champion of the people against privilege, reform's most doughty supporter. 'Vote for the two Bills,' was the reformers' slogan. To a monarch who prided himself on his impartiality and in fact found the principle of the Reform Bill of most questionable virtue, such applause was galling indeed. He was indignant when the Lord Mayor of London ordered illuminations in honour of the dissolution – and more indignant still when a mob broke the windows of those, like the Duke of Wellington, whose darkness was taken as betraying their distaste for reform. With chilling disdain he wrote to Grey: 'His Majesty admits that the expressions of loyalty and attachment to his person have been very general . . . but he cannot help ascribing these effusions of loyalty to the gratification of popular clamour by his sanction of a popular measure, rather than to any feeling upon which much reliance could be placed.'[38] Such cynicism hardly fits the conventional concept of a bluff buffoon who would do anything to win the plaudits of the mob.

With the prorogation the King had won time for the Whigs, given them a further chance to secure their precious reform. Now he felt it was Grey's turn to show goodwill. When Byam Martin complained to the King shortly after dissolution that the bill was too extensive, he replied: 'It ought to be made more moderate and I trust, by God, it will.'[39] To Grey he set out his ideas in more statesmanlike terms: 'a respite has been obtained; time is given for consideration and for revision, it may be remodelled.' Amendments, he argued, might now be introduced more freely than before the dissolution since, in victory, the Whigs could afford greater generosity.[40] Grey's reply was blandly non-committal. Changes there would be, but they would be minor ones – by definition unlikely to be of serious interest to the Tory hierarchy.[41]

The King had hoped his prime minister might have been more forthcoming but was by no means disposed to waver in his support. In May he confirmed this dramatically when Grey was given the blue riband of the Garter even though there was no vacancy in the order. '... a gross impropriety,' grumbled Wellington, '... not justified by services or by precedent.'[42] Most Tories dismissed the move as a *quid pro quo* for the ennoblement of the royal bastards – George FitzClarence became Earl of Munster in the same month. Cumberland and Gloucester were so indignant that they refused to attend the Chapter when Grey was invested; a foolish insult since the result, predictably, was to stiffen the King in his determination.

As always, everything stopped for Ascot. The King was bored to death with the races and his own horse broke down. After the races Greville dined at Windsor with forty other guests. 'What a *changement de décoration*,' he mused. 'No longer George IV, capricious, luxurious and misanthropic, liking nothing but the society of listeners and flatterers ... but a plain, vulgar, hospitable gentleman, opening his doors to all the world, with a numerous family and suite, with a frightful Queen and a posse of bastards, a Whig Minister, no foreigners and no Toad-eaters at all.' Idly he wondered how long this new order would endure. Not very long, he thought, as he watched the King: red-faced, portly, short of breath and visibly ageing as the strains of the monarchy took their toll. 'Queen, bastards, Whigs, all will disappear, and God knows what replace them.'[43]

So far as the elections were concerned, there was no hint that the Whigs were not in office for eternity. In virtually every constituency where there was any semblance of a popular vote the reforming candidate was returned triumphantly; in Huntingdonshire, for instance, an independent candidate won for the first time since 1688. Even where there was no question of a democratic result the borough-owners often went to great expense to ensure that government supporters replaced the sitting members. It was evident to everyone that the cause of reform had completely won the day so far as the House of Commons was concerned.

Curiously enough the Whig victory shook rather than strengthened the King's confidence in his ministers. For one thing the universities, against the trend, had returned anti-reformers to a man. Even Palmerston had been rejected for the Cambridge seat which he had held for twenty years. The King had always paid exaggerated respect to the cranky clerics who controlled the university seats and had told Princess Lieven that he would consider their judgment as the touchstone of the saner portion of his subjects.[44] The test had been made and the litmus paper had turned an emphatic shade of blue. For another, the elections had given rise to their usual crop of civil disorder; not as much as the gloomier prophets had forecast but still enough to upset the King. He felt the Whig triumph was tarnished by a tincture of demagoguery and coercion. 'It is impossible,' he wrote to Grey, 'that His Majesty should not have noticed with regret that there has, upon this occasion, been in many instances no real freedom of election; that violence and intimidation have had the effect of excluding it, that pledges have been called for and given by the candidate for popular favour to an extent which may be productive of extreme inconvenience to the Government hereafter . . .'[45]

But the real basis for his disquiet was simply that the Whig victory had been too complete. What chance was there, after his massive victory, that Grey would be disposed to compromise? Was it not all too likely that the very enormity of the enemy triumph would drive the Tories in the House of Lords into inveterate opposition? The cause of moderation and restraint had suffered a crippling blow. With the battle for reform in the House of Commons to all intents and purposes won, a new battle would now be waged between Commons and Lords. For the King this was the ultimate evil, 'an event the most prejudicial to the interests of the country at this period, and the most embarrassing to himself which could possibly occur.'[46] Ever since the fall of the Tory government he had fought to avert, or at least delay, the confrontation between reforming Commons and reactionary Lords. With the Whig triumph in May 1831 he realized that his time had almost run out.

CHAPTER XVI

Reform: the Second Phase

IN the summer of 1831 it seemed as if nothing could divert the British from their obsession with reform. Only one event, in fact, proved of comparable interest, at least as far as the capital was concerned. It was sad for the King that its theme should have been almost as vexatious to him as the battle for reform itself.

It is hard to be sure whether he had believed his words to be literally true when he told Lord Grey that his Coronation was over with the mere act of placing the crown upon his own head.* Certainly he would have liked it if the matter had been allowed to rest with such a sketchy ceremony. A full-dress affair, he considered, would be deplorably expensive and would foment the kind of agitation and excitement which he was most anxious to avoid.[1] He had gruesome memories of his brother's Coronation, with the injured Queen battering at the doors of Westminster Abbey.

His real objection to a Coronation was, however, far more fundamental. He considered it a pointless piece of flummery, a compound of superstition and sentimental antiquarianism which attempted to veil in mystery the perfectly straightforward relationship between a sovereign and his people. The King was a monument of unimaginative common sense. When the chaplain at Brighton prayed for rain his stentorian whisper, 'No good when the wind's in the south-east,' rumbled around the church. Similarly, he knew that he was king and that no amount of anointment with balm would make his kingship more real or permanent. At dinner when the ceremony was over he drily assured his court that 'he was not a whit more desirous than before taking the oath to watch over the liberties and promote the welfare of his people.'[2]

Hopefully he propounded an alternative project; that he should merely take the oath in front of the assembled Lords and Commons. He did not reckon with his more traditionalist subjects. Cumberland and Eldon seem to have launched the idea, partly no doubt out of

* See p. 189 above.

malice but also from genuine reverence for established forms. 'Their lunge,' wrote Holland to Lord Anglesey, 'was admirably parried by Grey and they are now manifestly afraid of provoking the King by swelling a matter disagreeable to him ... and ready, I suspect, to acquiesce in some compromise which will save H.M. from being greased by oil ...'[3] But the Duke of Wellington now took up the cause. The ceremony and the whole ceremony, was, he insisted, essential – anything less would be to cheat the people of their rights.[4]

Under protest the King agreed. He did, however, succeed in having it done more or less on the cheap. The 'Half Crownation' as it was commonly called dispensed with the usual banquet in Westminster Hall and the hire of a crown for the Queen. The Earl Marshal's pages were resplendent in 'blue frock coats, white breeches and stockings, a crimson silk sash and a small, ill-shaped hat with an ostrich feather', but since they paid for their costumes themselves, the Treasury could afford to be tolerant.[5] The most sumptuous carriage belonged to Prince Esterhazy, a foreign ambassador. 'The Coronation expense is limited to £20,000', wrote Mr Jekyll, '... so perhaps Gunter will contract for the whole of it ...'[6] The final cost, in fact, was a little over £30,000, against £240,000 for King George IV. This royal frugality was laughed at but also generally approved; the people, like the King, were not in the mood for pompous displays of wealth. They would no doubt also have endorsed his indignant refusal to let himself be kissed by the bishops, but this he was not allowed to get away with. 'As I expected,' recorded Greville, 'the Prelates would not stand it; the Archbishop remonstrated; the King knocked under ...'[7]

In spite, or perhaps because of, this cheese-paring, all passed off well on September 8. Everyone agreed that the Queen played her part well: 'with wonderful grace and dignity', said Macaulay. The King, too, did better than Lady Wharncliffe expected, but was 'very infirm in his walk, poor man, and looked oppress'd with the immense weight of his robes and crown'.[8] Brougham looked particularly absurd. 'His ugly features, his twitching nose, his Chancellor's wig hanging on each side of his face, surmounted by his coronet, made him resemble the lion in the Royal arms ...'; so much so that even the decorous Queen Adelaide did not dare look at him for fear of bursting into laughter.[9] In honour of the day the 'New Avenue', later to be known as The Mall, was illuminated and, though not yet completed, opened to the public. 'The coronation went off well,' summarized Greville, 'and whereas nobody was satisfied before it everybody was after it. No events of consequence.'[10]

One by-product was that the King was left with a grudge against the Tories; both for forcing the ceremony on him in the first place and then for their churlish behaviour when it took place. At one time, indeed, they threatened to boycott the service. The King treated their bluster with masterly indifference; 'he anticipates from it,' Taylor told Grey, 'greater convenience of room and less heat.'[11] But he nevertheless noticed with disapproval that Peel and Hardinge were among prominent Tories who did not attend, and it was a long time before he forgot the slight.[12]

In another way the Coronation also served the ends of the Whigs. 'Out of Evil comes good,' noted Lord Holland sanctimoniously, 'and the foolish Coronation . . . facilitates the elevation of a batch of peers.'[13] Certainly reinforcements were badly needed but the half-dozen or so creations did little more than underline the hopeless disadvantage under which the government laboured in the upper house. As the cheering died away and the crowds dispersed, government and opposition took up their battle positions while the King, no less dismayed at the prospect for being duly crowned, looked nervously from one side to the other, hoped for the best and waited for the worst.

*

Between June and September, 1831, the second Reform Bill was piloted through the House of Commons. The Tories hotly contested every clause. They did not really believe that they could introduce useful amendments in committee but were mistakenly convinced that, if time were won, the reforming fervour in the country would die down. Though Prince Leopold of Saxe-Coburg described the fury and activity with which the King's family sought to subvert his resolution and turn him against his ministers, William remained tranquilly on course.[14] 'All seems to me fair and above board,' wrote Lord Holland after a week-end at Windsor, and any stories to the contrary stemmed from the wishful thinking of the enemies to Reform.[15] But Grey was not at ease. In September a certain Colonel Torrens made an inflammatory speech against the House of Lords. Not unreasonably, the King deplored such conduct by a serving officer, and wanted him cashiered. Grey agreed the speech was intemperate and indecent but suggested to Taylor that it would be going too far to dismiss a loyal officer for a single indiscretion.[16] Both points of view were tenable but it is hard to see that Grey had any real grounds for writing gloomily to Holland on the same day: 'The affair of Torrens convinces me that the people who compose the King's private society have had some effect.'[17] The trouble about consistently expecting the worst is that sooner or later one is likely to make it come to pass. Grey, constantly taking the temperature at Windsor and broadcasting what he found there in pessimistic bulletins to his friends, did much to create the suspicion and distrust which he wished so anxiously to dispel.

To the King Torrens's speech was deplorable above all because it was calculated to stir up a spirit of resentment among the lower classes. The ultimate evil arose when those classes organized themselves to achieve a common purpose. Any form of union among such people was to be deplored unless properly supervised by a member of the local gentry, and he drew no distinction between unions designed to promote economic ends and those with wider political purposes. Nor, it is only fair to say, did most of those involved in the unions themselves. His Whig ministers shared the King's distaste for organized labour but Lord Melbourne at least showed greater *sang-froid* when it came to assessing the risks involved. Strikes for higher pay impressed him as particularly absurd. He cited to the King the case of some labourers in the north of England who were striking to have their wages raised from 25/- a week to 30/- a week. A twelve week strike would cost them £15 and even if they won their 5/- it would be more than a year before they made up the loss. 'This is so clearly a losing game,' concluded the Home Secretary with magnificent confidence, 'that its disadvantage must in time become obvious to the most vulgar understanding.'[18]

Melbourne, however, did not pretend that the same elementary arithmetic could be relied on to curb the unions if they were deprived of the reform which they had been promised. Indeed the Whigs saw some profit in making the King's flesh creep with visions of an outraged electorate rising in arms to defend its rights. Even in the Dorsetshire Yeomanry, Melbourne darkly informed the King, the spirit of party was so strong that their loyalty could not be relied on if the Bill were dropped or even substantially amended.[19] This echoed the King's starkest fears. He could never escape the conviction that any union of the lower classes, whatever its guise, was bent upon outrage and revolution. It was an illusion which was to plague his anyway half-agreeing ministers for the rest of his reign.

*

The certainty of an eventual clash between Lords and Commons had existed since the first Reform Bill had passed the House of Commons. King William had continued to assure both himself and his prime minister that a confrontation could be averted by a few judicious concessions. Grey he totally failed to convince; it is doubtful if he even managed to delude himself. The alternative, however, he resolutely declined to contemplate and Grey shrank from forcing him to do so until it was absolutely necessary. Correspondence between King and prime minister was curiously artificial, both men skirting around the issue which in fact preoccupied them both.

The Tories assumed that the pass was already sold: 'We hear every day of peers to be created,' wrote Wellington to Buckingham in July, 'and I confess that I concur with you in thinking that Lord Grey will stick at nothing. There can scarcely be a question about the King, considering what His Majesty has done by *dissolution*.'[20] The high Tories seemed to have evolved a singular image of the King – some sort of zombie, enslaved by malign Whig influences, allied with 'the mob, the Radicals, the Dissenters of all persuasions', against the Gentlemen of Property and the Church (revealingly cited by Wellington in that order).[21] Yet the concept was little more inaccurate than the Whig fantasy of a reactionary monarch seeking to destroy his ministers and open to every kind of right wing influence. Alarmed, bemused and trying desperately to be fair, the King buried his head in the Windsor sands and pretended that no crisis was at hand.

In October it arose. The Second Reform Bill was defeated decisively in the House of Lords. The opposition's majority of forty-one included twenty-one bishops. The King's reaction was unsurprising. Obviously, he told Grey, this was likely to happen if the Whigs made no concession to their enemies. Then for the first time he came to the crux of the matter – in terms that would have amazed and delighted the Duke of Wellington. '. . . the evil,' he wrote, 'cannot be met by resorting to measures for obtaining a majority in the House of Lords which no Government could propose and no Sovereign consent to, without losing sight of what is due to the character of that House, to the honour of the Aristocracy of the country, and to the dignity of the throne.'[22] In short, he would not contemplate the creation of enough peers to force through the measure.

Given the history of the next nine months it is curious to note the extent to which his ministers not only accepted this decision but positively welcomed it. As early as September 3 the cabinet had considered a proposal to make what Grey, in a slightly tendentious phrase, referred to as 'an inordinate number of peers.'[23] Lansdowne, Graham and Stanley had said they would rather resign, only Brougham was whole-heartedly in favour and he already was pursuing courses so devious as to have forfeited the trust of many of his colleagues. When defeat came in the Lords Grey's first reaction was said to have been relief at its scale, since 'no one now could ask him to make peers.'[24] To Herbert Taylor he said bluntly, 'the amount of the majority puts all notion of an attempt to counteract it by a further creation of Peers quite out of the question.' He would anyway, he added for good measure, have been extremely reluctant to resort to such a measure, even if a mere handful of peers had been involved.[25] Althorp agreed, writing to his father that the country would never accept so massive a creation.[26] Those people who criticized the King for being so reluctant in the spring of 1832 to coerce the Lords by the threat of a mass creation should remember that only a few months before the prime minister and other champions of reform had assured him that such a step was unthinkable.

Instead the Whigs contemplated resignation. The only chance for reform in the Lords seemed to be that it should be brought forward by its enemies. If the King had encouraged them in such a course the history of British politics in the nineteenth century might have read very differently. But he did not; on the contrary he told Grey that he would view the retirement of ministers as a great evil and urged him not even to consider it. Nervously the Whigs concurred. They would remain in office, they would continue the battle for a substantially unamended measure of reform, they would not seek to tamper with the structure of the House of Lords. To the King the programme must have seemed wholly acceptable; if he suspected also that it was too good to be true then he kept his suspicions to himself.

*

At this moment, when it was so necessary for King and prime minister to work together in mutual confidence, the relationship was soured by a silly and unnecessary squabble. The affair of Lord Howe was in itself of minimal importance, the rancour which it created between court and ministers inflated it into something close to a national disaster.

Lord Howe was one of those curious individuals whose actions, letters and reported speeches stamp them as so insufferable that it is impossible to understand the powerful charm which they apparently

held for some of their contemporaries. He was fatuous, foppish and
ineffably vain. At Eton he had been known as 'Miss Curzon', notorious
for his effeminacy and silliness. His subsequent career had done nothing
to prove his schoolmates wrong. Yet the King liked him and valued
his judgment, while Queen Adelaide, whose Lord Chamberlain he
was, doted on him. Greville saw the relationship as one in which Howe
gave all and the Queen coolly received the homage; Howe was 'like a
boy in love with this frightful spotted Majesty'.[27] This, however, was
not the popular view. Adelaide was believed to be besotted with her
Chamberlain and the two were often alleged to be lovers – 'Oh Lord
Howe wonderful are thy ways', as Lord Alvanley remarked when
rumours spread that the Queen was enjoying a belated pregnancy.[28]
No one who knows anything of the Queen could credit so absurd an
accusation, but everything indicated that she felt bound to her Chamberlain by strong romantic ties.

Unfortunately Lord Howe found it impossible to behave with the
discretion which this relationship and his office should have imposed
upon him. He was a convinced Tory; an aberration which Grey would
have been prepared to swallow if he had been modestly prudent in his
political activities but found hard to tolerate when Howe insisted on
playing a prominent role in opposition. In May, 1831, Grey protested
when Howe signed an Address from the people of Kent against the
Reform Bill. He wanted the King to rebuke his erring servant and
Taylor promised that this would be done if the subject came up. Somewhat disingenuously he added that this might easily never happen:
'Indeed Politics are not the Topic of Conversation here.'[29]

Unabashed, Howe now signed a similar declaration from the people
of Warwickshire. Taylor realized that things were going too far and
wrote him a stiff letter passing on the King's displeasure. But he did
so with some disquiet. '. . . the knowledge of my communication,'
he told Grey, 'has given extreme uneasiness to the Queen who dreads
the loss of Lord Howe's services . . .'[30] Howe contemplated resignation
and consulted the Duke of Wellington who counselled him to stay in
office and act with prudence.[31] Conceivably Howe would have followed
this sage advice if he had not been enraged by the leaking of Taylor's
rebuke to The Times,[32] Furiously he wrote to Wellington of a Whig
plot to separate the King from all his true friends: 'Nothing shall now
induce me to resign. I have the King's leave to vote as I like; my opinions
are firmly but temperately declared; and my Lord Brougham may yet
find me a thorn in his side.'[33]

Given this belligerent attitude it is surprising that battle was not renewed until October of the same year. Then Howe was responsible for – or, at least, was not prepared to disavow – a letter strongly attacking the government in the *Standard*. Grey insisted that Howe must go and had his way. 'All is right at Windsor,' he wrote jubilantly to Lord Anglesey, 'and Lord Howe's resignation has been accepted.'[34] But all, as he was soon to find, was far from right. Queen Adelaide interpreted the dismissal of her favourite as a direct insult. Almost overnight she was transformed from a demure housewife into a virago, determined to avenge the martyr in the blood of his adversaries. 'Never was so fierce a foe as the Greatest Lady in the Land,' wrote an awe-struck Lady Holland, who was no mean performer as a foe herself.[35] The Queen's diary, normally the most humdrum of documents, in this one entry reveals her depth of feeling.

'. . . I had trusted in, and built firmly on the king's love to me. But unfortunately he has not been able to resist the representations of his Ministers, and yielded, and I fear it will be the beginning of much evil. May God support us and protect and shield this country and save the king from ruin. I had a hard struggle before I appeared at table, after this blow, which I felt deeply as an insult, which filled me with indignation. I felt myself deeply wounded both as wife and queen . . .'[36]

Lord Grey was the principal victim of her wrath. When he went to Windsor the King carefully shielded him from Queen Adelaide and even two months later the prime minister found her polite enough but 'her civility at freezing point'. More serious, she seemed intent on rallying the Tory opponents of reform into a kind of Queen's party.[37] 'The Queen continues to pout. I know not why but I know *How* . . .' wrote Holland archly in October,[38] and at the end of the year she was still complaining angrily about the insult she had suffered.[39] Lord Anglesey, who was usually a reliable reporter, saw the King in March, 1832 and pointed out the dangers of being surrounded exclusively by Tory relations and courtiers. According to Anglesey the King agreed but said that it was all the Queen's fault. He led, he complained, a life of the damned.[40] The remark seems strangely out of character; William was usually hot in defence of his Queen. If he ever did speak in such a way however it could only have been at this moment, in the few months after Howe's dismissal, when Adelaide's rancour made her an embarrassment and a nuisance to her husband.

The dismissal of Howe as Chamberlain did not entail his exile from court; on the contrary, he seemed to be there as much as ever. In April, 1832, with the crisis over reform nearing its height, he abandoned his invalid wife to spend a week at Windsor. 'To say the *least* it is very indiscreet in the Great Lady,'[41] chided Lady Holland. The Queen wrote to him when he was away, assuring him early in 1832 that the King's eyes were now open to the perils around him. '. . . but I am afraid,' she concluded sadly, '[he] has the fixed idea that no other administration could be formed at present . . .'[42] With astonishing impropriety she suggested that Howe show the letter to the Duke of Wellington. The Duke at least knew what conduct was becoming from a Queen. His reply was brusque, lapidary and discouraging. 'I can do no more in Parliament,' he concluded. 'I can do nothing out of Parliament. Remember me most kindly to Lady Howe . . .'[43]

Though Adelaide's importunity sometimes annoyed the King it was not without its effect. The more he considered it, the more he felt that he had been badly treated, that Howe's dismissal had been a poor return for his loyal support of ministers. He showed his displeasure by refusing to prorogue Parliament in person.[44] Grey, answering the intention rather than the word, stressed the great pain he had felt at having to interfere in the composition of the Queen's household. He besought the King to relent.[45] William yielded but Grey can have been left in little doubt that the injury had not been forgiven or forgotten.

Within a few days the King was given fresh reason to deplore the activities of his ministers. In a reply to a motion of thanks from the Birmingham Union, Lord John Russell indulged in some fine polemical flourishes and enquired rhetorically whether it was conceivable that the whisper of a faction should prevail against the voice of a nation. To the King, who considered that the main preoccupation of the Whigs should be to conciliate the House of Lords, it seemed that to categorize their vote as 'the whisper of a faction' was perverse and provocative. Grey, who was anyhow disposed to agree, persuaded Russell to apologize and to assure the King that he had not meant to refer to the whole of the House of Lords but only the lunatic Right.[46]

William's confidence in his ministers was shaken. Lady Louisa Percy dined at the Pavilion at the end of November. She found that: 'The poor King looked worried to death. Tory as I am I could not help pitying him. When one looks at him with his good-humoured, silly countenance, it does strike one that Fate made a cruel mistake in placing him where he has to ride the whirlwind and direct the storm.'[47] Increasingly distrustful of his ministers, tortured by doubts about the wisdom of their policy, plagued by his Queen and courtiers, confronted by the certainty of that clash between Lords and Commons which he had sought so earnestly to avert, it would have been surprising if he had not at least half shared Lady Louisa's sentiment. The joys of kingship, which had seemed so bright only a year before, were now burning dim indeed.

*

There was little in the state of the country to comfort him. Generalizations about 'the people' are always suspect but if ever they can properly be said to have reacted as an entity it was to the defeat of the Reform Bill by the Lords in the autumn of 1831. A wave of indignation washed over all but the most feudal and traditionalist enclaves of the British Isles. In London the shops closed, there was a run on gold and a monster meeting in Regent's Park. The following day one of the mightiest processions ever seen in London presented Lord Melbourne with an address to the King. The provinces did not linger far behind, all over the country meetings of protest were held, the homes of noted anti-Reformers attacked, the Bishops' palaces singled out for particularly unfriendly attention. In Derby the Borough Gaol was stormed, in Nottingham the castle set on fire. But these were trifling incidents compared with the holocaust which engulfed Bristol three weeks later when the arrival of the deeply disliked Recorder, Sir Charles Wetherell, led to three days' rioting in which a large part of the city was gutted and many people killed.

At least, noted Greville sagaciously, the tragedy would open people's eyes; not that that would do much good with 'a mob-ridden Government and a foolish King, who renders himself subservient to all the wickedness and folly of his Ministers.'[48] The question remained, to what their eyes were opened? To ministers the riots showed the vital need of quickly giving the people the reform which they craved. To the King it suggested even more strongly that the greatest evil was to incite the masses and that it was his duty to patch up some understanding between Whig and Tory which would stop the controversy being thus carried into the public forum. Yet the riots did not cause him half as much uneasiness as the growing strength and activity of the political unions and the support given them by the radical press. Things, he felt, were reaching a pass when the unions would be more powerful than the government itself.[49]

Such fears were, of course, grotesquely exaggerated, but the growth of the unions had indeed been striking. At first springing up in the north and north-west they had quickly spread over most of the country – gatherings of earnest and, for the most part, eminently well-intentioned citizens bent on asserting their opinion in the only forum in which they had a voice. They were credited with a far greater degree of organization than they in fact possessed and, by the Tories at least, were believed to be in intimate contact with revolutionary elements on the continent. On this subject the King was as Tory as any of the opposition. He urged the prime minister that the Bristol riots should be made the occasion of banning unions over the whole country.[50] Grey saw force in the King's arguments; indeed most of the Whig ministers were as alarmist as their Tory counterparts. He would have been more than human, however, if he had resisted pointing out that, while he would do his best to discourage the unions, their success was the inevitable consequence of the folly of the House of Lords.[51]

Now Wellington thundered into the fray. Appropriately selecting the fifth of November as the date to take alarm, he wrote to the King of 'a great crisis' which seemed to be approaching. The Birmingham political union, he claimed, was being supplied with arms; revolution could only be a step away.[52] The King replied in friendly but noncommittal terms[53] and passed the letter to Grey. To his prime minister he said that he had told Wellington that he thought the latter had 'very unnecessarily taken alarm',[54] but in fact his reply read as if he shared the fears of the duke. Certainly Wellington referred to it approvingly as 'very stout'[55] and Grey objected that a simple acknowledgment would have been more in order. Grey was able to show that Wellington's 'evidence' did not stand up to examination and the net result of the exercise was to diminish the duke's influence over the King.

Nevertheless, on November 21, a proclamation banned political unions or, at least, those which were organized on a basis designed to equip them for rapid recourse to arms.[56] The King grumbled that the trades unions were not included and urged still greater vigour: '. . . the present moment,' he told Melbourne, 'is propitious for any measure which is calculated to put down lawless combinations.' To act would be to help, not impede, the Reform Bill since it would confound those who associated its progress with all sorts of unconstitutional and dangerous projects.[57] Still, with all its faults, the proclamation at least showed that ministers were not blind to the dangers. '. . . the King is quite satisfied and goes on with them as well as ever !' recorded Wellington peevishly.[58]

*

The worse things grew in the country, the more the King hankered after some compromise on reform. He found allies in a group of moderates among the Tories. The Waverers, as the group was soon christened, were led by Lords Wharncliffe and Harrowby. Ingenious, industrious and well-meaning, these two lords toiled for months to establish a consensus between the parties. Their weakness was that, in the last resort, they spoke for nobody except themselves. Wellington approved their efforts in general terms but would enter into no commitment to accept any particular measure of reform.[59] On the other side, while certain Whigs, pre-eminently Palmerston, were ready to contemplate quite substantial concessions, none of them was prepared to put them forward so that the Tories could pocket them and then seek to negotiate from their strengthened position.

The King did all he could to ease the bargaining. To Grey he defined his role by quoting Bolingbroke's prescription for the Patriot King when reforms were demanded: 'to render by his influence the proceedings more orderly and more deliberate'.[60] But he interpreted this role pretty liberally, not hesitating to press his minister to make specific concessions. He forwarded approvingly to Lord Melbourne a letter from 'the respectable tradesmen of London' which urged that those with large property should be granted additional votes.[61] Melbourne himself was hardly a champion of the proletariat but he replied with surprising firmness that any such measure would give an unfair influence to property.[62]

The crux of the matter was that few Whigs were disposed to concede anything which might be of real interest to their adversaries. Grey himself might have supported Palmerston but with Russell, Durham and above all Brougham surveying his manoeuvres with sharp distaste, he knew that he could not get away with anything of substance. In November he sent the King a formidable catalogue of the points of principle which separated Whigs and Waverers.[63] The King was undeterred. Even after the revised Bill had been introduced into the House of Commons he went on trying. At the beginning of 1832 he received Lord Wharncliffe several times and warmly applauded his initiative. 'I agree with every word you say,' he told his gratified but still despondent ally. 'We are indeed in a scrape, and we must get out of it as we can. I only wish everybody was as reasonable and as moderate as you . . .'[64] Brougham did his best to convince the King that the bill could not be modified,[65] patiently Grey pointed out the arguments against every proposed amendment – nothing would convince the King that a modicum of reason on either side would not quickly resolve the differences.

To Brougham, however, he did admit that he thought the likely results of the change were greatly exaggerated; 'once the Bill was passed, things would slide into an easy and quiet posture as before.'[66] The day after the King expressed himself so cheerily Wellington told Wharncliffe that: 'neither Lord Grey nor any nobleman of his order, nor any gentleman of his cast, will govern the country six weeks after the Reformed Parliament will meet, and that the race of English gentlemen will not last long afterwards.'[67] Posterity can judge whether monarch or duke came nearer to understanding the realities of their country.

CHAPTER XVII

Reform: Lords against Commons

AND SO, in the early months of 1832, the battle for the Reform Bill entered its final phase. Most of the protagonists were clearly identified: the Whigs sticking to the essentials of their Bill, the Tory Lords intransigent in opposition, the Waverers fluttering ineffectively between the two. Only the position of the King was in doubt; only he, in the last resort, could coerce the House of Lords into acquiescence. By creating peers out of accredited Whigs he could at any moment drown the built-in majority which the Tories could normally rely on in the Upper House, yet by so doing he risked destroying the fabric of the House itself. It was a prospect which appalled him. For almost twelve months he had lived in the consciousness that sooner or later this would be asked of him – always he had thrust it to the back of his mind in the hope that something would turn up to avert the need. Mainly because he too was aghast at the idea, Grey had done nothing to provoke the issue. At last, however, silence was no longer practicable as a course of action.

It was Sir James Graham, First Lord of the Admiralty, who precipitated the matter. He pointed out in cabinet that as recently as October 8 the prime minister had assured Taylor that a mass creation of peers was out of the question.[1] Now it seemed clear that the bill could not otherwise be passed. Unless the issue was put before the King he threatened to resign. Brougham supported him – if the King could be persuaded to agree in principle, he argued, then it was highly unlikely that the need to create peers would ever arise in practice.[2] On the other wing of the Cabinet, Lansdowne, Melbourne, Palmerston and Richmond seemed to consider the surrender of the bill a lesser evil than the destruction of the House of Lords. Reluctantly and after much anguished dithering, Althorp and Grey rallied to the activists.

On January 3 Grey called on the King at Brighton. His instructions – which he carried out with barely concealed distaste – were to press for a small immediate creation of peers, more as a token than anything else, and a promise to create as many more as might be necessary when and if the time came. He was strikingly gloomy about his prospects. 'The King, you are aware,' he told Holland, 'would dislike the thing to the greatest degree, and I have less hope of surmounting his repugnance, which will be confirmed by the concurrence in his opinion of some of the most important members of the Government ...'[3]

As so often, he misjudged the King. William was not prepared to abet the total frustration of reform by a reactionary House of Lords. Grey had come to Brighton proposing to speak in generalities, the King disconcerted him by switching to the particular. How many peers would it be necessary to create? Would not the very fact of creation alienate the moderate opposition and thus increase the majority against the bill? Would the government undertake to promote only the eldest sons of existing peers and thus preserve the present structure of the House of Lords? He ended with a plea. If he supported the government, would they in turn support the prerogative of the crown if it was threatened in the future? He was not conscious, he said wistfully, 'of having betrayed any disposition to an extravagant display of dignity or splendour, or to the exercise of despotic and arbitrary power.' Surely then, he should be protected against that 'growing fancy for *Liberalism*' which was menacing all the institutions of the country?[4]

Grey was quite unprepared to answer the royal questionnaire and could only undertake to refer the various points to his colleagues. He found them jubilant. The King's 'substantial acquiescence in the measure,' noted Lord Holland, 'and his unexpected ... disdain of diluting it, if resorted to, by not giving us a sufficient number, has, I hope, reconciled ... some of the more timid among us.'[5] But though encouraged, they found it difficult to reply. They had not the remotest idea how many new peers might be needed. The King had talked of twenty-one and had indicated that he would be ready to make this number straight away and thus end the matter. His ministers had an ugly suspicion that in the long run more than twice as many might be called for. All they were prepared to proffer by way of advice was that it would be best to wait and see but that, if the crisis came, the King should 'allow them the power of acting at once up to the exigency of the case.'[6]

Meanwhile the Tories fumed at what they took to be the surrender of the King. Lord Salisbury delivered a solemn warning; Lords Wharncliffe and Harrowby buzzed busily around the court, murmur-

ing that only minor concessions were needed to reach a solution satisfactory to everyone. Buckingham pleaded with Wellington to take
up the charge but the duke refused. What hope was there, he asked, of
persuading the King to dismiss his ministers and embark on a new
course when the risks of such a course were so clearly overwhelming?
'... the great mischief of all,' he concluded, 'is the weakness of our
poor King, who cannot or will not see his danger, or the road out of
it when it is pointed out to him ...'[7]

Undismayed, Buckingham decided on direct assault. Lord Chandos,
eldest son of the duke, sent Herbert Taylor a long letter intended for
the King which set out the arguments against a creation of peers.
Taylor passed the letter to Lord Grey, 'to be communicated to the
King by him if he should think so fit'. Blandly he told Lord Chandos
that such, he supposed, had been the latter's intention. 'This was
meeting the thing capitally and really makes as good a joke of it as I
ever heard,' wrote Althorp appreciatively to Lord John Russell.[8]

But clumsy though the efforts of the Tory lords might be, it should
not be forgotten that the arguments against a creation of peers carried
a great deal of weight – not only with the King but with all but the
most extreme of the Whig leaders. To overrule and radically refashion
one House at the behest of the other was, after all, to tinker with an
essential element of the constitution. 'What becomes then,' asked
Wellington, 'of the independence of the House of Lords? After such a
precedent, it could be of no use to the existence of the monarchy, none
to the democracy. It would be the ridicule of the public and a disgrace
to itself.'[9] The thought would not have been very differently expressed
by Palmerston or Melbourne. What was more, as the King himself
pointed out to Grey, the introduction of a cohort of peers nominated
by the government to act as their docile instruments, would be contrary to the principle of the very Reform Bill which it was supposed to
help. To pass a bill dedicated to the abolition of nomination boroughs
by creating a bevy of nomination peers was a recourse which smacked
of the ridiculous, if not the actively dishonest.[10] None of this, of course,
affected the essential point – that only the creation of peers, or at least,
the threat to do so, would make possible the passage of even modestly
radical legislation – but it still seemed of immeasurable significance
to the doubters and moderates of 1832.

It was not, therefore, a light request which was being made of the
King. Even after his encouraging reception at Brighton Grey was by no
means certain which way the cat would jump. When he read the

opening paragraphs of the King's reply his heart must have sunk still further. William stressed the importance he attached to the House of Lords: 'he looks,' he wrote, 'to that House principally . . . for the support of the Monarchy, and for the exertion of due vigour in resisting popular clamour . . .'[11] He had agreed, he said, to dilute that House by the creation of twenty-one new peers. Now he was being asked for *carte blanche*: 'the King is required to surrender into the hands of his Ministers this important prerogative, to be exercised without any other reserve or limit than that which their calculation or anticipation of the difficulties or opposition they may have to encounter shall produce . . . ' So far so bad, then came the twist for which Grey must have been praying. At the last the King relented. Provided it was first shown unequivocally that the bill would otherwise fail, provided his condition was met about heirs to peerages furnishing the vast majority of the new recruits, then he would accept his ministers' advice. Echoing the words of Lord Grey's letter he pledged that he would empower them to act 'up to the full exigency of the case'. In other words the Whigs could have as many new peers as they felt they needed. Grey had been given all that he had asked for and far more than he had expected.

*

In the middle of January, therefore, the King promised the Whigs to create peers when the need arose. Less than four months later he accepted the resignation of his ministers rather than create the peers they asked for. Treachery is an accusation which has frequently been flung at him; inconsistency, at least, is a charge from which he can hardly be acquitted. Yet when one surveys the tangled history of that intervening period – the irresolution and endless conscience pangs of Grey; the dubious manoeuvring of Lord Brougham; the arcane juggling of the doubters and moderates on both sides of the party line; the tactless blundering of the Whig leaders; the unscrupulous nerve-warfare of certain Tory propagandists – it is hard to decide how the burden of blame should be apportioned.

For the King the most disconcerting factor was certainly the conduct of Lord Grey. If ever a letter called for a brisk and grateful acknowledgment followed by silence it was this one. Grey should have left the King alone, tactfully reminded him from time to time of his undertaking, and sent in the bill when the time arose. Instead he replied in a massive letter of more than two thousand words, rehearsing the various

weaknesses in his own case. Within a few weeks he was dwelling on the
'repugnance, amounting to aversion' which he felt for the measure,
then, almost in the same breath, threatening to precipitate a creation
even before the government was defeated.[12] A few days later he was
ready to take almost any risk to avoid such a step,[13] and by March 12,
having thoroughly alarmed the King to no good purpose, he announced that, after all, the government had decided to wait and see
what happened when the bill was debated.[14]

But Grey's greatest folly was yet to come. Althorp questioned the
decision to defer the creation and Grey wrote to him arguing that his
tactics were the best. In this letter he rehearsed with apparent relish
all the objections which existed to swamping the House of Lords with
a new creation. 'It is a measure of extreme violence,' he concluded.
'There is no precedent for it in our history; ... it is a certain evil,
dangerous itself as a precedent; and, with all these objections, in my
opinion very uncertain of success.'[15]

Evidently pleased with his felicity of phrasing, he forwarded a copy
of the letter to the King. William saw all his worst fears set out by the
very man who had urged him into so unpalatable a commitment. True,
Grey in the end concluded that a creation of peers might be the least
of many evils, but by that time the harm was done. The King was not a
subtle man and it was the obtrusive doubts which impressed him in
Grey's letter, not the underlying certainty in the correctness of the
conclusion. If Grey, a partisan, could argue thus, how much more
should the King think twice and then think again. It is impossible to
establish any precise chronology in the development of William's
views, but the sharp change apparent in the second half of March must
in part at least reflect Lord Grey's well-meant but disastrously ill-
timed honesty.

The Tory Waverers, just because they were Tories, could not hope
to achieve results as dramatic as the Whig leader. Wharncliffe and
Harrowby, however, contributed their mite of mischief. Lady Wharncliffe, staying with the royal family at Brighton, was agreeably surprised at the style with which life was conducted.

'I have also been surprised,' she went on, 'to see how much his
mind seems *préoccupé*. I am sure he is very much annoyed and dissatisfied with the state of things – but he can no longer extricate
himself . . . His absent fits and melancholy countenance at Commerce
sometimes, from which he rouses and exerts himself to be gay and

K.W.

sociable, proved to me *at once* that he was *thinking* a great deal more than we give him credit for.'[16]

For this disquiet her husband was largely responsible. Lord Wharncliffe denounced any proposal to make peers and eventually told Taylor bluntly that, if such a creation took place, he and all his allies would oppose the second reading of the bill in the House of Lords.[17] This threat confirmed the King's blackest suspicions. How could he know that any given number of new peers would prove sufficient? 'The step might therefore have been resorted to,' he wailed to Grey, 'twenty-five or thirty Peers added, and the Bill might still be lost . . .'[18] Grey commented gloomily that, even if the bill did scrape through at the second reading, it would probably be mauled in committee and a belated creation would then, after all, be necessary. This horrified the King, who had visualized the passage of the bill on the second reading as the ultimate horizon beyond which he would at last find peace. Surely in committee the government would be ready to make whatever concessions were needed to protect the essence of the bill?

Still, towards the end of February, as the bill ground once more through the House of Commons, it must have seemed to the Whigs that things were going reasonably well. A fair number of peers who had voted against the bill on the last occasion, had now promised to switch or, at least, abstain. Lord Munster told Hobhouse that the general opinion at court was that the bill would pass, even though it was not expected that the government would long survive their triumph. Most important of all, Lord Melbourne believed that the King was now better disposed towards the measure: 'i.e.,' commented Greville cynically, 'they have got the foolish old man in town and can talk him over more readily.'[19]

Then came the affair of Queen Adelaide and the bishops. The bishops presented an Address to the Queen and, in her oral reply, she included the phrase: 'I trust you will strenuously exert yourselves, as you have hitherto so honourably done, for the preservation of our Church and State. Believe me, that I am heart and soul devoted to your maintenance.' Unfortunately the bishops' most strenuous exertion to preserve the State over the last few years had been to vote as a bloc against the Reform Bill. The Queen's speech was greeted with outrage by the Whig newspapers and provoked a mildly reproachful letter from Grey.[20] The King's riposte was indignant, as always when his wife was attacked. Adelaide's reply had been 'as unexceptionable in all respects, and as free from political allusion as possible'; her conduct over the last few months had been notably cautious and guarded.[21] Grey, it was implied, should have leapt to her defence, not passed on the slurs of the gutter press as though they deserved serious attention.

On March 26 the amended Reform Bill, duly passed by the Commons, was remitted to the Lords. The final count down had begun. The King was working busily to avert disaster. The Archbishop of Canterbury who, in theory at least, could powerfully influence his fellow churchmen, was a principal target but all the bishops came in for an unwonted share of royal attention. The Bishop of Worcester rallied to the cause;[22] Lord Glasgow promised that he would at least stay away; heavy, though in the end unsuccessful pressure was brought on the Commander-in-Chief, Lord Hill.[23] But there were limits beyond which William would not go; as when he declined Lord Ferrers' offer to vote with the Government if his former mistress, now wife, were only received at court.[24] Grey observed the King's manoeuvres with the patronizing approval of a parent whose child is engaged in a creditably convincing game of make believe. More and more he was becoming convinced that a few votes here and there would make little difference; even if the second reading passed his troubles would barely have begun.

At the end of March the cabinet, in what appears to have been a totally unnecessary minute calculated to alarm the King and resolve nothing, again raised the spectre of a narrow majority which would lead to subsequent defeat in committee. The King reiterated that he would be ready to create peers if the need arose but added the ominous proviso: 'subject to His Majesty's consideration of the nature and extent of the addition.'[25] If the bill were defeated, he commented, the government should consider recasting it to fit in with the ideas of the moderate opposition.

Thoroughly alarmed, Lord Grey hastened to Windsor. The King was affable enough, indeed reassuring in a non-committal sort of way, but on the issue which really preoccupied his prime minister he refused to budge. He would not commit himself to create peers if the opposition tampered with the bill in committee. Grey considered resignation; but to surrender before battle had even been joined seemed craven to his colleagues if not to him. No course was left but to wait and see – and while away the time by further discussing with William details of the measure which he prayed would never be necessary and which he feared the King would not agree to even if it were. Would it not be

possible, he asked, to include a few commoners among the new peers?
Certainly not, said the King. There were plenty of Whig lords whose
eldest sons had not been included on the list. What, for instance, about
Grey's own son, Howick? He was ready to sacrifice himself, surely his
ministers could do as much?

On April 14, with a majority of nine, the House of Lords voted for
the second reading of the Reform Bill. Thirty-nine peers switched their
vote, either to active support or at least to abstention. The result was a
triumph for the persistence and persuasiveness of Lord Grey, but it also
reflected the zeal with which the King had canvassed for the measure.
Brougham reported that he was 'prodigiously up . . . and took great
credit to himself for having always predicted that it would be so.'[26]
The Whigs too were gratified, but with the more restrained enthusiasm
of those who knew that every silver lining has a cloud. Their apprehension was quickly justified. As soon as the Easter recess was over, discussion of the bill began in committee. Lord Lyndhurst at once proposed that discussion of Schedules A and B, the lists of boroughs to be
disfranchized, should be deferred until later in the debate. It is doubtful
if the Tory leaders meant to do more than remind the government of its
weak position and thus fire a warning shot across its bows. Grey,
however, preferred to interpret it as an overt declaration of intent to
destroy the bill. When the amendment was passed by thirty-five votes
he promptly adjourned the House. A cabinet next morning on May 8,
decided that it must resign unless the King would immediately create
as many peers as might be necessary to pass the bill in its entirety.[27]
Armed with this ultimatum, Lord Grey once more took the road to
Windsor.

*

It is hard to speak with any confidence about the state of the King's
mind; probably he himself was far from sure what he ought to do.
His original aversion to the creation of peers, never allayed, had now
returned redoubled.[28] He told Lord Verulam that 'to destroy one
branch of the Legislature for any particular purpose, sanctioned only
by the other . . . would be a flagrant violation of my coronation oath';[29]
and when this hoary spectre began to trouble the royal conscience,
ministers could be certain that their troubles were great indeed. What,
from the point of view of the Whigs, was even worse was that he
poured out his doubts to all and sundry, even to such casual visitors
as the surgeon, Keate. 'Is there no way,' asked Brougham in despair, 'of

suggesting to him that this is sure to destroy the Bill? . . . he had much better turn us out than cut our throats in this way.'[30]

In part at least his change of heart may have been due to the relentless pressure of his entourage at Windsor. 'All the Royal Family, bastards and all, have been incessantly *at* the King,' wrote Greville.[31] Queen Adelaide had decided that the present issue was too important to allow of any scruples. She preached the iniquities of the bill to anyone who would listen, freely asserting that, rather than have the King yield, she would see him by the side of the exiled Bourbon, Charles X, in Holyrood House.[32] Her relations by marriage were no more reticent, even the notoriously feather-headed Duchess of Gloucester was supposed to be active in the campaign. 'From what I know of Her Royal Highness,' wrote Taylor drily to Grey in one of the few letters which he ever admitted had not been shown to the King, 'I should doubt Her ever bothering Her head about Politics . . . But you are aware that, with one exception,* the Members of the Royal Family, Male and Female, are Hostile to it and I have no doubt that Her language may be influenced by this feeling . . .'[33]

In April, also, a sharp disagreement over foreign policy; notably towards France, had driven Grey to the edge of resignation. Monster open-air meetings in Edinburgh, London, Birmingham and other cities contributed to the spirit of brooding disaster and confirmed the King in his fear that the Whigs had given birth to a monster which they could not control. But the best explanation of his attitude towards ministers was that stated by Taylor to Lord Grey. '. . . the continued agitation, during fourteen months, of a question which has assumed so many features, and has been the occasion of almost uninterrupted worry, uneasiness and embarrassment. It is natural that all this should have produced some irritability and impatience . . .'[34] Nothing was left, as Brougham put it in a curiously poignant phrase of 'their first good fellowship and fun,'[35] and, in the circumstances of 1832, a correct but chilly relationship could not be enough. The pity for Grey was that the virtual breakdown of his rapport with the King should have occurred at the moment when William's support was most needed to see the bill through its final stages.

Two considerations above all must have been uppermost in the King's mind when he mused over the demand of his prime minister. The first was that he did not think things had yet reached a point where such a demand could be justified. The Tories had not even sought

* Sir Herbert Taylor was presumably referring to the Duke of Sussex.

to amend the bill, had merely used a procedural device to ensure that the most controversial part should be discussed the last. If and when they tried seriously to change the substance of Schedules A and B it would be time enough to batter them into submission by a creation of peers. Grey, in fact, was probably right when he judged that to surrender on this point would be to lose control of the bill and open the way to innumerable damaging amendments but many of his own followers also doubted the wisdom of his timing.

The second consideration was potentially far more dangerous for the Whigs. For the first time the King believed that an alternative course existed which might save the essential features of the Reform Bill and yet avoid the need to create peers. If a Tory government could only be induced to sponsor the bill on the plea that, in their hands, the worst effects at least might be mitigated, then all difficulties would be smoothed over. At what date this curious scheme first occurred to the King is uncertain. It had been mooted by the Queen as early as January, in a highly subversive correspondence with Lord Howe. 'His [the King's] eyes are open,' she wrote, 'and see the great difficulties in which he is placed. He sees everything in the right light, but I am afraid he is fixed that no other administration could be formed at present among your friends . . . I should like to know what the Duke of Wellington thinks.'[36] Howe eagerly entered into the plot. In March he was writing to Wellington: 'Pray, my dear Duke, DEPEND UPON THE KING. Assure your party, if they will be *staunch*, he will be so.'[37] By the time Grey called at Windsor, the King must have been assured that Wellington would indeed be staunch – there was at least a chance of forming a Tory administration pledged to reform.

When Grey made his request on May 8, the King asked for a night to think it over. It was probably more the phrasing of his reply which preoccupied him than its nature. His final answer took the form of a terse letter regretting that he did not find it compatible with his duty to create as many peers as were needed to pass the bill. He softened this bleak reply with a personal letter to Grey, written most exceptionally in the first person, in which he spoke of the sincere and heartfelt regret which he felt at losing Grey's services and his gratitude for the prime minister's exemplary conduct.[38]

He was probably sincere; he respected, trusted and liked Lord Grey. But he was far from overcome by his grief. Mary Clitherow, dining that night at Windsor, found him '. . . cheerful but silent . . . The Queen certainly in particular good spirits . . .'[39] His chief reaction must surely have been relief at having at last arrived at a decision. He recognized that difficulties still lay ahead, but was satisfied that at least he could meet them with a quiet conscience. The audience at which he next day received his departing ministers was a more doleful occasion. 'The King was much affected, and was in tears repeatedly . . .' reported Stanley.[40] But through his tears he contrived to launch an initiative which he had privately decided to try before turning to the Tories. 'Perfidious Billy,' noted Creevey, was 'the outside of graciosity to Grey', but he reserved his most particular attentions for the Chancellor, urging Brougham to remain behind after the levee and confer with him in the closet.[41]

The fact was that he hoped to persuade Brougham, Richmond and perhaps one or two other ministers to remain in office and carry through a modified plan of reform on the lines sketched out by Ellenborough in the House of Lords. It is a striking commentary on Brougham's reputation that the King could make such an offer to the man who should have been considered the out-and-out champion of the bill whole and undiluted. Not for nothing had Sydney Smith remarked, when the Chancellor arrived for a performance of *The Messiah*, 'Ah, here comes counsel for the defence'. But this time at least Brougham did not play his colleagues false. He told the King that it was out of the question and when William, once again reduced to tears, appealed to him not to abandon his monarch at such a moment, replied firmly that it was rather the monarch who was abandoning him.[42]

The King cannot have been much surprised or even, one feels, disappointed. His hands were now free and he could turn to the Tories. He chose as his go-between Lord Lyndhurst who, as a former Lord Chancellor, was deemed to be above, or, at least, to one side of domestic politics. The selection of this devious and two-faced intriguer was deplored even by those who supported the object of the manoeuvre. 'This was not well done,' Greville commented, 'for besides the character of the man, which makes him the least fit to form an administration, it was a sort of insult to his ex-Ministers to send at once for the person who had been the immediate instrument in turning them out.'[43] Lyndhurst's instructions were clear: he was to establish whether a Tory government could be formed which would be ready to pass the Reform Bill substantially unamended.

Peel's reaction to this proposition was immediate and decisive. '. . . I do believe,' he wrote to Croker, 'that one of the greatest calamities that could befall the country would be the utter want of confidence in the declarations of public men which must follow the adoption of the Bill of Reform by me as a Minister of the Crown.'[44] In the light of contemporary political morality this view is so obviously correct that it is hard to see how such a monument of integrity as the Duke of Wellington could have reached a contrary conclusion. Somehow, however, he convinced himself that such was his duty and he addressed himself to the painful, even humiliating task of manufacturing the knife with which he could cut his own throat.

After Peel's refusal it was obvious that Wellington alone could take the lead. At one time there seems to have been a suggestion that Manners Sutton, the Speaker, should at least in title fill the office. 'Well, Sir,' the King addressed him bluffly, 'so you are to form part of my new Administration. You recollect that my servants must carry as extensive a Reform as the present.' 'Sire!' replied Sutton, 'I believe tham I am to have the honour to be First Lord of the Treasury.' 'Oh, no,' said the King, 'the Duke of Wellington must have that. I won't trust myself in anyone's hands but his.'[45] And that, so far as Sutton, Baring or other possible candidates were concerned, was that.

The enterprise was doomed from the moment of its conception. 'I have a sort of feeling that it cannot succeed ...' wrote Lyndhurst gloomily[46] and where the leaders doubted, the rank and file despaired. Even the most pessimistic, however, hardly foresaw the outburst of vilification which now struck the King. From popular hero he became, almost overnight, bogeyman of anyone with even a trace of liberal feelings. He was hissed as he drove up from Windsor on May 13 and clods of dirt were thrown at his carriage. The only people who surpassed him in disfavour and thus to some extent shielded him from the worst abuse were the Queen and the Duke of Cumberland. 'Only a week back,' declaimed Orator Hunt, 'omnibuses and coaches and all were christened Adelaide. Half the boys and girls too who were born were christened Adelaide: and now the name was all at once wiped out from the omnibuses, and the boys and girls were ashamed of it.'[47]

Britain, indeed, was as close to revolution as it had come for many years or was ever to come again. A run on gold and threats of refusal to pay taxes showed that the economy was not exempt while mass meetings all over the country proved that law and order could still more easily be overthrown. Worst of all, it was uncertain how reliable the troops would be in case of trouble. When men of the Scots Greys at Birmingham were informed that they might have to act to check a giant march they told their officers that they would prevent riots or attacks on property but would do nothing to hamper a constitutional protest made in a cause with which they were in total sympathy.[48] 'I never before,' wrote Cockburn, 'actually *felt* the immediate presence of a great popular crisis . . . There was nothing to distract the attention, or to break the terrible silence – nothing but grave looks and orderly public proceedings, unconquerable resolution, and the absolute certainty that, if any accident had made resistance begin anywhere, it would have run like an electric shock in a moment.'[49]

The Whigs for the most part had been taken by surprise. Even when Grey was at Windsor receiving his dismissal, Lord Holland was telling Anglesey that the King would certainly agree to create peers.[50] Now, in consternation, they had to decide what tactics to adopt. Many favoured all-out attack but the leaders argued that a great party should care more for measures than for men and that reform must be supported however base its champions. When the House of Commons met on May 14, therefore, speaker after speaker reviled the Tories but said that they would support the bill. It took a Tory, and a high Tory at that, to destroy the whole shabby conspiracy in a few phrases. If what was rumoured was true, said Sir Robert Inglis, he would regard it as 'one of the most fatal violations of public confidence which could be inflicted'. His speech crystallized a body of decent Tory opinion which could not see that a measure which was fundamentally wrong became any better if sponsored by its enemies. The storm grew and Baring virtually abandoned the cause. Wellington had still not been able to job together a workable Government; the disappearance of one of its principal members put an end to his hopes. When the House rose Peel, Croker, Baring and the Speaker drove to Apsley House to persuade the duke that he must renounce his efforts; the following morning Wellington went to St James's and formally notified the King that the attempt was over.

*

Defeat seemed total. The King, however, still would not accept that all was lost. On May 15, blandly ignoring all that had gone before, he wrote to Grey hoping that the difficulties might be removed, 'by passing the Bill with such modifications as may meet the views of those who may still entertain any difference of opinion on the subject.'[51] Grey would have been naïve indeed if he had countered this piece of effrontery with anything other than a flat refusal to contemplate changes of substance. He would only return to office if he was guaranteed sufficient support to pass the bill unamended. The following day William received the Whig leaders. He was polite enough but spent most of the time defending himself against the charge that he had betrayed the cause of reform. The visitors, noted le Marchant, 'were but moderately satisfied with the interview. It was evident that the King regarded them as forced upon him by the country.'[52] No absolute assurance was yet forthcoming that William would create the requisite number of peers.

Tension had slackened when Wellington withdrew from the ring but a feeling of incipient crisis still hung over the country. Extravagant rumours were abroad and won credence from all but the most levelheaded. One such tale was told by Hobhouse to the radical, Francis Place. The Queen, it was said, had persuaded the King 'to leave the country clandestinely and run away to Hanover.' Once there he would have dissolved parliament and called upon the more authoritarian powers of Europe to help him restore his land to sanity.[53] It is possible that such a 'cruel, heedless, dishonest project,' as Place described it, might have occurred to Queen Adelaide in one of her less lucid moments; one can conceive, though with difficulty, that she might have found the courage to broach it to her husband; but under no circumstances can one imagine King William greeting it with anything except anger or derision. Fanatically patriotic, loathing foreigners, totally committed to his constitutional responsibilities – he would no more have invoked the old Europe to redress the balance of what he unenthusiastically accepted to be the new than he would have appealed to the French to invade his land and take belated revenge on the Duke of Wellington. British problems required British answers, and no one felt himself more British than King William IV.

By May 16, however, two days after the debacle in the House of Commons, such a solution had still not been found. At Windsor Lord Munster was playing a role as disreputable as it was imprudent. Every few hours he coaxed from his father a statement of his latest doubts and fears, then dashed off another report to the Duke of Buckingham. Just before Grey arrived for his interview Munster dispatched his latest bulletin. Nothing, he said, would make the King create peers. 'He is *most stout*. For God's sake be sure, if the King is driven to the wall, of *Peel*.' After the interview he reported that nothing whatever had passed between Grey and the King. Buckingham passed the messages on to Wellington, informing him that 'the person' was to see the King again that night and would then 'press him to put the case on this footing into your hands.'[54]

Wellington, to his credit, paid not the slightest attention to these bulletins. He considered that the battle against reform was lost and that all that remained was to decide how best to negotiate the surrender. The King's position is harder to assess. He would not deliberately have misled his son, yet it is difficult to believe that he was still in any serious doubt as to his future course. Lady Erroll saw him on what was probably the following morning and was struck by the change in his appearance. She guessed that he had made up his mind to recall Grey on the latter's terms, 'which proved true – and ever since he has been in roaring spirits'. In London the joke was that Grey had frightened the King into submission. 'The poor old man fell upon his knees begging for *one desire* only – that he might not be *forced* to sign the marriage articles between Lord Howick and Princess Victoria!'[55]

The King's decision was to ensure that enough lords stayed away to ease the passage of the bill. Sir Herbert Taylor was instructed to write to a dozen or so of the more influential peers asking them to declare that they would drop their opposition – if this was done, they were told, there would be no question of a creation. Similar messages were sent by other means; Frederick FitzClarence, for instance, lobbying his friend Lord Glengall.[56] The results were not always happy – Londonderry, for one, exploding into rage and publishing the letter – but on the whole the King was reassured that he had done enough. The Whigs were less sure. In the debate of May 17, the Tory peers confined themselves to abuse of ministers and a mass exit without any promise about future behaviour. 'You see,' said Lord Strangford as he left the House, 'Sir Herbert Taylor's famous letter did no good.'[57] The news was brought to the House of Commons and Hobhouse whispered it into the ear of Althorp. 'Well, so much the better ...' commented that most admirable of country gentlemen. 'Now I shall have my shooting.'[58]

He was over-optimistic. Resistance was still alive but it was in its death throes. On May 18 Grey and Brougham went to St James's. For Brougham it was 'one of the most painful hours I ever passed in my life, because the King evidently suffered much, and yet behaved with the greatest courtesy to us. It is, however, the only audience I ever had in which he kept his seat, and did not desire us to sit down.' Once more the Whig leaders pressed for an unconditional undertaking that peers would be created. 'Well, now it must be so, and I consent,' said the King. Brougham then went on to ask that the promise should be made in writing and Grey, with some reluctance, backed this demand. 'Do you doubt my word?' grumbled the King angrily as he prepared to comply. As they left the palace Grey told Brougham that he was 'perfectly shocked' with his colleague's unfeeling behaviour. On the contrary, retorted Brougham, 'this written promise may render the measure of creation unnecessary.'[59]

All the evidence suggests that Brougham's precious assurance was in fact superfluous. The great mass of the Tory peers had by now decided not to cut their own throats by further opposition. The King made one further faint attempt to induce Grey to accept a few amendments.[60] He can have had little real hope that this plea would succeed. Grey rejected it out of hand, pointing out that, even if he believed the suggestions to be improvements, feeling in the party and the country was now such that anything resembling a concession to the Tories would give rise to near revolt. The bill raced through committee at almost indecent speed and, on June 4, only twenty-two diehards mustered to oppose the third reading.

William had one last opportunity to demonstrate his pique. Ministers were anxious that the royal assent to the bill should be given by the King in person so as to show the world that he was reconciled to reform. Many Tories were anxious that he should do the same and thus regain in some measure his former popularity; the stronger the King's position, the easier it would be for him to dispose of his government in the future. But the injuries inflicted on the King were too deep. Taylor's letter to Brougham, urging the Chancellor not to press the matter, reveals the bitterness which the King still felt – bitterness not so much against the Whigs as against his subjects. Nothing on earth, wrote Taylor, would induce the King to make a public demonstration of his support for reform 'in deference to what is called the sense of the people or ... the dictates of the press, its ruler, after the treatment he has experienced from both ...' It was his belief that 'he had been misrepresented, calumniated, and insulted; that the insults had not been confined to him – they had been heaped upon his Queen, on all belonging to him ... Was he to cringe and bow? Was he to kiss the rod held out *in terrorem* by the mob?'[61] The same spirit inspired King William's letter to Melbourne insisting that government offices should not be illuminated and there should be no fireworks in the royal parks.[62] Public order was his professed concern but revenge his evident preoccupation.

No amount of royal sulking, however, could dim the rejoicing of the country and almost against his will William found himself to some extent restored to popular favour. As so often the convenient fiction was invoked that all a monarch's sins were the result of bad advice, but on this occasion the advice was deemed to have come not from ministers – the usual villains – but from his courtiers, his relations and, above all, his wife. 'My cranky old sailor,' Queen Adelaide was made to designate him.

> *'My cranky old sailor is worse than a Taylor,*
> *His bill by commission was signed t'other day;*
> *I'm a Germany stormer, I hate a reformer,*
> *Confusion to Billy, his Broom and his Grey!'*

A cranky old sailor was what the British wanted their King to be and, if he gave them a chance, he would revert to it from the Mephistophelean role he had played so clumsily over the last few months.

*

Viewed from today, viewed indeed in 1832 from almost any vantage point except that of the royal palaces, it is obvious that the King's conduct was inept and ineffective. He forfeited the confidence of his ministers, the goodwill of his people and his own reputation for straight dealing to gain nothing except a dubious conviction that he had acted according to his conscience. In the end he had managed to escape with remarkably little damage either to his country or to the monarchy, but this was due more to good luck and the forbearance of the politicians than to his own dexterity.

The question of whether he behaved dishonourably is more difficult to answer. 'His Majesty's case was a bad one,' concluded Peel, after studying the documents.[63] Juridically it is hard to agree. The King had gone back on no precise undertaking. His original promise to make peers had been made when it appeared that only twenty or so creations would be needed. Gradually the total had edged up until the demand seemed to be for fifty or sixty with no guarantee that even this would be enough. Furthermore, he had promised to create peers only if the future of the bill was threatened. He found himself called upon to honour his promise when the passage of something pretty close to the original bill seemed assured and all that was immediately at stake was a question of timing within the debate itself. In such circumstances it was not unreasonable to contend that the original assurance no longer applied; certainly no court of law would have been likely to convict on such evidence.

Nevertheless it is difficult to escape the feeling that, though the King was not guilty of treachery or dishonesty, he still behaved pretty badly to the Whigs. He had led them to believe that he would stand by his ministers until the final show-down. The final show-down came and he deserted them. He had many excuses but, though excuses can mitigate an offence, they cannot remove it. His certainly did not stink to heaven but it still left a faintly unpleasant aroma in the corridors of Whitehall. Those who respect him as a King and as a man must regret his failing.

The final word can be Grey's. Writing to Lord Anglesey about the King's acceptance of his resignation, he commented: 'There seems to me every reason to suspect that this has been brought about by a deep and long-planned intrigue, of which the King himself was not aware, but in the snares of which he was involved by too much good nature towards those about him, too little suspicion of their designs, in part also by his own secret dislike of the measure of Reform and his fear, not unnatural in a King, of too great an ascendency of popular influence in the Government of the country.'[64]

If the chief victim of the King's action can speak thus, there is no need for posterity to be conspicuously less charitable.

CHAPTER XVIII

Foreign Affairs

FROM the foregoing chapters the reader might be forgiven for presuming that, during the previous eighteen months, King and ministers had been exclusively preoccupied with parliamentary reform. In fact, for much of the time the King was more concerned with foreign affairs. Though his interest in all that happened at home was intense, sometimes obsessive, he felt that the proper conduct of Britain's international relations was more directly his responsibility. On diplomatic questions he spoke with greater authority and expectation of being obeyed and, though his prejudices were no less marked, his appetite for detail and grasp of fundamentals were considerably more impressive. He was, in fact, well-informed and thoughtful; his arguments cogent and to the point. The fact is worth stressing, if only because of the popular vision of King William as a buffoon and lightweight incapable of forming a reasoned judgment on anything more complex than the most desirable colour for a naval uniform.

The prejudices, however, existed and with only the most minor adjustments could be tailored to serve in any situation. They can be briefly stated. First: no foreigners were to be trusted. Second: the French, for perfidy, were nevertheless in a class of their own. Third: legitimate and conservative governments were in all circumstances preferable to the revolutionary or radical régimes which might replace them. Fourth: as a corollary of the third, Britain should never seek to export her liberal habits and institutions to other, less enlightened lands.

To the student of international affairs this summary will seem intolerably facile. King William, however, was a simple man who saw things in black and white. It was his misfortune, or perhaps Lord Palmerston's, that for most of his reign he had a foreign secretary who had a similar propensity but tended to see white where his monarch saw black, and black where he saw white. Palmerston, of course, was incomparably more intelligent than the King but little more flexible in his views. He too had small use for foreigners as a class but was inclined

to think the French among the better. Though not above defending
a tyrannical régime if the national interest so required, as a general rule
the more conservative a foreign government, the more he deplored it.
He found it not only his duty but his pleasure to export the more liberal
features of the British way of life to the lesser breeds without the law.
Given so fundamental a divergence of outlook it is remarkable that the
two men got on well together. The King was sometimes indignant
at the iniquities of his foreign secretary but on the whole admired him
and supported him through his by no means infrequent difficulties.
Palmerston was often impatient of the King but liked and respected
him and treated his views with proper seriousness.

King William's chauvinism, his assumption that every foreigner was
seeking to do Britain down and that, in any dispute, his country must
inevitably be right, was shared by his advisers. His obsessive hatred of
France was another matter. In part it stemmed from the memory of
twenty-five years' almost uninterrupted war, in part from revulsion at
the fact that the Citizen King owed his throne to revolution and the
expulsion of the legitimate monarch. When Talleyrand pleaded that
we should send the royal yacht to Cherbourg during a visit by Louis
Philippe, the King flatly refused. Grey pointed out that we would be
forfeiting an excellent chance of spying on the French fleet. Taylor
replied that he had already made this point, but to no purpose. ' – I
have found it on this occasion and others . . . impossible to overcome
the prejudices which His Majesty entertains towards Louis Philippe
and his Family. There are certain early impressions which He cannot
shake off . . .'[1]

Many of the King's more serious disagreements with Palmerston
rose from this obsession. Frequently the government thought it essential for the success of our foreign policy that we should co-operate
closely with the French. Almost always the King objected. With
devastating honesty he admitted that, 'he entertains a prejudice, so
rooted, that he cannot help seeking for an *arrière pensée* in every assertion
and every measure of the French Government'.[2] Herbert Taylor, who
favoured a French alliance, was totally unable to influence his master.

His revulsion showed itself in various guises; from the dismissal of
the French pastry-cooks at Windsor to insults directed at whatever
French ambassador might be in London. About Talleyrand's appointment in 1830 his reaction was predictable. 'There are few Individuals,'
he wrote to Aberdeen, the Tory foreign secretary, 'whose Career
appears to His Majesty to have been more disreputable and although the

King does not question his Talents, especially for Intrigue, He does not consider the Selection of a Man of His Character ... to be either creditable to Himself or Complimentary to His Majesty.'[3] Even when he was magnanimous he accompanied the gesture with a sneer. The French were anxious that the ashes of Napoleon should be returned to France. 'His Majesty never quarrels with the Dead,' he wrote to Palmerston, 'and cannot see any objection ...' It was very natural that France should feel 'desirous of possessing and of *parading* the remains of the Individual under whose Auspices its Vanity had been so widely gratified.'[4]

His prejudices were, of course, mutually supporting and sustaining. France was the more detestable for being a revolutionary régime and encouraging others; revolutionary régimes were the worse for being the friends of France. He saw himself as champion of the monarchical principle. But he was never an extremist. In 1833 he spoke with disapproval of Metternich's lingering hope that 'England should become a Member of the Crusade which would probably long since have been set on foot against France if the wiser policy of England had not kept her aloof ...' He disliked revolutionary principles and designs, he said – which can hardly have been news to Palmerston – but, 'He has never been an Advocate for the Arbitrary Principles on which the Holy Alliance was founded, or for the oppressive Measures they would produce ...'[5]

His reluctance to engage in a crusade against France was a reflection of his wider belief that it was not our business to interfere in the domestic affairs of other countries. His belief that the French made it their business to stir up trouble in neighbouring states was one of his strongest charges against them,[6] and his outrage was extreme when he detected his foreign secretary engaged in the same pursuit.

'Deeply impressed as The King is,' he wrote to Palmerston, 'with the Value of the Principles on which the Constitution of this Country is founded ... He has always been of Opinion that He would not be justified in encouraging any Attempt to introduce these Principles into States whose other Forms of Government have long been established and still prevail and where the Character and the Habits of the Population may little fit them for Institutions under which the British Nation has prospered.'[7]

His words have rung down the ages and found a curious echo in the mouths of those who berate as foolish idealism the export of West-minster democracy to peoples unfortunate enough not to share our alleged wisdom and stability.

In the course of his reign the King enunciated this principle with wearying repetition. About Spain where he remarked that '. . . the proportion of its population which . . . is ripe for Liberal institutions is *very small*'.[8] About the Papal States, in which context he muttered balefully, '*The Spirit of the Age*, although it may be called Liberal, is *Revolutionary* and its Tendency is the Overthrow of all that is estab-lished, whether good or bad.'[9] About Germany, where he was alarmed lest we might unnecessarily commit ourselves in support of the '*Liberal* or Revolutionary feeling' which had found its way into that area.[10] Such are the cries of reactionaries throughout the centuries. It is not necessary to accept them to recognize that they are worthy of respect, perhaps even that they contain as many grains of truth as the dogmas of the wholly dedicated progressives.

*

It would mercifully be far beyond the scope of this book to follow in detail the various controversies which engaged William's attention during the first few years of his reign. Four areas of conflict however bulked so large that they cannot be ignored. First, both chronologically and in its intrinsic importance for the British, must rank the Belgian Question. Two million northerners, predominantly Dutch speaking and agrarian in interests, found themselves linked with three and a half million in the south whose tongue was French and whose economy was steadily becoming more industrial. Possession of the throne by the Protestant House of Nassau assured that the minority group enjoyed an unhealthy preponderance of power. The rising of the Catholics which gathered steam in the summer and autumn of 1830 soon grew into full-scale revolution seeking partition, and the formal exclusion of the House of Nassau from the throne of what was henceforward Belgium. Towards the end of 1830 the King of Holland appealed to the great powers to regulate the affairs of his country. In November a Con-ference was convened in London. From then on the British role was to be decisive.

Having propounded the principles on which King William IV based his foreign policy it is galling to have so quickly to disavow them. The Belgians were making war against legitimate authority; worse still, they were the protégés of the French. The King should therefore have supported the Dutch, to whom we had long been bound by sentiment and mutual interest. The Queen was ferociously of that mind; 'all fire and flame against the Conference,' reported Princess Lieven.[11] But William was disconcertingly open-minded. He recognized that the United Netherlands had not worked. '. . . a Reunion of Belgium and Holland has, by the Force of Events, become impossible,' he wrote bluntly to Palmerston in December, 1830;[12] all that remained was for the Conference to establish how the two countries should most equitably be divided and then cajole or bully the protagonists into acquiescence.

The King of Holland was the greatest single obstacle; 'Absurd, narrow-minded, shuffling and impolitic,' King William described his conduct.[13] At one time William was in favour of a possible compromise which would have nominated the King's son, the Prince of Orange, as head of the new State. The opportunity passed, however, and Leopold of Saxe-Coburg, widower of King George IV's daughter Charlotte, became the official British candidate. King William was doubtful. 'It will be said that England contended for the House of Orange so long as no Prince immediately connected with or dependent upon itself was brought forward, but abandoned that cause for a selfish object . . .'[14] His scruples were stilled as it became evident that the Prince of Orange was totally unacceptable to the Belgians and, still more, when a French candidate, the Duc de Nemours, entered the fray.[15] Nothing in the King's eyes could have been a more miserable outcome than this last, and he soon switched his support to the eventually triumphant Leopold.

In February 1831 the provisional *Bases de Séparation* were agreed by the great powers. Neither Belgians nor Dutch were satisfied but the Dutch were the more indignant and in July they attacked their neighbours. The French came to the rescue and their troops surged over Belgium. William was suspicious. 'He cannot disguise His Fears that France is not acting and will not act with good Faith . . .' he told Lord Grey.[16] He was not being wholly absurd – Talleyrand was known to be flirting with a project for the partition of Belgium[17] – but in the circumstances French intervention had been essential.

The unity of the great powers was now in tatters. Russia, Prussia and Austria – the Eastern Powers – began to line up behind Holland while France became ever more hot in its championship of the Belgians. This division put a disagreeable strain on the relationship between King and ministers. Palmerston wished to join in unequivocal support of Belgium; the King felt it could not be right that we should act in concert with the French against the legitimate powers of Europe. To Princess Lieven he is alleged to have said 'it is most desirable that we four powers should all appear to France as holding together, and of good intelligence one with the other.'[18] Gleefully, Princess Lieven passed the story back to Lord Grey. He may not have believed it wholly but he knew well that it was uncomfortably close to the King's real views.

On October 14, 1831, the Five Powers agreed the Twenty-four Articles which were supposed to provide the basis for Belgium's independence. Prolonged negotiations then began to work out the economic details, with the Dutch meanwhile obstinately refusing to evacuate the citadel of Antwerp. By the following year it was clear that only heavy pressure would bring them to reason. The King agreed, but with reservations: 'His Majesty does not forget the hatred heaped on Charles the Second and his Ministry, for assisting France against Holland ... and is also of opinion the British nation is decidedly against War with Holland.'[19] His favoured solution was economic sanctions.[20]

Even when he was convinced that some form of armed coercion was essential he objected to any co-operation with France beyond the naval. Grudgingly he conceded that some movement by the French army might be necessary but he was adamant that this should be confined to an assault on Antwerp. Anything more extravagant, he was convinced, would provoke the Eastern Powers into retaliation.[21] On one point he laid particular emphasis, a point which he was to reiterate in different circumstances throughout his reign. If we had to take active steps then let us at least do so on a scale which would ensure that they were effective. If a blockade was essential 'we must man and equip every Ship that can swim ... There should be no delay, as much will depend upon the first impression.'[22]

By mid-October Lord Holland was reporting cheerfully that the King was now fully reconciled to some sort of co-operation with the French and did not blame his ministers for forcing it upon him.[23] Certainly William had agreed that something of the kind was necessary but he was far from sanguine about the outcome. Even when the French behaved impeccably and withdrew their troops after the surrender of Antwerp, the King continued to grumble. In a letter to Grey he reiterated, 'His extreme aversion to the thoughts of any Continental Combination of Policy and Measures between this Country and France ...' which might suggest to our 'ancient Allies' that we were deserting them.[24]. Grey gloomily underlined the passage; since the 'ancient Allies' were presumably Russia, Prussia and Austria, who were doing all in their power to defeat British policy in Belgium, he can be forgiven for feeling a mild despair.

The Tories tried to make all the capital they could out of the war which they claimed the Whigs were needlessly courting. They were not particularly successful in panicking the public. Even in the City their meeting was a failure: 'The first resolution,' wrote Grey with splendid disdain befitting a champion of the people, 'was seconded, I believe, by a Stock Broker . . .'[25] But the King had good reason to believe the businessmen of the country by no means so unconcerned as Grey suggested. The country would not have liked a war with Holland, and the King was doing no more than reflect the feelings of his people when he said the same to Lord Grey.

By the spring of 1833 the crisis was over, an uneasy peace settled over Holland and Belgium. But the King could never altogether escape his obsession. Even a year later he was still suspecting plots to divide Belgium between Prussia and Holland, with '*France* coming in for her share of the Spoil'.[26] In foreign as in domestic matters, once the King had got an idea into his head, it was exceedingly hard to get it out again.

*

It was Palmerston's support for liberal movements in Germany which caused the most serious breach between him and the King. The pattern was set farther east. The Poles had risen against their Russian rulers. The Tsar was legally within his rights in quelling the insurrection and at first no Whig leader contemplated more than a few mildly sympathetic noises about the fate of the rebels. The King did not even go as far as that; if Princess Lieven is to be believed he said to her, 'Madame, you cannot desire more than I do the triumph of your Emperor, for it concerns me very closely.'[27] However, the singular brutality with which the Tsar put down the revolt, made it more and more difficult for Palmerston to pursue his policy of restraint.

He accepted his new role with relish. When the Tsar was abused in the House of Commons and the Foreign Secretary might have been expected at least to deprecate the harshness of the attack, he remained coldly and significantly silent. In private he argued in favour of strong remonstrances against the Russian behaviour. The King too was now prepared to say that he felt sympathy for Poland. But it was another matter when it came to an official protest. For one thing, we would have to associate ourselves once again with the French and thus ensure that Prussia and Austria would rally to Russia's side. This would harm the Poles rather than help them. His main reason, however, was his ingrained dislike of futile gestures. He did not object, he told Grey, to

> 'mild representations in a moderate and conciliatory tone, but opposes holding a language which this Country was not determined and prepared to support . . . He considers it unbecoming this Country to show its teeth without biting, or when it must be considered that it has neither the Power nor the Intention to bite.'[28]

In the event we contrived to annoy the Russians and gained nothing for the Poles. Palmerston noted the setback and resolved that it would not occur again.

As it happened developments were already offering an opportunity to recoup his losses. The July Revolution in France had been followed by turmoil in Southern and Western Germany. Hesse, Baden and Bavaria were among the states which had received new constitutions. The Whigs, or at least Palmerston, welcomed the new entrants to the family of democracy with avuncular approval. Metternich, the reactionary Austrian Chancellor, was as much dismayed. The King found himself closer to the Austrian position than that of his own foreign secretary: the South German states, it seemed to him, were 'strongly impregnated with Revolutionary Ideas and Feelings' and 'under the Influence of a Press almost as licentious and unbridled as the Press in this country . . .'[29] In June, 1832, Metternich forced through the German Diet the notorious Six Resolutions, imposing censorship on the Press and curbing further liberal excesses on the part of the state governments. Palmerston was dismayed, seeing Metternich as a monomaniac seeking to dragoon all Europe into passive submission; to the King the Resolutions were no more than the 'Application of Engagements already Contracted, dormant hitherto, but which the deed of Revolution has brought into Operation.'[30]

It was inevitable that soon there should be an open clash. It came over the position of Hanover. Though William was King of Hanover, Palmerston had no responsibility for its foreign policy. When its government supported Metternich he could only utter futile protests. Yet, in the eyes of Germany, the voice of Hanover was deemed to be the voice of England. Palmerston tried to put matters right by an angry speech which declared that constitutional States were, *ipso facto*, the natural allies of Britain.[31] The King was outraged. He was convinced that few Germans had any interest in the controversy, and that the clamour was confined to 'Journalists, Lawyers and speculating Members of some of the Universities.'[32]

His letter stating this formed part of a prolonged battle between King and government on the form of Palmerston's celebrated dispatch of September 7, 1832, in which he lectured the Austrian and Prussian governments on their improper policies. The King fought hard, secured some amendments, but could not veto the dispatch altogether. He was temporarily re-united with his ministers when the Prussian foreign minister, Ancillon, in a moment of vainglory, refused to receive the note – a very offensive proceeding, stormed the King – but in reality the breach was still as deep as ever.

It was revealed again in the autumn of 1833 when the German states were summoned by Metternich to a conference in Vienna. Broglie, the French foreign minister, was anxious that Hanover should take the lead by refusing the invitation. Palmerston eagerly seconded the proposal. But when the Duke of Cambridge, William's viceroy in Hanover, announced that he had accepted, the King backed him fully. Britain had failed to protect Hanover in the past, he pointed out, and would no doubt fail again in the future. When the conference opened at Vienna the Hanoverian envoy was conspicuous for his fawning acquiescence in everything Metternich suggested.

*

In Spain and Portugal the King's dislike of France once again went far to thwart his ministers' policy. In Portugal the corrupt and inefficient Pedro, exiled King of Brazil, was battling for the rights of his daughter Maria against his brother Miguel, equally corrupt and inefficient but barbarously cruel as well. The other European powers grouped themselves around this happy family. The French, impressed by Pedro's vaguely constitutional ideas, supported the cause of Maria; the Eastern Powers and Spain, even more impressed by Miguel's fanatical opposition to constitutionalism, were energetically behind the usurper. The Whigs, outraged by Miguel's excesses, found themselves with some reluctance drawn into championship of Pedro and Maria. In this posture the King felt little inclination to join them.

In the spring of 1832 Pedro launched his long meditated attack on Portugal. In spite of protests from the Eastern Powers, a sharp reaction from Spain, and the frequently expressed doubts of King William, the British fleet hung about the mouth of the Tagus, ensuring that Pedro's fleet got safely to land and the ring was kept clear for the two contestants to batter themselves and Portugal to pieces. Unfortunately, in the opening months, Pedro came off much the worse; indeed by September he seemed well on the way to defeat. The pressure was then to some extent relieved by an abrupt reversal of policies in Madrid. King Ferdinand dismissed his ministers and formed a new government intended to win the support of the middle classes. Such a government, Palmerston hoped, would surely support the Constitutionalists against the iniquitous Don Miguel.

The war lingered on through 1833. Miguel launched a great offensive designed to destroy Pedro utterly. After an interlude of uncharacteristic despair Palmerston rallied. 'To defeat the Holy Alliance in the arena which they themselves have chosen would be no common victory' he wrote belligerently.[33] But it was Charles Napier, late of the Royal Navy and now Pedro's admiral, who routed the Miguelites and restored his new master's position. His feats were a credit to the service in which he had been trained but the King, somewhat surprisingly, took the achievements of this 'unprincipled Firebrand and Adventurer of the most dangerous description',[34] as a personal affront.

The fact that Pedro owed his survival to Napier did much to disenchant the King with his cause. When Pedro occupied Lisbon and Palmerston urged that we should immediately recognize Maria as Queen, he insisted on caution. Grudgingly he agreed that Lord William Russell, the British representative, should be given discretion to recognize if Pedro had clearly won but added the insulting proviso that Russell must first obtain the active concurrence of the British naval commander in the area, Admiral Parker.[35] Needless to say Lord William, who was not a Russell for nothing, paid little heed to such vexatious restrictions and briskly recognized Maria without waiting for the formality of a victory.

King William stood by the consequences of his minister's action and, when Queen Maria visited England he resolved to do his duty. Indeed, to Taylor's alarm, he showed signs of doing even more. 'The King has ordered His Carriage to meet them at Bagshot ... which is all right,' the alarmed private secretary wrote to Grey, 'but He has added a Guard of Honor to receive them in the Castle Court, which is wrong as they are His Guests in His own personal Residence ... His Majesty being in a speaking mood I dread His committing Himself more than is desirable ...'[36] The visit was in fact something of a debacle. The King said he had never seen a more uninteresting girl than Donna Maria while Prince George of Cumberland thought she looked like an immense doll. After two days the young Queen lost some of her shyness and began to romp with Princess Augusta. 'I did not think the change improved Her,' wrote Lady Bedingfeld tartly, 'for her Voice sounded Ugly and her whole manner was uncouth, as I could expect that of a Princess from the Sandwich Islands . . .'[37] After her departure Princess Augusta fell ill with gout while the Queen retired to bed and slept for fifteen hours.

In January 1834 Don Pedro, despairing of finishing off the war singlehanded, appealed to the British to intervene. Grey strongly favoured the idea and persuaded the King to give cautious and qualified agreement, subject to his usual proviso that, if we were to intervene, it must be effectively.[38] But Grey now found that he could not carry his own cabinet with him; Althorp, apparently on financial grounds, for once coming out strongly against his leader. Grey felt that his only course was to resign. The King, Taylor told the prime minister, had rarely been 'more annoyed or more taken by surprise'.[39] Grey hastened to the Pavilion where he was lectured on his duties and assured of the King's total trust and affection. The royal remonstrance and the pleas of his colleagues prevailed; Grey withdrew his resignation but lost his point. Don Pedro was going to have to fight his own battles for a little longer.

Two months later a solution was at last imposed. Spain and England reached agreement on a settlement which would involve the eviction of both Miguel and Pedro from Portugal and the guarantee of Queen Maria's throne by the interested powers. Palmerston insisted that the French must be associated with the treaty. Inevitably the King balked at the idea but even he could see the advantages of a co-operation which would probably avert the need to use armed force. With some reluctance he agreed and in April 1834 the treaty was signed. The results were decisive. Miguel's army collapsed, Pedro's regency ended and Queen Maria was left to reign over a moderately stable and modestly constitutional state. Even William could not deny that things might have gone a good deal worse.

*

Last in this sketchy *tour d'horizon* must come a brief mention of the Eastern Question, in practice a complex of questions to none of which an answer was forthcoming. The trouble arose from the putrefaction of the Ottoman Empire. Its moribund carcass was under attack by Mehemet Ali, ruler of Egypt. The clash between the Porte and Mehemet,

wrote the King to Grey in January, 1833: 'appears to Him to involve
the direct interests of this Country, both political and commercial,
and to affect eventually the Existence of its Empire and Possessions in
India.'[40] William's preferred solution was that we should bolster up
the Turks. Though Palmerston was more sympathetic to the insurgent
Egyptians he too believed that the Porte must be saved from total
collapse. The problem was how best this could be done. The nearest to
a policy that the King could define was that Britain should take whatever steps were possible to place itself 'in a Condition to hold with
Effect the Language which its Dignity and its Interests prescribe'.[41]
With this daring proposition his ministers could hardly disagree.

The manoeuvring of France and England on the one side, Russia
and Austria on the other, would take a volume to describe. The King,
as always, sought to avoid entanglement with the French. Russia and
France should be allowed to 'growl at each other and bicker,' while we
kept the ring.[42] Russian intervention on behalf of the Porte, however,
made the King better disposed towards Mehemet Ali. In the long run,
he believed, it would be in Egypt's interest to remain firm friends with
England. His reasons were prescient and characteristically practical.
'It has been shown lately,' he wrote to Palmerston, 'that Communica-
tions by Canal and by Steam Vessels might be established from Cairo
to Suez and the Red Sea.' Since we, as owner of India, would make
incomparably greater use of such a canal than any other power, we
must inevitably be Egypt's closest ally.[43] The facts were relevant and
valid, the deduction from them perhaps less so. Whatever the force
of the King's reasoning it is fair to say, however, that left to himself, Palmerston would probably never have considered the point at
all.

By the end of the year war seemed more likely than not. The Duke
of Cumberland was supposed to have gone to Berlin so that, as the
King cynically remarked, 'He might be in the way to secure Hanover
for Himself in the Event of Prussia taking a part ...'[44] In the final
analysis, however, nobody wanted war. The Tsar certainly had no
intention of pushing things too far. 'I am *Chevalier Anglais*,' he announced, pointing to his Garter decoration. 'I shall repeat to all who
question my conduct especially respecting Turkey, "*Honi soi qui mal y
pense*".' Nor were the French disposed to back Mehemet Ali in his
more extravagant projects. An uneasy agreement evolved between
Turks, Egyptians and the great powers which settled little but at least
ensured that events should not be allowed to get out of hand. It would

be too much to say that a peaceful solution was imposed, but somehow, more by good luck than good management, disaster was averted.

*

A series of snapshots is no substitute for detailed analysis. Foreign
affairs are not composed of a multitude of unrelated fragments. It goes
without saying that all the protagonists were influenced in their
approach to the various problems by what had happened or was
happening in other parts of Europe, as well as by their domestic
strength or weakness. Any such study would however be far beyond
the scope of this book; in a biography of King William IV all that can
be done is to establish the way in which he considered the various international problems and the lines along which he sought to resolve them.
It will be seen that his style differed little from that with which he
handled affairs at home. Dogmatic, obstinate and truculent, the words
'imagination' or 'sensitivity' meant little to him. He lacked the objectivity and the intellectual powers to put himself in the place of other
people or to conceive long-term policies as part of a co-ordinated
whole. But he possessed a dogged common-sense. He could assess
with some shrewdness the needs and wants of his own people. He was
not to be deflected from the course that he deemed right by the
promise of temporary advantage. Above all, he abided by fundamentally decent standards of honour and loyalty. He always played
fair, whether with his own minister or foreign powers. He could never
have been described as a great statesman, hardly, indeed, as a statesman
at all, but his persistence, his honesty, his consistency – indeed his very
limitations – made him a valuable touchstone for a foreign secretary
who was not always in close touch with the realities of life in his own
country. As an absolute ruler William would have been disastrous;
as an element in the policy-making machine his value was considerable.

CHAPTER XIX

The Irish Question

With the passage of the Reform Bill the focus of political interest within the British Isles switched to Ireland. First however there was a breathing space while the parties regrouped, licked their wounds and prepared for the forthcoming election. If the King had had his way there would have been no election to prepare for. At the best of times he considered them unseemly carnivals; in the ferment of 1832 he felt that the result would be disorder on a scale so far undreamed of.

About a month before the bill was finally passed William had enquired whether it contained provision for an automatic dissolution because, if so, he felt that it would infringe his prerogative.[1] Melbourne answered reassuringly and thought no more about it. Then Brougham chanced to make some remark about the forthcoming election. 'What election?' snapped the King. To their consternation the Whigs discovered that he envisaged a long cooling-off period before an election was held – two and a half years according to Sir Henry Halford.[2]

Patiently Brougham and Grey explained that, since the House of Commons had persistently proclaimed over the last eighteen months that its composition made it incompetent to perform its duties, it could hardly now prolong its life. The King found the point hard to grasp. In the end it took a threat of resignation from Grey to push him into acquiescence and even then the elections were not to take place before the end of the year.

This difference of opinion was only one of several reasons why the King at this period looked on his ministers with marked distaste. It would indeed have been surprising if he had shown any real affection for the Whigs, who had been the cause of his recent humiliation, but he would quickly have forgiven them if things had gone well. Things did not. A month after the Reform Bill he was hissed at Ascot. Stones were thrown and one would have cut him badly if he had not been saved by the padding in his hat. On August 16 Hobhouse watched the King return to the palace. 'It was like a funeral procession: scarcely a hat taken off and positively no cheering.'[3] At the end of May William had complained bitterly to Althorp about his ministers' failure to protect him from unfair attack.[4] Now his indignation was renewed with a sharper edge.

Gloomily the Whigs anticipated disaster. Lord Durham, who looked on the King as 'little short of mad', predicted a fearful struggle when William sought to throw out his ministers and return to the bad old days of Tory rule.[5] Durham, it may be argued, was little better than his monarch when it came to madness but Hobhouse, who was almost tediously sane, also considered the King 'an irreconcilable enemy of the Ministers'.[6] Few people believed that he would court a second defeat so soon after his recent set-back but it was widely felt that he would do all he could to make things unpleasant for his ministers. At this unpropitious moment Grey chose to revive the question of the Queen's former Chamberlain and present favourite, Lord Howe. Once again a trivial affair assumed false significance because of the harm it did to the King's relations with his prime minister.

Grey's naïve intention had been to conciliate the Queen. In August 1832 he suggested that, now the Reform Bill was out of the way, Howe could resume his duties. His only condition was that Howe should not overtly oppose the Government.[7] The King was delighted and congratulated Grey on his 'good sense and good taste'.[8] But good sense, it seems, was not widely diffused among his courtiers. The negotiations were left to Taylor and Howe, who loathed each other. Taylor wrote Howe a correct but stuffy letter which offended the latter's delicate sense of his own dignity.[9] Howe fired back at Taylor a defiant salvo claiming that the Queen's household should not depend on the whim of a minister.[10] His letter showed 'bad spirit and great wrongheadedness', commented Princess Lieven[11] and Taylor, with some relief, treated it as tantamount to a flat rejection of the invitation.

But this was not at all Lord Howe's intention. He now began to climb down and the King, to Taylor's dismay, seized the opportunity. Howe was to be allowed to vote against the government provided he maintained a 'prudent reserve' in his opposition.[12] Shamefacedly Taylor broke the news to Grey. He admitted that the compromise did not place the matter exactly on the footing on which it ought to stand, but was sure, he said, that things would turn out for the best.[13] In fact he had few such hopes and the prime minister still less. Both men were by now heartily sorry that the issue had ever been revived. As Howe increased his concessions so Taylor stepped up his demands and this envenomed *pas de deux* did not end until almost the end of the year. Howe then finally refused office and the affair concluded with all the chief protagonists convinced that they had been monstrously misused.

One disagreeable by-product was a revival of rumours about Howe's relationship with Queen Adelaide. Greville described him as wooing the Queen like an ardent young lover, pursuing her everywhere and gazing at her with languishing devotion[14] while Princess Lieven claimed that Lady Grey became really angry when she failed to convince the company that Howe was Adelaide's accredited lover. 'Fancy,' wrote the Princess, with consternation unconvincing in so vile a gossip, 'the wife of one of the King's Ministers trying to persuade a foreign Ambassadress that the Queen is a harlot!'[15] Probably no one believed the story, but it made for enjoyable conversation and gave the FitzClarence bastards plentiful opportunities to air their spite. 'They are a bad set,' commented Greville, 'with a good deal of the *coulisses* in their dispositions, and all squabbling with and hating each other. A strange court, with an odd mixture of vulgarity, folly, *tracasserie* and magnificence.'[16]

When Grey went to Brighton towards the end of November, he found the atmosphere chilly and Lord Howe in high favour. The gathering was wholly Tory.[17] He could eliminate his more active enemies from among the royal officials but could do nothing to select the royal friends. It was not till January 1833 that Grey could feel the affair had been forgiven. The Queen had spoken kindly to him, a new and suitable Chamberlain had been appointed, and the King went out of his way to make him feel at ease. William's methods, however, were, to say the least, idiosyncratic. 'At the Commerce table the King sat by him, and was full of jokes; called him continually "Lord Howe", to the great amusement of the bystanders and of Lord G. himself.'[18] The joke, the prime minister might reasonably have felt, was in doubtful taste.

There was more difficulty when Grey found it necessary to intercede with the King on behalf of his brother the Duke of Sussex. This strange, shambling giant, half sage, half buffoon, with his multitude of piping bullfinches, his library of fifty thousand volumes and fifteen pairs of spectacles to read them by, his Negro page called Mr Blackman, was in serious disfavour at court. This was partly the work of his son, D'Este, who believed that his father's marriage was valid in Hanover and that, consequently, he must be high in the line of succession to the throne.

He pursued his claim by attacks of extreme offensiveness on the royal family and the formation of an alliance with the Irish revolutionary, O'Connell. His father found himself to some extent guilty by association.[19]

But the Duke's real offence came in the spring of 1832 when he sided with the ultra-radical supporters of reform and tried to present at court a sharply worded petition from the political union at Birmingham. 'There are fears,' noted Hobhouse, 'that the Duke of Sussex means to play the part of the Duke of Orleans.'[20] The King can hardly have taken the threat very seriously but Sussex was forbidden the court. Grey busied himself with bringing about a reconciliation; pleading that the Duke's conduct stemmed from inadvertence and not meditated disrespect.[21] He was successful but, as is so often the lot of mediators, won himself little favour with either party.

At the end of 1832 a more substantial issue contributed to the alienation of King and ministers. The King reverted to his demand that the government should suppress the political unions. He conceded that, so far, the unions had done little mischief but, 'it is to the Principle of *tolerating* such Societies that he objects.' They posed a threat to the future which could not be taken lightly by anyone who valued law, order and the constitution; 'which it is the object of these self-constituted Engines to resist, to undermine, and to destroy.'[22]

Grey was second to few in his dislike of the political unions but he had no intention of creating a new race of martyrs by suppressing them. His arguments, however, only provoked a longer and still more intemperate letter from the King. In his covering note Taylor assured the prime minister that William was, if anything, understating his views. 'He never misses an Opportunity of uttering them to Me,' added Taylor gloomily, 'and I am convinced that He would consider a French invasion the least Evil of the two.'[23] Suddenly it was all too much for Grey: the illness of his son-in-law, Captain Barrington; constant disputes with the King over the Belgian question; the Howe and Sussex affairs; and now this sequence of royal thunderbolts. In a poignant letter to Taylor he wrote of his distress. The King, he said, exhibited 'such strong marks of discontent and dissatisfaction with the conduct of the Government ... as to make me doubt whether it is possible for me to bear up against all the difficulties which press upon me.'[24]

Grey's cry of pain worked wonders. The King did not like the Whigs but he knew perfectly well that he must work with them.

Himself quick to take offence, he was perpetually surprised when others did the same, and was now quite genuinely distressed to see what woes he had inflicted on a man he respected and found in most ways reliable and sympathetic. His reply reassured Grey and gently rebuked him for over-sensitivity:

'... it cannot be considered extraordinary that a difference of Opinion should occasionally arise, and some Allowances should also be made for the continued existence of principles, some may call them prejudices, early imbibed and which it is not always easy to sacrifice, or to reconcile to Circumstances or Measures. These have occasionally, and may possibly again, lead to the strong expression of His Majesty's Feelings and Sentiments upon certain Subjects of Domestic and Foreign Policy, but His Majesty cannot allow that the Statements, or the Maintenance of such should bear the stamp of strong dissatisfaction, still less does he admit that His Adherence to Opinions, of which the fallacy remains to be proved, has tended to embarrass his Government . . .'[25]

Meanwhile the elections had come and gone. They had been heralded with extravagant gloom by all who thought they had a lot to lose. 'The Government of England is destroyed,' wailed Wellington. 'A Parliament will be returned, by means of which no set of men whatever will be able to conduct the administration of affairs, and to protect the lives and properties of the King's subjects.'[26] The King foresaw nothing quite so hideous but he was alarmed by the bloodshed and disorder which he felt the elections would provoke as well as by the radical riff-raff whom he believed would sweep the country.

In the event he was pleasantly surprised. The elections were certainly no more disorderly than those in earlier eras – and the members returned – except, perhaps for Mr Gully, the retired prize-fighter and book-maker, looked disconcertingly like those in previous parliaments. Still, he was not prepared to be too easily talked out of the more lurid of his fears. When Grey wrote exultantly about his victory he replied that the prime minister underrated the radical threat; he would find that many of his so-called supporters would prove to be opponents when issues of popular interest were debated. He was particularly glad that Colonel Grey had been elected; not so much because he was son to his prime minister as that he had prevented the return of Mr Disraeli.[27] Grey did not pretend that the future was entirely bright. 'The Black Spot on our horizon is Ireland,' he told Taylor, 'and there, I am sorry to say, the Elections appear to be taking as bad a turn as possible.'[28]

*

With the grant of Catholic Emancipation in 1829 most English politicians had deluded themselves that they could forget about Ireland. For three years they had not been proved wrong. O'Connell, now by far the most influential of Irish leaders, had devoted himself to the battle for parliamentary reform. In Ireland the victory of the Whigs became the triumph of O'Connell and the elections which followed reflected his accomplishment. The way was clear for him to move on to the next stage, the repeal of the union. The demand was as yet hardly articulate, no more than a vague ideal billowing in the mind of every Irishman with a sense of romance or of history, but it was already a potent force. Quite what it entailed no one knew. Certainly O'Connell's dream stopped short of total independence and separation from the Crown. It was noteworthy that, while he showered every English politician with Billingsgate abuse, he treated the royal family with marked tenderness.

King William did not reciprocate this courteous treatment. Even if O'Connell had not attacked the union the King would have considered him a rascal; as it was he was promoted to the status of anti-Christ. For the King the union possessed the sacred inviolability of everything even tenuously connected with his Coronation Oath. When he got to the point in the King's Speech in which he reaffirmed his intention to defend it he thundered the words, 'in a tone of voice which might have been heard at Charing Cross.'[29] 'Mr O'Connell's personal Character,' he told Melbourne, 'is as cowardly and contemptible as His Political Conduct is factious and seditious.'[30] As so often in such colonial or quasi-colonial situations the English persuaded themselves that if only one agitator could be removed everything would revert to benign tranquillity. When O'Connell was arrested in January, 1831, William rejoiced; when he was acquitted the King's disappointment was correspondingly bitter. He found comfort in the fact that at least we had played fair: 'that distinguishing feature of British Law and Justice, that if any doubt arise the Person concerned shall have the benefit of it,' had been conscientiously observed.[31]

At the beginning of 1833 the Whigs found themselves free to concentrate on Ireland. The dispensation appeared even then a doubtful blessing. They concluded, however, that there was one field in which they must take swift action and another in which they could introduce liberal reforms. The first was law and order, the second the Irish Church. Concessions made on the second would, they believed, make palatable the rigorous measures called for under the first.

The King was, of course, keener on law and order than reform. It was more than forty years since he had first declared that force was the only way to deal with Ireland and his opinions had not evolved noticeably in the interim. When the government introduced a Coercion Bill, suspending Habeas Corpus and introducing virtual martial law, he was delighted. But tough though it was, the bill still seemed to him too modest. Within a few months he was urging that any attempt at repealing the union should be made high treason and punished accordingly.[32]

Now it was the turn of the Church of Ireland. Reform was badly overdue. In a population of almost eight million, well under a million Irish were members of the established church, yet this relatively tiny band supported 1385 benefices (more than forty of which contained no member of the established church at all) and twenty-two bishops and archbishops. Pluralities were rife and, though the annual revenues of the church were some £750,000, £150,000 of this was the perquisite of the prelates. The trouble, of course, was that the established church did not, in fact, support its imposing hierarchy; the tithe system meant that the Catholic peasant, already pinned at or below subsistence level, was forced to give part of what little he had to support the Anglican clergyman in luxurious idleness. Of course not all Anglican priests were idle or lived in luxury, indeed the inefficiency of the system was such that the expense of extorting tithes from the peasantry was often greater than the resulting income; but the situation was too often that described by Sydney Smith where: 'the bell of a neat parish church often summons to worship only the parson, and an occasionally conforming clerk, while two hundred yards off, a thousand Catholics are huddled together in a miserable hovel, and pelted by all the storms of heaven.'[33]

In February, 1833, Althorp's bill for the reform of the Church of Ireland proposed the radical overhaul of the whole tithe system, the reduction of the number of bishoprics by ten and the abolition of a crop of sinecures. Even O'Connell considered it radical enough to merit his support. The King was less enthusiastic. He had been converted to the need for some reform, had indeed assured Grey that he highly approved the references in the speech from the throne,[34] but this was going further than he had expected. He might be betraying the most loyal of his subjects. Cumberland, self-appointed champion of the militant Orangemen, cunningly suggested he would be acting in breach of his Coronation Oath. For once this magic incantation failed to work, but his conscience was still not at ease.[35] Could it be right that the Anglican establishment should be deprived of privileges which it had enjoyed so long? What concerned him quite as much was that he saw on the horizon the dread spectre of another clash between Commons and Lords. Hopefully he suggested to Grey that the measure might be suspended; the interval before it was introduced could be used to establish 'by what Modifications, not essentially injurious to the Principles and the Objects of the Bill, its opponents . . . might be reconciled to it.'[36]

For both King and Grey there was a dismal flavour of déja vu about the situation. A measure of reform to which the government was pledged; the King acquiescent but unenthusiastic; the implacable opposition of a majority in the House of Lords; the search for concessions which would satisfy the Tories and yet not outrage the conscience of the Whigs: it was 1832 and the Reform Bill all over again. Brougham finally pointed up the grisly parallel. Early in June he wrote to the King urging the immediate creation of three or four peers known to favour reform and a clear intimation that as many more would be created as were needed to force through the Bill.[37] The King's reaction was predictable. 'No person,' wrote Taylor, 'can view the effects of a collision [between Lords and Commons] with greater apprehension than his Majesty, but he dreads also, in a yet greater degree, the effect of any measure which may degrade the House of Lords.' The former evil would be temporary, the latter permanent. All the old arguments were taken out, dusted and re-deployed. 'Upon the whole,' concluded Taylor, with that striking grasp of the obvious which was his hall-mark, 'the question is full of difficulty.'[38]

As it happened, Brougham had argued beyond his brief. Apart from his personal repugnance to the proposal, Grey knew that his government would fall to pieces if any creation of peers was suggested. Some other way must be found. Anglesey wrote to the King to plead for his active intervention on behalf of the bill; if this were not forthcoming then the government must resign.[39] He was pushing at an open door; the King had already shown his readiness to help his ailing ministers. n early June, when the government had been defeated on Wellington's motion in the House of Lords criticizing their Portuguese policy, he had stood firm and criticized the duke with unprecedented vigour.[40] What was more, he wrote a sharp letter to the Archbishop of Canterbury protesting that the bishops had no business to intervene in party politics.[41] 'Never was there such a proceeding, so unconstitutional, so foolish,' stormed Greville. 'I think, as far as being a discouragement to the Tories, and putting an end to their notion that he is hankering after them, it may be of use . . . But what an old Fool he is.'[42]

The Tories were indeed discouraged. 'The King has no disposition to run any more risks,' wrote Ellenborough in dismay. 'He will make 60 peers rather than allow his Ministers to resign. He has neither discernment nor firmness.'[43] Before Brougham even put his proposals to the King, all but the most die-hard Tories had decided that resistance on the Irish issue would be futile. But the King was resolved to leave nothing to chance. His letter to the Archbishop of Canterbury had not achieved the effect it should have because that cautious prelate kept it to himself. A copy was therefore sent to the Archbishop of York and the word discreetly passed to the opposition leaders. By the time the bill came to the House of Lords no Tory leader could doubt that the King wished to see it passed.

The tactics worked. As the King had obstinately continued to predict against the opinion of his ministers, the Tories preferred to surrender rather than cut their throats. The bill was passed. But there was an increasing conviction on all sides that this could not go on indefinitely with the government tottering from crisis to crisis and the House of Lords each time being coerced into truculent submission. The King cast around for some more permanent solution. He found it, to no one's surprise, in that favourite will-o'-the-wisp of a coalition of all right-minded Britons.[44] Brougham, to whom the suggestion had this time been made, rejected it out of hand as wholly impracticable.[45] William accepted the advice, but this brusque dismissal of his favourite dream left him resentful of his Chancellor and, to a lesser degree, of the whole Whig government. Grey visited him at Windsor in September, 1833 and was heartened by his friendly reception.[46] But his comfort was illusory. Each new crisis sapped the King's confidence in the ability of the Whigs to provide the stability and security which he felt the country above all things needed. He did not quite know what but something, he became more and more sure, would have to be done.

*

The next round of the battle over the Irish church could not be long delayed. In the spring of 1834 the more radical members of Grey's government revived the question – postponed a few months before – of appropriating the surplus revenue of the church for lay purposes. The establishment was outraged and in May a group of Irish bishops presented a petition of protest which had been signed by more than fourteen hundred clerics. In an apparently impromptu reply all the King's fears and doubts boiled over:

'You have a right to require of me to be resolute in defence of the Church. I have been, by the circumstances of my life, and by conviction, led to support toleration to the utmost extent of which it is justly capable, but toleration must not be permitted to go into licentiousness; it has its bounds ... which I am resolved to maintain ...' This was not, he concluded, 'a speech which I have got by heart; no, I am declaring to you my real and genuine sentiments ... The threats of those who are enemies of the Church make it the more necessary for those who feel their duty to that Church to speak out. The words which you hear from me are indeed spoken by my mouth, but they flow from my heart ...'[47]

Grey was alarmed when he heard reports of the King's words, aghast when it was published in the papers. It was not that the speech contained anything precise to which he could object, but the tone and timing were disastrous. To all who asked him he said bluntly that he had not advised the speech and had first heard about it from the newspapers.[48] Even Taylor admitted that the King's conduct had not been entirely discreet.[49] But this was only one of Grey's troubles. Edward Stanley, former Secretary for Ireland and known to most as Sir Benjamin Backbite, resigned rather than accept what he deemed misappropriation of the funds of the Irish church. With him went Richmond, Ripon and Graham. Grey was ready to throw in the sponge and declare his ministry at an end.[50]

It was Brougham who held the government together. He demanded an interview with the King and almost persuaded his sceptical monarch that the government would be the stronger for the resignations. Certainly he convinced him that it could survive them. But William was unhappy and perplexed. 'I feel more and more doubtful as to the possibility of our going on,' wrote Grey mournfully to Brougham.[51] The sentiment was one which the King would have echoed.

'The Whigs cannot exist as a party without taking in Lord Durham,' wrote Disraeli, 'and the king will not consent to it.'[52] The King was indeed obsessed by the fear that the recent resignations must herald a move towards the radical wing of the party. Grey, Althorp and to a lesser extent Melbourne he considered trustworthy; Palmerston and Lansdowne were respectable enough; but Brougham became increasingly unpredictable; Russell was anathema; and the dread Durham could tip the balance between the unliked and the intolerable. He wrote to Grey to urge the need for compromise. Then he went on to hint at his darker doubts. In Lord Grey, he said, he had perfect confidence and his present advisers were responsible. But about the future he was less certain: 'the Apprehension of Changes in His Councils, under certain Contingencies which Earl Grey has led Him to entertain, causes Him to engage with extreme Caution in any Measure which may be productive of Changes in the Constitution.'[53] Grey was already tired and demoralized; this sombre warning can have done nothing to raise his spirits.

*

It was the renewal of the Coercion Act, not the reform of the Irish church, which proved Grey's downfall. Though the details of the affair are now established, one is still left guessing about the motives of the various protagonists. 'A foolish dispute . . . about some Irish job,' was Campbell's tart summary;[54] and for the purposes of this book, there is little more to say. Grey committed himself to the view that the Coercion Act should be retained in full force. Wellesley, the new Lord Lieutenant, first encouraged him in this view, then changed his mind. Brougham played a part certainly devious, perhaps treacherous and Grey found himself isolated in the Cabinet. Even Melbourne took the line that he must bow to necessity and sacrifice his principles.[55] He had had enough. On July 7 he told the King that he must resign and recommended Melbourne as his successor.[56] He had cried 'Wolf' so often in the past that now it took time before anyone believed him, but he at least knew that his decision was irrevocable.

'My life for the last eight months,' he told Princess Lieven, 'has been one of such unhappiness as nobody can imagine, and as far as I am personally concerned, I rejoice at having escaped from so painful and so thankless a situation. But I feel, deeply feel, for the difficulties of the King . . .'[57]

CHAPTER XX

The Constitutional Coup D'État

✿

THE first of the difficulties of the King was to decide whether the government was in or out. Althorp had resigned when Grey held out for the retention of the Coercion Act in its full fury. Did this still stand? Did the prime minister's resignation carry with it that of his ministry? The last question was particularly perplexing. It so exercised the Duchess of Dino, niece and hostess of Prince Talleyrand, that she plucked up her courage and asked Grey himself. 'In theory, yes; but in fact, no,' he answered lucidly.[1]

In fact it was up to the King to decide. If he had wanted to treat the government as out of office and had sent for the Duke of Wellington, no one would have complained that he was acting unconstitutionally. That he found such a course of action tempting cannot be doubted. In a perceptive passage Brougham described him as:

'Sick of a Government that was urged on to make changes, of which he had had quite enough – still more sick of being urged on by that Government to consent to fresh changes; panting for the quiet of a Tory Ministry, the natural favourite of all kings; not relishing a set of Ministers who looked to popular support rather than to Court favour; still less liking a Ministry which almost every month spoke of breaking up (as under Lord Grey had been too often the case), and leaving him in the position of all others to all kings the most hateful and even alarming, that of being left for a time without a Government . . .'[2]

In such a frame of mind the King was naturally inclined to consider the government as being, *de facto* if not *de jure*, dissolved.[3] Brougham claims that, when he called on him after Grey's resignation, he found him determined that the Whigs should not be allowed to soldier on without some reinforcement. He argued the King out of his resolve, then clinched the matter with a fighting speech in the House of Lords in which he proclaimed that the government not only could but would carry on unimpaired. The King 'yielded a sullen compliance' wrote the Chancellor, but never forgave Brougham for thus bullying him out of what he was always to believe had been the right decision.

The story appears to be largely fiction. Brougham's meddling served to complicate rather than simplify the issue since he left the King with the strong impression that he saw himself as the future leader of the administration and planned to bring in a rabble of radicals in his train.[4] Nothing could more have appalled the King and it confirmed him in his conviction that the responsible elements of the Whig party were not strong enough to keep the left in check. But he never, as Brougham seems to have believed, seriously contemplated turning out the Whigs and substituting a Tory administration. He had accepted, reluctantly but finally, that no government could survive long against a determined majority in the House of Commons. He believed that the Whig majority was crumbling, would in time vanish altogether, but that so long as Althorp remained to rally his supporters in the Commons it would be too early to apply the *coup de grâce*.

But though the new government must be substantially, it need not be exclusively Whig. With a spasm of excited optimism the King determined to revive his pet project of a coalition; under Melbourne's leadership, certainly, but with a more conservative bent than the rump of Lord Grey's administration could provide.[5] Surely Peel and Wellington, in the dire circumstances which then reigned, would sacrifice their personal convictions in the interests of national union? Melbourne had no illusions about the futility of such a venture and told the King so bluntly when asked to open negotiations with the Tory leaders.[6] He went through the motions, as directed, but if ever a question was prefixed by the celebrated *num* – expecting the answer no – it was to be found in the invitations which he addressed to Wellington and Peel. The 'nos' duly came, in the case of Wellington with devastating finality: 'It must be obvious that a Union of Public Men in your Majesty's councils who appear not to concur in any one principle or policy . . . , whether Foreign or Domestic, cannot promote your Majesty's service, cannot conciliate the confidence of the public, or acquire the support of Parliament, and must lead to the most disastrous results.'[7] Even the King wistfully accepted that such an answer must be deemed conclusive.

A Whig government under Melbourne therefore seemed the only possibility. Brougham had it that the King was deeply prejudiced against his new prime minister because of some vestigial loathing of Melbourne House inherited from George III.[8] He may once have felt some such distrust but by the middle of 1834 it had long been forgotten. Melbourne's years as Home Secretary had shown him that he deserved almost total confidence. Calm, cautious, conservative, deeply disapproving of radicalism or 'democracy', he was indeed a man after the King's heart. His celebrated comment to Tom Young on being offered the premiership, that 'he thought it was a damned bore and that he was in many minds what he should do', was characteristic of his sustained attempt to create the image of a man without ambitions. By far the most skilled and professional politician of his age, he succeeded remarkably in investing himself with the aura of the disenchanted amateur. The King used to refer to him as 'a great gentleman', meaning by this talismanic phrase not only that he was honourable and patriotic, but that he eschewed all visionary clap-trap about equality or the rights of man. He was safe and, in matters of principle, predictable; and these were characteristics which the King prized highly.

But he was not so confident that Melbourne was strong or agile enough to control his radical wing. The King's primary object was to ensure that no one unsuitable was slipped into his counsels. When Melbourne argued that nothing could be more dangerous than a 'principle of exclusion', William retorted that, on the contrary, 'a System of indiscriminate Admission' would be infinitely worse. But his objections, he stressed, were to people and not to principles and he was sure that he would not be asked to accept the unacceptable.[9] On the whole his confidence was justified: the ministry had not changed to any marked extent. Most important was that Althorp – 'the Tortoise on which the world now rests', as Melbourne called him – agreed to rejoin the government. But though the faces might be the same, the loss of Grey meant that such men as Russell were markedly increased in power. The accession of Melbourne meant that the government shifted decidedly towards a more radical policy.

No one saw this more clearly than the King. After their first crucial meeting Melbourne noted that he had seemed agitated and annoyed. The new prime minister was left in no doubt about William's views. In a memorandum to Melbourne of July 13, 1834, he expanded on his political philosophy. He concluded that he would always oppose: 'Attempts to introduce Changes and Innovations which, however they may be considered by some to have become necessary elsewhere, must be admitted by reasonable minds to have ceased to be so here, provided the existing Constitution and Laws be duly observed and administered . . .'10

The King tempered this somewhat daunting message with an assurance that he recognized his obligations to his ministers but this can not have been much comfort to Melbourne. If William proposed to consider any new piece of legislation as a mischievous innovation inimical to the best interests of the country, then the lot of his prime minister was likely to be troublesome. What was more, the King was convinced that the country was behind him. '. . . the general feeling of the Nation,' he told Melbourne, 'is in favour of the more moderate and safe course, and to the Principle which advocates *letting well alone* . . .'11 Melbourne suspected that, if the King really believed he spoke for the nation, he would be more ready to risk a clash with the House of Commons and an ensuing election. Almost Melbourne's first act as prime minister was to scuttle the projected Coercion Bill and announce a new version shorn of those harsher clauses which Grey had believed essential. To William, who had felt that even the original bill had been too weak, this was an ominous portent of the wrath to come.

*

In October, 1834, the Houses of Parliament were destroyed by fire – divine retribution, concluded Queen Adelaide with satisfaction. Next day the King and Queen walked around the still-smoking ruins; the King alarming his courtiers by vigorously prodding the tottering walls with the evident intention of completing a task which had been well begun. He mourned the loss but his gloom was illumined by the radiant hope that now at last he might escape from Buckingham Palace.

When William IV succeeded to the throne the conversion of Buckingham Palace to something near its present form was almost complete. The expense was vast; the original estimate of half a million pounds had already proved totally inadequate. King William had loathed it from the start; its combination of pomposity and flamboyance providing an extravagant paradigm of all that he found most distasteful about his brother's reign. Sir John Sebright had told him it was a dog-hole; he was inclined to think this uncharitable to the dog. It might, however, be good enough for a soldier. In 1831 he suggested that it should be turned into a barracks to accommodate the fifteen hundred Foot Guards shortly to be expelled from Knightsbridge. Only when Grey refused to sanction the additional expense did he reluctantly authorize the present barracks in Birdcage Walk.[12]

It was not until 1833 that he conceived the idea of turning the palace into the Houses of Parliament; 'the present Houses of Parliament and their Appendages might be converted into a Residence for the Lord Chancellor, and into Courts of Law'. If the conversion work proved too costly, part of the garden could be sold for private development. Grey replied, with total insincerity, that the idea was a splendid one; if only it had been put forward earlier it might well have been practicable but so much money had now been spent that he feared the public would not stand for it.[13]

Given this background it was not surprising that Hobhouse should have found the King surveying the ruins, 'gratified as if at a show'. Gleefully he revived his former project. 'It would be the finest thing in Europe,' he promised lavishly. Surely, with their home destroyed, the Commons would now see the merits of his offer? As he was leaving he called Hobhouse and the Speaker over to his carriage. 'Mind, I mean Buckingham Palace as a permanent gift!' he stressed. 'Mind that!'[14]

Melbourne hurriedly asked the architect Blore for a report and to his relief got a categorical assertion that the plan was hopeless; 'so thoroughly inexpedient and ... attended with so many disadvantages and inconveniences that a worse selection could not well be made'.[15] The enraged King denounced the report and claimed that it was his prerogative to appoint the place at which Parliament should meet.[16] The prime minister counter-attacked. The Commons, he said, were thoroughly suspicious about the royal intentions and, if the matter were pressed, would be certain to put forward irritating proposals for St James's Palace and Marlborough House. More subtly, he argued the perils of rebuilding on a more extensive site; '... it will be very difficult to avoid providing much larger accommodation for Spectators as well as for Members, and Lord Melbourne need not recall to Your Majesty's mind the fatal effects which large Galleries filled with the Multitude have had upon the deliberations of public Assemblies.'[17]

The King gave way, but with bad grace. What injured him most was that his gesture – which, to be fair, was meant in part at least philanthropically – had been so misrepresented by his enemies. He complained that the Press 'with its usual malignity and venom,' had portrayed him as selfishly seeking to shift his private expenses on to the shoulders of the public.[18] Though he did not believe that his prime minister had himself helped to propagate the slander, he felt that more could have been done to protect him.

Such bitterness was doubly dangerous since it came at a time when relations between the King and his ministers were seriously deteriorating. The traditional honeymoon period after the change of administration had proved brief. 'The King is . . . perfectly satisfied and well pleased with his Ministers,' wrote Palmerston complacently to his brother in August 1834. No other form of government was even a possibility.[19] Disraeli was more perceptive when he noted that the King had asked his ministers to dinner and concluded, cynically, that he must therefore be about to dismiss them. 'He evidently, for he is very cunning, does not wish them to say when out that they were never *once* asked, during the whole administration, to the royal table.'[20]

The truth was that relations between King and ministers would remain placid so long as the latter steered a prudently inactive course. But however much such a policy might have suited Melbourne it was not acceptable to his more activist colleagues. In particular Russell was determined to launch a fresh assault on the entrenched interests of the Irish church. This, the King was resolved to oppose. Inevitably, therefore, a clash lay only a little way ahead. But there were more immediate reasons for the King's growing hostility to his ministers.

The most serious were the antics of Lord Brougham. Melbourne, in one of the most brutal letters that a prime minister can ever have written to a former colleague, was later to tell him bluntly that his conduct had been one of the principal causes of the dismissal of the ministry and that it provided the most popular justification for such a move.[21] In the summer of 1834 he seems to have gone slightly off his head. He had convinced himself not only that he was saviour of the government but master of the realm as well. Melbourne was his nominee, the King his puppet. In this euphoric mood he packed up the Great Seal and embarked on a tour of Scotland, drunk with vainglory and occasionally with whisky toddy. His speeches were extravagant, still more so were the letters which he wrote to the King reporting his various triumphs. 'There could not indeed be a more revolting spectacle,' commented *The Times* tartly, 'than for the highest law officer of the empire to be travelling about like a quack doctor through the provinces, puffing himself and his little nostrums, and committing and degrading the Government of which he had the honour to be a member.'

It is hard to be sure whether he really behaved so very badly. Reports of his speeches do not sound exceptionally bombastic for a politician. He·himself considered that he had been hardly used and made the scapegoat for the government's failure: '... is it common fairness to blame me because *the Court makes my proceedings a pretext* for doing what you all know it had resolved to do?'[22] But there was no doubting the King's outrage at his conduct. It served a double purpose; both discrediting the ministry of which he was a senior member and satisfying the King that Melbourne could not control his colleagues. Linked with other internal quarrels it provided a convincing portrait of a party in disarray and a government in the last stages of disintegration.

*

When the final crisis broke in November, 1834, it therefore did not, as some historians have implied, come from the blue; a sudden and whimsical decision on the part of the King to dismiss his ministers. Over the months since the resignation of Grey the King's antipathy to his ministers had ripened, through a series of doubts and suspicions, into a genuine conviction that they were no longer fit to rule. His entourage, scenting that victory might now be within reach, were working on him with particular vigour. Lady Cowper described him as badgered and bullied on all sides[23] while Miss Eden watched in dismay as Lady Sydney, Miss D'Este, the Howes, the Brownlows and the rest of the high Tory court party worked busily on his fears.[24]

At another time their efforts might have had less effect. Many people had noticed, however, that the King had been more than usually depressed and exhausted during that summer and autumn. The Duke of Cumberland said roundly that he was insane and a regent should be called for.[25] Princess Lieven wrote to her brother of strange scenes which she had recently had with him; she had concluded, and Wellington had agreed, 'that the King of England seems to me in a fair way to become as mad as his father.'[26] In May, Queen Adelaide had gone on a visit to Germany. Just before she left the King had suffered a frenzy of excitement, hinting darkly at the bachelor joys he would savour when she was away. Then abruptly he switched and could hardly bear to let her go. Adelaide told the Duchess of Dino that her absence would make it easier for the King to change his ministers, some people feared that it might make it easier for him to lose his wits.[27]

There is not much in this. William was far from demented, whatever his brother might hopefully broadcast to his cronies. He dismissed the

Whigs because he believed they could no longer carry on. His judgment was wrong, and the strains under which he laboured may have helped to warp it, but it was based on perfectly sensible premises and was concurred in by a large number of people whose sanity and prudence were in no way in question. To some extent, at least, it was concurred in by Lord Melbourne himself.

The final crisis began early in November, 1834, when it became clear that Lord Spencer was dying. Rarely can the death throes of an aged peer who had long out-lived his years of usefulness have been attended with greater foreboding. When he died, Althorp would be translated to the Lords. The prime minister told the King that he was anticipating 'most serious difficulty and embarrassment',[28] and William saw no reason to doubt his word. Even if Althorp could be cajoled into remaining an active politician – which seemed unlikely since he had repeatedly rejected the idea of playing a role in that 'Hospital for Incurables', the House of Lords – his vital influence would be lacking in the Commons and the balance of power in the government would slip still farther towards the activist left.

To fill Althorp's gap as leader in the Commons Melbourne suggested Lord John Russell. To this William strongly objected.[29] Contumelious as all his clan, Lord John had made it plain to the King that he considered him a third-rate mind performing a second-rate function with a style of striking gracelessness. But worse than this, Russell was identified with the policy of further encroachments on the Anglican church in Ireland. Such a man, felt the King, should be expelled from government, not promoted. Melbourne had anticipated such an attitude and was armed with other suggestions. With gradually diminishing enthusiasm he put forward Abercromby, Spring Rice, even Hobhouse. All seemed to the King equally or still more inadequate.

The fact is that King William had made up his mind that Althorp was irreplaceable and Melbourne could have named every man in his party without finding a substitute acceptable to the King. This view was perhaps extravagant but it had been instilled in him by the very men who were now arguing the contrary. It was Lord Grey who had first told him that the removal of Althorp from the Commons 'would be, of itself, a sufficient reason for breaking up his Administration'.[30] It was Melbourne himself who had written gloomily to the King as late as November 12, '. . . the Government in its present form was mainly founded upon the personal weight and influence possessed by Earl Spencer in the House of Commons . . . That Foundation is now withdrawn . . .'[31] After such a preparation it was hardly surprising that the King was sceptical when ministers showed signs of remaining in office.

When Melbourne called on the King at Windsor on November 13 and explained his plans for the future, William is supposed to have said: 'Then it appears to me that further concessions will be required from the Church?' Melbourne agreed, whereupon the King retorted, 'For that I am not prepared, and therefore the Ministry is at an end!'[32] In fact he said nothing of the sort, but went to bed; yet his putative retort exactly summed up his thinking. His lack of confidence in the whole administration and his dislike of Russell were the background to his decision but it was his fear of a further attack on the church which drove him to the final, fatal step. He was fortified by Melbourne's admission that resignations from the government would follow if measures of reform were introduced. Only an undertaking that the revenues of the Irish church would be protected could have won back royal support. Such an undertaking Melbourne would not have been allowed to give.

At dinner that evening Lady Brownlow thought Melbourne, 'less talkative and agreeable than usual, but the King was in great spirits and laughed heartily at Lord Adolphus' jokes.'[33] King William was never happier than when he had made up his mind to some decisive course of action and at that moment he can have been in no doubt that he was about to turn to the Tories. Formal confirmation came after breakfast next day. In a letter which the King presented to his departing minister he restated all the arguments which had led him to lose confidence in the Whigs and brought him to the sad conclusion that it would not 'be acting *fairly* or *honourably* . . . to call upon His Lordship for the continuation of his services in a Position of which the Tenure appears to the King so precarious.'[34]

Melbourne accepted his dismissal with extreme amiability. Guessing that the King would wish at once to appeal to the Duke of Wellington he cheerfully volunteered to carry any message there might be. Their parting, indeed, was exceptionally affectionate and Melbourne had hardly left the Castle before King William was writing him a letter in his own crabbed and arthritic hand: 'After the very *painful* Conversation for *both* Parties this morning and so *honourably* disinterested in Viscount Melbourne the King *cannot* permit the Day to pass without assuring his Lordship that H.M. will *never* forget those Words that fell from Viscount Melbourne during the Audience His Lordship had with the King . . .'[35] Though he had no doubts that the course he had adopted was the right one, he must have wondered, as Melbourne departed, whether he would find a man to replace him who by temperament and habit would suit him half as well.

*

On November 15, before ministers had even been told of what had happened, *The Times* carried an indignant paragraph informing its readers that: 'The King has taken the opportunity of Lord Spencer's death to turn out the Ministry, and there is every reason to believe the Duke of Wellington has been sent for. The Queen has done it all.' Probably Edward Ellice, a junior minister and Grey's brother-in-law, leaked the information.[36] Lord Holland saw it at breakfast. 'Here's another hoax,' he commented cheerfully; then posted off to the cabinet meeting to find that it was all too true.

At Windsor the paragraph, particularly because of its – in this case at least – totally unjustified slur on the Queen, caused an explosion of rage. The King was already closeted with Wellington when Taylor brought in the paper. 'There, Duke!' exclaimed the King. 'You see how I am insulted and betrayed. Nobody in London but Melbourne knew last night what had taken place here . . .; will your grace compel me to take back people who have treated me in this way?'[37] His anger did not last long but he was confirmed in his impression that he had done well to rid himself of this indiscreet and intemperate rabble.

The duke was less sure. To Peel he regretted that the King had acted so precipitately; if Melbourne had been given enough rope he would assuredly have hanged not only himself but the whole Whig party as well.[38] But it was no use lamenting what might have been. The King had got himself into a mess and the duke had no doubt that it was his duty to help him out of it. On one point he insisted. His experience in 1832 had taught him the folly of trying to run the country from the Lords with a hostile majority in the House of Commons. If the Commons were to be managed successfully the prime minister must come from that House. Peel was the only possibility. The King concurred, on the understanding that Wellington would fill the gap while Peel was being fetched home from holiday on the continent. A court official, Disraeli's 'Hurried Hudson', was sent scurrying across Europe to bring back the wandering leader. He missed him in Paris, tracked him down in Rome, set off with Peel's reply without even spending a night with his quarry, chartered a fishing boat to get back across the

THE CONSTITUTIONAL COUP D'ÉTAT 257

channel and posted back to Windsor, to be sharply reprimanded for spending a few hours in bed in London on the way. The answer he bore was a cautious consent.

On November 17 Wellington was sworn in as Lord Treasurer; in rapid succession he then took the oath as home secretary, foreign secretary and secretary for war. Lyndhurst was lent the Great Seal, but with no promise of being subsequently made Lord Chancellor. No other appointment was made. For one giddy moment a single states-man had engrossed all the executive offices of government. At the first meeting of the privy council the outgoing ministers came face to face with the collection of Tories whom the duke had scraped together for the purpose. Greville noticed with approval that perfect civility was observed all round except in the case of Brougham who stalked through the ranks of his enemies 'looking as black as thunder and took no notice of anybody'.[39] He made his feelings even clearer when he omitted to hand over the Great Seal in person but instead sent it to the King wrapped up in a bag 'exactly as a fishmonger might have sent a salmon for the King's dinner.' William is reported to have said that he never wished to see Brougham's ugly face again – a piece of schoolboy invective of which he may only too easily have been guilty.[40]

'The dismissal of the Ministers has been most offensive in the mode, so abrupt, so unlike anything gentlemanlike. To those who had very active affairs it was really most inconvenient.'[41] Lady Holland's un-characteristically genteel protest was by no means typical of the Whig rank and file. They had been robbed of office, betrayed by a nefarious plot. The Queen was a favourite target for their abuse; headed by the royal bastards, every discontented supporter of Melbourne seemed to delight in suggesting that her head had been predominant in the constitutional *coup d'état*. Erroll, the King's son-in-law, was so out-rageous on the subject in a public coffee-room that a gentleman stand-ing by cried out: 'Shame! Shame!'[42] But the Queen was only surro-gate for the greater sinner. Though public indignation was not so marked as in 1832, the King's reputation in Westminster had rarely been lower. It seemed that his popularity had gone for ever. It remains to establish whether this loss of favour was deserved.

*

To dismiss a popular government is a dubious proceeding for any monarch; to dismiss a popular government which commands a large majority in the House of Commons might seem wholly unjustifiable.

K.W.

Those who have sought nevertheless to justify it have argued that
Melbourne had laid such emphasis on the future weakness of his government as to convince William that it could never carry on; that in all
but the last formal rites he had indeed resigned. The argument has
some validity. Both Melbourne and Grey did emphasize the difficulties
ahead; Melbourne did show a marked lack of enthusiasm for continuing in office, did admit that there might be secessions, did accept
his dismissal with alacrity, almost relief. But this is still far from volun-
tary resignation. On November 19, Taylor wrote to Melbourne on
the King's instructions; putting formally on record that:

> '. . . not a word fell from You . . . which could justify the Assertion
> in the *Standard* that You "had said to the King that the Government
> must necessarily fall to Pieces in Consequence of its own differences
> before the Meeting of Parliament . . ." The King has ordered me to
> be thus explicit that Your Lordship may possess a Document of
> which You may make such Use as Your own good Judgement and
> Discretion shall prescribe. No man is more desirous than is His
> Majesty that Justice should be done to Your Conduct.'[43]

In the light of this generous letter the more fanciful accounts of Melbourne's interviews with the King can clearly not be sustained. He did
not minimize his difficulties but, equally, did not suggest that they
would prove impossible to surmount.

Grey pondered the situation at length and concluded that he could
not blame the King for his decision. In his opinion, he told Russell, it
was 'impossible for the present Government to go on.'[44] Nor was
Melbourne himself any more partisan. In a letter of striking moderation he told Grey:

> 'I am not surprised at his decision, nor do I know that I can entirely
> condemn it. You know the motives which have led him to form it
> as well as I do. His great distrust of the majority of the members of
> the present Cabinet; his particular dislike to John Russell . . .; the
> recent conduct of the Chancellor, and the absolute disgust and
> alienation which it has created in the King's mind; his lively appre-
> hension of the measures which he expected to be proposed to him
> with respect to the church . . . these considerations . . . have led
> him to this conclusion; and it is impossible to say . . . that all these
> feelings are unreasonable and unfounded. It is almost superfluous to

state to you that towards me personally the King's conduct has been most fair, honourable and kind; and I owe it to him to say that, whether his decision be right or wrong, I feel confident that he has come to it conscientiously, upon his own conviction that it is best, and unbiased by any other advice or influence whatever.'[45]

Counsel for the defence could hardly have put the case more kindly.

No defence, however, can gloss over the King's blunders. The first of these was his misjudgment of the Whig party. He believed, with excellent reason, that the party was subject to serious strains from within but he did not realize that the surest way to relieve those strains was to push them into opposition. Left in office they might have disintegrated; Melbourne's dismissal rallied them in enthusiastic if largely illusory unity.

But second, and more serious, was the King's misjudgment of his own strength. When the Duke of Wellington took office William reminded him of the not wholly dissimilar crisis of 1784. The administration which was then put in had lasted for seventeen years; he hoped that the same might prove true of this new Tory ministry.[46] The analogy was a revealing one; for he was referring to the celebrated occasion when the genius of Pitt and the obstinate support of George III had destroyed the cohorts of Fox and North and turned an insignificant minority in the House of Commons into a triumphant majority. It had been the final flourish of the 'King's Friends'; the last time that a monarch had been able to transform the Lower House according to his wishes. That William should now hint that this might happen again showed a complete misunderstanding of the constitutional position. Even in 1784 very special circumstances had helped the King; since then the royal influence in the House of Commons had been steadily eroded and the Reform Bill had done no more than apply the *coup de grâce* to an already dying system. William's actions betrayed an alarming misconception of his position, and of his influence in parliament and in the country.

Injudicious, therefore, his actions certainly were; their failure proved what anyway was evident to most contemporaries. Dishonourable, unconstitutional, dictatorial: they were not. In the apologia which he prepared for Peel he shows that he was conscious of the argument that he should have allowed the Whig government to tear itself to shreds. He did not do so, he said, because to have sanctioned the nomination of Lord John Russell would have been tacitly to accept his designs on the Irish church. By taking the line he did, he adopted 'the plain and simple course' which became him.[47] King William was a plain and simple man. Given his political principles, his reaction was inevitable. If he had reacted differently he would certainly have proved himself a shrewder politician but he would also have shown himself a different and perhaps a lesser man.

CHAPTER XXI

The Tory Interlude

PEEL's administration was doomed before it had really started; like an embarrassed spectre it flitted across the stage of history, aware that it had entered on the wrong cue and uneasily suspecting that it was in the wrong play altogether. More than any other government since 1784 it owed its existence to the King. He told Wellington that he was 'resolved neither to flinch nor falter, but having embarked with them, to nail his flag to the mast, and put forth all the constitutional authority of the Crown in support of the Government.'[1] This very manifest presence of the King aboard the ship temporarily blinded many observers to the more serious deficiencies of crew and bottom but it was not long before the illusion wore thin. It is conceivable that a monarch more skilled at the political game might have made a better showing but the cruel truth was that no King could have altered and few even delayed the final disastrous outcome.

Peel returned to England on December 9, 1834. In the meantime the Duke of Wellington – 'His Highness the Dictator,' as Grey angrily described him – continued to provide singlehanded virtually the entire machinery of government.[2] Peel took over the task with reluctance; he was more sceptical than his colleagues about the extent of the royal influence and had few hopes that he might gain converts from the Whigs. His only chance, as he saw it, lay in winning the support of the moderate Canningite rump which lingered on uncertainly between the two main parties. Almost his first move was therefore to turn to Stanley.

He was quickly disappointed. Stanley was far too prudent to commit himself to so hazardous an enterprise. He and his followers decided to wait and see. By so doing they made certain the rapid return of the Whigs to power. Peel was downcast, the King less so. 'As He wishes at all times to find the good Side of a Question,' he told Peel with awe-inspiring optimism, he concluded that Stanley's refusal, would tend 'to the more easy Settlement of the general Arrangements'.[3] In a sense he was right. With no Stanleyites to fit into the government, Peel went quickly on to form an administration of his own and Wellington's supporters. It was homogeneous but, based as it was on what Grey described as pure, unmixed and unmitigated Toryism, it was in for a rough time in the House of Commons.

Peel had no intention of submitting it to such a test until he had tried to improve the complexion of the House's membership. A general election was called for early January. The campaign was memorable for Toryism and for England since in it Peel first enunciated the principles of a new conservatism designed to satisfy the needs of the nineteenth century. He would show the electorate, he told the King, that he had the power to do as much in the way of real salutary reform, as any friend to such reform could wish.[4]

King William was delighted, and applauded with equal fervour Peel's celebrated letter to the electors of Tamworth which enshrined the new philosophy. Its 'Frankness and Manliness', he told Peel, 'are not more creditable to His Character than the good Sense and sound Judgement which distinguish it.'[5] His enthusiasm may seem to contrast oddly with the apparent revulsion from reform which had led him so recently to dismiss the Whigs. In fact there had been little change. His concern was always more with personalities than principles. Softened by the bland, business-like tones of Peel even an assault on the established church might have been palatable; the same measure presented more stridently by Lord John Russell would have been outrageous radicalism and would certainly have called in question the Coronation Oath. This attitude was not entirely foolish – the doctrine that 'it ain't what you do but the way that you do it' has as much validity in the political as any other field – but it betrayed him into many illogicalities and produced results strikingly unfair to those of his ministers who were unwise or unfortunate enough to lose his confidence.

Peel's new crusade came too late to save the Tories. There had, however, been some movement in their favour and, a week after the polls had closed, Peel was still claiming that any small majority against him would quickly melt away when parliament met. 'I have never allowed Myself to doubt it,' replied the King grandiloquently, 'or to consider it possible that We should not go forward in the execution of Our noble course, in spite of temporary Obstruction or Difficulty . . .'[6] He remained in this cheerful mood even when an analysis of the results began to disquiet the Tory leaders, assuring his prime minister, on unstated authority, that some of the doubtful would certainly prove

supporters and some opponents no worse than doubters.[7] With im-
partial observers suggesting that there might be a majority of a hundred
against him, Peel was less and less inclined to share his monarch's
optimism.

The only security of the Tories lay in the apparent impossibility of
forming any other administration. The only practicable alternative was
for Melbourne to return and this, to most people, appeared out of the
question. They could not look the King in the face again, commented
Hobhouse, 'nor he them, after such a clear intimation on his part that
he disliked them . . .'[8] That a former minister with some claims to
radicalism should consider so inconceivable the prospect of forcing a
government on a reluctant King shows how far the traditions and the
realities of power had grown apart in the England of 1835.

The King's illusions were dispelled with cruel rapidity. Sutton had
proved perfectly adequate as Speaker of the House of Commons.
Though a Tory, he would normally have been re-elected unopposed.
The opposition, however, determined to prove their power by un-
seating him. They nominated the dull, grave Abercromby – a man of no
greater merit but a committed Whig. The elder statesmen of the party
deprecated the move as inexpedient and ungentlemanly – 'How the
devil does John Russell make out the question of the Speakership to be
one of principle?' asked Grey indignantly[9] – but they were unable to
control the rank and file. It seemed that the adherents of out-and-out
opposition might have over-reached themselves. Peel told William
he was tolerably confident: 'His Majesty cannot bring Himself to
entertain a doubt on the Subject,'[10] retorted the King, whose resolute
refusal to contemplate the inevitable, always remarkable, now bordered
on the manic. The defeat of Sutton by ten votes left him little scope for
further self-deception.

The King was now forced to admit that his gamble might have failed.
The discovery promised much personal humiliation and, as he saw it,
still graver peril for the country. If the Tories were defeated, he told
Peel, it would be a 'direct Censure passed upon His Majesty's Conduct
by a Party avowing its determination to force itself upon Him . . . in
opposition to His declared Principles and Sentiments, His Wishes and
His Conscience.' He might have, he said ominously 'to sacrifice
feelings, Comfort and rooted Opinions and to bow under the over-
powering weight of this Evil, but it is impossible that He can give His
Confidence to Men so introduced to His Councils . . . They may
become his Ministers, but never His Confidential Servants. He would

receive all their Advice with Jealousy and Suspicion . . .'[11] Such objurgations offered a poor prospect for domestic harmony when the Whigs returned to power.

It was rumoured that Peel had proposed and William agreed to a further dissolution in a last desperate bid to redeem his position. The Whig leaders did not believe that Peel would be so bold or the King so foolish.[12] Since they were right about the Prime Minister, the King was not put to the test. If he had been, he might have yielded. The factious opposition of the Whigs seemed to him disloyal, almost treasonable; it confirmed his conviction that any step he might take to keep them out would be in the best interests of the country. A few days after Sutton's defeat Adolphus FitzClarence reported that his father was determined to stand by his ministers to the last,[13] and in the hectic spring of 1835 few would have ventured to predict at what point 'the last' would come.

The next blow came when the Commons debated the nomination of Lord Londonderry as ambassador to Russia. The Whigs were enchanted to humiliate this caricature reactionary whose arrogance and bile had made him the most hated man in England after the Duke of Cumberland. Not only did they condemn the appointment but even Stanley and his followers voted against the government. Defeat was total and Londonderry renounced his embassy. The King met this disaster with magnificent if misplaced *sang-froid*. He rejoiced, he told Peel, that Londonderry's well-judged withdrawal had saved the government from embarrassment and derived obscure satisfaction from his belief that 'the teazing Proceedings' of the opposition betrayed 'a sense of growing weakness' and a fear that they could not seriously injure the government.[14]

By the end of March, as the government tottered from defeat to defeat, Peel was almost pleading with the King to relieve him of his responsibilities. It was bad for the country, he argued, to see a House of Commons totally out of the control of the executive. This might be tolerated if the position of ministers seemed gradually to be growing stronger but such was not the case. The House of Commons – a point which he knew well would appeal to the King – would thus become 'habituated to the exercise of functions not properly belonging to them.' The royal prerogative would be the first and most important victim.[15] The King's reply was twenty-five pages of rambling sadness, concluding inevitably with the wistful hope that Peel would unite all the honourable men of every party into a coalition.[16]

It was now merely a question of when the Whigs would apply the *coup de grâce*. Peel had every virtue except resignation, said the wits, but he was resolved to remedy this as soon as possible. Wellington was disposed to stick it out a little longer but recognized that the end was certain. The King told Lord Wharncliffe that he was 'stout as a lion', but bemusedly he began to perceive that no amount of stoutness would meet the case.[17] He still saw one chance to save face and keep out the radicals. He turned to Grey and besought him to take on the government again. Melbourne, of all people, was selected as go-between.[18] What he thought of this errand is uncertain but he performed it gracefully – no doubt the more so because he knew nothing would induce his former leader to return. Sure enough, Grey declined. 'I should sink under a burden which I have not strength to maintain,' he wrote plaintively.[19] Instead he recommended the King to send for Melbourne and Lansdowne, promising to ease what might otherwise be a somewhat disagreeable meeting by sitting in and helping to jolly things along.[20]

*

'I will have no more of these sudden changes,' King William is alleged to have told a naval friend. 'The country shan't be disturbed in this way, to make my reign tumble about, like a topsail sheet-block in a breeze.'[21] Since he more than anybody else had been responsible for steering the country into the present hurricane the remark showed some lack of sensitivity. Nor was he going to have much to say about the shape of the next government. Melbourne was in a position to dictate terms and had no intention of forgoing an iota of his advantage. He made his conditions with painful clarity.[22]

First, there was to be no more trouble with the royal households. Melbourne remembered only too well the tribulations which he and Grey had endured and did not intend to let them recur. There need be no immediate resignations but all officers with seats in the Lords or Commons would be expected to support the government and any vacancies would be filled on Melbourne's recommendation. To this the King took no exception. Second, there must be an immediate creation of peers. About this the King was more hesitant. It was, after all, unusual to greet the arrival of a new ministry with a salvo of ennoblements. A few might be made but, he emphasized, such consent would not imply readiness to agree to a creation of peers of the kind visualized in 1832: 'His Majesty should declare most positively that under no circumstances will He ever again consent to a Proposal having in the most remote degree such a Tendency.'[23]

Melbourne was too wise to be drawn into dispute over so hypothetical an issue but he was more concerned when the King announced that he would veto certain names if they were put forward for ministerial appointments. He stated firmly that he would be unable to accept any 'Principle of Exclusion'. The King was equally firm in refusing to abandon it. Deadlock was avoided by common sense on both sides. With Lord Grey as honest broker Melbourne let it be known that he would not put forward any names to which the King had a rooted objection; the King for his part told Grey that only O'Connell, Sheil and Hume would be wholly unacceptable.[24] Since Melbourne had no intention of offering a job to any of them he was able gracefully to concur. If he had wanted to have Brougham back as Chancellor, William would probably have been disgusted but acquiescent; as it was the prime minister regarded his former colleague with vengeful loathing. He wished, however, to avoid turning him into too inveterate an enemy and so left the post vacant and put the Great Seal into commission. The King grudgingly accepted that all things considered, Melbourne had made the best of what was, and was likely to remain, an outstandingly bad job.[25]

One serious disagreement had still to be settled. In his answer to Melbourne's original ultimatum the King had dropped dark hints about the problems of the Irish church.[26] Melbourne was uncertain what the letter implied – probably the King himself was no more certain – but it was enough to make him ill at ease. After all, it was this issue that had been primarily responsible for his dismissal four months before. The House of Commons, Melbourne reminded the King, had resolved that the surplus revenues of the Irish church should be devoted to general education for children of all religions. To this – the notorious Appropriation Clause – the Whigs were pledged and no government could they form unless royal approval was guaranteed.[27]

The King shuffled and fell back on his last line of defence, the Coronation Oath. There is no reason to doubt that his scruples were genuine – for the Defender of the Faith it is, after all, no light thing to approve an assault on the established church – but Melbourne found it hard to sympathize, especially when the King announced that he wished to consult the fifteen judges. With something less than his usual suavity the Whig leader retorted that the matter was of great importance and urgency. The King's scruples were a matter of conscience, not of law, and the fifteen judges had nothing to do with it. Dubiously, he agreed that it would not be improper for William to lay his doubts before the outgoing Chancellor, Lord Lyndhurst.[28]

But Lyndhurst was far too sly to become involved in such an imbroglio. He pleaded that he was only temporarily acting as Chancellor and knew nothing of the proposed bill. In such circumstances he refused either to relieve or to arouse still further the royal conscience. 'The Lord Chancellor positively declines giving any opinion *whatsoever* to the King,' wrote William to Melbourne in some indignation.[29] He had now decided, he said, that since he would have to give his consent to the bill in the end, there was not much to be gained by refusing to do so in the early stages. The logic was impeccable, though Melbourne might reasonably have wondered why it had not occurred to the King a little earlier.

The last obstacle had now been removed and Melbourne's government was duly installed. 'The King in reappointing us was manifestly nervous and constrained but civil . . .' noted Lord Holland.[30] He paid little attention to anyone except Lord Howick, Grey's eldest son, to whom he was particularly polite, both as his father's son and as a new minister not tainted with the sins of his colleagues. No more could have been expected, worse had been feared. But it was a cool start to a new relationship.

CHAPTER XXII

The Declining Days

In April 1835 it might reasonably have been expected that the King should be dejected, almost, indeed, distraught. In every aspect of his life things seemed to have gone wrong. His policies were in ruins. He had been defeated and humiliated, the Tories whom he had befriended had been shattered, men had been forced upon him whom he was resolved to treat with jealousy and suspicion. The security of the country, the sanctity of its constitution, even the very existence of the monarchy, seemed to him in jeopardy.

There was little in his private life to redeem these catastrophes. Though Queen Adelaide was only forty-two years old and theoretically could have borne him another child, in fact all hope that King William might sire an heir to the throne of England had long since been extinguished. Apart from anything else it seemed hardly likely that he was now physically capable of fathering a child, so much so that when it was rumoured in January, 1835, that the Queen was again pregnant the sniggering gossips calculated how long it was since Lord Howe had last been at Windsor. 'Damned stuff,' growled the King when the tale of his wife's pregnancy was passed on to him and damned stuff it turned out to be. Damned stuff too was the poisonous prattle about the Queen's infidelity, though her conduct had certainly been indiscreet. Impressionable, indeed gullible, Adelaide would hold in exaggerated esteem the most unworthy objects. A quack doctor in Brighton was another of her idols – a totally innocent relationship which neverthe-less gave rise to lubricious speculation on the part of the idle and the malicious.[1]

For the King, with the corridors of Windsor swarming with his bastards and their progeny, it must have been especially galling to reflect that not one legitimate child of his remained. To his heir, Princess Victoria, he was genuinely attached; given a chance he would indeed have delighted in her almost as if she had been his own child, but a foolish and embittered quarrel with the Duchess of Kent deprived him even of this consolation.

Nor could he feel completely confident about the future of the little princess after he died. The Duke of Cumberland was known to feel strongly that he would make a better king than his brother, and his son George than any mere princess. His *aide-de-camp* recorded a curious evening at Windsor when the King and Cumberland dined together. From the next room he heard the duke grow more drunken and more quarrelsome till finally he called in his suite and proposed a toast to: 'The King's heir, God bless him!' William paused, collected his wits, and called out: 'The King's heir, God bless her!' then, throwing the glass over his shoulder, exclaimed – somewhat cryptically – : 'My crown came with a lass, and my crown will go with a lass.' Cumberland stormed from the room. The same authority relates that when King William was almost on his death-bed rumours were heard of a *coup d'état* planned by Cumberland. Wellington and Melbourne were involved in midnight consultations and plans were laid to frustrate the attempt.[2] If the threat ever existed it is hard to believe that it was taken seriously, but Cumberland's black resentment of Princess Victoria must have disquieted the King.

William got great pleasure from his grandchildren and Queen Adelaide could hardly have been kinder to them if they had been her own. Windsor seemed always to have its contingent of small Kennedys, Sydneys or Falklands with a few FitzClarences, depending on which of the sons happened at that moment to be on speaking terms with their father. They lisped 'Dear Queeny' or 'Dear King' in a suitably in-gratiating manner, scampered up and down the corridors and gave the great morgue a little of the life it lacked so sorely.[3] But there was precious little other satisfaction to be had from the royal children. His daughters were fond enough of him but resented and were dis-courteous to the Queen while Lord Erroll quarrelled with the Queen, insulted her publicly and cut her on her own terrace at Windsor.

It was his graceless sons, however, who caused the King most distress. The more he sought to do for them the more they demanded and the less gratitude they showed. Rapacious, arrogant, disqualified by vanity and incapacity from undertaking anything useful by them-selves, they harried their wretched father with a ferocity which dispels the sympathy one would otherwise have felt for them. The King was constantly trying to secure them pensions or perquisites, pestering his unfortunate ministers with often extravagant requests. 'His Majesty is persuaded,' wrote Taylor, 'that Earl Grey will consider His desire to provide for His children very reasonable . . .' The word 'reasonable' was smudged and Taylor confessed subsequently that he had started to write 'natural' before it struck him as an unfortunate word to choose.[4]

Lord Munster was the most exigent of the brothers, already showing that paranoiac sense of persecution which was in the end to drive him to suicide. After he had been installed as Constable of the Round Tower and a privy councillor he had been reconciled with his father, but this had not lasted long. Soon he was complaining that his position was intolerable, that nothing could prevent his utter ruin, that his relations with his father-in-law, Lord Egremont, had been disastrously embroiled and that for this, as for everything, his father was to blame.[5] Munster had a power to distress the King enjoyed by no one else and he used it without inhibition. When William offered to have his portrait painted for him he refused scornfully on the grounds that it would soon be in a pawnbroker's shop.[6] His visits were dreaded by all who felt for the King. 'Lord Munster is, I understand, coming here next week . . .' wrote Taylor to Grey, 'and I fear that his Presence will be a Source of constant Excitement and Irritation. Indeed, the effects of the last Visit are still very perceptible.'[7]

Augustus FitzClarence was little better. He rejected a prebendal stall at Worcester as not being grand enough, and almost rejected a canonry of Windsor for the same reason. He grabbed all the money that was offered him without ever expressing thanks for that or any other favour. When he heard that his sister was to be married under the King's roof he refused to conduct the ceremony. Frederick FitzClarence, for his part, protested bitterly that his sisters were being given a fortune more or less equal to his own. He first demanded to be made a major general in the Hanoverian army, then, with still greater vehemence, a peer of the United Kingdom, threatening, whenever he failed to get his way, that he would stand for parliament. 'The whole of your reasoning,' concluded Taylor after indignantly tabulating the iniquities of the brothers, 'strives to establish that the King is to be thanked for nothing, and that between him and his Sons gratitude is a sentiment which cannot exist.'[8]

Nor was the King's health good. His hands were almost crippled by arthritis and any movement caused discomfort and even pain. His asthma, which had given relatively little trouble over the previous decade, was now far worse again and June was a month to be dreaded alike by King, family and ministers. His liver was enlarged and hardened, a condition which must certainly have given him much trouble. Worst of all, he seemed less able to control his never very equable temper. Outbursts became more frequent in which he would grow literally purple with rage and pour out whatever – fortunately often incoherent – abuse might come into his head. 'The King is all but crazy,' snapped Melbourne in a moment of irritation and fatigue.[9] He was exaggerating but certainly there were now occasions on which William could no longer be said to be in command of his faculties. The King recognized this growing weakness, deplored it, and like all the sons of King George III, was haunted by the memory of his father's madness.

Adolphus FitzClarence left a portrait of his father which accords well with his sombre chronicle. The King, he said:

'sleeps in the same room with the Queen, but in a separate bed; at a quarter before eight every morning his *valet de chambre* knocks at the door, and at ten minutes before eight exactly he gets out of bed, puts on a flannel dressing-gown and trousers, walks into his dressing room and goes at once to the water closet. Let who will be there, he never takes the slightest notice of them till he emerges from the temple ... At half-past-nine he breakfasts with the Queen, the Ladies, and any of his family; he eats a couple of fingers and drinks a dish of coffee. After breakfast he reads *The Times* and *Morning Post* commenting aloud on what he reads in very plain terms, and sometimes they hear "That's a damned lie" or some such remark, without knowing to what it applies. After breakfast he devotes himself with Sir H. Taylor to business till two, when he lunches (two cutlets and two glasses of sherry); then he goes out and drives till dinner; at dinner drinks a bottle of sherry – no other wine – and eats moderately, and goes to bed soon after eleven. He is in dreadfully low spirits, and cannot rally at all; the only interval of pleasure which he has lately had was during the Devonshire election, when he was delighted at John Russell's defeat.'[10]

And yet this picture of an ill, angry, frustrated old man does not in the last resort convince. Too many accounts show him patently getting fun out of life: guiding Miss Eden around the gallery at Hampton Court, 'just like a housekeeper with a story for each picture. It was pitch dark so it does not much matter if the pictures were as improper as the stories ...';[11] making bawdy jokes in council about Poulett Thomson being a cuckold; prosing on endlessly to bored but helpless

guests. At a dinner party on the anniversary of the battle of Camper-
down the Queen was about to retire when the King asked the ladies to
stay as he had something to say. He began by noticing the first invasion
of Britain by Julius Caesar, passed on rapidly to the landing of the
Danes, moved on through the intervening years from the days of
Elizabeth to William III and finally released the ladies after a lengthy
analysis of the more recent wars. He was mortified when it was later
pointed out to him that he had forgotten to mention Anson's victory
off Cape Finisterre.[12]

Certainly he felt chagrin, even dismay, at the course of politics, yet
there was still a lot of satisfaction to be got out of being King. He enjoyed the consequence, he enjoyed doing generous deeds for his
friends, he believed that even with an administration of Whigs – perhaps especially with an administration of Whigs – the King had an
important constitutional function to fulfil. He even got a certain satisfaction out of his feud with ministers; regretted his outbursts yet
enjoyed letting himself go. He was on the whole a happy man; and
though his happiness was often ruffled and trials came thick and fast,
he would not have changed his lot for any other.

*

'The King dines at the Duke of Wellington's tomorrow,' wrote
Londonderry on June 7, 1835, 'and is said to continue his sovereign
ill-humour and disgust with his Ministers.'[13] Their relationship over
the next few months was one of chilly aloofness punctuated by spas-
modic and sometimes fearful rows. It is hard to be sure what the King
hoped to gain from this guerrilla warfare. Some people detected a
carefully laid plot; a determination to wear down his ministers, to
break their spirit, as Palmerston put it, 'by finding fault with everybody and everything connected with the Administration, and trying
to pick holes in all our matters';[14] eventually, to force them to resign.
It seems unlikely that any such malign intent existed. The King knew
perfectly well that no alternative administration could be formed and
that it would take more than a few shows of pique from the King to
conjure it into existence. He had learned, painfully, the limitations to
his power. This humiliating knowledge lent fresh bitterness to his
resentment. Paradoxically, if he had been in a position seriously to
injure the Whigs, he would have treated them with greater generosity;
his acrimony was the measure of his impotence.

It was also the measure of his failure to control himself; a failure which alarmed responsible Tories as well as ministers. Peel wrote to Taylor to urge that the King should act with restraint. Taylor's reply is a striking commentary on the limits of his influence. He always preached moderation to the King, he said. 'At times I have succeeded ... and at others failed, or His Majesty has been led away by the excitement of the Moment to Use of language which is much to be lamented ... Unfortunately ... I stand almost alone in this respect and am often counteracted by others, who, in the violence of Party feeling and personal Prejudice, wholly overlook the bounds of reason, discretion and Safety.'[15] The King never took amiss Taylor's efforts to deflect him but too often he was deaf to reason, or could be brought to hear it only after the outrageous letter had been dispatched or the insulting remark flung at some wretched minister. It was a harrowing period for this pattern of the modern civil servant whose sole preoccupation was to ensure that the business of the country was carried on smoothly and with expedition.

In most of the conflicts between King and ministers William had some right on his side, but rarely enough to excuse his churlishness. An early example occurred when Durham was to be sent as special ambassador to Russia. The Emperor of Russia was consulted before the matter had even been broached with the King. This was a point on which monarchs were notoriously touchy and it was inevitable and not unreasonable that William should have been displeased. There was no need, however, to carry his displeasure to the pitch of what Melbourne called 'censure of Palmerston so violent that I know not how I can acquiesce under it'.[16] There was still less excuse for his assault on the innocuous Lord Torrington, a lord of the bedchamber who, when presenting someone at the levee, described him as 'Deputy Governor'.

'Deputy Governor?' demanded the King. 'Deputy Governor of what?'

'I cannot tell your Majesty as it is not upon the card.'

'Hold your Tongue, sir. You had better go home and learn to read!'[17]

The offence just did not merit the rebuke, any more than the presentation of Major Stanhope as usher of the black rod without first getting royal assent was, 'the most outrageous insult ever offered to a monarch'.[18]

But pin-pricks like these were insignificant compared with the bludgeon blows which the King launched at the head of Lord Glenelg. The target was not undeserving; Glenelg was strikingly inept, con-

demned by his own colleague John Russell for indolence and irresolution.[19] But there was a flavour of the vendetta about the royal attitude,
explained in part, perhaps, by the active part which Glenelg had played
in opposing the grant for Queen Adelaide's outfit shortly after the
succession. Whatever its origin, however, his dislike came to a head on
an issue on which he felt the strongest possible qualms of principle.

The future of Canada was in question. The King believed that the
government had plans for the colony which would move it a few
tentative paces down the path towards self-government. To Lord
Gosford, the newly nominated Governor, he exploded: 'I must call
your Lordship's attention to Canada. *That Colony must not be lost to this
Country, which must be the inevitable consequence of making the Legislative
Council there elective* . . . I do not consider the present Cabinet as Mine,
and I caution You what You do. By God if they adopt any such
dangerous course, *I will have them impeached* . . . I believe You are a
Gentleman, so I give You this caution to be on Your Guard . . . Does
Your Lordship understand me? *Canada must not be lost to this
Country* . . .'[20]

The cabinet discussed this outburst and decided it had best be
ignored. The King, however, had no intention of letting the matter
rest. When Glenelg submitted Gosford's instructions he stormed
through them angrily: 'No, my Lord, I will not have that word,
strike out "conciliatory", strike out "liberal".' A compromise was
agreed but two days later he made fresh difficulties and denounced
Glenelg, both in private and in a speech at council.[21] The cabinet was
indignant, the more so as only a little time before the King had been
almost as outspoken in an audience with Sir Charles Grey. 'A mass of
muddle and impropriety,' Melbourne called the royal diatribe, 'such
as never, probably, was equalled before.'[22] A solemn remonstrance was
drawn up recording the concern which ministers felt at William's
address to Grey and his strictures on Glenelg. By criticizing to officials
or outsiders advice given by ministers in the closet, he was under-
mining the position of his government in a way which could not be
tolerated.[23]

The King was contrite and somewhat alarmed. He assured Melbourne
that he wished his ministers well but had been overcome by the strength
of his feelings. His penitence, though real, did not, however, run very
deep. Next year, when the question of holding elections in Lower
Canada was once more mooted, he restated 'his *determination* and fixed
resolution *never* to permit any despatch to be sent to his Majesty's

representative in Canada or any other colony . . . that can for a moment hold out the most distant idea of the King *ever* permitting the question to be entertained by his Majesty's confidential servants of a most remote bearing relative to any change in the manner of the appointment in the King's Councils . . .'[24] Few vetoes could have been expressed in so conscientiously comprehensive a style and, followed as it shortly was by a fresh hail of insults at Glenelg, it did little to cheer Lord Melbourne.

*

The reverberations of the Canadian contretemps had not died away before King and ministers were again embroiled. This time it was over the introduction of a bill to reform municipal corporations in England and Wales. The King objected that he had not been properly consulted; also, somewhat more seriously, that the bill was altogether too drastic in its provisions.[25] Melbourne retorted that the King had sanctioned the introduction of the bill when he had referred to it in the Speech from the Throne. True, said William mildly, but this did not mean that he agreed with it or that he was precluded from putting forward reasoned counter arguments.[26]

Melbourne could hardly quarrel with so dulcet an exposition of the royal case but he did not conceal his fear that sweet reason from Windsor might be translated into something more raucous in the House of Lords. His fears were justified. In August, 1835, the Tory lords led by Lyndhurst assailed the bill in almost every particular. Knowledge of the King's attitude put heart into their revolt, but William was dismayed when he saw that another direct clash between Commons and Lords was in prospect. Fortunately Peel, and less enthusiastically, Wellington came to the rescue. Peel saw that, until opinion in the country had swung to the right, it would be worse than futile to force the government into resignation. For the moment the Whigs must not be provoked too far.[27] The hot-heads were called to heel and the bill, modestly amended, passed through the Lords.

Melbourne saw the King's point more sympathetically when the latter protested at Lord Mulgrave entertaining O'Connell at Viceregal Lodge – 'an irreclaimable blackguard . . . unfit for any gentleman to associate with.'[28] Rather sheepishly the prime minister pleaded that it was Mulgrave's duty to entertain every member of parliament when he passed through Dublin and that to make an exception of O'Connell would have been to adorn him gratuitously with a martyr's crown.[29] What alarmed William was that he knew how heavily Melbourne relied on the tacit support at least of O'Connell and his supporters to sustain his majority in the House of Commons. The government was thus open to blackmail – and any proposals which it might make concerning Ireland were doubly suspect as having been previously approved by that revolutionary brigand.

The Mulgrave administration was making a determined effort to court the Catholics and in this at least the King supported them wholeheartedly. They were, he said roundly, 'as loyal and as well affected as any other Class',[30] and should be treated with all the dignity and equity merited by every British citizen. Eagerly, the Duke of Cumberland nominated himself patron of the Orangemen and devoted himself to thwarting his brother's will. The King treated him with aloof courtesy punctuated with bursts of bad temper: reporting to Melbourne with some pride that, even though the duke had paid a visit of some hours to the Pavilion, he had managed to avoid any tête-à-tête.[31] But the duke was assiduous and by no means unsubtle; though his poison might work deviously, in the end much of it soaked through. The Queen was a willing instrument in his hands and Cumberland persuaded her to write very violently to the King on the subject of the Irish church bill.[32] Discredited but still dangerous, his sullen presence loomed over the royal circle; the mischief he made lingered long after he himself was safely away.

Mutual distrust of Cumberland was not enough to restore King and ministers to harmony. Hostilities reached their height in the summer of 1835 when the King was forced to consent to a bill reducing the strength of the militia. His resentment was shown in council when he suddenly launched into a passionate philippic against government policy. 'I am an old man,' he said, 'older than any of Your Lordships, and therefore know more than any of you.' Next session, he insisted, he would have a new and better bill introduced '*whoever may be, or whoever are Ministers*'. The council heard the speech – especially the threat in its peroration – in glum silence. Melbourne especially looked black and haughty.[33]

In his more rational moments William felt concern about this protracted war of attrition between King and ministers. He sought to put it in perspective when he told Russell: 'There is this difference between the English and the French; here we may differ on certain points; you and I may differ; but we all of us mean well and have but one object. I have my view of things, and I tell them to my Ministers. If they do not adopt them, I cannot help it. I have done my duty.'[34] An admirable sentiment, and undoubtedly sincerely meant; yet in fact it was only half the truth. Again and again the King showed that he could not forgive his ministers for having defeated him. This was not just personal pique – it was the very function of monarchy which he believed had been affronted – but the consequence for the government was the same. They were given the benefit of no doubt, extended no tolerance, treated as enemies to be held at bay with cold courtesy and destroyed when the opportunity arose. William was a fair man, but he treated Lord Melbourne's second administration unfairly. Greville – no lover of the Whigs – referred regretfully to the King's 'unwise, irksome and degraded' posture.[35] The phrase is harsh but not wholly unfair. All that remains to be added is that, though ministers were irked as much as or more than the King, it was William who was degraded.

*

For another battle which he waged over this period it is possible to have far greater sympathy. It is the duty of the biographer to be conspicuously charitable to his subject's enemies; yet in his warfare with the Duchess of Kent it is impossible not to feel that it was the King who was most sinned against. It would have been regrettable but not altogether surprising if William and Adelaide had resented the existence of their sister-in-law whose ostentatiously flourishing daughter seemed constantly to reproach them for their own failure to produce an heir. The very reverse was true. Until 1830 Queen Adelaide and the duchess had been close friends; Adelaide had done much to comfort the widow after the death of her husband. But with the accession of King William all changed. The Duchess of Kent seems to have considered his reign as an undesirable and inconsiderately protracted interregnum between the black wickedness of the Georges and the radiant paradise to open with the accession of Queen Victoria. She longed to be regent herself and, under the influence of her malign toady, Sir John Conroy, seemed determined to act as such even before the occasion offered. In her person the status of 'mother to the heir-presumptive' – not hitherto one which had enjoyed particular prestige in the British hierarchy – took on a new lustre.

William and Adelaide were anxious to make much of their niece. When King William first opened parliament, Queen Adelaide watched from the garden opposite St James's Palace, with Princess Victoria beside her. People saw her and shouted 'The Queen! The Queen!' In response she picked up the princess and put her on the wall beside her. 'God save Both Queens!' someone shouted, and so it might have been.[36] But the Duchess of Kent would have none of it. She had always been uncivil to King William's children, now she refused to have any intercourse with them. When she was staying at Windsor, George FitzClarence blundered into the room where she was breakfasting. At once she fled and rejected the Queen's pleas to return. She made this accidental meeting with her host's eldest son a reason for giving the royal palaces a wide berth, and sought to keep Princess Victoria totally apart in case her innocence might be sullied by a similar outrage.

What was offensive when done in the family became grossly impolitic when performed in public. Early in 1831 the duchess refused to allow her daughter to attend the royal drawing-rooms. Eventually, and with exceedingly bad grace, she gave way but resolutely refused to let Princess Victoria be present on the Birthday. The King professed to be satisfied with the compromise. He was above all anxious, he told Grey, to avoid giving colour to stories 'that Disunion and Jealousy prevailed where they did not'.[37] But he could not forget the offence. His chance to strike back came six months later when the duchess wanted Conroy to be made a baronet. Resentfully he told Grey that he 'would do nothing for the Duchess of Kent and Her Protégés while She continued to take every opportunity of slighting and insulting Him . . .'[38]

Perhaps if the King had been more conciliatory things might have gone better, but he was not one to turn the other cheek. The conflict simmered restlessly for two more years, then exploded again in 1833. The duchess decided that her daughter should see something of her future realm. They embarked on a series of progresses around the country. It is never agreeable to a monarch to be reminded of his incipient demise, especially when the reminder comes with the brutality preferred by the Duchess of Kent. She arrogated to herself a range of salutes and honours normally reserved to the King alone, made free use of the royal yachts, and conferred 'Royal Distinction and Her Style' on a regiment of yeomanry without first obtaining the King's sanction.[39] William retaliated by imposing irritating restrictions on her movements. The luckless Grey, caught between these two royal rowdies, sought helplessly to achieve a compromise. 'Nothing can be worse than the terms on which their Courts are together,' noted Lady Holland sagely. 'Yet I believe the rising sun is more to blame in the contest than the elders.'[40]

Things were not improved when the two young Princes of Württemberg came to stay with the duchess. The King politely invited them to

Windsor but was told that, on the day suggested, the princes unfortunately had an engagement elsewhere. In the event they went to
the London Zoo.[41] His sense of injury was redoubled when, in March
1834, he heard that a marriage was projected between Princess Victoria
and the elder of the two princes. Indignantly he wrote to Grey recording his '*decided* and *unalterable* Objection to this most *indecently* and *dis-
respectfully* proposed Union.'[42] The King, Taylor remarked to the
prime minister with his characteristic flair for under-statement, was
'not a little nettled'.[43] Grey hurriedly replied that reports of a match
were premature and the King subsided, still urging his ministers to
'keep a watchful Eye upon the Designs of the Duchess of Kent, who
may not scruple to sacrifice the Interests of this Country to personal
Considerations.'[44]

In March 1835 a fresh outbreak occurred over Princess Victoria's
confirmation. Thinking the Archbishop of Canterbury was away the
King asked the Duchess of Northumberland to find out what the
Duchess of Kent wanted. The duchess refused to pass any message on
the subject except through the archbishop and William, with equal
pig-headedness, refused to change his emissary. The question was one
of authority, he told Melbourne; 'altho' there may be Obstinacy on
both Sides, His Majesty conceives that which *He* shows to rest on sound
Principles . . .'[45] The duchess gave way but promptly counter-attacked
by announcing another grand progress around the north. The King
wrote sternly to his niece: '. . . I hope the newspapers will *not* inform me
of your travelling *this* year. I *cannot* . . . approve of your flying about
the Kingdom as you have done the last three years and this, if attempted,
I *must* and *shall* prevent . . .'[46] But when it came to the point he found
himself powerless and could only vent his rage by ordering troops not
to show the duchess the usual courtesies on their journey north.

Hostilities came to a head with the appalling scene at Windsor in
August 1836. The duchess had caused great offence only a few days
before when she had totally ignored the Queen's birthday; the King
was anyhow more than usually indignant because he had just come
from Kensington where he had found that the duchess had appropriated
a suite of seventeen rooms which the King had expressly reserved for
himself. Through the long banquet the hundred-odd guests watched
apprehensively as King William steamed like a pressure cooker under
excessive strain. At last came the explosion. As soon as his health had
been drunk he rose to speak:

'I trust in God,' he began, 'that my life may be spared for nine months longer, after which period, in the event, no Regency would take place. I should then have the satisfaction of leaving the royal authority to the personal exercise of that Young Lady [pointing to Victoria] ... and not in the hands of a person now near me, who is surrounded by evil advisers and who is herself incompetent to act with propriety in the station in which She would be placed. I have no hesitation in saying that I have been insulted – grossly and continually insulted – by that person, but I am determined to endure no longer a course of behaviour so disrespectful to me. Amongst many other things I have particularly to complain of the manner in which that young lady has been kept away from my Court ... I would have her know that I am King and that I am determined to make my authority respected ...'[47]

To insult one's sister-in-law in such terms at one's own table and before a hundred guests cannot be called praiseworthy, yet it is hard to read the royal philippic without feeling some of the exultation experienced when Mr Micawber turned and rent Uriah Heep or the Rev. Josiah Crawley crushed Mrs Proudie. The Duchess of Kent had invited outrage and it is impossible to feel much pity for her. For Princess Victoria it was another matter; the unfortunate child burst into tears while her mother sat in silence. After this, a shocked calm settled over relations between Windsor and Kensington. The King privately knew that he had gone too far, the duchess was dismayed by the storm she had provoked. Both were resolved that it should not happen again. No true reconciliation was possible but a frigid courtesy in future governed their intercourse. It was hardly satisfactory but at least it was better than what had gone before. Before he died King William had met Prince Albert, liked him and referred to him as one of the handsomest young men he had ever seen.[48]

*

By the end of 1835 the worst of William's resentment against ministers had died away. In November ministers attending his council were told that they would also be expected to dine with the King;[49] early in 1836 Palmerston took comfort from the King's readiness to appoint a Chancellor and create three new peers.[50] 'I hear the King is behaving well,' a friend wrote to Durham. 'His Majesty said to a person, to whom he speaks unreservedly, he could not understand the views of the Opposition, or what it was they sought. The country, he added, was never more prosperous or more contented. What, then, could they desire?'[51] The question may not indicate any very profound knowledge of the ambitions of politicians but it must have fallen cheerily on the ears of the Whigs.

Lord Melbourne's divorce suit offered the King an unusual chance to show his feelings. Melbourne found himself cast as the accused on a more-or-less trumped up charge of criminal connection with Caroline Norton. Almost certainly he was as innocent as the Court in due course found him, though both he and Mrs Norton had been indiscreet. With its usual talent for believing the worst, the British public, however, concluded Melbourne was guilty long before any jury had had a chance to find him innocent. While the gossip was at its height Melbourne asked the King whether he should resign. William briskly rejected the idea. He had a good nose for a put-up job and was confident enough in his judgment of the prime minister to be sure that he had not done anything particularly dishonourable. If he had believed Melbourne guilty he would have insisted that he be driven from office; because he did not and cared nothing for the slanderous chatter of London society, he was equally determined to keep him there. When the Duke of Cumberland came bearing tales he sent him about his business and complained that it was really too much to hear his ministers subjected to such unsavoury personal abuse.[52]

The King's benevolence may, of course, have been prompted partly by the fear that, if he were to lose Melbourne, Russell would be the successor. With such a fire around him, who would not cling for dear life to the frying pan? Even more, however, it was a sign of a general mellowing, due as much to fatigue as to a change of heart. At the age of seventy he was losing the appetite for battle. At a levee in May, 1836, a guest found him 'shrunk both in mind and body'. When he woke from his habitual nap after dinner he would shake violently and find difficulty in getting to his feet. '. . . the medical men consider the decay of age is fast coming upon him.'[53] For the first time he felt himself an old man; viewed the prospect of his duties with dismay and of his pleasures with sadly reduced enthusiasm. The end might not be in sight but the hill was steep and the going fast becoming tougher.

CHAPTER XXIII

The Last Chapter

THOUGH old age might have brought a measure of resignation the King had not learnt to love his ministers. He was not reconciled to them, nor was going to be. But at least he had learnt to live with them.

It was the King's old butt, Lord Glenelg, who precipitated the most violent clash of that summer. The King was anxious to confer an honour on Lord Aylmer, who had been active in standing up for the King's views while serving in Canada. Glenelg had no particular grounds on which to object but dithered futilely when it came to putting the King's wish into practice. Melbourne, presumably unaware of this, chose the moment when the King's irritation was at its worst, to propose Lord Southwell for the Riband of St Patrick. Indignantly the King replied that he would agree to nothing of the sort till 'the *vacillating* and *procrastinating* Lord Glenelg' had done his duty.[1] Melbourne took umbrage at such abuse of one of his senior ministers. He protested to the King, who replied, with what can only have been feigned surprise, that the letter was strictly private and that, though the epithets used were perhaps a little strong, they had not been intended to give offence.[2] How a letter from the sovereign to his prime minister taxing a senior member of the government with idleness and inefficiency could be described as 'strictly private', was not explained. Melbourne was once more dismayed. He wrote ominously to Russell: 'In his present mood, having got rid of Parliament and having five months before him, he would not be unwilling, I think, to drive me to a resignation. Much allowance ought to be made for his infirmities of all kinds, but it will not do to bear too much.'[3]

*

It was unfortunate for everyone – most of all for Glenelg – that his offence coincided with a crisis in Spain which upset the King and led him into further disagreement with his ministers. A civil war had been dragging on for several years between the legitimate government under the Queen and the Carlists under the Queen's violently reactionary uncle, Don Carlos. The Eastern Powers supported Don Carlos, the English and the French the Queen. It would, of course, have been more efficacious if the Queen's supporters had agreed to act in concert but William, as always, would not hear of any such co-operation. The royal cause was instead sustained by a rickety combination of Roths-childs and the British Legion and there seemed no reason why the war should ever end.

In the summer of 1836 a *coup d'état* forced a relatively liberal consti-tution upon the Queen. The Whigs, or at least Palmerston, were gratified; the King was outraged. When he came on a passage in the draft Speech from the Throne which was cautiously optimistic about the chances of the royalist cause, he indignantly struck it out. 'He has not the least Confidence in the Queen's Government,' he told Mel-bourne, 'no Opinion of the Patriotism of the Spanish Nation, and he does not believe that . . . Her Catholic Majesty's Allies will succeed in rescuing Spain from the State of frightful Disorder and Anarchy in which it is placed by the Imbecility of its Rulers and the unprincipled and atrocious proceedings of every Class of its Population.'[4]

This might have seemed strong enough, but there was worse to come. The King now decided that the constitution forced upon Queen Isabella had so radically changed the situation that all previous agree-ments must be void. The Quadruple Alliance was a dead letter and should be formally buried.[5] Palmerston hurried down to Windsor. He found the King unresponsive to any argument and an unhealthily Tory house-party in residence – Wharncliffe, Howe and Winchelsea among the more conspicuous. For two days he darted around the ante-rooms, trying to get to grips with his evasive monarch. In the end he was forced to put his case on paper. The mere fact that the Spanish constitution had been changed, he pointed out, could not affect our treaty obligations. We were stuck with the Quadruple Alliance, whether we liked it or not.[6]

In the event British policy to Spain went on very much as it had before. But the King never altogether abandoned his position. When the time came to review the Foreign Enlistment Order by which British citizens were allowed to serve in the British Legion in Spain, he opposed it ferociously. He claimed, among other things, that British troops in Spain had been grossly ill-treated. In that case, retorted Palmerston, there would be no problem since they would not want to re-enlist. The King declared that the character and credit of Britain would be endangered by the renewal of the order, Palmerston said that, on the contrary, they would only be endangered by a failure to renew it. In the end, and as usual, the King gave way; though he saved some face by insisting that renewal should be for one year only. 'A very good Stern-chaser to cover a Retreat,' commented Palmerston; a metaphor which William would hardly have appreciated but would have understood only too well.[7]

The crisis differed from those of previous years in that it blew up abruptly in a period of relative calm and passed with equal suddenness. By November all was sunshine again. When Melbourne wrote to propose a day for the meeting of parliament the King agreed with alacrity: '. . . He begs that everybody will dine with Him after the Council, and drink two bottles of wine a man . . .'[8] A year before, ministers would have been lucky if they had been offered a glass of water in the guard-room.

This reconciliation, though real enough, was still not enough to set the King's mind at rest on foreign affairs. The appointment of a new and overtly anti-British government in Paris had renewed all his suspicions of the French: rioting and other disturbances led him to the not wholly ungratifying conclusion that a new and still bloodier revolution was on the way. He told Melbourne that he did not 'apprehend the Contagion for this Country, being convinced that the good Sense and the good Feeling of the great Mass of the People and the strong Conviction of the blessings They enjoy would preserve it from such a Calamity . . .'[9] But this consoling vision of a contented proletariat did not relieve his worries. Danger would still arise if we were drawn into a war. Our only safety lay in standing aloof, isolating ourselves from the contamination behind a *cordon sanitaire* of white cliffs and proper principles.

Melbourne received this not very striking conclusion with patient courtesy. He had, indeed, nothing much else to suggest; even Palmerston was prepared to concede that, if France was riven by internal conflict, neutrality was our only course. The correspondence ended with a splendidly robust reaffirmation by the King of his faith and code of conduct. '. . . Jealousy of the Prosperity and Grandeur of this country,' he said, 'is the dominant feeling of France and of every state on the Continent . . . We should therefore be guided in Our Proceedings with respect to them by Circumstances and by a Consideration of what is best suited to Our Interests, always however bearing in mind that, in

Transactions between States as between individuals, "Honesty is the Best Policy".[10]

The exchange is of interest because of the widely held belief that King William was more or less senile in the last year of his reign. There is no evidence in his letters to support this. He was prolix certainly, but verbosity had always been one of his weaknesses; impervious to new ideas, but on most issues his mind had been resolutely closed for fifty years; stubborn, but no more so than he had always been. He remained emphatically aware of what was going on; often indeed too much so for his ministers' comfort. He was as quick as ever to detect assaults on the prerogative; as ready to resist the insidious inroads of radicalism. What he had to say was usually to the point and quite often the point was worth making.

Taylor had no greater hand than before in the formulation of policy. Certainly the lack-lustre style, the flabby adjectives, the absence of wit or elegance, betray the hand of that otherwise admirable amanuensis. But the views put forward were those which William had always held, the prejudices invariable. Taylor would hardly have had to spend so much time writing his own letters which sought to make the King's views more palatable if his role had been much more than that of privileged pen-pusher. King William, as is indeed borne out by every reliable eye-witness report, was still in command of his memory and his powers of reasoning. He showed no serious signs of failing until the final illness.

*

In January, 1837, the reform of the Irish municipalities again became an active issue. William pleaded that it should be approached prudently and step by step. Those in opposition should first be won over, the way should be prepared by the prior introduction of a poor law.[11] His counsel was ignored and when he read the draft Speech from the Throne he found that he was to stress the urgent need for such a measure. He argued no more but instead pleaded the illness of his cousin, the Duchess of Gloucester, as an excuse for not opening parliament in person. It was a muted, sulky riposte to what he would once have deemed intolerable provocation. Almost one could feel that he was washing his hands of the affairs of state.

Much the same happened two months later when the government introduced a bill to abolish church rates. The Archbishop of Canterbury objected strongly, and under his expert guidance the King was induced to do the same. The King put forward a bevy of amendments which would have reduced the bill to a caricature of its former self.[12] Melbourne dismissed them with his habitual brisk courtesy. At once the King retreated. He had had no intention of objecting to the introduction of the bill, he assured his prime minister; he only wished to ensure that his views were known.[13]

It seemed, indeed, that Melbourne now saw less need to mollify and manage his royal master. In January, 1837, the King told him that he wanted to create his son, Adolphus FitzClarence, Ranger of the Home Park. Melbourne replied firmly that the King had long ago given away the right to dispose of the appointment. When William wrote of his 'mortification and disappointment',[14] Melbourne proved inexorable. There was no doubt that he was in the right but even a year before he would have tried harder to bend the law in the King's favour.

The King's attitude towards politics in general had now sunk into a settled gloom. On April 13 Taylor told Melbourne that he had now lost faith even in his most cherished dream, that of a coalition.[15] Certainly it had never seemed more distant. The Tories, clinging obstinately to their illusion that the King was in a mood to dismiss his ministers and the country to tolerate it, had no intention of boarding a sinking ship. The Whigs, more than half inclined to agree that their ship was about to founder, were still resolved to drown with dignity or to tread water till some better vessel came along. Surveying this melancholy scene the King prepared for the worst or perhaps more accurately, accepted that the worst had almost come and prepared instead for the grave. A sad miasma clings around his last months; a mood of fatalistic resignation which ensured that anyone who expected dashing or resolute action would be doomed to disappointment. The King, if yet another nautical metaphor can be forgiven, was adrift, and he lacked the will power even to try to get under way again.

*

In the family, too, things went badly. In April, Queen Adelaide was dangerously ill. She had been to Meiningen to be present at her sister's death bed and on her return came disturbingly close to her own. Raikes said that her recovery was considered doubtful;[16] no one else suggests that things were quite so serious but certainly she had to ask Princess Augusta to hold her drawing-room for her – a confession of weakness to which she would have resorted only in dire need. It must have disturbed her the more because the King was deeply in need of her comfort. A week before, his daughter Sophia, Lady de L'Isle, had died suddenly in childbirth. Sophia had probably been his favourite child-'. . . divine, so good-looking, so clever and so lively that my "withered nut" was in danger,' one admirer wrote archly of her.[17] In fact she seems to have had a sharp tongue, a malicious wit and little capacity for gratitude or generosity, but she was gay and by no means bad-natured and she knew how to make herself acceptable and useful at her father's court. The King, wrote Taylor, was 'very much shaken and affected' by the tragedy; only the death of Queen Adelaide herself would have grieved him more.

It seemed as if this black cloud might bear an exiguous silver lining in the form of a reconciliation with his son, Lord Munster. On hearing of Sophia's death Munster wrote a letter of condolence to his father. No one else would have deemed this more than the minimum which courtesy required, but the King was desperately anxious to reunite his family. At once he sent back a warm reply, thanking his son for this 'additional proof of that goodness of heart which I know you possess and for which at all times I have given you credit.'[18] He urged Munster to return to his father's roof as soon as he felt inclined.

Receiving such a letter from a seventy-one-year-old father, known to be in bad health, with a sick wife and distracted by the death of a favourite daughter, few children would have failed to respond warmly. Munster was victim to no such sentimental impulse. In a reply of querulous self-righteousness he declined to be reconciled with his father until 'justice' had been done him. '. . . death has already com-menced his havoc amongst us,' he concluded tactfully, 'and . . . the time may be short, in which I may yet have even the gratification, or possi-bility, of a thorough reconciliation with your Majesty.'[19] For a while the exchange continued but gradually the King abandoned all hope of welcoming back his eldest child and, on May 22, 1837, he brought the 'painful correspondence' to a close.

*

By the time of his last letter the King was himself gravely ill. In April his annual bout of asthma had struck him with especial violence. For several weeks he had virtually no sleep. He insisted on carrying out his full programme but did so with increasing difficulty.[20] On May 17, when he returned to Windsor from the levee, he could hardly climb the stairs and collapsed, breathless and exhausted on a sofa. A few days later he was eating nothing and fainted both at lunch and dinner. He was never to leave the private apartments again. Though he managed to attend the council on May 27, he arrived in a wheel-chair. The day before Taylor had written in distress to the prime minister:

'Yesterday was a very bad day with the King, and his Daughters who are *all* here were much alarmed, nor have they much control over their feelings ... The Queen is the best and the quietest Nurse I ever saw and I only dread her knocking herself up, as she does not undress at night and is frequently up.' The King was a bad patient and the doctors had the greatest difficulty in keeping him even slightly quiescent. 'The fact is that He is most anxious to be considered not seriously ill, and better than He is, and this leads to His doing that which encreases illness; to His sending for Numbers of Persons whose Attendance and Business is *perfectly immaterial*, to his holding a Council here tomorrow . . .'[21]

He had one comfort. On May 24 Princess Victoria came of age. The threat that the abhorred Duchess of Kent might one day be Regent was at last removed. The King was unable to attend the ball given at St James's in her honour but sent her a grand piano as a present. He also dispatched Lord Conyngham to offer her an establishment independent of her mother. Conyngham, on the King's precise instructions, delivered the letter to the princess, ignoring the outstretched hand of the indignant mother. The reply, a highly qualified acceptance, was not what either Victoria or the King would have wanted but the offer had driven a wedge between Princess Victoria and her mother which was never to be removed.[22]

So far the public knew little of what was going on within the walls of Windsor but on June 6 the Queen went alone to Ascot. The sacrifice cost the King little, for racing bored him, but the Ascot race-meeting had by then become one of those hallowed feasts at which the tribal chief ritually immerses himself in the convocation of his subjects. Its omission possessed an awful significance for every Briton. The following day a plan to remove the King to Brighton was abandoned by the doctors, and all the guests at the traditional Ascot house-party were sent home. Reluctantly the King agreed to a bulletin being issued. It was couched in typically misleading terms, seeking to present an ephemeral rally as the first step towards permanent recovery.

It is doubtful whether the King believed it. Colonel Clitherow, who saw him on June 3, found him 'cheerful and chatty' and busily making plans for the future,[23] but those who knew him best were not deceived.

Among the courtiers hope was dying. By June 15 Taylor was admitting bleakly to John Russell that he saw no prospect of the King recovering his strength.[24] In Whitehall officials were reminding themselves of the requirements for a royal funeral and even beginning to cast furtive glances at the dusty files which dealt with Coronations.

On June 16 came the next stage in the laborious ritual. The Archbishops of Canterbury and York and the Bishop of London met to discuss prayers for the King's recovery. 'There was no display of feeling on the part of these most reverend prelates,' noted Hobhouse sourly, 'but they went through their work in a business-like manner.'[25] Business-like was perhaps hardly the word. In a moment of bureaucratic economy the form of prayer was dispatched to all clerics by the twopenny post. It appeared in the newspapers on Saturday evening but had been received by few of the London clergy in time for morning service on Sunday.[26] On the same Sunday the Archbishop of Canterbury administered the sacrament to the dying King. Queen Adelaide had by then not been to bed for more than ten days. The strain was beginning to tell and, when the blessing was given, she broke down. 'Bear up! Bear up!' said her husband kindly, showing more concern for her distress than he had done for all his own suffering.

June 18 was Waterloo day. 'Doctor, I know I am going,' the King had greeted Dr Chambers a few days before, 'but I should like to see another anniversary of the battle of Waterloo. Try if you cannot tinker me up to last out that day.' 'I know I shall never live to see another sunset,' he told his doctor that morning. 'I hope your Majesty will live to see many,' replied Dr Chambers in what he presumably considered to be a bedside manner. 'Oh, that is quite another thing,' said the King tersely. Medically, indeed, it was astonishing that he was still alive. At the time of his death his lungs were turgid with blood, the heart valves ossified, the liver enlarged, the spleen double its normal size.[27]

By will power alone he preserved a tenuous grip on life throughout the day. 'The King dies like an old lion,' wrote Disraeli.[28] As June 19 dawned the doctors said he could hardly survive more than a few hours. Propped up in his heavy leather chair to ease his breathing he fought to prove them wrong. By the late afternoon he was unconscious. His last articulate word was the name of his valet. At two-twenty a.m. on the morning of Tuesday, June 20, what little was left to him of life flickered out.

The heading in the daily ledger at Windsor for June 18 had referred to 'Their Majesties' Dinner'. By June 19 it had changed to 'Her

Majesty's Dinner'. The following day it had discreetly altered once more to 'Dinners at Windsor Castle'. It was not until August 22 that the new era dawned with 'Her Majesty's Dinner' again. By such trivia does one measure the passing of kings.

*

'The King is dead. Long live the King!' is so much part of the myth of sovereignty, that the curtains fall with chilling speed about the body of the departed monarch. When England awoke on June 20 the eyes of a nation turned to Kensington Palace where a shy but self-possessed princess was moving with determination towards the centre of the stage. All who were left at Windsor to tend the corpse were a mourning Queen, a few of the bastards – for the most part more concerned with the pickings they could secure for themselves than the memory of their father – and a handful of devoted courtiers. Always the rising sun obliterates the memory of what has gone before. In 1837 there was a conviction that a new age had dawned which consigned Victoria's predecessor to oblivion with a speed and completeness even unkinder than is the wonted fate of monarchs.

The politicians, of course, went through the appropriate motions. 'A monarch of the strictest integrity that it had ever pleased Divine Providence to place over these realms,' proclaimed Melbourne in the House of Lords. Wellington praised his 'firmness, discretion, candour, justice and spirit of conciliation' while Peel struck the truest note when he said that it would be impossible to find a man 'who felt more pleasure in witnessing and promoting the happiness of others'. Probably they meant what they said – one usually does feel benign about the newly dead – but their orations were a debt hurriedly paid to the past before they turned with alacrity to the future. The note of authenticity rings more truly in the cool regret of Victoria in a letter to her beloved Uncle Leopold: 'Poor old man! I feel sorry for him; he was always personally kind to me, and I should be ungrateful and devoid of feeling if I did not remember this.'[29] And true pain is only to be found in the scrawled note which Queen Adelaide wrote to her niece the day of her husband's death. 'Excuse my writing more at present,' she ended, 'my heart is overwhelmed and my head aches very much. Accept the assurance of my most affectionate devotion, and allow me to consider myself as your Majesty's most affectionate Friend, Aunt and Subject.'[30]

On one more occasion King William was to occupy the centre of the stage. On July 8 he was buried at Windsor. He would hardly have gained much satisfaction from the ceremony. A wretched mockery, Greville described it. The service was long and tedious and miserably read by the Dean of Windsor. A host of persons of all ranks and stations loitered around, chattering and sniggering. 'I saw two men in an animated conversation, and one laughing heartily at the very foot of the coffin as it was lying in state.'[31] 'I certainly did not see a tear in any eye,' commented Hobhouse, 'not even in Sir Herbert Taylor's.'[32] Only the guardsmen holding tapers and torches in their hands wore expressions of proper solemnity, and they knew only too well what fate awaited them if they allowed themselves for a moment to relax.

And so the coffin was consigned to the vault and the mourners turned briskly to more important matters. Adelaide left Windsor to install herself once more at Bushy. The FitzClarences scattered to make what lives they could for themselves without their father's protection. A new reign began in earnest.

*

All kings, as every schoolboy knows, are great, good or bad. Great kings win wars, found empires, remodel constitutions. William did no such things. Bad kings are harsh, unjust, trample on their people; or else are weak, pay *danegeld* and are probably homosexual. Here too the descriptions hardly fit. Was William then a good king?

Certainly it can be argued that he was a good man. As a youth he sometimes seemed the worst kind of Hanoverian princeling: arrogant, insensitive; half buffoon, half bully. In later life he had at least one considerable weight upon his conscience in his treatment of Mrs Jordan. Yet the total picture was by no means discreditable. He was honest, he was generous, he was brave. He might hurt people by his temper or his tactlessness but if he realized what he had done his contrition was genuine and he would do all that he could to put the matter right. He blundered on, but they were venial blunders, springing from a warm heart and a hot head. He was straightforward almost to a fault; guileless; plain spoken. He was loyal to his friends yet never unforgiving to his enemies; usually, indeed, he was incapable of remembering that somebody *was* his enemy unless constantly reminded of the fact by fresh marks of hostility. He was a faithful and affectionate husband; for many years, indeed, showed himself as loyal a lover. As a father he was understanding and tolerant. He was what few kings were, a man to trust and depend on. He would never betray the individual in the interests of the State; indeed, a state that could only thrive on such a basis would have been, to his mind, hardly worth the pains of serving. Honour is a highflown word to apply to a figure so humdrum, yet King William was honourable beyond cavil; not the honour which causes a man to hitch his wagon to a star but the honour which keeps him on earth toiling in a harsh and often unrewarding furrow. He never spared himself in the cause of what he believed was right.

A formidable catalogue of qualities; yet are they those which are called for in a king? Would William have done a better job if he had been less kindly, less decent; had had instead greater ambition, greater subtlety, the vision of a Napoleon, the guile of a Henry VII, the charm of a Charles II? Perhaps, but then the job would have been a different one. He had inherited a throne which, because of the excesses of his predecessor, had become almost uniquely discredited. To re-establish it called for time and King William was satisfied that several years of total inactivity were what was needed. Temperamentally it was a course for which he was well suited. To do very little as slowly as possible was his pattern of good government. In the England of 1830 he was convinced it was the only prudent policy.

It was not to be. His reign coincided with the explosion of a pent-up and long-frustrated yearning for innovation. He was confronted, almost as soon as he had acceded to the throne, with a demand for reform so radical as to seem to all those of a conservative cast of mind to amount virtually to revolution. He himself found it little less dreadful. Yet he convinced himself that this was what the vast majority of his people wanted; that their wishes, though extravagant, were nevertheless legitimate; and that, as King, it was his duty to see that they had their way. In reaching this conclusion he exhibited an awareness of the realities of constitutional monarchy far beyond the grasp of his father or his eldest brother.

At a banquet he gave late in his reign for the American minister King William declared that it had always been a matter of serious regret to him that he had not 'been born a free, independent American, so much did he respect that nation, which had given birth to Washington, the greatest man that ever lived.' Such rhetoric smacks too much of the diplomatic dinner to be taken at face value; nevertheless, it cannot be ignored. King George IV could not have brought himself to make such a remark, any more than he could have brought himself to support the Whigs when the old establishment was under threat. If he had lived another ten years, or if the Duke of York had succeeded him, there would have been a direct confrontation with all the progressive forces in the country. 'If ever William comes to the throne,' George IV used balefully to remark to the Duke of York, 'he will bring about a revolution.'[33] So, in a sense he did. But it was not at all the revolution which King George IV had anticipated, nor was it the revolution which George IV would have provoked if he had been put to a similar test.

To conceive King William as the champion of revolution is, of course, grotesque. It is impossible to understand his political philosophy, impossible indeed to give it such admiration as it deserves, unless one realizes the repulsion which he felt for many of the measures he was compelled to sponsor. Constantly he acted against his personal predilection, often against his better judgment, sometimes even against his conscience. This he conceived to be his highest duty. But it was also his duty, as he saw it, to make the best of a bad job, to bring some common sense into the idealist folly of his ministers, above all to ensure that such radical legislation as had to be passed was passed without too brutal a clash with the opposition. It was peculiarly the task of a King, William believed, to work for a consensus between the various interests in his country; to preach the virtues of compromise; to mollify; to transmute points of principle into points of detail and finally to conjure them altogether out of sight and out of mind.

Such a task called for more dexterity than was within King William's range. His cherished dream of a coalition never survived for even a moment in the light of day, he failed to convince either Whig or Tory that they should sacrifice any serious matter of principle in the interests of achieving a consensus. But this did not mean that he served no useful purpose. His function was admirably set out by Bolingbroke in his celebrated essay, *The Idea of a Patriot King*[34] – a tract which William claimed had been one of the formative influences of his life:

'. . . as every new modification in a scheme of government and of national policy is of great importance, and requires more and deeper consideration than the warmth, and hurry, and rashness of party conduct admit, the duty of a prince seems to require that he should render by his influence the proceedings more orderly and more deliberate, even when he approves the end to which they are directed . . .'

To King William, who rarely approved and often deplored the end to which the efforts of his ministers were directed, this rule of conduct was *a fortiori* applicable. So precisely do the words fit his attitude that one wonders whether it was them that Grey had in mind when he declared that, 'if ever there was a Sovereign entitled to the character,

His Majesty may truly be styled the Patriot King.' Confronted with the reforming legislation of his government he did not oppose it but instead sought to buy time for further consideration, to let tempers cool on both sides, to give the moderates a chance to exert their influence. If change must come, let it at least come slowly and with deliberation. It was hardly a dashing or an inspiring principle, but perhaps it was none the worse for that. The brake is not the most exciting feature of a motor car, but heaven help the driver who has to do without one.

There is no sure scale by which to judge his success. In his short reign, however, there was put forward a programme of legislation as dynamically radical as that passed by any other great reforming ministry of this conservative nation. Other governments may have innovated as vigorously, none has more completely overthrown the patterns of the past. And yet this dramatic activity was carried out with decorum and received, on the whole, with good temper. There was no violent revolution, little bloodshed. Except by a handful of irreconcilables, the new order was accepted as a tolerable basis for future life. The establishment weathered the storm, built busily on its new foundations and found that things were really not so different after all. To claim that this was entirely the work of King William IV would be absurdly extravagant but to deny him any credit would be almost as irrational.

To say of somebody that others would have done worse may not seem lyrical as praise, yet for a king it is sometimes the truest flattery. None of his brothers would have done so well as William in the Britain of the 1830s; with the possible exception of the Duke of Cambridge it seems indeed unlikely that any of them would have survived seven years without provoking violent reaction from some portion of their subjects. King William had a line of extreme difficulty to follow; he followed it not by subtlety or skill but by the surer methods of honesty, generosity and good will. He inherited a monarchy in tatters, he bequeathed to his heir the securest throne in Europe. For that Queen Victoria at least should have been grateful. It would seem churlish to deny that, from his country, too, he had deserved well.

The Children of King George III and Queen Charlotte

1. George, Prince of Wales, Prince Regent, King George IV, 1762–1830
2. Frederick, Duke of York, 1763–1827
3. William, Duke of Clarence, King William IV, 1765–1837
4. Charlotte, Queen of Württemberg, 1766–1828
5. Edward, Duke of Kent, 1767–1820.
6. Augusta, 1768–1840
7. Elizabeth, 1770–1840
8. Ernest, Duke of Cumberland, King of Hanover, 1771–1851
9. Augustus, Duke of Sussex, 1773–1843
10. Adolphus, Duke of Cambridge, 1774–1850
11. Mary, 1776–1857
12. Sophia, 1777–1848
13. Octavius, 1779–1783
14. Alfred, 1780–1782
15. Amelia, 1783–1810.

The Children of the Duke of Clarence and Mrs Jordan

1. George Augustus Frederick FitzClarence *b.* 29th January 1794; *d.* 20th March 1842. Married Mary Wyndham, natural daughter of Lord Egremont.
2. Henry Edward FitzClarence *b.* 27th March 1795; *d.* September 1817.
3. Sophia FitzClarence *b.* August 1796; *d.* 10th April 1837. Married Lord de L'Isle and Dudley.
4. Mary FitzClarence *b.* 19th December 1798; *d.* 13th July 1864. Married Charles Richard Fox, natural son of Lord Holland.
5. Frederick FitzClarence *b.* 9th December 1799; *d.* 30th October 1854. Married Lady Augusta Boyle, daughter of Lord Glasgow.
6. Elizabeth FitzClarence *b.* 17th January 1801; *d.* 16th January 1856. Married Lord Erroll.
7. Adolphus FitzClarence *b.* 18th February 1802; *d.* 17th May 1856.
8. Augusta FitzClarence *b.* 17th November 1803; *d.* 8th December 1865. Married, firstly, John Kennedy Erskine, second son of the Marquess of Ailsa, who died on 16th March 1831; secondly, Lord Frederick Gordon.
9. Augustus FitzClarence *b.* 1st March 1805; *d.* 14th June 1854. Married Sarah Elizabeth Catherine, eldest daughter of Lord Henry Gordon.
10. Amelia FitzClarence *b.* 21st March 1807; *d.* 2nd July 1858. Married Lord Falkland.

Notes

The place, date of publication and full title of a book is only mentioned if the book is not cited in the bibliography.
Abbreviations employed:
NRS Naval Records Series, London
RA   Royal Archives
RA. Add.   Royal Archives, Additional Manuscripts
Add. mss.   Additional Manuscripts (in the British Museum)
Parl. Hist.   Parliamentary History
Later Correspondence [of George III]

CHAPTER I (pp. 11-21)

1. Walpole. *Letters to Sir Horace Mann*. Vol. I p. 41.
2. Fitzgerald. *Royal Dukes and Princesses*. Vol. I p. 25.
3. D'Arblay. *Diaries and Letters*. Vol. III p. 28.
4. D. Stuart. *Daughters of George III*. p. 9.
5. Wright. *William IV*. Vol. I p. 15.
6. Huish. *George IV*. p. 15.
7. *Mrs Papendiek's Journal*. ed. Mrs Broughton. Vol. I p. 41.
8. *The Letters and Journals of Lady Mary Coke*. Vol. II p. 97.
9. D'Arblay. Vol. III p. 31.
10. *Annual Registers*. 1773-75. *Court and City Register*. 1773.
11. Lady Mary Coke provides the most useful source. David Duff, in his *Edward of Kent* has much of interest.
12. Clitherow. *Glimpses of King William IV*. p. 48.
13. Coke. Vol. IV p. 129.
14. *Ibid*. p. 113.
15. Wright. p. 17.
16. *Memoirs of Mrs Chapone*. p. 55.
17. *Later Correspondence*. Vol. I p. xvi.
18. D. Stuart. *Daughters of George III*. p. 81.

CHAPTER II (pp. 22-36)

1. These statistics, grossly over-simplified, are derived from Professor Michael Lewis's invaluable *A Social History of the Navy 1793-1815*. London, 1960, chapter I.

2. Earl Dundonald. *Autobiography of a Seaman*. London, 1860–61. p. 32.
3. *Midshipman Easy*. Captain Marryat's novels provide an excellent picture of naval life at this time.
4. *A Social History of the Navy*. Chapter VIII.
5. Frederic Chamier. *The Life of a Sailor*. London, 1833. pp. 23–4.
6. July 12, 1778. *Naval Miscellany* (NRS). Vol. I p. 225.
7. July 15, 1778. RA. Add. 16/146.
8. May 27, 1779. *Naval Miscellany* (NRS). Vol. I p. 226.
9. Huish. *George IV*. Vol. I p. 244.
10. George III to Budé. June 11, 1779. RA. Add. 15/460.
11. Fitzgerald, *William IV*. Vol. I p. 7.
12. Preserved at the National Maritime Museum.
13. June 11, 1779. *Naval Miscellany* (NRS). Vol. I p. 226.
14. June 11, 1779. RA. Add. 15/461.
15. *Journal of Thomas Addison. Naval Miscellany* (NRS). Vol. I p. 343.
16. William to George III. November 24, 1779. RA 44606.
17. RA. Add. 21/1. 2.
18. November 24, 1779. RA 44606.
19. George III to William. November 29, 1779. RA. Add. 21/1. 5.
20. Rodney to the Admiralty. January 9, 1780. cit. Wright. *William IV*. Vol. I p. 38.
21. January 26, 1780. RA 44611.
22. Anecdote of Col. Drinkwater. cit.Wright. Vol. I p. 47.
23. March 3, 1780. RA 44615.
24. Byam Martin. *Letters and Papers*. Vol. I p. 8.
25. William to George III. August 6, 1780 and April 11, 1781. RA 44619 and 24.

CHAPTER III (pp. 37–53)

1. July 10, 1781. RA. Add. 21/1. 17.
2. July 13, 1781. RA 44625.
3. August 21, 1781. RA 44628.
4. *Ibid.*
5. William to George III. September 27, 1781. RA 44630.
6. *Ibid.* September 28, 1781. RA 44632.
7. William to George III. March 28, 1782. RA 44638.
8. *The Writings of George Washington*. ed. Jared Sparks. Vol. 8 p. 261.
9. Mrs E. Stuart Wortley. *A Prime Minister and his Son*. London, 1925. p. 174.
10. George III to William. August 6, 1782. RA. Add. 21/1. 24.
11. December 30, 1782. RA. Add. 21/1. 28.
12. Majendie to Hood. October 27, 1782. RA 16307.
13. Digby to George III. October 29, 1782. RA. Add. 15/719.
14. Hood to George III. February 5, 1783. RA 16334.
15. April 16, 1783. RA 16346. c.f. George III to William. April 16, 1783. RA 16344.
16. George III to William. April 16, 1783. RA 16344.
17. March 20, 1783. RA. Add. 15/749.
18. Cit. Wright. *William IV*. Vol. I p. 84.
19. Nelson to Capt. Locker. February 25, 1783.

20. Cit. Huish. *William IV*. p. 141.
21. Walpole to Lady Ossory. July 15, 1783.
22. *Later Correspondence*. Vol. I p. xvii.
23. *Correspondence of Prince of Wales*. Vol. I p. 131.
24. August, 1784. *Later Correspondence*. Vol. I p. 77.
25. August 20, 1784. RA 44668.
26. January 2, 1784. RA 44650.
27. William to Prince of Wales. April 23, 1784. *Correspondence of Prince of Wales*. Vol. I p. 144.
28. September 23, 1783. RA. Add. 15/468.
29. October 7[?], 1783. *Later Correspondence*. Vol. I p. 124.
30. October 7, 1783. RA. Add. 15/470.
31. John Maude to William. December 30, 1783. RA. Add. 4/24.
32. Baron Reichenbach. *Caroline von Linsingen and King William IV*. London, 1880.
33. April 1, 1785. RA 44674.
34. July 23, 1784. RA 44664.
35. January 4, 1785. *Later Correspondence*. Vol. I p. 120.
36. December 29, 1783. RA. Add. 21/1. 47.
37. April 1, 1785. *Later Correspondence*. Vol. I p. 152.
38. April 1, 1785. *Later Correspondence*. Vol. I p. 152.
39. May 13, 1785. RA 44676.
40. George III to William. May 6, 1785. *Later Correspondence*. Vol. I p. 157.
41. Wright, *William IV*. Vol. I p. 113.

CHAPTER IV (pp. 54-64)

1. Lord Ellenborough. *The Guilt of Lord Cochrane*. London, 1914. p. 2.
2. William to George III. November 6, 1785. RA 44685.
3. August 4, 1785. *Later Correspondence*. Vol. I p. 175.
4. Wright. *William IV*. Vol. I p. 123.
5. *Ibid.* p. 147.
6. Fitzgerald. *William IV*. Vol. I p. 70.
7. Huish. *William IV*. p. 141.
8. William to Prince of Wales. November 25, 1785. *Correspondence of Prince of Wales*. Vol. I p. 202.
9. November 6, 1785. RA 44685.
10. Byam Martin. Vol. I p. 20.
11. January 20, 1786. *Correspondence of Prince of Wales*. Vol. I p. 215.
12. William to Prince of Wales. December 1, 1786. *Ibid.* p. 264.
13. Roger Fulford. *The Royal Dukes*. p. 90.
14. Capt. G. K. Elphinstone to Martin. February 3, 1786. Byam Martin. Vol. I p. 209.
15. Undated. *Ibid.* p. 206.
16. William to Martin. January 31, 1786. *Ibid.* p. 208.
17. William to Prince of Wales. December 1, 1786. *Correspondence of Prince of Wales*. Vol. I p. 264.
18. February 10, 1786. *Ibid.* Vol. I p. 219.

19. March 3, 1786. *Later Correspondence*. Vol. I p. 247.
20. William to George III. September 21, 1786. *Later Correspondence*. Vol. I p. 247.
21. William to Prince of Wales. December 1, 1786. *Correspondence of Prince of Wales*. Vol. I p. 264.
22. December 24, 1786. *Nelson's Letters to his Wife*. (NRS) 1958 p. 39.
23. November 27, 1786. *Ibid*. p. 37.
24. January 3, 1787. RA 44730.
25. J. Fidge to Captain Elphinstone. February 18, 1788. RA 44818.
26. William to Prince of Wales. May 20, 1787. RA 44769.
27. RA 44818.
28. Broughton. *Recollections*. Vol. IV p. 158.
29. Byam Martin. Vol. I p. 70.
30. Nelson to Captain Locker. December 29, 1786.
31. *Ibid*. February 14, 1787.
32. Joseph Yorke to Charles Yorke. October 8, 1786. *Later Correspondence*. Vol. I p. 251n.
33. *Gentleman's Magazine*. 1787. Vol. I p. 357.
34. William to Prince of Wales. May 20, 1786. *Correspondence of Prince of Wales*. Vol. I p. 226.
35. Byam Martin. Vol. I p. 25.
36. April 18, 1787. *Nelson's Letters to his Wife*. p. 58.
37. Byam Martin. Vol. I p. 56.
38. William to George III. May 20, 1787. *Later Correspondence*. Vol. I p. 290. The whole story, including *Prince William's Narrative*, is contained in 'Prince William and Lieutenant Schomberg 1787-88'. *The Naval Miscellany*. Vol. IV. (NRS) 1952. cf. Byam Martin. Vol. I pp. 67-70.
39. December, 1786. *Nelson's Letters to his Wife*. p. 56.
40. *Despatches and Letters of Lord Nelson*. ed. Nicolas. Vol. I p. 238.
41. January 1, 1788. *Prince William and Lieutenant Schomberg*. p. 291.
42. December 3, 1787. *Prince William and Lieutenant Schomberg*. p. 289.
43. December 26, 1787. *Ibid*. p. 290.
44. October 8, 1787. *Correspondence of the Prince of Wales*. Vol. I p. 323.
45. August 19, 1787. *Later Correspondence*. Vol. I p. 317.
46. *E.g.* Wright. Vol I p. 156. Gore-Allen. p. 34.
47. William to Prince of Wales. December 27, 1787. *Correspondence of Prince of Wales*. Vol. I p. 329.
48. October 8, 1787. *Ibid*. p. 323.
49. *Dyott's Diary*. ed. R. W. Jeffery. p. 37.

CHAPTER V (pp. 65-75)

1. William to Prince of Wales. January 30, 1788. *Correspondence of Prince of Wales*. Vol. I p. 334.
2. February 16, 1788. *Ibid*. Vol. I p. 336.
3. Byam Martin. Vol. I p. 116.
4. *Ibid*. p. 120.

5. William to Prince of Wales. June 14, 1788. *Correspondence of Prince of Wales.* Vol. I p. 340.

6. Byam Martin. Vol. I p. 123.

7. August 20, 1788. *Later Correspondence.* Vol. I p. 388.

8. William to Keats. September 13, 1788. Keats mss.

9. Byam Martin. Vol. I p. 125.

10. *Dyott's Diary.* ed. R. W. Jeffery.

11. McKenzie Porter. *Overture to Victoria.* London, 1962. p. 78.

12. October 26, 1788. RA 44850.

13. See, in particular, *George III and the Mad Business.*

14. January 24, 1789. *Correspondence of Prince of Wales.* Vol. I p. 453.

15. Lady Minto. *Life and Letters of Sir Gilbert Elliot.* Vol. I p. 272.

16. Byam Martin. Vol. I p. 133.

17. See Huish. *George IV.* Vol. I p. 309.

18. Princess Augusta Sophia. cit. Stuart. *The Daughters of George III.* p. 130.

19. *Farington Diary.* Vol. VI p. 264.

20. Michael Joyce. *My Friend H.* London, 1948. p. 207.

21. RA 45240. Undated.

22. *Creevey Papers.* Vol. I p. 51.

23. *Farington Diary.* Vol. IV p. 205.

24. Watkins. *William IV.* Vol. I p. 773. cf. *Farington Diary.* Vol. III p. 64.

25. Walpole to Lady Ossory. September 26, 1789.

26. *Ibid.* October 9, 1789.

27. Selwyn to Lady Carlisle. November 1790. Hist. mss. Comm. Carlisle mss. London, 1877. p. 694.

28. *Ibid.* September 5, 1789.

29. Glenbervie. *Diaries.* Vol. I p. 63.

30. *St James's Chronicle.* March 10, 1791. cf. William to Duke of Sussex. September 23, 1791. RA. Add. 9/147.

CHAPTER VI (pp. 76–85)

1. Unless otherwise stated all facts about Mrs Jordan are to be found in the latest and by far the best of her biographies, that of Brian Fothergill.

2. *Dramatic Essays.* London, 1894. p. 79.

3. E. V. Lucas. *Life of Charles Lamb.* London, 1905. Vol. II p. 13.

4. London, 1895. p. 69.

5. October 13, 1791. *Correspondence of Prince of Wales.* Vol. II p. 208.

6. August 17, 1790. *Correspondence of Prince of Wales.* Vol. II p. 88.

7. William to Prince of Wales. September 5, 1790. *Correspondence of Prince of Wales.* Vol. II p. 90.

8. William to Prince of Wales. May 15, 1790. RA 44859.

9. RA. Add. 40/34.

10. Glenbervie. Vol. I p. 71.

11. William to Thomas Coutts. December 1, 1797. *Mrs Jordan and her Family.* p. 40.

12. *Mrs Jordan and her Family.* p. xiv.

13. October 18, 1797. M. W. Patterson. *Sir Francis Burdett and his Times.* p. 83.

14. *Correspondence of Prince of Wales.* Vol. II pp. 131 and 148.
15. *The Great Illegitimates.* p. 36.
16. Horace Walpole to Miss Berry. August 26, 1795.
17. *The Courier.* August 23, 1806.
18. *The Journal of Mary Frampton.* p. 137.
19. Glenbervie. Vol. I p. 122.
20. RA. Add. 39.
21. June 10, 1809. RA. Add. 39.
22. *Political Register.* September 6, 1806.
23. February 11, 1813.
24. *Farington Diary.* Vol. V p. 113.
25. September 24, 1792. *Correspondence of Prince of Wales.* Vol. II p. 286.
26. *The Jockey Club, or, a Sketch of the Manners of the Age.* Anon. London, 1792.
27. Roger Fulford. *Royal Dukes.* p. 109.
28. Fitzgerald. *William IV.* Vol. I p. 118.
29. Jonah Barrington. *Personal Sketches of His Own Times.* Vol. II p. 48.
30. William to Collingwood. May 21, 1808. *Correspondence and Memoirs of Lord Collingwood.* p. 357.
31. W. F. Hall. *William IV, Thomas Pearse and the Rumbelows.*
32. *Bon Ton Magazine.* cit. Fothergill. p. 166.
33. James Boaden. *The Life of Mrs Jordan.* Vol. II p. 13.
34. Glenbervie. Vol. I p. 414.
35. August 20, 1795. *Correspondence of Prince of Wales.* Vol. III p. 93.
36. *Letters of Lord Granville Leveson-Gower.* Vol. II p. 284.
37. Huish. *William IV.* p. 433.

CHAPTER VII (pp. 86-100)

1. D'Arblay. Vol. V p. 11.
2. *A Diary of the Royal Tour in June, July, August and September, 1789.* London, 1789. p. 20.
3. *Ibid.* p. 73.
4. D'Arblay. Vol. V pp. 170-74.
5. Wraxall. *Memoirs.* Vol. III p. 154.
6. December 6, 1792. Add. mss. 34903 f 98.
7. Farington. *Diary.* Vol. IV p. 205.
8. *Correspondence of Charles, 1st Marquess Cornwallis.*
9. Mrs Aubrey Le Blond. *Charlotte Sophie, Countess Bentinck.* London, 1912. p. 165.
10. *Letters of Lord Granville Leveson-Gower.* Vol. II p. 63.
11. *Later Correspondence.* Vol. I p. 645.
12. Lady Anne Hamilton (att.). *Secret History of the Court of England.* London, 1832. Vol. II p. 348.
13. Elliot. *Letters.* Vol. I p. 320.
14. Add. mss. 46358 f 4.
15. July 24, 1791. *Correspondence of Prince of Wales.* Vol. II p. 177.
16. Moira to Loughborough. June 6, 1796. Loughborough mss.
17. June 11, 1796. *Correspondence of Prince of Wales.* Vol. III p. 222.

18. William to Duke of Sussex. June 14, 1793. RA. Add. 9/166. cf. Byam Martin. Vol. I p. 15.
19. Glenbervie. Vol. I p. 59.
20. *Parliamentary Register*. XXXVI p. 272.
21. To Duke of York. August 4, 1793. *Correspondence of Prince of Wales*. Vol. II p. 368.
22. December 1, 1793. *Nelson's Letters to his Wife*. p. 96.
23. March 15, 1794. cit. Fitzgerald. *William IV*. Vol. I p. 93.
24. Moira to Prince of Wales. September 18, 1793. *Correspondence of Prince of Wales*. Vol. II p. 389.
25. June 7, 1796. *Later Correspondence*. Vol. II p. 486.
26. October 3, 1796. Add. mss. 34904 f 400.
27. William to Keats. June 1799. Keats mss.
28. William to Keats. April 25, 1800. Keats mss.
29. William to Keats. August 28, 1800. Keats mss.
30. William to Sir T. Sinclair. cit. Fitzgerald. *William IV*. Vol. I p. 97.
31. February 25, 1804. Goff. mss.
32. February 10, 1801.
33. November 3, 1801. *Parl. Hist*. Vol. 36 p. 161.
34. William to Keats. December 1, 1802. Keats mss.
35. May 23, 1803. *Parl. Hist*. Vol. 36 p. 1501.
36. May 24, 1806. *Farington Diary*. Vol. III p. 237.
37. November 1, 1808. RA 44966.
38. Queen Charlotte to Prince of Wales. March 2, 1795. *Correspondence of Prince of Wales*. Vol. III p. 35.
39. May 3, 1792. *Parl. Hist*. Vol. 29 p. 1349.
40. February 5, 1807. *Hansard*. Vol. 8 p. 664.
41. To Duke of York. April 14, 1793.
42. William to Nelson. August 4, 1799. Add. mss. 34913 f 45.
43. Liverpool to William. July 10, 1799. Add. mss. 38416 f. 312.
44. Macaulay to Miss Mills. June 1, 1799. *Life and Letters of Zachary Macaulay*. London, 1900. p. 22.
45. *Ibid*. June 20, 1799.
46. To Sir Samuel Hawker. Goff. mss.
47. Huish. *William IV*. p. 437.
48. *Correspondence of Prince of Wales*. Vol. IV. p. 41n.

CHAPTER VIII (pp. 101–111)

1. *Mrs Jordan and her Family*. p. 176.
2. William to Hawker. September 28, 1810. Goff. mss.
3. William to George FitzClarence. October 19, 1810. RA. Add. 39/49.
4. Glenbervie. Vol. II p. 130.
5. December 20, 1810. *Hansard*. Vol. 18 p. 235.
6. To Miss Mercer. *The Letters of Princess Charlotte*. p. 7.
7. January, 1811. [?] *Mrs Jordan and her Family*. p. 181.
8. July 31, 1809. RA. Add. 39/20.

9. RA. Add. 39/94.
10. RA. Add. 4/40.
11. J. and H. Robinson. *The Life of Robert Coates*. London, 1891. p. 37.
12. Lady Charlotte Bury. *The Diary of a Lady-in-Waiting*. Vol. I p. 83.
13. *Letters of Lord Granville Leveson-Gower*. Vol. II p. 415.
14. Mrs Jordan to William. August 1, 1811. *Mrs Jordan and her Family*. p. 196.
15. Boaden. *Mrs Jordan*. Vol. II p. 271.
16. *The Letters of Princess Charlotte*. p. 8.
17. October 19 [?] 1811. *Mrs Jordan and her Family*. p. 207.
18. October 27 [?] 1811. *Ibid*. p. 211.
19. October 13, 1811. *Ibid*. p. 206.
20. October 20, 1811. *Ibid*. p. 209.
21. October 19 [?] 1811. *Ibid*. p. 208.
22. William to Mayo. RA. Add. 4/38.
23. Auckland to Colchester. November 30, 1811. Abbot. *Diary*. Vol. II p. 347.
24. December 10, 1811. *The Letters of Princess Charlotte*. p. 17.
25. *Letters of Lord Granville Leveson-Gower*. Vol. II p. 415.
26. December 16 [?] 1811. *Mrs Jordan and her Family*. p. 220.
27. *The Letters of Princess Charlotte*. p. 25.
28. December 28 [?] *Mrs Jordan and her Family*. p. 222.
29. November 6, 1817. RA. Add. 39/288.
30. *Personal Sketches of His Own Times*. Vol. II p. 48.
31. *Journals and Correspondence of Miss Berry*. p. 463.
32. Mary Hobkirk. *Queen Adelaide*. p. 131.
33. *Mrs Jordan and her Family*. p. 178.

CHAPTER IX (pp. 112-123)

1. *Diaries of a Lady of Quality*. London, 1864. p. 279.
2. *Letters of Lord Granville Leveson-Gower*. Vol. II p. 355.
3. Hon. Amelia Murray. *Recollections*. London, 1868. p. 19.
4. *Letters of Harriet, Countess Granville*. Vol. I p. 208.
5. John Gore. *Creevey's Life and Times*. p. 158.
6. *The Unpublished Diary and Political Sketches of Princess Lieven*. p. 34.
7. Princess Charlotte to Miss Mercer. January 4, 1814. *The Letters of Princess Charlotte*. p. 101.
8. William to George FitzClarence. December 15, 1813. RA. Add. 39/176.
9. Princess Charlotte to Miss Mercer. January 11, 1814. *The Letters of Princess Charlotte*. p. 103.
10. William to McMahon. March 23, 1814. *Letters of King George IV*. Vol. I p. 416.
11. *The Autobiography of Miss Knight*. p. 160.
12. *The Taylor Papers*. p. 138.
13. William to Liverpool. January 19, 1814. Add. mss. 38190 f 110.
14. William to McMahon. February 12, 1814. RA 45020.
15. William to McMahon. February 18, 1814. RA 45027.
16. Prince Regent to Liverpool. Add. mss. 38245 f 104.
17. RA 45074.

18. May 27, 1814. RA 45100.
19. William to McMahon. June 1, 1814. RA 45110.
20. William to McMahon. June 9, 1814. RA 45114.
21. William to Melville. June 10, 1814. RA 45123.
22. William to George FitzClarence. RA. Add. 39/190.
23. Byam Martin. Vol. I p. 18.
24. November 18, 1815 [?] RA 42536.
25. September 21, 1815. *The Letters of Princess Charlotte.* p. 207.
26. RA. Add. 4/40.
27. William to Lord Mayo. RA. Add. 4/35.
28. May 26, 1813. RA. Add. 39/151.
29. Moira to McMahon. October 26, 1816. *Letters of King George IV.* Vol. II p. 170.
30. Hastings to Bathurst. September 3, 1817. Hist. mss. Comm. Bathurst mss. London, 1923, p. 439.
31. D'Arblay. Vol. VII p. 241.
32. Prince Regent to Queen Charlotte. December 16, 1817. *Letters of King George IV.* Vol. II p. 223.
33. William to Queen Charlotte. December 16, 1817. *Ibid.* p. 227.
34. Liverpool to Bloomfield. *Ibid.* p. 236.
35. William to George FitzClarence. February 18, 1818. RA. Add. 39/296.
36. William to Barton. RA. Add. 21/1. 67.
37. *The Journal of the Hon. Henry Edward Fox.* p. 87.
38. Greville. *Memoirs.* Vol. III p. 84.
39. William to George FitzClarence. March 21, 1818. RA. Add. 39/300.
40. Lady Jerningham to Lady Bedingfeld. February 27, 1818. Oxburgh mss.
41. Duchess of Gloucester to Prince Regent. *Letters of King George IV.* Vol. II p. 243.
42. Add. mss. 38574 f 42.
43. William to George FitzClarence. March 5, 1818. RA. Add. 39/298.
44. Liverpool to William. March 2, 1818. Add. mss. 38574 f 15.
45. Electoral Prince of Hesse Cassel to Duke of Cambridge. March 1, 1818. *Letters of King George IV.* Vol. II p. 247.
46. April 16, 1818.
47. William to George FitzClarence. January 11, 1818. RA. Add. 39/292.
48. William to George FitzClarence. March 21, 1818. RA. Add. 39/300.

CHAPTER X (pp. 123-132)

1. *The Life and Times of Queen Adelaide* by Mary Sanders (London, 1915) remains the best book on the subject. Mary Hopkirk's more slapdash study, *Queen Adelaide* (London, 1946) adds little of real importance.
2. *Letters of Harriet, Countess Granville.* Vol. I p. 242.
3. RA. Add. 21/1. 68.
4. *Barnard Letters.* p. 272.
5. May 29, 1818. *Correspondence of Charlotte, Lady Williams Wynn.* p. 211.
6. William to George FitzClarence. April 6, 1818. RA. Add. 39/301.

7. July 4, 1818. RA 45135.
8. *Correspondence of Charlotte, Lady Williams Wynn.* p. 211.
9. October 10, 1818. RA. Add. 39/316.
10. E. H. Coleridge. *The Life of Thomas Coutts, Banker.* Vol. II p. 192.
11. *Count Münster's Memorandum.* RA. Add. 21/18.
12. William to George FitzClarence. September 18, 1818. RA. Add. 39/311.
13. *Ibid.* March 8, 1819. RA. Add. 39/348.
14. William to J. R. Daniell. August 19, 1818. Goff. mss.
15. November 14, 1818. Goff. mss.
16. Duke of Kent to George FitzClarence. November 21, 1818. RA. Add. 39/319.
17. *Count Münster's Memorandum.* RA. Add. 21/18.
18. August 2, 1819. Add. mss. 38190 f 116.
19. *Jerningham Letters.* Vol. II p. 187.
20. William to Prince Regent. December 10, 1820. RA 45148.
21. Horace Twiss. *Life of Lord Chancellor Eldon.* Vol. II p. 411.
22. *The Journal of the Hon. Henry Edward Fox.* p. 50.
23. William to Daniell. March 2, 1821. RA. Add. 4/110.
24. Add. mss. 37232 f 90.
25. William to Liverpool. March 8, 1822. Add. mss. 38190 f 126.
26. April 9, 1822. *Letters of George IV.* Vol. II p. 523.
27. RA. Add. 39/419.
28. Mary Hopkirk. *Queen Adelaide.* p. 58.
29. Lord Albemarle. *Fifty Years of my Life.* p. 294.
30. *Memoirs of the Duchess of Dino.* Vol. I p. 81.
31. *The Diary of Henry Hobhouse.* p. 30.
32. Sir Joseph Arnould. *Memoir of Thomas, First Lord Denman.* Vol. I p. 175.
33. *The Creevey Papers.* Vol. I p. 339.
34. Vol. V p. 571.
35. *Letters of Harriet, Countess Granville.* Vol. I p. 238.
36. January 28, 1822. *Correspondence of Sarah, Lady Lyttelton.*
37. Colchester to Wilbraham. June 20, 1820. Abbot. *Diary.* Vol. III p. 142.
38. *Elizabeth, Lady Holland, to her Son.* p. 17.
39. William to Daniell. June 29, 1826. Goff. mss.
40. William Beattie. *Journal of a Residence in Germany.*
41. June 30, 1826. *The Private Letters of Princess Lieven to Prince Metternich* p. 372.
42. RA 45142. cf. *Hobhouse.* p. 122, where the gift is put at £15,000.
43. December 31, 1826. RA. Add. 39/425.
44. January 21, 1827. *The Private Papers of Sir Robert Peel.* p. 93.
45. John Gore. *Creevey's Life and Times.* p. 234.
46. Liverpool to George IV. February 8, 1827. *Letters of George IV.* Vol. III p. 198.
47. RA 45165.

CHAPTER XI (pp. 133-144)

1. April 21, 1827. *The Diary of Henry Hobhouse.* p. 131.
2. July 15, 1827. Hist. mss. Comm. Bathurst mss. London, 1923. p. 641.
3. Bathurst to Charles Arbuthnot, July 17, 1827. Quoted in A. Aspinall *The*

Formation of Canning's Ministry, 1827. Camden Series, LIX. London, 1937. p. 264.

4.   *A Narrative of my Professional Adventures.* Sir William Dillon. Vol. II p. 482.

5.   Add. mss. 41368 f 116.

6.   J. C. Herries to Arbuthnot. April 16, 1827. Add. mss. 40340 f 142. cf. *Hobhouse.* p. 131.

7.   Taylor to Grey. December 18, 1831. RA. Add. 15/1647.

8.   See p. 62 above.

9.   May 6, 1827. Abbot. *Diary.* Vol. III p. 495.

10.   Sir John Barrow. *An Autobiographical Memoir.* p. 340.

11.   *The Private Diary of the Duke of Buckingham and Chandos.* Vol. I p. 5.

12.   Gabriele Von Bülow. *A Memoir.* p. 135.

13.   Henry Moses. *Visit of William IV when Duke of Clarence as Lord High Admiral to Portsmouth in the Year 1827.*

14.   Barrow. *Memoir.* p. 342.

15.   Lady Brownlow. *The Eve of Victorianism.* p. 128.

16.   January 15, 1828. RA 45190 and January 19, RA 45191.

17.   William to Sir E. Codrington. July 16, 1827. Codrington mss.

18.   *The Unpublished Diary and Political Sketches of Princess Lieven.* p. 131.

19.   At the National Maritime Museum.

20.   William to Mayo. November 12, 1827. RA. Add. 4.

21.   November 19, 1827. *Memoir of the Life of Admiral Sir Edward Codrington.* Vol. II p. 115.

22.   George IV to William. November 11, 1827. Add. mss. 46358 f 50.

23.   Gore to Codrington. November 12, 1827. *Codrington.* Vol. II p. 113.

24.   Gore to Codrington. November 14, 1827. *Codrington.* Vol. II p. 118.

25.   July 10, 1828. Wellington. *Despatches.* Vol. IV p. 517.

26.   Ellenborough. *Political Diary.* Vol. I p. 159.

27.   July 10, 1828. Fitzgerald. *William IV.* Vol. I p. 181.

28.   William to Wellington. July 11, 1828. *Despatches.* Vol. IV p. 520.

29.   July 13, 1828. *Letters of George IV.* Vol. III p. 411.

30.   RA 24522.

31.   William to George IV. July 17, 1828. Wellington. *Despatches.* Vol. IV p. 535.

32.   August 5, 1828. Hist. mss. Comm. No. 76. Bathurst mss. London, 1923. p. 655.

33.   August 3, 1828. *Despatches.* Vol. IV p. 573.

34.   August 8, 1828. *Ibid.* p. 578.

35.   August 9, 1828. *Ibid.* p. 581.

36.   August 11, 1828. *Ibid.* p. 595.

37.   Croker. Vol. I p. 429.

38.   August 23, 1828. *Despatches.* Vol. IV p. 653.

39.   Barrow. p. 367.

40.   Fitzgerald. *William IV.* Vol. I p. 198.

41.   September 1, 1828. *Codrington.* Vol. II p. 432.

42.   August 8, 1828. Ellenborough. *Diary.* p. 193.

43.   Bransby Cooper. *The Life of Sir Astley Cooper.* Vol. II p. 384.

44.   See, in particular, Sir John Briggs. *Naval Administrations 1827 to 1892.* London, 1897. cf. C. J. Bartlett. *Great Britain and Sea Power, 1815-1853.* Oxford, 1963.

45.   December, 11, 1827. RA. Add. 39/429.

46. January 12, 1829. Abbot. *Diary*. Vol. III p. 593.
47. May 26, 1827. Add. mss. 41367 f 256.
48. *Croker*. Vol. I p. 401.
49. *Creevey*. Vol. II p. 104.
50. February 23, 1829. Ellenborough. *Diary*. p. 357.
51. G. M. Willis. *Ernest Augustus, Duke of Cumberland*. p. 181.
52. April 28, 1830. *The Diary of Philipp Von Neumann*. Vol. I p. 209.
53. *Memoirs of Sir William Knighton*. Vol. II pp. 116-17, 118, 124, etc.
54. June 22, 1830. Gore. *Creevey's Life and Times*. p. 321.
55. From the transcript of Queen Adelaide's diary in the Royal Archives.
56. Lord Anglesey. *One Leg: The Life and Letters of the First Marquess of Anglesey*. p. 226.
57. A story told with many variants. e.g. *The Journal of Mary Frampton*. p. 348.
58. Broughton. Vol. IV p. 33.

CHAPTER XII (pp. 145-155)

1. E. J. Hobsbawm and G. Rudé. *Captain Swing*. London, 1969.
2. See A. Aspinall. *The Cabinet Council 1783-1835. Proceedings of the British Academy*. Vol. XXXVIII. London, 1952.
3. January 8, 1851. *Brougham* mss. cit. Aspinall.
4. December 2, 1835. RA. Melbourne mss.
5. See *English Historical Documents Vol. XI, 1783-1832*. Introduction. A. Aspinall and E. A. Smith. London, 1957.
6. RA 50594. Undated.
7. July 16, 1830. *Letters of Dorothea, Princess Lieven, during her Residence in London*. p. 230.
8. August, 1830. *Miss Eden's Letters*. p. 198.
9. Cit. Fitzgerald. *William IV*. Vol. I p. 224.
10. *Creevey*. Vol. II p. 228.
11. Grace Thompson. *The Patriot King*. p. 169.
12. Taylor to Grey, June 20, 1832. RA. Add. 15/1916.
13. Broughton. Vol. IV pp. 40 and 49.
14. *The Journal of Mary Frampton*, p. 366.
15. Greville. Vol. II p. 9. cf. Ellenborough. Vol. II p. 319.
16. *Correspondence of Charlotte, Lady Williams Wynn*. p. 377.
17. Gabriele von Bülow. June 27, 1830. cit. Fitzgerald.
18. Buckingham. *Memoirs of the Courts and Cabinets of William IV and Victoria*. p. 75.
19. Ellenborough. September 16, 1831. *Three Early Nineteenth Century Diaries*. p. 128. cf. Wellington. *Despatches*. Vol. VII p. 520.
20. Broughton. Vol. V p. 49. *The Diary of Philipp von Neumann*. Vol. I p. 253. Albemarle. *Fifty Years of my Life*. p. 294.
21. *Correspondence of Charlotte, Lady Williams Wynn*. p. 376.
22. Albemarle. p. 290.
23. Countess of Münster. *My Memories and Miscellanies*. p. 22.
24. *Letters of Charles Lamb*. ed. A. Ainger. London, 1904. Vol. II p. 272.
25. *Letters of Dorothea, Princess Lieven, during her Residence in London*. p. 224.

CHAPTER XIII (pp. 156-167)

1. Greville. Vol. II p. 3.
2. Mary Frampton. p. 371.
3. Duchess of Dino. Vol. I p. 4.
4. *Lieven-Grey Correspondence*. Vol. II p. 495.
5. Wellington. *Despatches*. Vol. VIII p. 422.
6. Clifford Musgrave. *Royal Pavilion*. London, 1959. Chapter XII.
7. Barry O'Brien. *The Life and Letters of Thomas Drummond*. London, 1889. p. 42.
8. May 14, 1832.
9. Greville. Vol. II p. 92.
10. RA. Add. 39/493.
11. From the transcript of Queen Adelaide's diary in the Royal Archives.
12. July 18, 1831. RA. Add. 39/523.
13. July 19, 1831. RA. Add. 39/524.
14. *The First Lady Wharncliffe*. Vol. II p. 99.
15. Wellington. *Despatches*. Vol. VII p. 106.
16. G. M. Willis. *Ernest Augustus, Duke of Cumberland*. p. 204.
17. Greville. Vol. II p. 4.
18. *Admiralty Circular*. July 10, 1830.
19. June 4, 1835. RA. Melbourne mss.
20. *Letters of Dorothea, Princess Lieven, during her Residence in London*. p. 236.
21. *Lieven-Grey Correspondence*. Vol. II p. 49.
22. Brougham. Vol. III p. 305.
23. Lady Shelley. *Diary*. Vol. II p. 249.
24. Greville. Vol. II p. 197.
25. *Ibid*. Vol. II p. 14.
26. July 28, 1831. Paget mss.
27. Contained in the *Memoirs of Baron Stockmar*. Vol. I p. 315.
28. Ellenborough. Vol. II p. 287.
29. *Letters of Dorothea, Princess Lieven, during her Residence in London*. p. 254.
30. Brougham. Vol. III p. 96.
31. July 14, 1830. Add. mss. 40301 f 74.
32. July 19, 1835. Add. mss. 40303 f 239.
33. *Grey-William Correspondence*. Vol. I p. xiv.
34. Greville. Vol. II p. 3. Croker. Vol. II p. 66.
35. Le Marchant. *Althorp*. p. 246.
36. Taylor to Peel. October 27, 1830. Add. mss. 40301 f 249.
37. Ellenborough. Vol. II p. 420.
38. *Ibid*. p. 435.
39. *Ibid*. p. 428.
40. *Letters of Harriet, Countess Granville*. Vol. II p. 65.
41. Clitherow. p. 14.

CHAPTER XIV (pp. 168-178)

1. November 22, 1830. From the transcript of Queen Adelaide's diary in the Royal Archives.
2. Ellenborough. Vol. II p. 438.
3. Brougham. Vol. III p. 420.
4. Duchess of Dino. Vol. I p. 65.
5. Greville. Vol. II p. 62.
6. November 16, 1830. *Lieven-Grey Correspondence*. Vol. II p. 121.
7. November 18, 1830. Stuart Reid. *Life and Letters of the First Earl of Durham*. Vol. I p. 216.
8. Grey to Holland. November 16, 1830. cit. G. M. Trevelyan. *Lord Grey of the Reform Bill*. p. 241.
9. Brougham. Vol. III p. 78. cf. Croker. Vol. II p. 80.
10. Le Marchant. *Diary*. p. 6.
11. Greville. Vol. II p. 69.
12. November 23, 1830. RA. Add. 15/1183.
13. December 29, 1830. *Lieven-Grey Correspondence*. Vol. II p. 129.
14. November 26, 1830. *Grey-William Correspondence*. Vol. I p. 5.
15. November 27, 1830. *Grey-William Correspondence*. Vol. I p. 6.
16. December 2, 1830. RA. Add. 15/1191.
17. Grey to Brougham. January 31, 1831. Brougham. Vol. III p. 93.
18. Taylor to Grey. February 4, 1831. *Grey-William Correspondence*. Vol. I p. 93.
19. February 11, 1831. *Hansard*. 3rd Series. Vol. II p. 152.
20. Taylor to Peel. July 19, 1830. Add. mss. 40301 f 123.
21. Byam Martin. Vol. I p. 158.
22. Raikes. Vol. I p. 243.
23. On the genesis and passage of the Reform Bill I have relied heavily on J. R. M. Butler's admirable study *The Passing of the Great Reform Bill* which still, after more than fifty years, remains the best authority on the subject.
24. January 13, 1831. *Grey-William Correspondence*. Vol. I p. 51.
25. January 14, 1831. *Grey-William Correspondence*. Vol. I p. 54.
26. January 16, 1831. *Ibid*. p. 66.
27. January 17, 1831. *Ibid*. p. 70.
28. January 12, 1831. *Ibid*. p. 47.
29. January 15, 1831. *Ibid*. p. 60.
30. E. J. Littleton. *Diary*. p. 156.
31. *Tales of my Father*, by A. M. F. London, 1902. p. 33.
32. Croker. Vol. II p. 113.
33. RA. Add. 15/1250.
34. Croker. Vol. II p. 104.
35. January 19, 1831. Brougham. Vol. III p. 99.
36. At any rate if Croker is to be believed. Vol. II p. 139.
37. Paget mss.
38. Roger Fulford. *Royal Dukes*. p. 130.
39. Grey to Anglesey. February 4, 1831. Paget mss.

40. February 2, 1831. Paget mss.
41. *Grey–William Correspondence*. Vol. I p. 94.

CHAPTER XV (pp. 179–191)

1. See, in particular, E. and A. Porritt, *The Unreformed House of Commons*. London, 1903.
2. Croker. Vol. I p. 372.
3. Monypenny. *Disraeli*. Vol. I p. 324.
4. August 3, 1832. Broadlands mss. RC/A/127.
5. William to Palmerston. August 7, 1832. Broadlands mss. RC/A/129.
6. *Lieven–Grey Correspondence*. Vol. II p. 191.
7. March 20, 1831. *Grey–William Correspondence*. Vol. I p. 156.
8. March 21, 1831. *Grey–William Correspondence*. Vol. I p. 177.
9. March 20, 1831. *Grey–William Correspondence*. Vol. I p. 174.
10. Buckingham. *Memoirs*. Vol. I p. 272.
11. April 4, 1831.
12. April 10, 1831. Paget mss.
13. *Life and Letters of Lord Macaulay*. London, 1876. Vol. I p. 203.
14. Durham to Grey. March 22, 1831. *Grey–William Correspondence*. Vol. I p. 193.
15. William to Grey. March 23, 1831. *Grey–William Correspondence*. Vol. I p. 194.
16. Grey to Anglesey. March 24, 1831. Paget mss.
17. Creevey. Vol. II p. 225. cf. Greville. Vol. II p. 134.
18. Grey to Lady Grey. April, 1831. Howick mss. cf. *Lieven–Palmerston Correspondence*. p. 25.
19. Ellenborough. pp. 79–80.
20. April 19, 1831. *Grey–William Correspondence*. Vol. I p. 214.
21. April 19, 1831. *Grey–William Correspondence*. Vol. I p. 218.
22. April 20, 1831. Paget mss.
23. William to Grey. March 20, 1831. *Grey–William Correspondence*. Vol. I p. 163.
24. April 24, 1831. *Grey–William Correspondence*. Vol. I p. 239.
25. Parker. *Peel*. Vol. II p. 178.
26. April 21, 1831. *Grey–William Correspondence*. Vol. I p. 227.
27. April 21, 1831. Paget mss.
28. Buckingham. *Memoirs*. Vol. I p. 296.
29. *The First Lady Wharncliffe*. Vol. II p. 77.
30. Lady Brownlow, *The Eve of Victorianism* p. 148.
31. April 22, 1831. From the transcript of Queen Adelaide's diary in the Royal Archives.
32. Brougham. Vol. III p. 115.
33. Albemarle. *Fifty Years of my Life*. p. 292.
34. *The Reminiscences of Captain Gronow*. Vol. I p. 288.
35. Brougham. Vol. III p. 118.
36. Greville. Vol. II p. 139. Quoting Lord Sydney.
37. Greville. Vol. II p. 139.
38. William to Grey. May 17, 1831. *Grey–William Correspondence*. Vol. I p. 265.
39. Add. mss. 41368 f 91.

40. William to Grey. April 24, 1831. *Grey-William Correspondence*. Vol. I p. 239.
41. Grey to William. April 25, 1831. *Grey-William Correspondence*. Vol. I p. 247.
42. *Despatches*. Vol. VII p. 449.
43. Greville. Vol. II p. 150.
44. *Letters During Residence in London*. p. 301.
45. May 17, 1831. *Grey-William Correspondence*. Vol. I p. 265.
46. William to Grey. May 28, 1831. *Grey-William Correspondence*. Vol. I p. 272.

CHAPTER XVI (pp. 192-204)

1. Taylor to Grey. July 2, 1831. *Grey-William Correspondence*. Vol. I p. 301.
2. Huish. *William IV*. p. 667.
3. July 6, 1831. Paget mss.
4. Wellington to Buckingham. July 22, 1831. Buckingham. *Memoirs*. Vol. I p. 333.
5. Buckingham. *Memoirs*. Vol. I p. 347.
6. *Correspondence of Mr Joseph Jekyll*. ed. A. Bourke. London, 1894. p. 274.
7. Greville. Vol. II p. 187.
8. Wharncliffe. Vol. II p. 83.
9. Brownlow. *The Eve of Victorianism*. p. 150.
10. Greville. Vol. II p. 196.
11. August 15, 1831. *Grey-William Correspondence*. Vol. I p. 331.
12. Ellenborough. p. 204.
13. Holland to Anglesey. July 24, 1831. Paget mss.
14. Littleton. p. 98.
15. Holland to Anglesey. July 28, 1831. Paget mss.
16. September 27, 1831. RA. Add. 15/1536.
17. G. M. Trevelyan. *Lord Grey of the Reform Bill*. p. 321.
18. September 26, 1831. RA. Melbourne mss.
19. October 25. 1831. *Ibid.*
20. July 22, 1831. Buckingham. *Memoirs*. Vol. I p. 333.
21. Wellington to Buckingham. July 28, 1831. *Despatches*. Vol. VII p. 478.
22. October 8, 1831. *Grey-William Correspondence*. Vol. I p. 362.
23. Palmerston to Melbourne. September 3, 1831. RA. Melbourne mss.
24. Ellenborough. p. 137.
25. October 8, 1831. *Grey-William Correspondence*. Vol. I p. 365.
26. Le Marchant. *Memoir of Viscount Althorp*. p. 354.
27. Greville. Vol. II p. 333.
28. *Elizabeth, Lady Holland*. p. 155.
29. Taylor to Grey. RA. Add. 15/1396.
30. May 16, 1831. RA. Add. 15/1412.
31. May 24, 1831. *Despatches*. Vol. VII p. 444.
32. May 23, 1831.
33. May 25, 1831. *Despatches*. Vol. VII p. 445.
34. October 11, 1831. Paget mss.
35. *Elizabeth, Lady Holland*. p. 136.
36. October 10, 1831. From the transcript of Queen Adelaide's diary in the Royal Archives.

37. See, for example, William Holmes to Mrs Arbuthnot. November 18, 1831. Arbuthnot mss. and Greenwood, *Hanoverian Queens of England.* Vol. II p. 383.
38. October 24, 1831. Holland to Anglesey. Paget mss.
39. Clitherow. p. 27.
40. Lord Anglesey. *One Leg: The Life and Letters of the First Marquess of Anglesey.* p. 257.
41. *Elizabeth, Lady Holland.* p. 132.
42. Wellington. *Despatches.* Vol. VIII p. 168.
43. *Ibid.* p. 169.
44. Taylor to Grey. October 10, 1831. *Grey-William Correspondence.* Vol. I p. 370.
45. Grey to William. October 11, 1831. *Grey-William Correspondence.* Vol. I p. 371.
46. Russell to William. October 18, 1831. Add. mss. 38080 f 54.
47. Wharncliffe. Vol. II p. 99.
48. Greville. Vol. II p. 212.
49. Taylor to Melbourne. November 1, 1831. RA. Melbourne mss.
50. Taylor to Grey. November 4, 1831. *Grey-William Correspondence.* Vol. I p. 400.
51. November 8, 1831. *Grey-William Correspondence.* Vol. I p. 410.
52. *Despatches.* Vol. VIII p. 30.
53. Taylor to Wellington. November 9, 1831. *Despatches.* Vol. VIII p. 43.
54. William to Grey. November 13, 1831. *Grey-William Correspondence.* Vol. I p. 417.
55. Wellington to Stuart de Rothesay. November 15, 1831. *Despatches.* Vol. VIII p. 63.
56. H.O. 41. 10.
57. November 22, 1831. RA. Melbourne mss.
58. Wellington to Buckingham. January 2, 1832. Buckingham. *Memoirs.* Vol. I p. 384.
59. Wellington to Wharncliffe. November 26, 1831. *Despatches.* Vol. VIII p. 98.
60. William to Grey. October 17, 1831. *Grey-William Correspondence.* Vol. I p. 381.
61. October 23, 1831. RA. Melbourne mss.
62. Melbourne to Taylor. October 25, 1831. RA. Melbourne mss.
63. November 30, 1831. *Grey-William Correspondence.* Vol. I p. 451.
64. Greville. Vol. II p. 254.
65. Brougham. Vol. III p. 142.
66. Brougham. Vol. III p. 145.
67. November 29, 1831. *Despatches.* Vol. VIII p. 110.

CHAPTER XVII (pp. 205-222)

1. See p. 197 above.
2. Brougham to Grey. December 29, 1831. Brougham. Vol. III p. 151.
3. January 1, 1832. *Eng. Hist. Doc.* London, 1959. Vol. XI p. 112.
4. Minute of Conversation. *Grey-William Correspondence.* Vol. II p. 68; and William to Grey. January 5, 1832. *Ibid* p. 73.
5. Holland to Brougham. January 7, 1832. Brougham. Vol. III p. 458.
6. Cabinet Minute of January 13, 1832. *Grey-William Correspondence.* Vol. II p. 96.

7. January 2, 1832. Buckingham. *Memoirs*. Vol. I p. 384.
8. January 7, 1832. *The Early Correspondence of Lord John Russell*. Vol. II p. 29.
9. *Despatches*. Vol. VIII p. 156.
10. Taylor to Grey. March 16, 1832. *Grey-William Correspondence*. Vol. II p. 257.
11. January 15, 1832. *Grey-William Correspondence*. Vol. II p. 108.
12. February 13, 1832. *Grey-William Correspondence*. Vol. II p. 207.
13. February 16, 1832. *Grey-William Correspondence*. Vol. II p. 229.
14. March 11, 1832. *Grey-William Correspondence*. Vol. II p. 262.
15. March 11, 1832. *Grey-William Correspondence*. Vol. II p. 262.
16. Wharncliffe. Vol. II p. 118.
17. February 8, 1832. *Grey-William Correspondence*. Vol. II p. 193.
18. February 12, 1832. *Grey-William Correspondence*. Vol. II p. 197.
19. February 23, 1832. Greville. Vol. II p. 263.
20. February 27, 1832. *Grey-William Correspondence*. Vol. II p. 239.
21. February 27, 1832. *Grey-William Correspondence*. Vol. II p. 241.
22. Taylor to Grey. March 21, 1832. RA. Add. 15/1769.
23. Taylor to Grey. March 17, 1832. *Grey-William Correspondence*. Vol. II p. 272.
24. RA. Add. 15/1436.
25. William to Grey. March 30, 1832. *Grey-William Correspondence*. Vol. II p. 292.
26. *Creevey's Life and Times*. p. 354.
27. *Grey-William Correspondence*. Vol. II p. 394.
28. e.g. Greville. Vol. II p. 282.
29. Wellington. *Despatches*. Vol. VIII p. 339.
30. Brougham to Grey. April [?] 1832. Brougham. Vol. III p. 172.
31. Greville. Vol. II p. 297.
32. *Elizabeth, Lady Holland*. p. 137. cf. Le Marchant. *Diary*. p. 245.
33. Taylor to Grey. April 22, 1832. RA. Add. 15/1818.
34. April 17, 1832. *Grey-William Correspondence*. Vol. II p. 371.
35. *Creevey's Life and Times*. p. 354.
36. Fitzgerald. *William IV*. Vol. II p. 102.
37. Fitzgerald. *William IV*. Vol. II p. 103.
38. May 9, 1832. *Grey-William Correspondence*. Vol. II p. 396.
39. Clitherow. p. 33.
40. Stanley to Anglesey. May 10, 1832. Paget mss.
41. *The Creevey Papers*. Vol. II p. 246.
42. Brougham. Vol. III p. 194.
43. Greville. Vol. II p. 293.
44. Parker. *Peel*. p. 206.
45. Le Marchant. *Diary*. p. 252.
46. Lyndhurst to Wellington. May 14, 1832. Fitzgerald. *William IV*. Vol. II p. 111.
47. May 21, 1832. *Hansard*. Vol. XII.
48. A. Somerville. *Autobiography of a Working Man*. London, 1858. p. 244.
49. *Journal of Henry Cockburn*. Edinburgh, 1871. Vol. I p. 30.
50. May 8, 1832. Paget mss.
51. *Grey-William Correspondence*. Vol. II p. 406.
52. Le Marchant. *Diary*. p. 259. The entry is undated and could possibly have referred to the interview of May 18.

53. Add. mss. 20749 f 88.
54. Wellington. *Despatches*. Vol. VIII pp. 260–329.
55. Lady Anglesey to Lord Anglesey. May 17 [?] 1832. Paget mss.
56. RA. Add. 15/1889.
57. Grey to Taylor. May 17, 1832. *Grey–William Correspondence*. Vol. II p. 423.
58. Broughton. Vol. IV p. 231.
59. Brougham. Vol. III p. 199.
60. Taylor to Grey. May 28, 1832. *Grey–William Correspondence*. Vol. II p. 447.
61. Brougham. Vol. III p. 211.
62. June 10, 1832. RA. Melbourne mss.
63. Croker. Vol. II p. 165.
64. May 10, 1832. Paget mss.

CHAPTER XVIII (pp. 223–235)

1. August 17, 1833. RA. Add. 15/5049.
2. Taylor to Grey. May 1, 1832. *Grey–William Correspondence*. Vol. II p. 385.
3. Taylor to Aberdeen. September 11, 1830. Add. mss. 43040 f 132.
4. March 1, 1834. Broadlands mss. RC/A/319.
5. William to Palmerston. June 1, 1833. Broadlands mss. RC/A/247.
6. Stockmar. *Memoirs*. Vol. I p. 340.
7. August 7, 1832. Broadlands mss. RC/A/129.
8. William to Grey. October 29, 1833. RA. Add. 15/5090.
9. William to Palmerston. March 23, 1832. Broadlands mss. RC/A/85.
10. William to Palmerston. July 23, 1832. Broadlands mss. RC/A/119.
11. *Lieven–Grey Correspondence*. Vol. II p. 260.
12. December 21, 1830. Broadlands mss. RC/A/4.
13. William to Palmerston. October 25, 1831. Broadlands mss. RC/A/57.
14. William to Grey. April 10, 1831. *Grey–William Correspondence*. Vol. I p. 210.
15. Stockmar. *Memoirs*. Vol. I p. 288.
16. August 19, 1831. RA. Add. 15/1492.
17. Webster. *Foreign Policy of Palmerston*. Vol. I p. 139 for summary of evidence.
18. September 14, 1831. *Lieven–Grey Correspondence*. Vol. II p. 277.
19. William to Palmerston. September 18, 1832. Broadlands mss. RC/A/146.
20. William to Palmerston. September 21, 1832. Broadlands mss. RC/A/149.
21. Taylor to Grey. October 14, 1830. RA. Add. 15/1998.
22. William to Grey. October 4, 1832. RA. Add. 15/1991.
23. Holland to Anglesey. October 13, 1832. Paget mss.
24. William to Grey. December 17, 1832. RA. Add. 15/2076.
25. Grey to William. December 4, 1832. RA. Add. 15/2055.
26. William to Palmerston. May 24, 1834. Broadlands mss. RC/A/341.
27. May 1, 1831. *Letters during Residence in London*. p. 302.
28. Taylor to Grey. August 11, 1832. RA. Add. 15/1960.
29. William to Palmerston. June 18, 1832. Broadlands mss. RC/A/99.
30. William to Palmerston. July 23, 1832. Broadlands mss. RC/A/119.
31. August 2, 1832. Hansard. Third Series. Vol. XIV.
32. Taylor to Grey. August 8, and 11, 1832. RA. Add. 15/1957 and 1960.

33. Palmerston to Lamb. May 21, 1833. cit. Webster Vol. I p. 376.
34. William to Palmerston. October 15, 1833. Broadlands mss. RC/A/286.
35. William to Palmerston. August 4, 1833. Broadlands mss. RC/A/261.
36. September 9, 1833. RA. Add. 15/5063.
37. Oxburgh mss.
38. William to Palmerston. April 2, 1834. Broadlands mss. RC/A/326.
39. January 15, 1834. RA. Add. 15/6071.
40. January 7, 1833. RA. Add. 15/3005.
41. William to Grey. January 29, 1833. RA. Add. 15/3049.
42. Taylor to Grey. July 2, 1833. RA. Add. 15/4093.
43. William to Palmerston. June 1, 1833. Broadlands mss. RC/A/247.
44. Taylor to Grey. November 13, 1833. RA. Add. 15/5097.

CHAPTER XIX (pp. 236–246)

1. Taylor to Melbourne. May 28, 1832. RA. Melbourne mss.
2. Parker. *Robert Peel*. Vol. II p. 178.
3. Broughton. Vol. IV p. 251.
4. Le Marchant. *Althorp*. p. 437.
5. June 2, 1832. Broughton. Vol. IV p. 239.
6. May 19, 1832. Broughton. Vol. IV p. 235.
7. Grey to Taylor. August 19, 1832. RA. Add. 15/1966.
8. Taylor to Grey. August 20, 1832. RA. Add. 15/1967.
9. Taylor to Howe. August 22, 1832. RA. Add. 15/1975.
10. August 25, 1832. RA. Add. 15/1976.
11. September 6, 1832. *Lieven–Grey Correspondence*. Vol. II p. 390.
12. Taylor to Howe. September 5, 1832. RA. Add. 15/1982.
13. September 10, 1832. RA. Add. 15/1984.
14. Greville. Vol. II p. 337.
15. *Lieven–Palmerston Correspondence*. p. 46.
16. Greville. Vol. II p. 337.
17. *Lieven–Grey Correspondence*. Vol. II p. 415.
18. Greville. Vol. II p. 341 cf. *Lieven–Grey Correspondence*. Vol. II p. 437.
19. Camden to Wellington. August 11, 1832. Wellington. *Despatches*. Vol. VIII p. 421.
20. Broughton. Vol. IV p. 235.
21. Grey to Taylor. August 19, 1832. RA. Add. 15/1966.
22. William to Grey. December 17, 1832. RA. Add. 15/2076.
23. William to Grey. December 21, 1832. RA. Add. 15/2080 and Taylor to Grey 15/2081.
24. December 22, 1832. RA. Add. 15/2082.
25. December 25, 1832. RA. Add. 15/2085.
26. Wellington to Buckingham. June 23, 1832. Buckingham. *Memoirs*. Vol. II p. 5.
27. Taylor to Grey. December 14, 1832. RA. Add. 15/2074.
28. December 16, 1832. RA. Add. 15/2075.
29. February 5, 1833. Wharncliffe. Vol. II p. 175.
30. January 26, 1831. RA. Melbourne mss.

31. February 9, 1831. RA. Melbourne mss.
32. William to Grey. November 9, 1833. RA. Add. 15/5092.
33. Cit. Anglesey. *One-Leg.* p. 260.
34. William to Grey. January 30, 1833. RA. Add. 15/3051.
35. Taylor to Grey. June 7, 1833. RA. Add. 15/4075, and July 22, 1833. 15/5010.
36. Taylor to Grey. June 11, 1833. RA. Add. 15/4082.
37. Brougham. Vol. III p. 280.
38. Taylor to Brougham. June 16, 1833. Brougham. Vol. III p. 281.
39. July 14, 1833. Paget mss.
40. Le Marchant. *Diary.* p. 332.
41. June 6, 1833. RA. Add. 15/4074.
42. Greville. Vol. II p. 385.
43. Ellenborough, p. 337.
44. Taylor to Brougham. June 16, 1833. Brougham. Vol. III p. 281.
45. Brougham to Taylor. June 18, 1833. Brougham. Vol. III p. 292.
46. Grey to Brougham. September 14, 1833. Brougham. Vol. III p. 305.
47. *Annual Register.* pp. 43-4.
48. Grey to Taylor. June 7, 1834. RA. Add. 15/7083.
49. Taylor to Grey. June 8, 1833. RA. Add. 15/7085.
50. Brougham. Vol. III p. 364.
51. Brougham. Vol. III p. 368.
52. *Lord Beaconsfield's Correspondence with his Sister.* p. 24.
53. William to Grey. June 10, 1833. RA. Add. 15/7091.
54. Campbell. *Lord Lyndhurst. Lives of the Lord Chancellors.* Vol. VIII p. 93.
55. Melbourne to William. July 15, 1834. Add. mss. 40303 f 205.
56. William to Grey. July 8, 1834. RA. Add. 15/8014.
57. July 10, 1834. *Lieven-Grey Correspondence.* Vol. II p. 506.

CHAPTER XX (pp. 247-260)

1. Duchess of Dino. *Memoirs.* Vol. I p. 118.
2. Brougham. Vol. III p. 399.
3. Taylor to Brougham. July 10, 1834. Brougham. Vol. III p. 402.
4. Taylor to Grey. July 10, 1834. RA. Add. 15/8017.
5. Stockmar. *Memoirs.* Vol. I p. 324.
6. Melbourne to William. July 10, 1834. Add. mss. 40303 f 198.
7. Wellington to William. July 12, 1834. RA. Add. 15/8020. cf. Peel to William. July 13, 1834. Add. mss. 40302 f 1.
8. Brougham. Vol. III p. 409.
9. William to Melbourne. July 15, 1834. RA. Melbourne mss.
10. William to Melbourne. July 13, 1834. RA. Melbourne mss.
11. July 22, 1834. Melbourne mss.
12. William to Grey. October 26, 1831. *Grey-William Correspondence.* Vol. I p. 389.
13. Taylor to Grey and Grey to Taylor. March 16, 1833. RA. Add. 15/3085 and 3087.
14. Broughton. Vol. V p. 23.
15. October 19, 1834. RA. Melbourne mss.

16.   William to Melbourne. October 31, 1834. *Ibid.*
17.   Melbourne to William. November 1, 1834. *Ibid.*
18.   William to Melbourne. November 2, 1834. *Ibid.*
19.   Palmerston to William Temple. August 1, 1834. Broadlands mss.
20.   August 20, 1834. *Lord Beaconsfield's Correspondence with his Sister.* p. 42.
21.   February 14, 1835. *Melbourne Papers.* p. 257.
22.   Brougham to Melbourne. February 15 or 16, 1835. RA. Melbourne mss.
23.   November 18, 1834. *Lieven–Palmerston Correspondence.* p. 65.
24.   November 25, 1834. *Miss Eden's Letters.* p. 248.
25.   Duchess of Dino. Vol. I p. 50.
26.   *Letters during Residence in London.* p. 372.
27.   Duchess of Dino. Vol. I pp. 95–108.
28.   November 10, 1834. Add. mss. 40303 f 215.
29.   Stockmar. *Memoirs.* Vol. I p. 329.
30.   Stockmar. *Ibid.* p. 332.
31.   Add. mss. 40303 f 221.
32.   *The Letter-Bag of Lady Elizabeth Spencer Stanhope.* Vol. II p. 154.
33.   *The Eve of Victorianism.* p. 190.
34.   Add. mss. 40303 f 227.
35.   November 14, 1834. Melbourne mss.
36.   *History of The Times.* Vol. I p. 335.
37.   Fitzgerald. *William IV.* Vol. II p. 307.
38.   November 15, 1834. Parker. *Peel.* p. 255.
39.   Greville. Vol. III p. 97.
40.   Campbell. *Brougham.* p. 460.
41.   *Elizabeth, Lady Holland.* p. 155.
42.   Clitherow. p. 56.
43.   RA. Melbourne mss.
44.   Russell. *Early Correspondence.* p. 59.
45.   *Lord Melbourne's Papers.* p. 224.
46.   Greville. Vol. III p. 105.
47.   Stockmar. *Memoirs.* page 336.

CHAPTER XXI (pp. 261–267)

1.   Greville. Vol. III p. 109.
2.   December 1, 1834. *Grey–Lieven Correspondence.* Vol. III p. 47.
3.   December 12, 1834. Add. mss. 40302 f 23.
4.   Peel to Taylor. January 12, 1835. Add. mss. 40302 f 184.
5.   William to Peel. December 17, 1834. Add. mss. 40302 f 69.
6.   January 15, 1835. Add. mss. 40302 f 224.
7.   January 21, 1835. Add. mss. 40302 f 243.
8.   Greville. Vol. III p. 144.
9.   Grey to Melbourne. February 3, 1835. RA. Melbourne mss.
10.   William to Peel. February 12, 1835. Add. mss. 40302 f 317.
11.   William to Peel. February 22, 1835, Add. mss. 40303 f 8.
12.   Holland to Anglesey. February 27, 1835. Paget mss.

13. Greville. Vol. III p. 165.
14. March 17, 1835. Add. mss. 40303 f 75.
15. March 29, 1835. Add. mss. 40303 f 106.
16. March 30, 1835. Add. mss. 40303 f 112.
17. Wharncliffe. Vol. II p. 248.
18. William to Melbourne. April 11, 1835. RA. Add. 15/8042.
19. Grey to Taylor. April 12, 1835. RA. Add. 15/8044.
20. *Lieven-Grey Correspondence*. Vol. II p. 99.
21. Huish. *William IV*. p. 672.
22. Melbourne to William. April 14, 1835. RA 50522.
23. April 15, 1835. RA 50525.
24. RA. Add. 15/8040.
25. William to Melbourne. April 17, 1835. RA. Melbourne mss.
26. April 15, 1835. RA 50525.
27. Melbourne to William. April 15, 1835. RA 50535.
28. Melbourne to William. April 15, 1835. RA. Melbourne mss.
29. April 16, 1835. *Ibid.*
30. Holland to Anglesey. April 21, 1835. Paget mss.

CHAPTER XXII (pp. 268–281)

1. e.g. see *Lieven-Palmerston Correspondence*. p. 89.
2. *Tales of my Father* by A. M. F. London, 1902 p. 2.
3. Gabriele Von Bülow. *A Memoir*. p. 53.
4. December 29, 1832. RA. Add. 15/2095.
5. March 24, 1834. RA. Add. 39/589.
6. Greville. Vol. III p. 127.
7. January 12, 1833. RA. Add. 15/3022.
8. February 24, 1837. *Taylor Papers*. p. 386.
9. August 20, 1836. Broughton. Vol. V p. 61.
10. Greville. Vol. III pp. 207–8.
11. *Miss Eden's Letters*. p. 244.
12. Barrow. *Memoirs*. p. 373.
13. Buckingham. *Memoirs*. Vol. II p. 186.
14. Palmerston to Granville. July 17, 1835. Granville mss.
15. Taylor to Peel. July 15, 1835. Add. mss. 40303 f 235.
16. Melbourne to Lansdowne. June 30, 1835. RA. Melbourne mss.
17. Greville. Vol. III p. 231.
18. Walpole. *Lord John Russell*. p. 240.
19. Russell to Melbourne. December 26, 1837. RA. Melbourne mss.
20. Memorandum of Lord Melbourne. *Ibid.*
21. Torrens. *Melbourne*. Vol. II p. 147. Greville. Vol. III p. 223.
22. Melbourne to Russell. July 5, 1835. Walpole. *Russell*. p. 240 n.
23. Draft, undated, in RA. Melbourne mss.
24. William to Melbourne. June 7, 1836. *Melbourne Papers*. p. 349.
25. William to Melbourne. May 31, 1835. RA. Melbourne mss.
26. William to Melbourne. June 2, 1835. *Ibid.*

27. Peel to Goulburn. August 1835. Parker. *Peel.* Vol. II p. 315.
28. Melbourne to Mulgrave. October 16, 1835. *Melbourne Papers* p. 293.
29. Melbourne to William. October 19, 1835. RA. Melbourne mss.
30. William to Melbourne. August 16, 1835. *Ibid.*
31. Taylor to Melbourne. January 27, 1836. *Ibid.*
32. Taylor to Peel. July 15, 1835. Add. mss. 40303 f 235.
33. Broughton. Vol. V p. 47 cf. Greville. Vol. III p. 254.
34. Broughton. Vol. V p. 40.
35. Greville. Vol. III p. 224.
36. Sanders. *Queen Adelaide.* p. 132.
37. William to Grey. February 17, 1831. RA. Add. 15/1303.
38. Taylor to Grey. September 4, 1831. RA. Add. 15/1831.
39. See, for example, Grey to Taylor, June 25, 1833 or Taylor to Grey, September 21, 1833. RA. Add. 15/4088 and 5066.
40. *Elizabeth, Lady Holland.* p. 158.
41. *Jerningham Letters.* Vol. II p. 369.
42. March 28, 1834. RA. Add. 15/7028.
43. March 28, 1834. RA. Add. 15/7021.
44. March 30, 1834. RA. Add. 15/7030.
45. July 17, 1835. RA. Melbourne mss.
46. August 22, 1835. *Ibid.*
47. Greville. Vol. III pp. 309-10.
48. *Tales of my Father.* p. 18.
49. Walpole. *Russell.* Vol. I p. 241.
50. January 18, 1836. *Lieven-Palmerston Correspondence.* p. 111.
51. Reid. *Durham.* Vol. II p. 103.
52. Broughton. Vol. V p. 54.
53. Reid. *Durham.* Vol. II p. 104.

CHAPTER XXIII (pp. 282-294)

1. William to Melbourne. August 25, 1836. RA. Melbourne mss.
2. Melbourne to William and William to Melbourne. August 26, 1836. *Ibid.*
3. August 26, 1836. Walpole. *Russell.* Vol. I p. 268.
4. August 18, 1836. RA. Melbourne mss.
5. William to Melbourne, August 26, 1836 and to Palmerston, August 23, 1836. *Ibid.*
6. Palmerston to Melbourne. August 27, 1836. *Ibid.*
7. Palmerston to Melbourne. May 19, 1837. *Ibid.*
8. Melbourne to Russell. November 26, 1836. Walpole, *Russell.* Vol. I p. 269.
9. Taylor to Melbourne. November 7, 1836. RA. Melbourne mss.
10. William to Melbourne. January 2, 1837. *Ibid.*
11. Taylor to Russell. January 2, 1837. Walpole. *Russell.* Vol. I p. 274.
12. William to Melbourne. February 12, 1837. RA. Melbourne mss.
13. February 14, 1837. *Ibid.*
14. January 7, 1837. *Ibid.*
15. April 13, 1837. *Ibid.*

16. Raikes. Vol. III p. 163.

17. *Correspondence of Mr Joseph Jekyll.* ed. A. Bourke. London, 1894. p. 271.

18. April 16, 1837. RA. Add. 39/599.

19. May 3, 1837. RA. Add. 39/600.

20. The most full account of William's final illness is that of J. R. Wood. *Some Recollections of The Last Days of King William IV.*

21. Taylor to Melbourne. May 26, 1837. RA. Melbourne mss.

22. Elizabeth Longford. *Victoria R.I.* London, 1964. pp. 56–8.

23. Clitherow. p. 65.

24. *Early Correspondence.* Vol. II p. 198.

25. Broughton. Vol. V p. 75.

26. Fitzgerald. *William IV.* Vol. II p. 384.

27. June 20, 1837. RA. Melbourne mss.

28. June 19, 1837. *Correspondence with Sister.* p. 66.

29. June 19, 1837. *The Letters of Queen Victoria.* ed. Esher. London, 1908. Vol. I p. 73.

30. June 20, 1837. London, 1908. *The Letters of Queen Victoria.* Vol. I p. 75.

31. Greville. Vol. III p. 382.

32. Broughton. Vol. V p. 84.

33. Byam Martin. (NRS). Vol. III p. 338.

34. *Collected Works.* London, 1809. Vol. IV p. 281.

Bibliography

Manuscript Sources

The most important collection covering the life of William IV prior to his accession and his private life as King are the Münster Papers (R.A. Add.Mss. 39). Other relevant collections are those of his secretary, Sir John Barton (R.A. Add.Mss. 21); his correspondence with his steward and related papers (Goff Mss.); the papers of General Budé (R.A. Add.Mss. 15); Letters of Mrs Jordan and other papers at Wemyss Castle (Wemyss Mss.); the Diary of Queen Adelaide at Windsor Castle.

His correspondence with naval colleagues is often a fruitful source of information, notably with Nelson (Add.Mss. 34902–21 and at National Maritime Museum), John Martin (Add.Mss. 41367–68), Keats, Codrington and Keith all at the National Maritime Museum. Also at the Maritime Museum are Prince William's Log Book and the Book kept by the Admiral's Steward of the *Prince George*.

Though stray volumes survive, the bulk of William IV's official correspondence as King was destroyed after the death of his secretary, Sir Herbert Taylor. Much of it can, however, be reconstructed from the collections of his ministers which often contain copies of replies as well as the letters to ministers from the King and Taylor. Of particular importance are the papers of Lord Grey (Howick Mss.), Lord Melbourne (at Windsor Castle), Lord Palmerston (Broadlands Mss) and Peel (Add.Mss. 40301–03). Other collections relevant to this period are those of Lord John Russell (Add.Mss. 38080), Lord Ripon (Add.Mss. 43,040), Place (Add.Mss. 27,794), Lord Aberdeen (Add.Mss. 43,040) and Lord Anglesey (Paget Mss.).

Other manuscript collections of value are those of Lord Wellesley (Add.Mss. 37414), Lord Liverpool (Add.Mss. 38190 *et seq.*), Huskisson (Add.Mss.38749, 52 and 56), Knightley (Add.Mss. 46358), Ellis (Add.Mss. 38626) the Bedingfeld family (Oxburgh Mss.), and Lord Hardwicke (Add.Mss. 35653 and 708).

Among the productions of the Historical Manuscripts Commission the most useful are those of Bathurst, Carlisle, Fortescue and Stopford Sackville.

Published Sources

Of the various books treating King William IV in whole or part the most nearly satisfactory is probably still that of Percy Fitzgerald. *The Life and Times of William IV* (2 Vols. London 1884). The most recent, that of W. Gore Allen, *King William the Fourth* (London 1960) is pleasantly written but historically worthless. The most perceptive and brilliantly written study of William is Roger Fulford's essay in his *Hanover to Windsor* (London 1960). Other books to mention are:

Ashton, J. *When William IV was King*. London 1896.

Clitherow, Mary. *Glimpses of King William IV and Queen Adelaide*. London 1902.
Hall, W. F. *William IV, Thomas Pearse and The Rumbelows*. Newbury 1960.
Huish, Robert. *History of the Life and Reign of William IV*. London 1837.
Maley, A. J. *Historical Recollections of the Reign of William IV*. Two vols. London 1859.
Molloy, Fitzgerald. *The Sailor King*. Two vols. London 1903.
Moses, Henry. *Visit of William the 4th when Duke of Clarence as Lord High Admiral in the Year 1827*. London 1840.
Reichenbach, Baron. *Caroline von Linsingen and King William IV*. Trad. T. G. Arundel, London 1880.
Thompson, Grace. *The Patriot King*. London 1932.
Watkins, J. *The Life and Times of William the Fourth*. London 1831.
Wood, J. R. *Some Recollections of the Last Days of King William the IV*. London 1837.
Wright, G. N. *The Life and Reign of William the Fourth*. Two vols. (pp. 1–609 reproduce the text of J. Watkins biog. *op. cit.*) London 1837.

Mrs Jordan has been better served by biographers. By far the best is Brian Fothergill's excellent *Mrs Jordan* (London 1965). Professor Aspinall's editing of some of her correspondence, *Mrs Jordan and Her Family* (London 1951), has proved invaluable. Other books of some value about her include:

Boaden, James. *The Life of Mrs Jordan*. London 1831.
The Great Illegitimate. The Public and Private Life of Mrs Jordan, By a Confidential Friend of the Departed. London 1831.
Jerrold, Clare. *The Story of Dorothy Jordan*. London 1914.

The best book about Queen Adelaide is still that of Mary Sandars: *The Life and Times of Queen Adelaide* (London 1918). Mary Hopkirk's *Queen Adelaide* (London 1946) adds nothing of importance.

There is a plethora of books about other members of the royal family and the court. Of pre-eminent importance are *The Later Correspondence of George III* (ed. Aspinall, Vols. I–III, Cambridge 1962–67); *The Correspondence of George, Prince of Wales* (ed. Aspinall, Vols. I–V, London 1963–70); *The Letters of George IV* (ed. Aspinall, Vols. I–III. Cambridge 1938). Other books of some value (listed under the subject) are:

Charlotte, The Letters of Princess. ed. A. Aspinall. London 1949.
Cumberland, Ernest Augustus, Duke of. G. M. Willis. London 1954.
Elizabeth, Letters of Princess. ed. Philip Yorke. London 1898.
George III, The Daughters of. D. M. Stuart. London 1939.
George III and the Mad Business. Ida Macalpine and Richard Hunter. London 1969.
George III, The Royal Dukes and Duchesses of the Family of. Percy Fitzgerald. London 1882.
George IV, Memoirs of. Robert Huish. 2 vols. London 1831.
Hanover to Windsor. Roger Fulford. London 1960.
Kent, Edward of. David Duff. London 1938.
Queens, Lives of the Hanoverian. Alice Greenwood. 2 vols. London 1911.
Royal Dukes. Roger Fulford. London 1933.
Victoria, The Letters of Queen. ed Benson and Esher. Vol. 1. London 1908.
Victoria, The Girlhood of Queen. ed. Esher. London 1912.
Victoria R.I. Elizabeth Longford. London 1964.

It is difficult to know what general works should be cited in this sketchy bibliography. *The Reign of George III* by Steven Watson (Oxford 1960) and *The Age of Reform* by E. L. Woodward (Oxford 1938) are pre-eminent as background. Other works which, for a variety of reasons, are worth citation are:

Aspinall, A. *The Cabinet Council 1783–1835.* Proceedings of the British Academy. Vol. XXXVIII London 1952.

Aspinall, A. *The Formation of Canning's Ministry, 1827.* Camden, Series LIX London 1937.

Bartlett, C. J. *Great Britain and Sea Power 1815–53.* Oxford 1963.

Briggs, Sir John. *Naval Administrations 1827–92.* London 1897.

Butler, J. R. M. *The Passing of the Great Reform Bill.* London 1914.

Fletcher, Benton. *Royal Homes Near London.* London 1930.

Gavin, C. M. *Royal Yachts.* London, 1932.

Roebuck, J. A. *History of the Whig Ministry of 1830.* London 1852.

Times, The History of The. Vol. I 1735–1841. London 1935.

Turberville, A. S. *The House of Lords in the Age of Reform.* London 1958.

Finally there is the great welter of biography and autobiography, diaries and letters, which provide so much of the raw material of this work. They are listed alphabetically according to the name of the subject. I have not included those of only passing interest, which are referred to in the notes, but have marked with an asterisk the dozen or so volumes which have proved of particular value.

Abbot, Charles. Lord Colchester. *Diary and Correspondence.* London 1861.

Albemarle, Lord. *Fifty Years of My Life.* London 1876.

Althorp, Viscount. *Memoir.* Denis le Marchant. London 1876.

Anglesey. *One Leg: The Life and Letters of the First Marquess of.* Lord Anglesey, London 1961.

D'Arblay, Diary and Letters of Madame. London 1854.

Barnard Letters. ed A. Powell. London 1928.

Barrington, Sir Jonah. *Personal Sketches of His Own Times.* London 1869.

Barrow, Sir John. *An Autobiographical Memoir.* London 1847.

Beattie, William. *Journal of a Residence in Germany.* London 1831.

Berry, Miss. *Journals and Correspondence.* ed. Lady Lewis. London 1865.

Bessborough, Lady, and her Family Circle. ed. Lord Bessborough. London 1940.

Boteler, Captain. *Recollections.* NRS LXXII. London 1942.

*Brougham, Henry, Lord. *Life and Times.* Written by Himself. London 1871.

*Broughton, Lord. *Recollections of a Long Life.* Vols. IV and V. London 1910–11.

Brownlow, Lady. *The Eve of Victorianism.* London 1940.

*Buckingham, Duke of. *Memoirs of the Courts and Cabinets of William IV and Victoria.* London 1861.

Buckingham, Duke of. *Private Diary.* London 1862.

Bulow, Gabriele Von. *A Memoir.* London 1897.

Burdett, Sir Francis, and his Times. M. W. Patterson. London 1931.

Bury, Lady Charlotte. *Diary of a Lady-in-Waiting.* London 1908.

Chapone, Mrs. *Memoirs.* John Cole. London 1839.

Codrington, Memoir of the Life of Admiral Sir Edward. ed. Lady Bourchier. London 1873.

Coke, Lady Mary. *Letters and Journals*. Privately Printed. Edinburgh 1889.

Collingwood, Lord. *Correspondence and Memoirs*. London 1829.

Cooper, Sir Astley, *Life*. Bransby Cooper. London 1843.

Cornwallis, Charles, First Marquess. *Correspondence*. ed. C. Ross. London 1859.

Coutts, The Life of Thomas, Banker. E. H. Coleridge. London 1920.

Creevey. *Papers*. ed. Sir H. Maxwell. London 1904.

Creevey. *Life and Times*. John Gore. London 1934.

Croker. *Papers*. ed. L. J. Jennings. London 1884.

Delany, Mrs. *Life and Correspondence*. Second Series. London 1862.

Denman, Thomas, First Lord. *Memoir*. J. Arnould. London 1873.

Dillon, Sir William. *A Narrative of my Professional Adventures*. NRS London 1956.

Dino, Duchess of. *Memoirs*. ed. Princess Radziwill. London 1909.

Disraeli, Benjamin, Lord Beaconsfield. *Life*. W. F. Monypenny, Vol. I. London 1910.

Disraeli, Benjamin, Lord Beaconsfield. *Correspondence with His Sister*. London 1886.

Durham, Lord. *Life and Letters*. Stuart Reid. London 1906.

Dyott's Diary. ed. R. W. Jeffery. London 1907.

Eden, Miss. *Letters*. ed. V. Dickinson. London 1919.

Eldon, Life of Lord Chancellor. Horace Twiss. London 1844.

Ellenborough, Lord. *A Political Diary*. ed. Lord Colchester. London 1881.

Ellenborough, Lord. *Three Early Nineteenth Century Diaries*. ed. Aspinall. London 1952.

Elliot, Sir Gilbert. *Life and Letters*. Lady Minto. London 1874.

A.M.F. *Tales of My Father*. London 1902.

Farington Diary. ed. J. Greig. London 1922–28.

Fox, Hon. Henry Edward. *Journal*. ed. Lord Ilchester.

Frampton, Mary. *Journal*. ed. Mundy. London 1886.

Glenbervie, Sylvester Douglas, Lord. *Diaries*. London 1928.

Granville Leveson-Gower, Lord. *Letters*. ed. Countess Granville. London 1916.

Granville, Harriet Countess. *Letters*. ed. Leveson-Gower. London 1894.

*Greville. *Memoirs*. ed. Fulford & Strachey. London 1938.

*Grey. *The Correspondence of the late Earl with His Majesty King William IV and with Sir Herbert Taylor*. ed. Henry, Earl Grey. London 1867.

Grey, Lord, of the Reform Bill. G. M. Trevelyan. London 1920.

Gronow, Captain. *Reminiscences*. London 1892.

Halford, Sir Henry. *Life*. William Munk. London 1895.

Hamilton, Lady Anne (attributed). *Secret History of the Court of England*. London 1832.

Harcourt, Mrs. *Diary*, Philobiblon Society. *Miscellanies Vol. XIII*. London 1871–72.

Harcourt, The, Papers. ed. E. W. Harcourt. Privately Printed. Oxford.

Hobhouse, Henry. *Diary*. ed. A. Aspinall. London 1947.

Hobhouse, John Cam. *My Friend H*. Michael Joyce. London 1948.

Holland, Elizabeth, Lady, to her Son. ed. Lord Ilchester. London 1946.

Jerningham, The, Letters. Ed. Castle. London 1896.

Keith, Admiral Lord. Alexander Allardyce. Edinburgh 1882.

Knight, Miss. *Autobiography*. ed. Fulford. London 1960.

Knighton, Sir William. *Memoirs*. London 1838.

Le Marchant, Sir Denis. *Three Early Nineteenth Century Diaries*. ed. Aspinall. London 1952.

Lieven, Princess. Correspondence of, with Lord Aberdeen. ed. Jones Parry. Camden, Series LX. London 1938.

*Lieven, Princess, Letters of Dorothea, during her Residence in London. ed. Robinson. London 1902.

*Lieven, Princess, Correspondence of, with Lord Grey. ed. Le Strange. London 1890.

Lieven, Princess, The Private Letters of, to Prince Metternich 1820–6. ed. Quennell. London 1937.

Lieven–Palmerston Correspondence 1828–56. London 1943.

Lieven, Princess. *Unpublished Diary and Political Sketches.* ed. Temperley. London 1925.

Littleton, Edward. *Three Early Nineteenth Century Diaries.* ed. Aspinall. London 1952.

Lyndhurst, Lord. *Life.* Lord Campbell. *Lives of the Lord Chancellors.* Vol. VIII. London 1869.

Lyttleton, Sarah, Lady. *Correspondence.* ed. Mrs Wyndham. London 1912.

Mackenzie, Frederick. *Diary.* Harvard 1930.

Marryat, Captain, and the Old Navy. Christopher Lloyd. London 1939.

Marryat, Captain. Oliver Warner. London 1953.

*Martin, Sir Thomas Byam. *Letters and Papers.* NRS London 1903.

*Melbourne, Lord. *Papers.* ed. Lloyd Sanders. London 1889.

Melbourne, Lord. *Memoirs.* W. M. Torrens (New Edition). London 1890.

Münster, Countess of. *My Memories and Miscellanies.* London 1904.

Nelson. *Life.* Captain A. T. Mahan. London 1897.

Nelson's Letters to His Wife. NRS London 1958.

Neumann, Philipp von. *Diary.* ed. Beresford Chancellor. London 1928.

*Palmerston. *Foreign Policy.* Sir Charles Webster. London 1951.

Palmerston, Lord. Jasper Ridley. London 1970.

Papendiek, Mrs. *Journals.* ed. Mrs Broughton. London 1887.

Peel, Sir Robert. *Private Papers.* ed. George Peel. London 1920.

Raikes, Thomas. A Portion of the Journal kept by. London 1856–57.

Russell, Lord John. *Life.* Spencer Walpole. London 1889.

Russell, Lord John. *Early Correspondence.* ed. R. Russell. London 1913.

St. Vincent, Lord. *Letters.* ed. Smith. NRS London 1922.

Shelley, Frances, Lady. *Diary.* Ed. Edgcumbe. London 1913.

Spencer Stanhope, Lady Elizabeth. *Letter Bag.* ed. Stirling. London 1913.

Stockmar, Baron. *Memoirs.* ed. Muller. London 1872.

Taylor, The, Papers. ed. Ernest Taylor. London 1913.

Tomlinson, The, Papers. ed. Bullock. NRS London 1935.

Traherne, Mrs. *Romantic Annals of a Naval Family.* London 1873.

Walpole, Horace. *Letters.* Yale University Press. 1941–70.

* *Wellington, Despatches, Correspondence and Memoranda of Field Marshal Arthur Duke of.* London. Vol. IV, 1871. Vol. VII, 1878. Vol. VIII, 1880.

Wellington, Correspondence of Lady Burgersh with the Duke of. ed. Lady Weigall. London 1903.

Wharncliffe, The First Lady, and her Family. ed. Grosvenor. London 1927.

Wraxall, N. W. *Posthumous Memoirs of His Own Times.* London 1836.

Wynn, Charlotte Lady Williams. *Correspondence.* London 1920.

Wynn, Miss F. W. *Diaries of a Lady of Quality.* London 1864.

Index

VICTORIA AND DISRAELI

'Mr Theo Aronson has given the best
impression of the Queen that I have read.
With much subtlety – and dead-pan humour –
he has used her relationship with Disraeli to
give us an insight into what she was really
like. His book is bright with intelligence and
human wisdom. Very strongly recommended.'
C. P. Snow, *Financial Times*

Theo Aronson, well known for his biographies
of the royal houses of Europe, is ideally
qualified to tell the story of the strange
partnership between the formidable Widow of
Windsor and the flamboyant Jew who once
wrote 'my nature demands that my life should
be perpetual love.'
But were they so ill-matched? Both needed the
intimate support of someone of the opposite
sex and each responded to the romanticism of
the other.
By the mid 1870s the personal and political
association between the imperialist Prime
Minister Disraeli and his Queen Empress was
in full flower. It was a relationship which
brought happiness and fulfilment to them
both.

'A sensitive and stylish account of their
relationship ... skilfully and sympathetically
described. Aronson has produced an
illuminating and entertaining book.'
Observer

0-304-31433-1